Ethnic Families in America

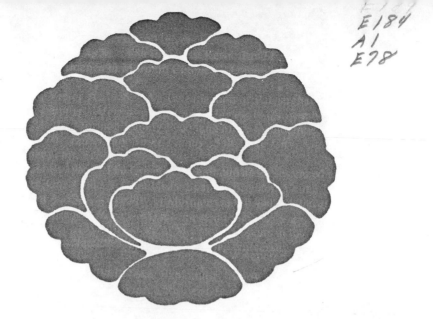

Ethnic Families in America
PATTERNS AND VARIATIONS

Edited by CHARLES H. MINDEL

and ROBERT W. HABENSTEIN

ELSEVIER

New York / Oxford / Amsterdam

ELSEVIER SCIENTIFIC PUBLISHING COMPANY, INC.
52 Vanderbilt Avenue, New York, N.Y. 10017

ELSEVIER SCIENTIFIC PUBLISHING COMPANY
335 Jan Van Galenstraat, P.O. Box 211
Amsterdam, The Netherlands

Library of Congress Cataloging in Publication Data

Main entry under title:

Ethnic families in America.

    1. Minorities—United States—Addresses, essays,
lectures. 2. Family—United States—Addresses,
essays, lectures. I. Mindel, Charles H.
II. Habenstein, Robert Wesley, 1914–
E184.A1E78   301.45'1'0420973   75-40654
ISBN 0-444-99022-4
      0-444-99025-9 pbk

Manufactured in the United States of America
Designed by Loretta Li

CONTENTS

PREFACE

The idea for this book was first conceived several years ago with the inability of one of the editors to find readings and lecture material on family patterns of America's ethnic minorities. In searching out the material it became apparent that most of the recent textbooks on the sociology of the family had begun to pay attention to some minority family types, especially the Black family, but that the overwhelming emphasis has been and probably will continue to be on the generalized white Protestant middle class American family.

Considering the fact that America, a nation of immigrants, still contains large numbers of families who see themselves as members of ethnic groups and for whom ethnic culture still has important behavioral consequences it seemed appropriate that a volume on these distinctive family types might be organized.

In planning this book the editors decided to try to include most of the major American ethnic groups, but at the same time it became apparent that to write this book ourselves would be a near impossible task, certainly beyond our expertise as well as the range of our ethnic—Jewish and German—experience. In addition, one of the deficits we and others have noted about most writings on race and ethnic studies is a tendency to examine only the negative or "problems" of minority families. Most frequently this is the case because the writers are not members of the group about which they are writing. In this volume we decided to take a more positive approach, examining ethnic family strengths as well as weaknesses, and to lodge these characterizations in historical socio-economic contexts. Consistent with this approach was our decision to seek out scholars who also happened to be members of the ethnic group about which they might be writing. The risk of getting an overly rosy picture of the ethnic group we felt to be more than offset by the benefits which include a greater penetration into the subjective meanings that group members attach to certain cultural traits or behaviors, and a depth of understanding that might not be so apparent to an outsider. Although we were not totally successful in securing authors who were also members of the ethnic group they wrote about, in those chapters where we do not have correlative ethnic authors (Amish, North American Indian, and Puerto-Rican) we do have experts who have worked for many years in and with their groups.

The decision was made at the outset to develop a common outline that each of the authors would follow so that a certain consistency would exist and that the book would be seen as an integrated whole rather than a collection of readings. To a large extent this goal was achieved but to a certain degree it was not. Rather than seeing this as a failing we prefer to see it as the consequence of the great heterogeneity of America's ethnic groups, and our agreement that contributing authors be allowed to develop those areas where they thought their respective ethnic group was most distinctive. If the chapters do not always follow the outline in every detailed respect we do not think on balance that it was necessarily a bad thing for the book.

Some contributors have raised the question of the use of "America" throughout the book. Inasmuch as the Western Hemisphere has been geographically divided into three "Americas," it may be questioned if our usage might not be erroneous at best, offensive at worst. Our decision rests on what we believe to be social usage and the common currency of "America" in everyday discourse to mean the country Kate Smith sings about in "God Bless America" and which graces the titles of thousands of books all referring, technically speaking, to the United States. Without our usage most authors in the end would have difficulty in expressing the ethnic linkage to the host culture, as in Chinese American, Mexican American, Polish American, Greek American and the like.

Attempting to acknowledge all those who over the last several years have facilitated our efforts would be impossible, but special thanks are in order first of all to all of the contributing authors who have worked patiently with us through the many edits and re-edits of their chapters. We also would like to specially thank Ellen H. Biddle for her extra contributions as well as Susan Elder and Jean Bailey for their assistance with the manuscript. To the staff of the Center for Research in Social Behavior we would like to acknowledge their cooperation in the task of typing, retyping, duplicating and distributing the manuscript in its many forms.

A final word of thanks are in order for William Gum of Elsevier who without white horse or shining armor rescued this pristine work from ravaging editors in another part of the publishing forest.

November, 1975

CHARLES H. MINDEL
ROBERT W. HABENSTEIN

LIST OF CONTRIBUTORS

DAVID ALVIREZ received his Ph.D. degree in sociology from the University of Texas at Austin in 1971. His major research interests are the Mexican Americans and demography, with a specific focus on fertility. Among his major works are articles on the Mexican American worker, the effects of religiosity on the fertility patterns of Mexican Americans, and census data problems with respect to the conceptual definition of the Mexican American population. He is currently associate professor and acting head of the Department of Behavioral Sciences, Pan American University, Edinburg, Texas.

FRANK D. BEAN is associate professor of sociology and associate director of the Population Research Center at the University of Texas at Austin. He received his Ph.D. degree from Duke University. His major research interests are in the areas of family and fertility, fertility differentials among ethnic groups, and the sociology of the family. He has published numerous articles, including several dealing with various aspects of fertility among Mexican Americans.

ELLEN H. BIDDLE received a B.A. degree from Wellesley College (Sociology) in 1950, an M.A. degree from Earlham College (Community Development) in 1952, and a Ph.D. degree from the University of Missouri at Columbia (Sociology) in 1969. Her fields of interest are minority groups, family, and gerontology. A book on urban Australian Aborigines, *Look Forward, Not Back,* of which she is co-author, was published in 1975. At present a research associate at the Center for Research in Social Behavior at the University of Missouri at Columbia, Dr. Biddle is conducting studies of the housing and health-care patterns of elderly persons.

BRUCE CAMPBELL received his B.A. and M.A. degrees from Brigham Young University in Child and Family Development. He received his Ph.D. degree in sociology at the University of Minnesota. His major research interests are aging and the family. Dr. Campbell is presently located at the Center for Family Life Studies, Department of Home Economics at Arizona State University.

EUGENE CAMPBELL, professor of history, received his M.A. degree from the University of Utah in 1940 and his Ph.D. degree in history from the University of Southern California in 1952. On the faculty of Brigham Young University since 1956 and department chairman, 1959–67, Dr. Campbell's major research emphasis is Utah and Mormon history. He is co-author of *The United States: An Interpretative History* and a contributor to *History of a Valley: Cache Valley.* Among his other publications are articles on important figures and events in Mormon political and social history.

ABDO A. ELKHOLY, a graduate of Princeton University, is considered an authority on the Arab Americans and Arab Canadians. He has written numerous articles, and his book, *The Arab Moslems in the United States: Religion and Assimilation,* is used by students of assimilation at many colleges and universities. He is well known in the Arab world as a leading authority on "manpower" utilization and mobilization. For the academic year, 1973–74, he was selected by both the Board of Foreign Scholarships and the Government of the United Arab Emirates to conduct sociological research in Abu Dhabi under the Fulbright–Hays Program of Senior Scholars. His current research interest is motivation for birth control in the Middle East. Dr. Elkholy is currently a professor of sociology at Northern Illinois University.

BERNARD FARBER received his Ph.D. degree from the University of Chicago in 1953. Since then, his major research interests have been in the sociology of the family and kinship. His books include *Family: Organization and Interaction* (1964); *Comparative Kinship* Systems (1968); *Mental Retardation: Its Social Context and Social Consequences* (1968); *Kinship and Class, a Midwestern Study* (1971); *Guardians of Virtue: Salem Families in 1800* (1972); and *Family and Kinship in Modern Society* (1973). He has also edited *Kinship and Family Organization* (1966) and has written a series of monographs on the effects of retarded children on family relationships. Currently, he is professor of sociology at Arizona State University, Tempe.

FRANCIS X. FEMMINELLA is associate professor of sociology and education at the State University of New York, Albany. His graduate work was done at Fordham, and at New York University where he received the Ph.D. degree. Specializing in ethnic studies professor Femminella is currently appointed to the National Advisory Council on Ethnic Heritage studies which advises the Secretary of H.E.W. and the U.S. Commissioner of Education.

JOSEPH P. FITZPATRICK received his M.A. degree in philosophy from Fordham University and his Ph.D. degree in sociology from Harvard. Much of his research has been devoted to a study of the Puerto Rican migration. He has published: *Puerto Rican Americans: The Meaning of Migration to the Mainland;* (with John Martin) *Delinquent Behavior: A Re-definition of the Problem;* and (with J. M. Martin and R. E. Gould) *The Analysis of Delinquent Behavior: A Structural Approach.* Dr. Fitzpatrick has been a faculty member at Fordham University in New York since 1949.

LAURENCE FRENCH was born, reared, and educated in northern New England. After serving in the U.S. Marine Corps, he attended the Church College of Hawaii, the University of Hawaii, and the University of New Hampshire, where he earned his degrees. His major academic and research interests are in durable groups, deviance, corrections, and criminal justice. He has published articles in major journals and is the co-author (along with Palmer and Humphrey) of *New Perspectives in Deviance.* Currently he is an assistant professor of sociology at Western Carolina University.

ROBERT W. HABENSTEIN began a delayed career in sociology after experiences in C.C.C. camps, armed forces, and industrial work in Cleveland, Ohio. His Ph.D. dissertation at the University of Chicago in 1954 dealt with funeral directing, and at the University of Missouri, where he has been on the staff since 1950, he has conducted a number of studies in the family and occupations and professions. He is the author or co-author of eight books. Currently he is professor of sociology and research associate in the University's Center for Research in Social Behavior where he conducts studies in social gerontology.

LUCY JEN HUANG, professor of sociology, was born in China. She received her Ph.D. degree at the University of Chicago in 1954. Before coming to her present position at Illinois State University in 1967, she taught sociology at Lake Erie College and Boston University. Her major interest in sociology is comparative family and alternate life styles in marriage and the family. Her major published works are in the area of changing family and sex roles in the Chinese family.

GERTRUDE ENDERS HUNTINGTON was born in Wooster, Ohio, on the edge of the largest Amish community in America. She did graduate work at Rochester University and received her Ph.D. degree from Yale, writing her dissertation on the Old Order Amish community. She has worked with religious minorities, particularly the Hutterites and the Amish. With John A. Hostetler she co-authored *The Hutterites in North America* (1967) and *Children in Amish Society* (1971). Her special interests are in the areas of child-rearing practices, the anthropology of education and the interactions among the community, and the family in its various forms. Currently Dr. Huntington is a visiting assistant professor in anthropology at the University of Michigan.

AKEMI KIKUMURA is a National Institute of Mental Health (NIMH) doctoral trainee in anthropology at the University of California, Los Angeles. She has co-authored an article on "Japanese American Interracial Marriage" and is currently working on the success of interracial unions and the effects on their children.

HARRY H. L. KITANO is currently professor of social welfare and sociology at the University of California, Los Angeles, and was formerly the director of the University of California Tokyo Study Center (1972–73). He received his Ph.D. degree from the University of California, Berkeley, and is the author of the following books: *Japanese Americans: The Evolution of a Sub-culture* (1969); *American Racism: Exploration of the Nature of Prejudice* (with Roger Daniels, 1970); and *Race Relations* (1974).

GEORGE A. KOURVETARIS received his Ph.D. degree from Northwestern University in 1969 and is currently an associate professor of sociology at Northern Illinois University. His major academic and research interests include political and military sociology, social stratification, intergroup relations, and comparative sociology. Among his most recent publications are: "The Greek Army Officer Corps: Its Professionalism and Political Interventionism," in Morris

Janowitz and Jacques Van Doorn (eds.), *On Military Intervention* (1971); *First and Second Generation Greeks in Chicago: An Inquiry into Their Stratification and Mobility Patterns* (1971); and *Social Origins and Political Orientations of Officer Corps in a World Perspective* (1973). He is founder and editor of the *Journal of Political and Military Sociology*.

BERNARD LAZERWITZ did his graduate work at the University of Michigan and has specialized in survey research and the study of ethnic minorities. He has taught at the University of Illinois, Brandeis University, the University of Missouri, and has been a visiting professor at Bar-Ilan University in Israel. Among his major works are studies of religion and social structure, trends in fertility rates of Jews and Arabs in Israel, an investigation of the components and consequences of religio-ethnic identification, a book on survey research, and the statistical design for the recently completed, first large-scale national sample survey of the American Jewish population.

HELENA ZNANIECKI LOPATA received her Ph.D. degree from the University of Chicago in 1954 and is currently professor of sociology and director of the Center for the Comparative Study of Social Roles, Loyola University of Chicago. Formerly she served as chairman of the Sociology Department at Loyola University, 1970–72. Her major works include: *Occupation: Housewife* (1971); *Widowhood in an American City* (1973); *Marriages and Families* (1973); and forthcoming, *Polish Americans: Status Competition in an Ethnic Community*. Currently Dr. Lopata is conducting a survey of the support systems for widows of all ages in urbanizing communities and is organizing a first stage of research into the identities and commitments of women to work, family, and other roles.

CHARLES H. MINDEL, born in New York City, received his B.A. degree at the State University of New York at Stony Brook and his Ph.D. degree in sociology at the University of Illinois in 1971. His research interests are in the areas of kinship, family, and aging. His recent works have included articles on "Extended Kinship Relations in Black and White Families" and "Kinship, Reference Groups and the Symbolic Family Estate: Implication for Social Mobility." He is currently an assistant professor in sociology at the University of Missouri and is engaged in a study of elderly and extended family living and a comparative study of Anglo, Black, and Chicano adolescents and their families.

JOHN A. PRICE is an urban anthropologist at York University in Toronto. He received his Ph.D. degree at the University of Michigan and has done field work in Japan, Mexico, America, and Canada. His last book was *Tijuana: Urbanization in a Border Culture* (1973), and his current book in press is *Native Studies: Toward a Humanistic Understanding of U.S. and Canadian Indians*.

JILL S. QUADAGNO is a doctoral candidate at the University of Kansas. She received her B.A. at Pennsylvania State University and her M.A. at the University of California at Berkeley. She currently is a social gerontology trainee with the Midwest Council for Social Research on Aging.

ROBERT STAPLES was born in Roanoke, Virginia, and educated in the state of California. He received his Ph.D. degree at the University of Minnesota. His major research interests are in the area of ethnic family systems, human sexuality, race relations, and urban sociology. His most recent book is entitled *Introduction To Black Sociology*. Among his major works are forty articles on Black family life and the books: *The Black Family: Essays and Studies* (1971) and *The Black Woman in America: Sex, Marriage and the Family* (1973). He is associate professor and chairman of the Graduate Program in Sociology at the University of California Medical Center at San Francisco.

Family Life Styles of America's Ethnic Minorities: An Introduction

This is a book about patterned differences in American families— differences based on the national, cultural, religious, and racial identification and membership of groups of people who do not set the dominant style of life or control the privileges and power in any given society. These differences are embedded in what are generally known as "ethnic groups." Ethnicity is usually displayed in the values, attitudes, life styles, customs, rituals, and personality types of individuals who identify with particular ethnic groups. Had these ethnic identifications and memberships no other effect on peoples' lives than to provide interesting variety within a country, sociologists would long since have described them in their variety and moved on to other matters. But identification with and membership in an ethnic group has far-reaching effects on both groups and individuals, controlling access to opportunities in life, feelings of well-being, and mastery over the futures of one's children.

CHAPTER ONE

BY

CHARLES H. MINDEL AND
ROBERT W. HABENSTEIN

ANALYSIS AND METAPHOR

Ethnicity and the analysis of ethnic groups have long been topics of discussion in scholarly and popular literature. Terms such as "melting pot," the metaphor embodying the notion that immigrants from all over the world somehow fuse together here in America, producing a new and better amalgam combining the best cultural contributions of each, was first coined by Israel Zangwill in a 1906 play of the same name. On the other hand, avid discussions about the virtues of maintaining a "cultural pluralism," that is, becoming "American" while at the same time retaining one's cultural heritage, have been going on since at least 1915, when

1

Horace Kallen first introduced the idea. Still others have claimed that really what we have here in America is a highly ethnocentric coercion toward "Anglo conformity," implying the downgrading and elimination of ethnic and the incorporation of the dominant Anglo culture. The element of conflict and the transformation of ethnic groups into politically conscious ethnic minorities are central to this approach.

In recent years there has been a decline in "melting pot" theories of racial and ethnic assimilation, and the notion of American society as a conglomerate of "unmeltable ethnics" existing in a somewhat tenuous societal pluralism has been gaining ground. The "salad bowl" metaphor has found favor in Canada where pluralism—the willingness of any one group to seek an amicable accord with any other, whatever hue or creed—has long been an article of national faith (Elkin, 1970; Ishwaran, 1971; Queen and Habenstein, 1974; Wade, 1960). Conflict theory has not yet developed an acceptable figure of speech to characterize American ethnic relations, but "cats in a bag" might not be totally inapplicable.

But the concept of assimilation historically has long enjoyed the status of what Gouldner (1970) has called a domain assumption, carrying with it a kind of value-laden ethnocentricism that presumes superiority on the part of the host culture in all respects and an inferior cultural baggage carried ashore by the newly arrived immigrants. True, "Americanization," the lingual epitome of an earlier twentieth-century social movement to detribalize and de-ethnicize the ubiquitous foreign element, has long since left the sociologist's lexicon, although its presence may occasionally be noted in a Fourth of July or Memorial Day public address.

Some of the enthusiasm for denigrating ethnic groups has lost its national appeal. The long-term rise in the standard of living and the disappearance of much physically demanding, toil-ridden work has made for fewer "dirty-work" occupations being associated with particular ethnic groups (Fuchs, 1968). The material success of some ethnic groups *qua* ethnic groups, Chinese, Japanese, Jews, and recently Cubans, has helped explode the myth that ethnics are somehow best equipped genetically and culturally to remain at lower or at best midlevels of America's economy.

A more recent and spectacular development in the sociopolitical realm has been the impressive growth of the civil rights movement, punctuated by fire storms of political activism and violence, with attendant proliferation of legislation and court rulings aimed directly at discrimination in all its guises. An expanding Black consciousness has for

2

millions of Americans reversed the onus of color: "Black" does not "stay back," "Brown" is not "down," and "white" is not necessarily "right."

In reviewing these developments of long and short duration, it is evident that there has been a growth of ethnic awareness of a different genre in America, whether it expresses itself in the comfort that older ethnic groups can now feel when proclaiming their Old World heritage or in the troubled and troublesome abrasiveness of the long-subjugated ethnic minorities searching for a status yet to be won. Both the achievers and the achieving, it remains to be added, face the universal problem of searching for, finding, and maintaining roots and tradition in face of the appeals of modernity and homogenized living in the burgeoning mass society.

Though all of these contrasting and seemingly contradictory views concerning American immigrant and minority groups, "Anglo conformity," "melting pot," and "cultural pluralism," or as sociologists often refer to them, assimilation, amalgamation, and accommodation (Rose, 1974: 66) have taken on a new relevancy today, we still lack an intensive yet broad-gauge study of American ethnic groups. The fact is that we know relatively little about American ethnic groups and even less about their family life.

Most textbooks on the American family's attempt to meet the challenge of ethnic diversity include in their work examples of one or two distinctive families (e.g., Nye and Berardo, 1973; Burgess, Locke, and Thomes 1963; Kephart 1972; Cavan 1969; Reiss 1971). However, while ethnicity continues to act as an important determinant of behavior for a significant number of people, it has often been treated by scholars and texbook writers *en passant,* either as a historical or residual category.

It may well be that in the long run ethnic differences will disappear, as Glazer (1954) and others have argued, but as Greeley (1969: 21) notes, "family, land and common cultural heritage have always been terribly important to human beings, and suspicion of anyone who is strange or different seems also deeply rooted in the human experience." It is the purpose of this book, then, to examine a wide variety of American ethnic groups, probing the historical circumstances that impelled them to come to this country; focusing on the structure and functioning of their family life to determine or at least to raise clues as to how and why they have been able or unable to maintain an ethnic identification over the generations; and, finally, looking ahead to speculate on what the future has in store for these groups and their constitutive families.

3

WHAT IS AN ETHNIC GROUP?

"Ethnic" derives from the Greek word *ethnikos,* meaning "people" or "nation." Members of some ethnic groups or their ancestors coming from the same country are often referred to as "nationalities." Members of other ethnic groups such as Jews or Gypsies, individuals whose identity was not restricted to a particular national boundary, are often referred to as "peoples" (Rose 1974: 13). In this general sense, *an ethnic group consists of those who share a unique social and cultural heritage that is passed on from generation to generation.* Gordon (1964: 24), varying the perspective slightly, sees those who share a feeling of "peoplehood" as an ethnic group. But the sense of "peoplehood" that characterized most social life in the past centuries has become fragmented and shattered. This has been occurring for a variety of reasons, it is suggested, including in the last few centuries massive population increases, the development of large cities, the formation of social classes, and the grouping of peoples into progressively larger political units. However, and as many other writers have noted, there has been a continuing need for individuals to merge their individual identity with some ancestral group, with "their own kind of people." Gordon proposes that the fragmentation of social life has left competing models for this sense of peoplehood, that men are forced to choose among them or somehow to integrate them totally. In America the core categories of ethnic identity from which individuals are able to form a sense of peoplehood are race, religion, and national origin, or some combination of these categories (Gordon, 1964). It is these criteria, emphasizing substantively cultural symbols and consciousness of kind, that are used to define the groups included in this book.

Minority Groups

Related, of course, but of a different genre is the concept of minority or minority group. "Minority" in the sociological as opposed to the statistical sense refers to a power or dominance relationship. Those groups that have unequal access to power, that are considered in some way unworthy of sharing power equally, and that are stigmatized in terms of assumed inferior traits or characteristics are minority groups. To be a member of a minority group, then, is to share a status relationship, and to act as a minority group member is to act power consciously. To be a

4

member of an ethnic group, on the other hand, is to share a sense of cultural and historical uniqueness, and to act as a member of an ethnic group is to express feelings or call attention to that uniqueness. It should be understood that the same individual at any one moment may act in either capacity. The Black student who complains about the student cafeteria food may be expressing (ethnically) a desire for dishes familiar to him from childhood, or he may be expressing (minority) resentment against being denied these foods on the basis of race and race alone.

ETHNICITY IN AMERICA

Part of the explanation for the lack of concern for ethnic differences among many scholars has been the feeling that these variations are only of a transitory nature; they will soon go away. Indeed, historically ethnic groups and ethnic communities might very well have served purposes that seem very much unnecessary today. In the past, ethnic communities served to preserve the familiar, the *gemeinschaft* of the old country for large numbers of people set adrift in an alien America. And America, from its very beginnings an ethnically diverse society, was not as a matter of moral principle hostile to the existence of distinct cultural groups.

Several writers have attempted to explain why ethnicity has remained important. Herberg (1955) and Greeley (1969) have both linked ethnicity with religion. Herberg's claim was that ethnic differences in America were being replaced by religious differences along a tripartite Protestant, Catholic, and Jewish dimension. This development was taking place ostensibly because Herberg felt that "religion was a more respectable way of maintaining ethnic primary groups than ethnicity itself " (Glazer and Moynihan, 1970: xxxviii). In like manner, Greeley (1969) suggests that religion and ethnicity are inextricably intertwined, and that the persistence of ethnic groups and ethnic identification is due to continuing religious identification.

Glazer and Moynihan (1970), in their excellent work on ethnicity, have also analyzed the evolution and persistence of ethnicity. They argue that "the adoption of a totally new ethnic identity, by dropping whatever one is to become simply American, is inhibited by strong elements in the social structure of the United States." These inhibitions range from labeling to brutal discrimination and prejudice as well as the "unavailability of a simple 'American' identity" (Glazer and Moynihan, 1970: xxxiii). Most positively seen, ethnic communities provide indi-

5

viduals with congenial associates, help organize experience by personalizing an increasingly impersonal world, and provide opportunities for social mobility and success within an ethnic context (Greeley, 1969: 30). However, while American ethnic groups have in a large measure become acculturated, that is, learned the manners and customs and language of the dominant culture, in only a few cases have they been assimilated to that point at which they can relate to members of other groups intimately on the primary group level (Greeley, 1969).

ETHNIC RESURGENCE

Glazer and Moynihan also offer some provocative suggestions to explain the increasing importance of ethnicity in recent years. They hypothesize that ethnic identities have replaced occupational identities, particularly working-class occupational identities that have lost much of their glamour in recent years. It is better to be Polish than to be known as a Polish assembly-line worker in a Detroit automobile plant. Second, they speculate that one's ethnic identity in America in large measure has become separate from events in the country of origin. Domestic happenings are more important than international events in evoking feelings of ethnic awareness. (They make an important exception for the Jews, a group whose ethnic identification increased dramatically in America with the creation of the state of Israel.) Third, they suggest, contrary to Greeley and Herberg, that religion as well as occupation and homeland have declined as a source of ethnic identification. That is due, they say, to declining religiosity in general and among the Catholics to the rather dramatic changes that have overcome the Catholic Church in the past decade. Ethnic groups (they concentrated on "Negroes, Puerto Ricans, Jews, Italians, and Irish of New York City") have become largely political, economic, and cultural interest groups (Glazer and Moynihan, 1970: xxxiv–xxxvi). Interethnic relationships, by the same token, become dynamic, tension laden, and carry seeds of potential conflict. The major cities remain the locus of interethnic unrest. Paraphrasing Max Weber, cultural relationships that are not powercentered give way to political relations that certainly are.

ETHNICITY AND FAMILY LIFE STYLE

The maintenance of ethnic identification and solidarity ultimately rests on the ability of the family to socialize its members into the ethnic culture and thus to channel and control, perhaps program, future be-

6

havior. The manner in which the respective ethnic families carry out this function we refer to as family life styles. Consequently, the distinctive family life styles that developed as a consequence of historical and contemporary social processes become the focal concern of this work. Authors were asked to examine the relationships and characteristics distinctive of ethnic family life; to look to the past for explanation of historical or genetic significance; to describe the key characteristics of the ethnic family today; and to analyze the changes that have occurred to the family and speculate as to what lies ahead.

It bears repeating that the historical experience of the ethnic group both with respect to when the group arrived on these shores as well as the conditions under which the members of the group were forced to live is a vitally important factor in the explanation of the persistence of the ethnic family and the ethnic group as well. It is for this reason that each chapter contains an important discussion on the historical background of the respective ethnic groups. In addition to the old-country settings each author was requested to summarize the major characteristics of the family as it existed previously or as it first appeared in America, in order that the subsequent changes and adaptations could more clearly be seen.

One of the most significant ways in which an ethnic culture is expressed is through those activities that we identify as family activities. The family historically has been a conservative institution, and those cultural elements concerning family life, if not affected by outside forces, will tend to replace themselves generation after generation (Farber, 1964). Experiences within the family are intense, heavily emotion-laden, and are apt to evoke pleasurable or painful memories for most individuals. For example, it is not accidental that in many of the ethnic groups to be discussed here "eating" and particularly eating "ethnic" food remains a significant part of the ethnic identity. These are activities that occur in a family context. If traditional ethnic values are to be found anywhere, they will be found in the family.

In addition to developing historical context, the authors were asked to discuss four major areas relevant to ethnic family life in which ethnic culture might either be generated, sustained, or have an impact. First were the demographic characteristics of the ethnic family. How does the ethnic culture get specific expression in fertility, marriage, and divorce rates? How does the group cope with the cultural matter of intermarriage? Intermarriage can be viewed as an important indicator of assimilation for the ethnic group and ranges in incidence from very low among the Black Americans and Amish to relatively high as among the Japanese Americans. Second is the question of the structure of the

7

family, which involves the distribution of status, authority, and responsibility within the nuclear family and the network of kin relationships linking members of the extended family. Most discussions of ethnic family life have focused on this area because many ethnic groups have been characterized as patriarchal or matriarchal or as having very close knit extended family relationships. It is in this context that we hear comments about Black matriarchy or the "Jewish mother." How much is cultural myth or ideology? How much is fact? What has been the effect of the American experience?

In addition to the cultural patterns that define family roles and statuses, rights and obligations, there are many attributes of an ethnic culture that are mediated through the family. These are cultural values that concern such issues as achievement, style of life, and educational or occupational aspirations. While many historical, economic and other factors such as discrimination and prejudice have limited the mobility of individuals in many ethnic groups, for many the possession of a cultural reservoir of motivations and skills has worked to their distinct advantage. For others the lack of this reservoir has worked to their disadvantage. The cultural tradition of the Jews, with its emphasis on literacy and education, has helped them immeasurably from a socioeconomic standpoint. On the other hand, the Poles have only recently begun to emphasize the importance of education to their family members. These cultural distinctions, while existing to some extent outside the family context, are for the most part developed within the family.

Finally, in discussing ethnic family life, it is important to examine the family at different stages of the family life cycle. In this collection of essays authors were requested to analyze those aspects of child rearing, adolescence, mate selection, and the place of the elderly in which ethnic culture has had significant influence. The culture of many groups usually specifies what the most desirable end product of the socialization process should be. Whether this product should be a good Mormon or Amishman, the family as the major force of socialization, especially in the critical early years, is the most responsible ethnic institution.

Most of the large-scale immigration to America has ceased, although as in the case of the Puerto Ricans, the Greek Americans, Arab Americans, and most recently the war refugees from Cuba and Indo-China there has been a continuing or sudden large-scale migration to this country. Is it then true, as many writers have suggested, that ethnic differences may very well be on the decline, and in the future they may be relatively unimportant distinguishing features of individuals? In this book the authors will conclude the chapters with a brief look into the

8

future of ethnic groups. For some, such as Black Americans and other racial groups, these differences and potential for tension and conflict appear destined to continue for some time. For others, such as Greek Americans, Irish Americans, or Polish Americans, these distinctions appear to be disappearing at a somewhat faster rate.

ETHNIC DIVERSITY AS THE CRITERION OF SELECTION

Although not randomly selected, the ethnic families presented in this book were chosen to represent a rather wide spectrum of distinguishable groups, ranging from the less than 100,000 Amish to the 22 million Black people, whose ethnicity continues to be expressed through identifiable institutions and, significantly, the family. Nevertheless, there *are* large numbers of Americans who find it possible to trace descent to foreign nations and cultures such as Germany, Great Britain, and Canada, yet who retain little if any of an Old World cultural heritage. Their life styles are largely indistinguishable from others of similar socioeconomic classes, and for this reason they have been excluded from this work.

While the possession of an ethnic heritage that continues to be expressed in a distinctive family life style is the common theme among all groups chosen in this work, the reasons both for their appearance in America (remembering that American Indians had precedence!) and their continued existence as an identifiable ethnic group remain to some extent unique. That groups migrating to America in great numbers in pre- and early nineteenth-century periods were responding to general social, economic, and class-oppressive pressures gave all immigrants of that time a measure of common status. Nevertheless, each has its own distinguishing features, contingencies, and value system to provide significantly different ethnic group life histories, and therefore, each has its own story to be told.

There is some justification, then, for adopting the kaleidoscope approach and simply jumbling all 15 family groups together without anything more ordered than what can be achieved by an alphabetical arrangement. Or, conversely, for those more compulsive about systematization, a set of formal ahistorical, all-inclusive categories might be constructed. We have chosen something less abstract through the pragmatically useful grouping of our ethnic families into four substantive categories: (1) Early arriving ethnic minorities, (2) recent and continuing ethnic minorities, (3) historically subjugated but volatile ethnic minorities, and (4) socioreligious ethnic minorities.

These categories help sort out the groups according to several dimensions, but they should in no way be taken as definitive, completely exclusive, or the only way to achieve a useful classification. The most important criterion in the minds of the editors has been that the categories appear to capture a particularly important contingency or group experience that has had a continuing influence upon its collective fate. Let us briefly discuss the scheme that we have chosen:

1. Early Arriving Ethnic Minorities

The importance of this category lies in the time dimension. Each of these ethnic groups has been in this country in substantial numbers for 75 to 100 years. Important questions for the study of these groups relate to the effects of time and generation on the cultural heritage but more particularly as they directly affect family life. The extent to which assimilation and acculturation has had an impact on ethnic identity and life style remains one of the key problems encountered by these groups of people. The first group includes the Polish, Japanese, Italian, Irish, and Chinese American families. Religion plays an important role in all these families, but it is not such a determining factor as for others dealt with in the final section.

2. Recent and Continuing Ethnic Minorities

The three ethnic minorities in this category are the Arab, Greek, and Puerto Rican immigrants who arrived in the late nineteenth and early twentieth centuries. These ethnic groups (who in small numbers may have come to America earlier) are characterized by a sizable number of recent as well as a continuing flow of immigrants. The problems they have faced include adjusting to a modern business cycle and war-plagued industrialized society and to constant infusions of new representatives from their respective countries of origin.

3. Historically Subjugated but Volatile Ethnic Minorities

These groups either preceded the arrival of the "Americans" or arrived later and were immediately or later placed in some form of bondage. Enslaved to the land, alienated from it, or bound in a latter-day peonage, Blacks, Indians, and Latins have in America the darkest and least savory group life histories from which to build viable ethnic cultures. In at least two of these three groups it will be noted that the role of

10

the family, whether truncated or extended, becomes crucial for ethnic survival.

4. Socioreligious Ethnic Groups

These four groups, the Amish, the Jews, the Mormon, and the French Canadian Americans, are categorized together because their identity and experience have largely been a result of or strongly influenced, if not dominated, by their respective religions. By no means later arrivals, they all sought in America a place to live that kind of social existence in which religion could continue to be vitally conjoined with all aspects of their life and livelihood.

A NOTE ABOUT THE AUTHORS

When we originally conceived the idea of preparing a book on family life styles of American ethnic groups, one option was to write the book ourselves. However, the task of understanding and grasping the essence of the historical and cultural experiences of each of the suggested ethnic minorities appeared a virtual impossibility. Rather than embark on what would most likely end up as an exercise in futility, we felt a better choice would be to approach scholars in the field who themselves had researched and experienced the culture of some particular ethnic minority group. The success of this approach may be measured in the fact that in twelve chapters the authors themselves are members of the ethnic group they are writing about, and a number of these are widely recognized in the area of ethnic studies. In the other three ethnic family chapters the authors have spent many years in one way or another concerned about and as students of "the" American family in its common and diverse features. The biographical sketches included herein may not present a Who's Who in sociology, but they most certainly will discourage any member of an ethnic group from asking about the author of a chapter, "Who's that?"

REFERENCES

Burgess, Ernest, Harvey J. Locke, and Mary M. Thomes. 1963. *The Family* (3rd ed.). New York: American Book.
Cavan, Ruth S. 1969. *The American Family* (4th ed.). New York: Thomas Y. Crowell.

Elkin, Frederick. 1970 *The Family in Canada: An Account of Present Knowledge and Gaps in Knowledge about Canadian Families*. Ottawa: The Vanier Institute of the Family.

Farber, Bernard. 1964. *Family Organization and Interaction*. San Francisco: Chandler.

Fuchs, Victor. 1968. *The Service Economy*. New York: National Bureau of Research. Distributed by Columbia University Press.

Glazer, Nathan, and Daniel P. Moynihan. 1970. *Beyond the Melting Pot* (2nd ed.). Cambridge, Mass.: M.I.T. Press.

————. 1954. "Ethnic Groups in America: From National Culture to Ideology." In Morroe Berger, Theodore Abel, and Charles H. Page (eds.): *Freedom and Control in Modern Society*. New York: Van Nostrand.

Gordon, Milton. 1964. *Assimilation in American Life*. New York: Oxford University Press.

Gouldner, Alvin. 1970. *The Coming Crisis in Western Sociology*. New York: Basic Books.

Greeley, Andrew M. 1969. *Why Can't They Be Like Us?* New York: Institute of Human Relations Press.

Herberg, Will. 1955. *Protestant, Catholic and Jew*. New York: Doubleday.

Ishwaran, K. (ed). 1971. *The Canadian Family: A Book of Readings*. Toronto and Montreal: Holt, Rinehart and Winston of Canada Ltd.

Kephart, William M. 1972. *The Family, Society and the Individual*. (3rd. ed.) Boston: Houghton Mifflin.

Nye, F. Ivan, and Felix Berardo. 1973. *The Family: Its Structure and Interaction*. New York: Macmillan.

Rose, Peter I. 1974. *They and We: Racial and Ethnic Relations in the United States*. (2nd. ed.) New York: Random House.

Queen, Stuart, and Robert W. Habenstein. 1974. *The Family in Various Cultures*. (4th ed.) Philadelphia: Lippincott.

Reiss, Ira. 1971. *The Family System in America*. New York: Holt, Rinehart and Winston.

Wade, Mason (ed.). 1960. *Canadian Dualism*. Toronto: Toronto University Press.

EARLY ETHNIC MINORITIES
(circa 1850-1920)

The Polish American Family

The main thrust of this chapter is upon the Polish American family as it exists within the developing and changing Polish ethnic community, an area Dr. Lopata refers to as Polonia. This emphasis is acknowledged to be different from much of the literature on ethnic groups, which is primarily concerned with individualistic assimilation and acculturation, and which attempts to determine the factors that impede or facilitate the absorption of peoples into a society. This chapter focuses on certain background characteristics of Old World Polish culture, especially in its peasant variations and of the historical trends in Polonia, which have created a unique ethnic community that persists into the 1970's. The Polish family must be seen in its relation to the continued existence of the Polish American community.

CHAPTER TWO
BY
HELENA ZNANIECKI LOPATA

HISTORICAL BACKGROUND

The Polish immigrants constituted one of the last two sizable groups to come from Europe prior to the immigration acts of the 1920s. The quota acts, culminating in the 1924 immigration law (which went into effect in 1929), limited the number of Polish entrants to 6,488 per year (U.S. Department of Justice, 1969: 1–10). Actually, the quota for Poland was not filled in most of the years since 1929 due to the changing political and socioeconomic situation both in the mother country and in America. World War II affected Poland strongly, with long-run effects on international relations and immigration to America. About six million Poles died, a minority in the fighting but a major number through purposeful extermination by the Nazis. Approximately the same numbers were deported to Siberia by the Soviets or to labor camps by the Nazis, or escaped over the borders to join the Allied fighting troops. Those who left were a heterogeneous amalgam, but heavily overrepresented by the intelligentsia, both Jewish and non-Jewish, and those of the upper

15

classes who were not exterminated (Szczepanski, 1962 and 1970). The aftermath of the war found many of those who survived unwilling to return to Poland because it was dominated by a restrictive Communist Party strongly affiliated with a traditional enemy. The American government passed several special laws allowing these displaced persons excombatants, and their families to immigrate here outside of the quotas.

Haiman (1948: 30), a major historian of Poles in America, divides the immigration into three periods: the "Colonial Immigration from 1608–1776 of artisans and adventurers;" the "Political Immigration from 1776–1865 of soldiers, writers, political exiles and noblemen:" and the great waves of the "Economic Immigration," starting in 1865 and involving mainly the subclasses of peasants and particularly the landless farm workers. The latter was accompanied by a lively back and forth movement across the ocean of political émigrées and men returning to Europe in preparation for World War I. The migrants returned frequently to escort their families to the land of their new settlement. Political refugees were forced out after attempts failed to free Poland from political control by Russia, Prussia, and Austria (countries that had partitioned Poland three times in the eighteenth century). The last partition actually removed Poland from the map of Europe in 1794. Estimations of the actual number of Polish immigrants who came here and who remained are problematic because of this back and forth movement, and because the American Immigration and Naturalization Service and the Bureau of Census kept changing their definitions of who was a Pole in response to the political situation in Europe. It is generally known that the two decades between 1900 and 1920, when Poland was not listed as a country of origin, are the very ones that witnessed the greatest Polish migration to America, the high point in numbers for a single year being recorded as 174,365 for 1912–13. (The year is computed on a fiscal rather than a calendar basis; Schermerhorn, 1949: 265.) World War I stemmed the flow, but it resumed after the situation settled down, mainly through the entrance of relatives of earlier immigrants. The decades 1900–19 are recorded by Haiman as witnessing 875,000 Polish immigrants to America (Haiman, 1949: 30). The post-World War II special immigration act included 162,462 Poles, who form what the Polish American community calls the "new emigration."

More detailed examination of the immigrants of 1909, a typical pre-World War I year, finds that most of the Poles came to join relatives, fewer joining friends, and only a handful venturing forth as pioneers or through the initiative of people whom they did not know from the homeland and to whom they were not related. Most of the immigrants that year, as throughout the economic phase of the "old emigration" period, were farm laborers, laborers of other kinds, servants, or wives and the children of these men. Only 102 had been farmers in Poland, that is, had owned their own land rather than renting their labor to farmers. In 1910, 35 per cent of the Poles entering America were illiterate, a proportion similar to that of Russians, Rumanians, Croatians, and Slovanians, and lower than other groups except the Italians (Lieberson, 1963: 72). Almost one-fourth as many Poles left America in those years as had entered it, and the outflow almost equaled the inflow in the years immediately preceding World War I (U.S. Department of Justice, 1909: 22–23, 68).

Most of the Polish immigrants, although peasants by background, settled in the urban industrial areas of Chicago, Detroit, and Buffalo, or in Pennsylvania mining towns such as Scranton or Erie. Few ventured South or West. Some settled along the Connecticut Valley and on farm land in Wisconsin, Michigan, and Minnesota. Recent survey estimates indicate there were 4,021,000 people in America of Polish origin in 1969, and that this total would increase to 4,941,000 in 1971. (U.S. Bureau of Census, 1969). The totals, of course, include the "new emigration." The presence of several different generations and of the two main "emigrations," the "old" and the "new," have contributed to the complexity and heterogeneity of Polonia as an ethnic community.

The Poles in America: Polonia

The Poles migrating to America resembled other migrant groups in that most were part of the lower classes in the mother country, came from rural and agricultural areas, had obtained little formal education, were restricted by a culture very foreign to the previously established American dominant one, lacked familiarity with the cosmopolitan world, had no "calling cards" guaranteeing positive social contact and interaction, and packaged all these characteristics into an ethnic style of life and minority status in the society.*

Although physically different from the established urban Americans because of cultural traits, the women stigmatized by a "babuszka" covering the hair and part of the wrinkled face and dark, shapeless dresses,

---

*Louis Wirth's (1945: 347) classic definition of minorities is undoubtedly used in other parts of this book, but it bears repeating here: "We may define a minority as a group of people who, because of their physical or cultural characteristics, are singled out from the others in the society in which they live for differential and unequal treatment, and who therefore regard themselves as objects of collective discrimination."

17

the men by a heavy walk and "dour" (Zand, 1956: 86) facial expression, symbolizing the fatalistic philosophy of peasants accustomed to a hard life, they had an advantage over Black and Oriental immigrants in that these differentiating characteristics were discardable through the acculturation process (Gordon: 1964). Like other immigrants, they tended to huddle together, usually in urban subcommunities within or near older ghetto areas, with clear physical or social boundaries isolating them from the foreign and generally hostile dominant society and culture. Both the local communities and superterritorial Polish American community became known as "Polonia." As true of other groups in the past and each new group in America, they were unable to reproduce the social structure and way of life of their homeland. Therefore, they reformulated their ideas, norms, and relations in the new environment, trying to retain measures of solidarity and social control while inventing new, stopgap measures to prevent complete "demoralization" (Thomas and Znaniecki, 1918–20, Part IV, Chap. 1). Gradually they built marginal communities of varying degrees of institutional complexity (Breton, 1964).

The Poles in America have been differentiated from other minority groups in several ways. First, they did not originally come here to stay, to settle and become "Americanized." They came to earn money, invest in property, wait for the right opportunity, then sell and return to Poland to buy land that would assure them a desirable social status within the familiar world of a limited reference group. Of course, there were other migrants who had dreamed of return to the homeland, but the Poles displayed an unusual lack of interest in American society, in learning its characteristics, and in acquiring traits that could gain them increasingly higher social status individually, in family units, or even as a subcommunity. Before the arrival of the "new emigration" the gradual process of settling down and becoming Americanized went largely unnoticed, while attention was focused on Poland and the internal competition for status within Polonia. Since all the ills of life in the home country could be blamed on foreign occupation, they did not even resent the upper classes as much as did immigrants from other European countries. Their relation with the mother country was, in fact, unique, and it strongly influenced Polonia's life.

Another distinguishing feature is that the culture that they brought with them was not only peasant but also very different from the American Protestant, English-based, Western culture. They were unsuited to immediate involvement in the life of society and experienced restricted interaction with its established members. For example, their religion

18

was Catholic, of ideosyncratic hue, with its own saints, Polish language during ceremonies and confessionals, and special ways of celebrating important events. Here they immediately entered into conflict with the Roman Catholic Church, which was controlled primarily by Irish priests, to the extent of having part of the community break away from this traditional identification to form the Polish National Catholic Church.*

The large number of Polish immigrants has been a very important factor in Polonia: Large size, paradoxically, contributes to social isolation, in that it aids in the creation of a relatively self-sufficient ethnic community and increases the probability of prejudice and discrimination from other groups. Closely related has been the complexity of the ethnic community that they developed, with a multiplicity of voluntary associations whose membership is drawn not from the elite but from all social layers. The complexity of the community has been maintained in large measure by the presence of a *highly developed status competition*. This has motivated even second- and third-generation Polish Americans into involvement with the community instead of "passing" into the dominant society, or at least into the "melting pot" (Gordon, 1964).

The Creation of Polonia as an Ethnic Community

Settlement of the Poles was fairly organized; most of the men (later followed by their families), who already knew someone in America, found a job and a place to live. Friends and family served as intermediaries to build ties between the newcomer and the social system. Gradually, with increasing numbers of Poles in a settlement, there arose a diversification of services and organizations designed to meet their unique needs. A few of the more affluent immigrants or their children opened neighborhood stores carrying Polish foods. Parishes were started and maintained with the help of a variety of newly created groups out of necessity rather than a tradition of organized action in Poland. Mutual-aid societies were created to ensure "a nice funeral" and help in illness since there were few wealthy people willing to extend traditional

---

*The Polish National Catholic Church, founded in the early years of the twentieth century, has as its main characteristics a lay board of control, marriage and family rights of priests, the use of Polish and later English language during the Mass, and rejection of the pope and the concept of papal infallibility. It never won over a high proportion of Polish Americans, but the very action of its creation and its continued presence in the community reinforce Polonian anticlergy attitudes by reminding them of the Irish control over Roman Catholicism and of the lack of Polish American representation in that hierarchy. It also contributed an additional status hierarchy to the system (Lopata, 1954).

charity. The combination of need and willingness to experiment with solutions in spite of a rigid and limited cultural background, and the presence of political émigrées and more settled immigrants assisted in the building of Polonia as a distinctive ethnic community. This community consists of local neighborhoods that were first predominantly Polish and then gradually Polish American, "settlements" combining more than one neighborhood (Breton, 1964), local communities combining several settlements, as in Chicago's Polonia, and the superterritorial (Thomas and Znaniecki, 1918–20) Polonia, the ethnic community that weaves together those scattered throughout America who have even minimal ties with it as well as those identified with the smaller territorial units.*

A period of intense patriotism, during which Polonia was known as the "fourth Province of Poland," lasted from the turn of the century till the early 1920s. It was followed by a gradually developing but cumulatively strong disillusionment and withdrawal. Poland after World War I went through a period of intense political conflict with which the Polish Americans could not identify and that spoiled their romanticized image of the mother country. Much of the money invested in businesses and in government bonds was lost, and the war-torn country kept needing more help. Also, Poland and Polonia did not really have as much in common as the patriotic years had portrayed. Contact was mainly personal, through correspondence with relatives and villagers left behind, occasional visits to "the old country," and a minimal sharing of a few items of folk or religious culture. The Polish Americans for the most past did not know Polish culture, and Poles in Poland were not interested in the ethnic culture Polonia was gradually developing. World War II brought renewal of the humanistic interest in the suffering of Poles, who were occupied again by the old enemies, Russia and Germany. The repressive acts of the Nazis won pro-Polish sympathy from Americans of all ethnic identification. Relief activity in Polonia continued even after the war in spite of its very strong anticommunist stand. In recent years, with

---

*I am using here the concept of ethnic community as developed in Caroline F. Ware's classic article in the first *Encyclopedia of Social Sciences* (11:607–13). She wrote "Ethnic communities are groups bound together by common ties of race, nationality or culture, living together within an alien civilization but remaining culturally distinct . . . Such communities vary according to their origin, their cohesive factors, the attitudes of the outer community, and the nature of the civilization of which they are part. The ethnic community in a large society can be geographically located in many different neighborhoods, and the term refers to both the local and the superterritorial unit. The concept of "Polonia" is of this nature as it refers to the community of identification binding all Polish-Americans to each other and to the press and organizations that involve them in communication and cooperative activities, even competitive ones.

the thawing of the Cold War there is an active traffic of people between Poland and Polonia. Also, in recent years, concern with status in America and the increasing level of education achievement of Polish American youth have resulted in a closer bond of interest in the national culture, dispelling some of the prejudice Poles have against the Polish Americans as frozen in an archaic folk culture and some of the prejudice descendants of the peasants have of the Poles as portrayed in current Polish jokes.

The Family Heritage of the Old Emigration

The Polish village system contained a complex class structure but one that was very insular, that is, psychologically and culturally isolated from the broader national culture society at the turn of the century when most of the immigration took place. Although the urbanized and particularly the Polish upper classes were highly nationalistic and organized into a society that ran across political boundaries of three states, most villagers limited their identities and interests to the local *okolica* (Thomas and Znaniecki, 1918–20), or the area within which a man's "reputation" is contained. The *okolica* includes the territory lived in and worked by his family and the other villagers of his community, and sometimes other villages if they were sufficiently close for repeated contact. This *okolica* was sufficiently heterogeneous in terms of family status to allow the development of a major aspect of Polish village culture: status competition. Polish families attempted to gather many items of high status in an ongoing competition vis-à-vis other families.

Although the basic unit which status was assigned in pre-World War I years in village Poland was the family, such a system was highly individualistic. Each person was born to a family with a certain more or less crystallized position vis-à-vis other families within the *okolica*. This ascribed status was cumulative and competitive; points were won by the acquisition of new prestige items and lost by negatively evaluated actions or by the loss of items from which prestige flows. A complicated status hierarchy within the village and a certain flexibility of social movement in its boundaries gave each family member the opportunity of playing the competitive game. At the same time, each person needed his family to provide him with a background and objects used for the status competition and to continue working together for the accumulation of new points. Thus, to the extent that each member was locked into the village and could not "make it on his own," and to the extent to which daily life and exceptional events were very public, family solidarity,

21

found to be a basic characteristic of the peasant social system, was a vital necessity. Each member of the family must earn his right to membership and continue earning it throughout life. Very strong measures of family social control were used to prevent deviation that might decrease the family reputation, and fear of shame extended to the whole household, which often contained grandparents, an aunt or other siblings of either parents, the parents, their unmarried siblings, still unmarried offspring, vagabond relatives resting for a time, traveling seers pausing to educate the young in the rudiments of schooling, and the owner and his wife (Finestone, 1964).* Family members who disgraced the unit were simply ignored or, in extreme cases, even legally disowned.

All of life in the village was flavored by the status competition. Marriage was not a matter of love but an arrangement guaranteeing the best status and economic position for the new unit. Because of the importance of the competition, all social actions were carefully observed and, through gossip, crystallized and added or subtracted from the status package that was always partially open to recrystallization within the life cycle. Personal reputations formed an important aspect of the individual's and the family's status and revolved around efficiency, specialization in an admired craft, intelligent use of property, personality, looks, and behavior. Official positions in the community political structure were an added source of social status, as was personal influence of the charismatic or associational types. This constant evaluation developed the feelings of independence, personal worth, and importance as a contributor to the unit's points.

Establishing the Family in America

The first members of a family to venture on the long journey overseas to a foreign land were young men, who had a better chance of finding employment, and who, once in America, were more free to experiment than men bringing their families over in the first crossing. Young single women also came to stay in homes of relatives, but they were fewer in

---

*Helen Merrell Lynd (1965) distinguishes between societies using guilt from those using shame as a means of socialization and social control. Guilt-based societies ensure that their members internalize generalized rules of behavior (see also Mead, 1934), which then operate as a "superego" so that a person stops himself from committing negatively sanctioned acts because he believes them to be wrong and feels guilt if he crosses into such behavior. Shame-based societies contain members who fear exposure and ridicule and thus stop from committing disapproved acts. In situations in which a family can be shamed by the action of any one of its members, strong social controls are applied by it during the socialization process of children, and pressure is constantly put on adults. There is also a constant effort to keep transgression from public knowledge.

22

number than the men. The location chosen by the immigrants for settlement in this vast land was not selected at random but followed the migration chain established by early pioneers who had been successful in finding employment and residence.

The villager in Poland learned through letters* or the grapevine of the opportunities in America, where an effort equal to, or even less than, that to which he was already accustomed produced economic benefits far outweighing what he was able to wrest from the homeland (Curti and Birr, 1950; Thomas and Znaniecki, 1918–20). He usually left for the New World in the company of other men from the same family or village and aimed for the town or city in which he knew someone already established. He usually boarded with friends or relatives. The few women who were part of the early migration waves ran such boarding houses since this was considered women's work and highly appropriate for those who were married, and because it allowed them to stay home while at the same time contributing income to the family welfare. "The boarders were frequently brothers or other near relatives of the husband or wife, or fellow townsmen from the old country, and so the household was something in the nature of an enlarged family" (Zand, 1956: 79).

The sex ratio of the pre-World War I immigration was heavily in favor of males, but the distribution evened out over the decades as more and more women joined the tide, mainly as wives and children of the male pioneers. Some men deserted their wives and children in Poland, never sending for them or bringing them over from the homeland; others vanished to another city in America after importing them here in search of a better job or in solution to many problems, but there are no figures as to the frequency of such practices (Zand, 1956: 78).

The most favored occupation for married women and girls was one that kept them in or around their homes or at least near other Poles. Wives contributed to the family income by maintaining boarding houses or "helping their husbands run a grocery store or a saloon" (Zand, 1956: 84). For unmarried girls, the most favored occupation was service in private households. "Young men married a girl who had been in domestic service more readily than one who had worked in a factory partly because they expected that she would be a better housekeeper" (Zand, 1956: 85). Factory work was also evaluated in traditional terms; if the girl had to work in industry, then it should be as close to the settlement

---

*It would be difficult to overestimate the importance of the letters exchanged across the Atlantic. Many were published in newspapers, others circulated hand-to-hand in the villages thus expanding an informal contact network.

23

and with as many other Poles as possible. Concern over morality in working conditions and the attitudes toward education for women severely restricted the occupational opportunities of this sex throughout Polonia's history. Young girls were supposed to stay home, help their mothers take care of younger children, and do housekeeping rather than "wasting" their time in any but primary parochial education. Obidinski (1968) found the negative attitude attached to education for girls still dominant in Buffalo, New York, in the 1960s among the lower-class members of the Polonian community and not absent among those he identified as of the upper class.

Emerging Family Relations in Polonia

Although the sex-role definitions of traditional Polonia rejected the idea of women leaving home and community social control for educational or work experience, even at the cost of decreasing the economic contribution they could make to the family, certain changes have been observed over time in the relations between men and women as a result of immigration life circumstances in America. In the first place, according to Zand (1956), women gained family power as a result of the processes of immigration and settlement. They became the sole heads of households when the men left for America or for a better job in another city once the family migrated here. The jobs the men were able to get usually required long hours of work, six days a week, so that the children did not see their fathers most of their waking hours. Women dominated the household. "This female hegemony was due in large part, no doubt, to the influence of the American family and social patterns in which women have far greater importance than in the Polish scheme (Zand 1956: 77). The traditional peasant living arrangement and family structure had necessitated the wife's leaving her family and moving into or near the home of her husband's family. Such a family living arrangement supported the patriarchal authority system, and the wife was relatively powerless until she accumulated her own reputation. Some of her symbols of status were brought with her from her family reputation and dowry; increasing age, and birth of children and acquisition of children-in-law, plus the increasing power of her husband over the other men in the family helped build her sphere of influence over time.

The situation in America, on the other hand, shortened the number of years required for a woman to gain power in her family since she was able to establish her own home without taking her husband's family into consideration. She was freed from the patriarchal, consanguine struc-

24

ture by the very fact that her husband's family was very apt to have remained back in Poland. In addition, as Zand (1956: 77) points out, so many of the pre-World War I immigrants were men, and the only women the single ones among them could marry were the daughters of more settled families. Under these circumstances, the young couples often lived with the wife's parents until they became economically independent, and those wives who were more acculturated than the husbands were able to influence family decisions to an extent much greater than typical of traditional village women. As late as the early 1950s Wood found women in Hamtramck to be the "first authority on domestic problems." In fact, "in families of the laboring class the wife not only has the final say in domestic matters, but also acts as manager and treasurer" (Wood, 1955: 207). In spite of the strong tradition of sex-segregated marital relationships. Obidinski (1968: 103) found a definite shift in decision-making responsibilities in the home among his Buffalo, New York, Polish American respondents of the 1960s. The adult respondents who compared their own homes to those of their parents claimed a strong trend from sex-segregated to sharing behavior between husband and wife in decisions regarding the budget, the discipline of children, the choice of recreation, even shopping, but not much in housekeeping.

PARENT CHILD RELATIONS. The traditional authority of the male parent over his offspring has been a recorded part of Polish family culture (Reymont, 1925; Thomas and Znaniecki, 1918–20; Finestone, 1964; Zand, 1956). Children were always expected to obey without question and to continually contribute to the family welfare. The following prayer, distributed by the Orchard Lake Seminary as late as the 1970s, printed in Polish on one side and English on the other, is indicative of the ideals of strength of family control and influence.

PRAYER OF CHILDREN FOR PARENTS

O Almighty God, who has given unto me my father and mother, and made them to be an image of Thy authority and tender watchfulness, and hast commanded me to love, honor, and obey them in all things, give me the grace to keep this law cheerfully and with my whole heart. Help me to love them fervently, to honor them truly, to yield a ready obedience to all their wishes, to study their happiness in everything, and to bear with patience the humility of their rebukes. May I in no lawful concern whatever offend my parents on earth, or displease Thee my Father, who are in heaven. Through Jesus Christ, our Lord. Amen.

Even in America, the child was expected to contribute everything he or she earned to the family income, to be distributed as the parents saw fit. This norm became one of the first and strongest sources of intergenerational conflict as soon as the young people learned of their own market value and the economic independence of children of other ethnic backgrounds. Many cases were brought to court by parents against their children because of the latter's failure to turn over income and their tendency to leave home because of conflict (Thomas and Znaniecki, 1918–20; Finestone, 1964). As noted before, any members not contributing to the family status position by virtue of uncooperative action or by shaming it in front of other families were removed from the membership list of this unit or forced through external social control agencies to mend their ways.

Obidinski (1968: 143) found strong class differences among Buffalo Polish Americans of the 1960s in the expectation that children should "supplement family income" in their parental home when they were growing up, with working-class and middle-class respondents having higher expectations than higher status respondents.

RELATIONS WITH THE ELDERLY. Much of the recorded bitterness in Polonia revolves around the economic obligations of the adults to the older parents. Hamtramck parents complained that "after they finished school, they got married, and they are not help for the parents at all. They leave home and forget about their poor old parents" (Wood, 1955: 215). The parents were not psychologically or financially prepared to maintain themselves independently of their adult children, who had adopted the more American view of the family man or women as having primary obligations to his or her own development, then to his or her family of procreation, rather than to the family of orientation.

A current study of widowed women in metropolitan Chicago (Lopata, 1973c) and a survey of the needs of older people by the Mayor's Office for Senior Citizens in 1972 (Lopata, 1973c) uncover an undercurrent or open expression of anger, helplessness, and hostility of the elderly toward their adult children and grown grandchildren for "abandoning them." Many of the older Polish Americans are still living in the old neighborhoods among Blacks, Puerto Ricans, and Mexicans with whom they have very unpleasant relations, while their offspring have moved to the suburbs or urban fringes. Simultaneously, however, they are pleased over being able to maintain an independent existence in a changing urban scene and over not having to work, even by their being able to help the younger generations with homemaking and child rearing. They express pleasure over having privacy and control over their own homes and lives, unusual in the history of the Polish immigrants and other older-generation Polish-American women.

SIBLINGS. Another area of possible family strains in Polonia besides those between husband and wife, parents and children, is within the family of orientation as siblings reach adulthood. The complexity of the community and of the American society and the decrystallization of status roles, accompanied by multiplication of status sources, have lead to uneven social mobility among brothers and sisters. Although feelings of obligation to the elderly parents, even if they are obviously of an inferior social status, are still sufficiently strong that some efforts for maintaining contact and assistance are made intergenerationally, in relations with other relatives they are less likely to survive as a viable source of support (Lopata, 1973a and b).

FAMILY DISORGANIZATION. In spite of strains between sexes and generations, the Polish American family has survived its first century of transition from being Polish to being American. Many observers of the Polish peasant immigrant in America, particularly Thomas and Znaniecki (1918–20) predicted extensive family disorganization, having observed many instances of conflict in the years surrounding World War I and its increase in the future. The old patterns of family and community control seemed to be weakening and not being replaced by new forms of self-control. The problems surrounding immigration and settlement in such a foreign country were taking their toll during these years: marital relations broke into open conflict and the young men of the second generation were coming into conflict both with their parents and with the American law enforcement system. Yet, the usual indices of family disorganization, divorce and crime have not supported these predictions. The Polish Americans have relatively low divorce rates and the juvenile delinquency rates decreased over time as the young men of the second generation grew into stabilized adulthood and the third generation displayed little tendency to repeat the pattern. There may be several reasons for the apparent infrequency of divorce among Polish Americans. One reason may be adherence to the Catholic religion, which has universally, and in Polish Catholicism especially, been opposed to divorce (Thomas, 1950; Rooney, 1957). A second could be the "moralistic fibre" of Polish culture, which contains a negative image of human nature (Finestone, 1964: 122–32; Zand, 1960; Thomas and Znaniecki, 1918–20) and emphasizes the importance of the

27

family as a means of controlling it. It is quite possible that even in the marginal Polish American community, a man and certainly a woman bring shame and ridicule on themselves if they resort to divorce. The woman, after all, is supposed to remain in the home (Zand, 1956) and not support herself and her children through paid employment. Also, if the status competition has been and continues to be as important in Polonia as suggested, even an open conflict between family members (between husband and wife particularly) might be offset, or at least balanced, by their mutual need for cooperative action vis-à-vis other families. Since the bond in marriage has not traditionally been love but mutual status benefit, it is hard to imagine any gain derived from "hedonistic" behavior. Finally, open and total family disorganization may have been prevented by the presence of the active and diversified community superstructure, involving not only the educated elite but even the rather uneducated men and women. David (1971: 124) reports that in 1921 "among the Poles it was estimated that 70 to 80 per cent of the men belonged to at least one society and that 50 per cent of the women have organizations of their own." Such social engagement may have taken attention away from marital problems and, combined with the advantages of team contributions to the status competition, thus added to marital stability. Of course, the absence of high rates of divorce does not preclude strain and conflict in husband-wife relations.

Recent Transitions in the Polish American Family

While Polonia has moved through its ideological changes from close identification with Poland into a more or less institutionally complete ethnic community of highly American sub-culture, its members have also changed. Concerned mainly with their own community life and status competition within it, they neglected the dominant American society and its status system until very recently. The elites, composed of the intelligentsia, political and organizational leaders and those who have become economically successful stay within their own companionate circles, while the rest of the community has become status decrystallized moving upward into higher positions of the blue collar world and even crossing into the white collar world. The various sources of information about the Polish Americans reflect many characteristics of transitional family movement up the socio-economic ladder and into the mainstream of American society, while still retaining vestiges of Polish folk culture and immigrant background.

PREMARITAL SEXUAL RELATIONS. Greeley (1971) found a decreasing double standard in attitudes toward the sexual behavior of the youth in his analysis of Catholic Americans. The Polish Americans registered approval of the male "when he is engaged" in kissing (95 per cent) and petting (70 per cent) but not in intercourse (13 per cent). Moreover, the proportions were similar for girls. Comparatively, Poles were much more permissive of petting while rejective of intercourse than other groups, the Jewish being permissive on all levels of sexual behavior (92, 63, 49 per cent, respectively), while the Italians were more rejective of both petting and intercourse, and the Irish, although more rejective of petting, were more permissive of intercourse for boys, but not for girls.

INTERMARRIAGE. The Polish-stock younger men (under 45 years of age) are twice as apt than are the older men to be married to native-born daughters of native parentage (53 to 22 per cent, respectively), but they are not at all likely to select brides identified as Black (.0001 per cent), Puerto Rican (.002 per cent), or of Spanish heritage (.01 per cent). Those married to foreign or mixed-parentage wives are, as might be expected, most inclined toward women born in Poland. Germany and particularly the U.S.S.R. are the places of origin of a large number of these women, not surprisingly in view of the above-mentioned problems of national identification. Only .07 per cent of the younger and .04 per cent of the older men are married to Italian-stock women, only .02 per cent of the younger and .01 per cent of the older men to Irish stock women. These figures do not support the Kennedy (1952) theory of the "triple-melting" pot, composed of the three major religious groups. In fact, the Polish-stock men are just as apt to marry women of the United Kingdom or of Canadian background, .04 per cent of the younger and .02 per cent of the older men having done so.

FERTILITY. Fertility rates for Polish American women have been dropping considerably over the years, particularly among those who are or have been married, who are now in the ages between 15 and 44, who live in urban areas in the central city, and who are working full time. The trends reflect those of American females in general. The Polish foreign-born women who were between 35 and 44 years of age in 1910 had the highest number of "children ever born" to a foreign-born white group of that age cohort: a total of 5,868 per 1,000 women. The rate for that age group dropped to 2,776 in 1960, ranking the Poles seventh out of nine foreign groups in fertility. By 1969 they had dropped to eighth place with

2,513 per 1,000, a rate far below that typical of women in 1969, since the national rate was 3,003 children ever born per 1,000 women (U.S. Bureau of the Census, November 1971: 20, Table 9). This figure stands in spite of identification with the Catholic religion, which officially forbids artificial contraception. Interestingly enough, Polish American wives existing on the lowest quartile of family income in America are not the ones who report the highest rate of children; the highest rate is recorded for women in the second from the lowest quartile. The figures, going from lowest to highest, of 1,985, 2,425, 2,304, and 2,138 probably reflect the health deficiencies of the poorest American mothers (U.S. Bureau of Census, November 1971: 20,226, Table 6).

RESIDENCE. In 1970, according to the U.S. Census *General Social and Economic Characteristics,* there was a total of 548,107 foreign born and 1,826,137 native born with one or both foreign-born parents who are identified as Polish Americans. Interestingly, only four-fifths of the foreign born list Polish as their mother tongue, while the number of second-generation Poles listing it as a mother tongue far exceeds those listing one or more parent as foreign born.

The heavy concentration of Polish Americans was still located, in 1970, in and around the central cities of the North east and North Central states, but there has been a definite movement from the cities to the urban fringes on the part of the native-born descendants of foreign or mixed parentage. That is, about two-thirds of the foreign born residing in metropolitan areas still live in the central city, while half of the native-born descendants live in the central city, the remaining located at the urban fringes. Relatively few native-born or second-generation Polish Americans live in small cities, most of the people outside of metropolitan areas residing in nonfarm rural areas. The most frequent listing of Polish as a mother tongue is interestingly among people who live in nonmetropolitan areas of the country. There is no difference between residents of central cities or urban fringes as to the proportion that list Polish as their mother tongue. In their urban-rural distribution the Poles resemble the Italians and Russians, who are also overrepresented in the urban areas in proportion to their contribution to the general population. The Poles are particularly underrepresented in rural farm locations.

EDUCATIONAL AND OCCUPATIONAL ACHIEVEMENT. The traditional peasant attitudes toward formal education were very negative, intellectual matters being defined as the province of the nobility and the intelligentsia; schooling was seen as an economic waste and a source of intergenerational problems (Thomas and Znaniecki, 1918–20; Reymont, 1925). The only school system the immigrants trusted to rear their children was the parochial one, which was expected to teach them Polish Catholicism and moral values. Education past the 14th, or other legal year of compulsory schooling meant deprivation to the family economic system, at least as seen through the traditional short range perspective (Abel, 1929; Miaso, 1971). As a result, few Polish Americans of the second generation, old emigration even finished high school, let alone entered college, the women being even less encouraged to schooling than were the men.

The lack of formal education beyond the minimum and the limitation of schooling to parochial schools which were not very intellectually oriented (Greeley and Rossi, 1969) resulted in a lack of occupational mobility between generations. The majority of the Polish emigration from pre-World War II Poland came from rural areas with agricultural skills and settled in urban centers requiring unskilled labor. The men went to the steel mills of Illinois and Indiana, to the packinghouses of Chicago, the automobile assembly lines of Detroit and the coal mines of Pennsylvania. A few became farmers in the Connecticut Valley or the midwestern states. Over time, they saved their money and moved slightly up the occupational scale, but their sons started out with a disadvantage in comparison to other immigrant groups because of the lateness of their father's arrival, his unskilled status and the tendency of the second generation to stay in the same general occupational area (Hutchinson, 1956; Lieberson, 1963; Duncan and Duncan, 1968). By the late 1960s and the 1970s these two generations of Polish stock men, at least those who survived, were in the top rungs of the blue collar world and their children or grandchildren were moving up into the lower rungs of the white collar world. The median family income of the Polish Americans has been recently rather high, compared with other groups of similar background, but it came more from the blue-collar than from the white collar jobs, because the latter are being held by the young, still new in their occupations. (Greeley, 1975). The occupational distributions for the whole ethnic groups, obtained by the United States Census of 1969 which asked for ethnic origin rather than country of birth of the self and of the parents reflects the polarization of these generations of Polish Americans with a high proportion of the men still in the craftsmen, foremen and kindred workers category (23 per cent) with 19 per cent still working as operatives and kindred workers, 18 per cent as professionals and 13 per cent as managers, officials and related personnel (U.S. Bureau of Census, *Current Population Reports,* 1971 P-20:249, T-7). The Polish American women reflect their lack of formal education in that 16 per cent are still in service occupations, 36 per cent in clerical job, 19 per cent working as operatives and only 13 per cent in professional occupations.

CHANGE AND ADAPTATION

The New Polish Americans

There is strong evidence in the form of census figures that the Polish Americans are undergoing dramatic change under the influence of an increasing interest in status within the broader society. In recent years the children of the financially well-positioned craftsmen, foremen, paid organizational officials, and managers have turned to the main means of upward mobility available in America: higher education. These facts are not reflected in the Greeley and Rossi (1968) study conducted in 1964, in Duncan and Duncan's (1968) analysis based on 1962 data, nor in the composite pulled together by Greeley (1973), which included studies in 1963, 1964, and two in 1965, but they are evident in the results of a special supplement to the November 1969 Current Population Survey (U.S. Bureau of Census, 1971). This survey not only asked for the country of birth of the father and mother and of the self and spouse, the mother tongue, and the language currently spoken at home, but also allowed the respondent to determine his or her own "origin or descent," a practice not followed by previous census survey but similar to that followed by the National Opinion Research Center. According to this report, "About 75 million of the approximately 200 million persons in the United States reported that they were of one of the seven specific origin categories covered" (221:1). Four million of these reported having a Polish "origin or descent." Of these, the older adults, or those 35 years of age or over, completed only 10.9 years of schooling, but the younger ones, between 25 and 34, completed 12.7. In this achievement they were topped only by the Russians, who have an average of of over 16 years of education. The Poles had a level of educational achievement higher than the English, the Germans, and the Irish, who had a higher level of educational achievement than the Poles among the older age groups. The 1969 survey shows the Polish Americans earning a family income of $8,849, which is higher than that of any other group included in the analysis with the exception of the Russians. The Russian group is heavily weighted by the presence of Jews who had been born in that country because the immigrant waves included mostly Jews and very few non-Jews. In the case of the Poles, although the presence of Jews

32

who identify Poland as their country of origin has an undoubted influence on the national educational statistics, the proportion is not as high in relation to the non-Jews as in the Russian subsample. It is thus probably safe to conclude that the non-Jewish Poles are also turning to education as a means of social mobility, although it took them longer than it took the Jewish Russians and probably the Jewish Poles.

The improved educational achievement of the Polish Americans and their movement into more prestigeful jobs has been assisted by the new emigrants, who, unlike most other immigrants to America, came with a higher and more diversified socioeconomic background. According to Taeuber and Taeuber (1967: 806), 42.5 per cent of the 108,930 people listing Poland as their country of birth who entered America between 1941 and 1950 were housewives or children. Of the remaining, 43.8 reported white-collar occupations. The proportion of white-collar immigrants dropped to 31.8 per cent in the years between 1951 and 1960. These were mostly people whose education had been interrupted by the war when schools were shut down or by removal to concentration and labor camps. Taeuber and Taeuber (1967) caution that generalizations about the foreign born in America should not lump together those who entered before World War II with those who came during and after that uprooting event. This is particularly true of Polonia, in which case new emigration did not lower the socioeconomic level. In fact, Mostwin (1969; 1971), whose self-selected 1,450 respondents are not a sample but probably the more educated and successful, demonstrates that at least they were able to make a relatively successful adjustment to American society.

Families in this new emigration who came to America were more likely to represent the upper strata than the lower, and although there is a definite sacrifice of status paid by the top two classes in Polish society in movement to the American society, many were able to retain at least some similarity of life style. "Over half of the respondents of the Polish upper class were found to be in the upper class in the United States while nearly 30 per cent of this group were found to be in the upper middle class in this country" (Mostwin: 1971: 182). Less successful were the members of the middle class, over 50 per cent of whom moved downward to the lower-middle class, mostly because they had been owners of small businesses or in occupations requiring prolonged retraining made difficult by their having reached America in the middle years of life without language skills.

The presence of the new emigration, or at least of those members who moved into Polonian neighborhoods or joined its social and organiza-

33

tional life, has probably affected the old emigration and their descendants in many ways. These new emigrants had been reared in Poland between world wars, which offered high status to its intelligentsia (Szczepanski, 1962; 1970). However, they gradually found many aspects of life in common with the descendants of the old emigration while still complaining that the first generation had been frozen into an idealization of a culture that no longer existed even in Polish peasant villages. They considered the language spoken in Polonia as "archaic," reflecting migration prior to the great educational push following World War I. The presence of these critics of Polonia may thus have influenced the youth to turn to education as a means of upward mobility. Both the short- and long-run effects of the "modernization" of Polonia with the help of the new emigration and the more educated descendants of the old emigration may be rather dramatic. Accustomed to the status competition within the community and to the use of all resources in this focus of life, the Polish Americans can be expected to now rapidly turn to this newly discovered and efficient means of upward mobility. As the sons and daughters, but particularly the sons, start demonstrating that higher education is an important status-gaining tool, the anti-intellectualism, or at least the anti-educational prejudice, can be expected to decrease.

SUMMARY

This chapter has examined the Polish American community, called Polonia, and its influence on the lives of members and families. It has tried to establish the importance of status competition as a central theme preserving the community through generations, uniting family members in spite of disorganizing pressures, and delaying concern with status in the American society. It is undoubtedly true that other ethnic communities also developed the hierarchies, motivation for involvement, and "game rules" necessary for maintaining a complex status competition among their individual, family, and other social units. However, the social structure of pre-World War I Poland, in which the immigrants and the parents, grandparents, and in some cases great-grandparents of the native-born Polish immigrants were socialized, and the culture and social structure that they founded, with modification, in America encouraged the development of status competition to a complex and personally meaningful level. The negative consequences of this focal emphasis of Polonia lay in its internal conflict, the underuse of resources for gaining higher status for the community and its members and prejudice against competing external groups. The combination of these effects resulted in a low and relatively long-lasting social status of the Polish Americans vis-a-vis other ethnic groups in America. This, in turn, encouraged a withdrawal of interest on their part from the larger society and concern only with internal status. The positive effects of this status competition have been to cushion the disorganization and "demoralization" consequences of migration into a very different country by a basically non-cosmopolitan, uneducated, rural- and village-based population. The various stages of change in Polonia, first in its development of a complex social structure, then in the creation of a political patriotic identity as the "fourth province of Poland," followed by its definition of America as containing nothing but ethnic groups lacking a "melted core," and finally now as a center for increasingly cooperative concern with external social status, have enabled it to survive almost a century. Assisted recently by the introduction of new members who strive to intellectualize identification with Polish culture, previously limited to a folk emphasis, and a highly developed communication system useful in building ever more complex personal and familial "reputations," Polonia has maintained itself as a marginal community with its own culture. Each person or family can draw from a variety of status-giving categories, including participation in voluntary associations, particularly as a "dignitary" (Thomas and Znaniecki, 1956 edition), prestige location of marriage partner or offspring, residence, occupation, income, ability to speak Polish, personal contacts, and style of life. Until recent years the Polish Americans have under-used education as a means of upward mobility both within the community and outside of it, rising into the elite rungs of the blue-collar world rather than crossing over to white-collar occupations, but there are strong indications that the significance of education as a tool for status competition has been "discovered" by the younger Polonians. If this trend continues, it can lead to dramatic changes in the community, since the highly individualistic and competitive subculture can be expected to move the group rapidly toward greater educational achievement. This would have consequences on all aspects of life style and family relations, making the Polish Americans more like the more established American ethnic group. It will be interesting to see what consequences the shifts in education, and then in occupation, will have on Polish American identities, family relations, attitudes toward other groups and the society at large, and the survival and the life style of Polonia as a community.

REFERENCES

Abel, Theodore. 1929. "Sunderland: A Study of Changes in the Group-Line of Poles in a New England Farming Community." In Edmund De.S. Brunner (ed.): *Immigrant Farmers and Their Children*. Garden City, N.Y.: Doubleday, Doran, 213–43.

Abramson, Harold J. 1971. "Ethnic Pluralism in the Central City." In Otto Feinstein (ed.): *Ethnic Groups in the City*. Lexington, Mass.: Heath Lexington Books, 17–28.

Adamic, Louis. 1945. *A Nation of Nations*. New York: Harper and Brothers.

———. 1942. *What's your Name?* New York: Harper and Brothers.

Barth, Fredrik. 1969. *Ethnic Groups and Boundaries*. Norway: Johansen and Nielsen Boktrykkeri: especially his introduction.

Blalock, Herbert H. 1967. "Status Inconsistency and Interaction: Some Alternative Models." *American Journal of Sociology* 73:305–15.

Blau, Peter M. 1964. *Exchange and Power in Social Life*. New York: Wiley.

Borkowski, Thomas. 1963. "Some Patterns in Polish Surname Changes." *Polish American Studies* XX, 1 (January–June):14–16.

Bott, Elizabeth J. 1957. *Family and Social Network*. London: Tavistock.

Breton, Raymond. 1964. "Institutional Completeness of Ethnic Communities and the Personal Relations of Immigrants." *American Journal of Sociology* 70 (September):193–205.

Brunner, Edmund De.S. 1929. *Immigrant Farmers and their Children*. Garden City, N.Y.: Doubleday, Doran.

Bugelski, B. R. 1961. "Assimilation Through Intermarriage." *Social Forces* 40:148–153.

Burton, Ronald. 1972. "Status Consistency and Secondary Stratification Characteristics in an Urban Metropolis." Unpublished dissertation, Michigan State University, Department of Sociology.

Cressey, Paul Frederick. 1938. "Population Succession in Chicago: 1898–1920." *American Journal of Sociology* XLIV (July):59–69.

Curti, Merle, and Kendal Birr. 1950. "The Immigrant and the American Image in Europe, 1860–1914." *Mississippi Valley Historical Review* XXXVII, 2 (September):203–30.

David, Michael M. Jr. 1971. *Immigrant Health and the Community* (Re-edited). Montclair, N.J.: Ratterson Smith, as part of Americanization Studies.

Diamond, Stanley, 1957. "Kibbutz and Shtetl: The History of an Idea." *Social Problems* 5, 2 (Fall):71–99.

Duncan, Beverly, and Otis Dudley Duncan. 1968. "Minorities and the Process of Stratification." *American Sociological Review* 33, 2 (June):356–64.

Emmons, Charles F. 1971. "Economic and Political Leadership in Chicago's Polonia: Some Sources of Ethnic Persistence and Mobility." Unpublished dissertation, University of Illinois, Circle Campus, Department of Sociology.

Finestone, Harold. 1964. "A Comparative Study of Reformation and Recidivism Among Italians and Polish Adult Male Criminal Offenders." Unpublished dissertion, University of Chicago, Department of Sociology.

36

————. 1967. "Reformation and Recidivism among Italian and Polish Criminal Offenders." *American Journal of Sociology* 72, 6 (May):575–88.

Ford, Richard G. 1950. "Population Succession in Chicago." *American Journal of Sociology* LVI (September):156–60.

Fox, Paul. 1922. *The Poles in America*. New York: Doran.

Gans, Herbert. 1962. *The Urban Villagers*. New York: The Free Press.

Geschwender, James A. 1968. "Status Inconsistency, Social Isolation and Individual Unrest." *Social Forces* 46, 4 (June):477–83.

Glazer, Nathan, and Daniel Patrick Moynihan. 1970. *Beyond the Melting Pot*. Cambridge, Mass.: M.I.T. Press.

Gordon, Milton M. 1964. *Assimilation in American Life*. New York: Oxford University Press.

Greeley, Andrew M. 1969. *Why Can't They be Like Us?* New York: Institute of Human Relations Press.

————. 1971. "Ethnicity as an Influence on Behavior." In Otto Feinstein (ed.): *Ethnic Groups in the City*. Lexington, Mass.: Heath Lexington Books, 3–16,

————. 1974. *Ethnicity in the United States*. New York: John Wiley.

Greeley, Andrew M., and Peter H. Rossi. 1968. *The Education of Catholic Americans*. Garden City, N.Y.: Doubleday (Anchor Books).

Haiman, Mieczyslaw. 1948. *Zjednoczenie Polskie Rzymsko-Katolickie*. Chicago: Polish Roman Catholic Union Press.

Handlin, Oscar. 1951. *The Uprooted*. New York: Grosset & Dunlap.

Hoff, Hannah Broen. 1936. "Problems of Post-War Immigration as Illustrated in the Chicago Area." Unpublished dissertation, University of Chicago, School of Social Service Administration.

Hughes, Everett C. 1943. *French Canada in Transition*. Chicago: University of Chicago Press.

————. 1944. "Dilemmas and Contradictions of Status." *American Journal of Sociology* 50:353–57.

————, and Helen H. Hughes. 1952. *Where Peoples Meet*. Glencoe, Ill.: The Free Press.

————. 1971. *The Sociological Eye*. Chicago: Aldine-Atherton: 141–50.

Hutchinson, E. P. 1956. *Immigrants and their Children*. 1850–1950. New York: Wiley.

Johnston, Ruth. 1969. *The Assimilation Myth*. The Hague: Martinus Nijhoff.

Kennedy, Ruby Jo. 1952. "Single a Triple Melting Pot: Intermarriage in New Haven." *American Journal of Sociology* 58:55–66.

Kiang, Ying-Cheng. 1968. "The Distribution of the Ethnic Groups in Chicago, 1960." *Research Notes, American Journal of Sociology* 74, 3 (November):292–95.

Kitagawa, Evelyn, and Karl E. Taeuber. (eds.). 1963. *Local Community Fact Book of the Chicago Metropolitan Area, 1960*. Chicago: University of Chicago Community Inventory.

Koenig, Samuel. 1952. "Second and Third-Generation Americans." In Francis J. Brown and Joseph S. Roucek (eds.): *One American*. New York: Prentice-Hall.

Kolm, Richard. 1969. "The Identity Crisis of Polish-Americans." *The Quarterly Review* XXI, 2 (April-June): 1 and 4.

Kotlarz, Robert J. 1963. "Writings about the Changing of Polish Names in America." *Polish American Studies* XX, 1 (January–June): 1–4.

Kruszka, Waclaw. 1937. *Historia Polska w Ameryce*. Milwaukee: Kuryer Press.

Landecker, Werner S. 1960. "Status Congruence, Class Crystallization, and Social Cleavage." *Sociology and Social Research* 54, 3 (April):343–55.

Lenski, Gerhard. 1954. "Status Crystallization: a Non-vertical Dimension of Social Status." *American Sociological Review* 19 (August):405–12.

———. 1956. Social Participation and Status Crystallization." *American Sociological Review* 27 (August):458–64.

———. 1966. *Power and Privilege: A Theory of Social Stratification*. New York: McGraw-Hill.

———. 1967. "Status Inconsistency and the Vote: A Four Nation Test." *American Sociological Review* 32, 2 (April):298–301.

Lieberson, Stanley. 1958. "Ethnic Groups and the Practice of Medicine." *American Sociological Review* 23, 5 (October):542–49.

———. 1963. *Ethnic Patterns in American Cities*. New York: The Free Press.

Lopata, Helena Znaniecki. 1964. "A Restatement of the Relation between Role and Status." *Sociology and Social Research* 49, 58–68.

———. 1954. "The Function of Voluntary Associations in an Ethnic Community: Polonia." Unpublished dissertation, The University of Chicago, Department of Sociology.

———. 1966. "Of Space and the Housewife: Initial Comments on the Relation Between Social Spaces and Social Roles." Paper given at the Miami meetings of the Society for the Study of Social Problems, August 1966 (incorporated in the *Occupation: Housewife* book).

———. 1973a *Widowhood in an American City*. Cambridge, Mass.: Schenkman.

———. 1973b. "The Effect of Schooling on Social Contacts of Urban Women." *American Journal of Sociology* 79:604–19.

———. 1973c. "Life Styles of Elderly Urbanites: Chicago of the 1970's." Paper given at the Gerontological Meetings, November 1973, to be published in *The Gerontologist*.

Lynd, Helen M. 1965. *On Shame and the Search For Identity*. New York: Science Editions.

Mead, George Herbert. 1934. *Mind, Self, and Society*. Chicago: University of Chicago Press.

Miaso, Josef. 1971. "Z Dziejow Oswiaty Polskiej w Stanach Zjednoczonych." *Problemy Polonii Zagranicznej*, VI. Warszawa: Polski Akademia Nauk, pp. 19–42.

Mostwin, Danuta. 1969. "Post World War II Polish Immigrants in the United States." *Polish American Studies* XXVI, 2 (Autumn):5–14.

———. 1971. "The Transplanted Family: A Study of the Social Adjustment of the Polish Immigrant Family to the United States after the Second World War." Dissertation, Columbia University, School of Social Work (microfilms).

Napolska, Sister Mary Remigia. 1946. "The Polish Immigrant in Detroit to 1914." Chicago: Polish Roman Catholic Union.

Obidinski, Eugene. 1968. "Ethnic to Status Group: A Study of Polish Americans in Buffalo." Unpublished dissertation, State University of New York (microfilms).

Polish American Congress News Letter. 1970. "Anti-Defamation Off to a Good Start." XI, 2 (July 20): 2.

Reymont, Ladislas. 1925. *The Peasants: Fall, Winter, Spring, Summer*. New York: Knopf (four volumes).

Rooney, Elizabeth. 1957. "Polish Americans and Family Disorganization," *The American Catholic Sociological Review* 18 March:47–51.

Schermerhorn, Richard A. 1949. *These Our People*. Boston: Heath.

Segal, David R., and D. Knoke. 1970. "Status Inconsistency and Self-Evaluation." *Sociometry* 33, 2 (September):347–57.

Suttles, Gerald. 1968. *The Social Order of the Slum*. Chicago: University of Chicago Press.

Szczepanski, Jan. 1962. "The Polish Intelligentsia, Past and Present." *World Politics* XVI, 3 (April):406–20.

——. 1970. Polish Society. New York: Random House.

Taeuber, A. F., and K. E. Taeuber, 1967. "Recent Immigration and Studies of Ethnic Assimilation." *Demography* 4:798–808.

Thomas, John L. 1950. *The American Catholic Family*. Englewood Cliffs, N.J.: Prentice-Hall.

Thomas, William I., and Florian Znaniecki. 1958. *The Polish Peasant in Europe and America*. (2nd ed.) New York: Dover (two volumes, originally published in five volumes, 1918–20).

U˙S. Bureau of the Census. 1971. "Characteristics of the Population by Ethnic Origin: November, 1971," In *Current Population Reports*. Series P-20, No. 221. Washington, D.C.; U.S. Government Printing Office; also, No. 220 "Ethnic Origin and Educational Attainment: November, 1969," and No. 226, "Fertility Variations by Ethnic Origin: November, 1971."

U.S. Bureau of Justice, Immigration Commission. 1911. Immigration and Crime, Report 36. Washington, D.C.: U.S. Government Printing Office.

U.S. Department of Justice. *Report of the Commissioner of Immigration and Naturalization*. Washington, D.C.: U.S. Government Printing Office, 1969, 1959, 1949, 1929, 1919, 1909.

Wagner, Stanley P. 1964. "The Polish American Vote in 1960." *Polish American Studies* XXI, 1 (January–June): 1–9.

Ware, Caroline. 1930. "Ethnic Communities." In R. A. Seligman (ed.): *Encyclopedia of the Social Sciences*, Volume VI. New York: Macmillan, pp. 607–13.

Wirth, Louis. 1945. "The Problem of Minority Groups." In R. Linton (ed.): *The Science of Man in the World Crisis*. New York, Columbia University Press, pp. 347–72.

Wood, Arthur Evans. 1955. *Hamtramck: Then and Now*. New York: Bookman Associates.

Zagraniczny, Stanley J. 1963. "Some Reasons for Polish Surname Changes." *Polish American Studies* XX, 1 (January–June); 12–14.

Zand, Helen Sankiewicz. 1956. "Polish Family Folkways in the United States." *Polish American Studies* XIII, 304 (July–December): 77–88.

———. 1960. "Polish American Wordways." *Polish American Studies* XXII, 1-2 (January–June): 41–48.

Zborowski, Mark, and Elizabeth Herzog. 1969. *Life is With People*. New York: Schocken Books.

Znaniecki, Florian. 1952. *Modern Nationalities*. Urbana, Illinois: University of Illinois Press.

The Japanese American Family

Japanese Americans, like most other minority racial groups in America, have suffered relatively high levels of discrimination and persecution. Similarly, they have maintained relatively high degrees of ethnic solidarity and identification. The Japanese Americans, in numbers a relatively small ethnic group in America, present to most Americans of European origin a quite distinct cultural tradition. Japanese culture, particularly its emphasis on the collective and loyalty to the group, has had and continues to have strong impact on family life. In combination, the impact of discrimination, persecution, and devotion to group cohesiveness has produced a family life style that remains distinctly Japanese. In the chapter to follow, Professors Kitano and Kikumura present the distinctive cultural elements of Japanese culture that play themselves out through the mediation of the family and discuss the impact of modern life on the present-day Japanese American family.

CHAPTER THREE
BY
HARRY H. L. KITANO AND AKEMI KIKUMURA

HISTORICAL BACKGROUND

Of the many ethnic groups discussed in this volume, one of the most stereotyped is the Japanese American. The notion of their relative homogeneity strongly reinforces the perception that there is a typical Japanese and a typical Japanese family, whereas in actual life, it would be difficult to identify such a phenomenon. Nevertheless, the temptation to stereotype them has been especially strong in America—from the "sly, sneaky" image of a past era to the "hard-working, conforming, cohesive family, and carrier of a traditional culture" representation of today (Ogawa, 1971; Sue and Kitano, 1973).

One of the basic reasons behind the facile generalizations remains the overall ignorance about this ethnic minority population. They are small in number. (1970 Census figures show 591,290.) They are mainly clustered in Hawaii (217,307) and California (213,280), and only recently have there been publications of a scholarly nature about them (Kitano, 1969; Petersen, 1971). An analysis of some of their past experiences indicates they have not been that unique:

> They came to the United States during the great industrial and agricultural expansion that took place after the Civil War and the beginning of World War I. Most were poor and had little capital to set up their own enterprises. Most were minimally educated, so that entrance into professions and fields of skill labor was denied them. The majority could not comminicate in English. Further most Japanese had unrealistic ideas about America; many expected to make their fortunes and return to the old country in a short period of time. They were often attacked by nativist and racist groups and were forced to settle in the slums. Inevitably, they started at the bottom of the occupational ladder, and felt too socially inferior to seek much intercourse with the majority group. (Kitano, 1969: 30)

These were conditions faced by most groups, and if these were the only problems, then the history of the Japanese might be similar to those of other immigrants (Daniels, 1962). However, there were a number of other factors that provided additional difficulties. First, they were non-white; second, they were soon to be identified as coming from an enemy nation and eventually an "enemy race." Third, they belonged to a "strange and unassimilable culture." Several groups have had one or two of these charges leveled at them, but never has an immigrant population been in the position of facing all three. The culmination of the hostility, prejudice, and discrimination against the Japanese took place during World War II when all of them, whether citizens or aliens, were evacuated from their homes on the West Coast and detained in "relocation centers."

Early History

Although there is evidence of Japanese in America prior to 1890, the significant immigration occurred after this date. The initial groups were relatively homogeneous in age (young); sex (male); occupation (laborers); education (four to six years of schooling); and general background, having been drawn from the primarily agricultural provinces (kens) of Hiroshima, Kumamoto, Wakayama, Fukuoka, and Yamaguchi.

Most settled along the Pacific Coast and found employment as laborers, especially in California agriculture. Some began establishing small businesses catering to ethnic needs (ethnic restaurants, hotels, barbers), so that an interdependent economic-social Japanese network began to be formed. When it came time to establish families, individual preferences and the lack of opportunity to intereact with majority-group females lead to the vast majority bringing wives from Japan. Many of them participated in the "picture bride" process, whereby the couple would initially meet through an exchange of pictures; however, the matching was not sheerly of a random nature. There was an attempt to "match" the couples on a number of characteristics, and if statistics on separation and divorce can be used as the criteria of the success of such unions, they were successful indeed. Rates of divorce for this immigrant group, called the *Issei*, show a 1.6 per cent rate (Kitano, 1969: 156).

The American-born children of the Issei, called the *Nisei*, were generally born between 1910 and 1945 and were primarily products of the American culture. They attended American schools and are currently in the middle years of their life. The children of the *Nisei*, called the *Sansei*, provide the great majority of the current school-age population. Although there are other groups, the Isei, Nisei, and Sansei provide the bulk of the Japanese population, and most of our generalizations are drawn with these groups in mind.

Role of Discrimination

It would be difficult to ignore the role of discrimination when discussing the history of the Japanese American. In common with most immigrants, they wanted to better their lives and were not content to remain on the bottom of the occupational ladder. But the idea of these "yellow men" wanting to share equally in the American dream was antithetical to many members of the majority group. The feelings of the American community can be summarized in an editorial in the *San Francisco Chronicle* (1910).

> Had the Japanese laborer throttled his ambition to progress along the lines of American citizenship and industrial development, he probably would have attracted small attention of the public mind. Japanese ambition is to progress beyond mere servility to the plane of the better class of American workman and to own a home with him. The moment that this position is exercised the Japanese ceases to be an ideal laborer.

The hostility against the Japanese was constant, harsh, and relentless. Further, the differentiation between the Japanese in Japan (the nation), the Issei, and the Nisei was blurred so that the behavior of the nation was linked to activities of all Japanese, whether American born or not.

Although the Japanese faced many barriers, the discriminatory laws were the most damaging. There were local nuisance laws such as special license fees; state laws such as the Webb-Heney Bill of 1913, also known as the California Alien Land Bill, which limited Japanese aliens from owning or leasing lands, and national legislation such as the immigration act of 1924, which forbade the further immigration of Japanese. There was also a celebrated incident in San Francisco in 1906 in which the school board was forced to rescind its order of segregating Japanese students through the intervention of President Theodore Roosevelt (Kitano, 1969).

World War II set the stage for a final solution to the "Japanese problem." All persons of Japanese ancestry were evacuated from their homes along the West Coast and placed in "relocation camps," a procedure that was adjudged legal by the United States Supreme Court. Various books are available covering this era of Japanese American history (Bosworth, 1967; Daniels, 1971; Girdner and Loftis, 1969; Kitano, 1969; Tenbroek, Barnhart, and Watson, 1970). There were some strident voices for sending them all back to Japan; milder solutions advocated resettlement as long as "they didn't come back to our state." But for a variety of reasons, the end of World War II brought about a change in the treatment of the Japanese Americans. The camps were closed, and many found employment in areas formerly denied them.

The group has made rapid progress since that time. They have been upwardly mobile; they have been successful in higher education; housing is no longer a major problem, and there are even Japanese American faces in Congress. Meanwhile, their rates of "deviant behavior," such as crime, delinquency, and mental illness. remain low (Hosokawa, 1969; Petersen, 1971; Kitano, 1969). Much of the explanation for this "success" has been attributed to the Japanese American family.

Japanese Culture

Prior to any discussion of the Japanese American family a brief analysis of the social structure in Japan must be presented. There are many problems in presenting information about Japan because it is so often piecemeal or exotic, contradictory or untranslated. Another problem is to choose an appropriate historical period to serve as a reference point. The majority of the Issei spent their developmental years in the Meiji era of Japan (1867–1912), whereas most of the available social-science writings of the Japanese family in English date from the allied occupation after World War II. Therefore, what is said about modern Japan may not be relevant to the experiences of the Issei and the culture that they brought over to America.

However, Nakane (1970) provides a number of concepts that describe the Japanese social structure in a fashion that Japanese Americans will recognize even today. There are, of course, many other ways of looking at the Japanese social structure, but a summarization of the Nakane framework will provide the background for understanding the culture that the Issei brought with them from Japan. The major components of this model are:

1. Japanese membership is by situation rather than by qualification. For example, in Japan an individual refers to the company that employs him (e.g., "I work for Sony") rather than by the qualifications that may have landed him the position (e.g., secretary, engineer). Nakane (1970; 1 ff.) calls this the "frame" structure of Japanese society, in which the Japanese tend' to identify with a particular institution, such as a company or a university, rather than a more universal identity that cuts across institutional lines. The "frame" tends to shape one's life since there develops a strong group consciousness (e.g., "my company") and a heavy dependence on the organization for economic, social, emotional, and psychological support. Conversely, there is an attempt to achieve an independence for each "frame" so that it can remain a relatively autonomous organization.

2. The *ie* or household unit is the most important frame for early socialization and upbringing. Nakane likens the *ie* to a corporate residential group that takes on the job of managing the affairs of its members. The model can be traced back to agricultural groups that banded together to form such units. Although kinship ties are important, the situation has even higher priority, so that sons and daughters who leave the *ie* for whatever reasons have less influence than the individuals and families who are currently a part of the "corporation." One consequence of such a structure is that neighbors become more important than relatives. There is a Japanese saying, "You can carry out your life without cousins, but not without your neighbors" (Nakane, 1970; 7).

   The families and other groups comprising the *ie* play a major role in the socialization of the young. Marriages are not between individuals but between families and *ies,* so that factors such as acceptable behavior, etiquette, morals, and training are a part of the reputation of an *ie*. Suitable marital choices are carefully screened to provide some degree of *ie* comparability.

3. The power of the group is one of the strongest elements in the

Japanese system. Group control of behavior extends into the shaping of ideas and the manner of behavior. In most cases it is a unilateral relationship, and employees, *ie,* or family members have few alternatives since their jobs and social life are so interwoven with the organization. The head of these units (by seniority) has absolute authority, and the organization is viewed as a permanent one (for life). Newly employed people are similar to the newborn: They must be socialized into the company's or *ie's* ways. Common techniques for social control emphasize the role of others: "What will other people think?" "They'll laugh at you." "Don't make such a fool of yourself in front of others.

4. The Japanese system encourages loyalty to one "frame." Japanese stories often depict the loyal retainer who would never think of switching masters, or one who gives his life to save his lord. "No man can serve two masters at the same time" (Nakane, 1970: 21) is a Japanese saying that also means that the almost total emotional participation within one group precludes much participation in another.

5. Rank and status are determined primarily by age, sex, and order of entrance, and the period of service, as contrasted to a model that rewards competence, additional training, or efficiency. Leadership positions are important but appear localized into specific groups. A leader cannot be easily replaced because recruiting from the outside is limited.

One term that describes this relationship is *oyabun-kobun,* literally, of parent to child. It is similar to the master-apprentice or tutor-learner models, and appropriate reciprocal behavior is expected from the respective parties.

The identification of rank and status within the frames is important because they determine the type of expected interaction within the unit. Rank and status cues are also important in determining the style of interaction with outsiders, so, as Nakane (1970: 31) says, "Without consciousness of ranking, life could not be carried on smoothly in Japan for rank is the social norm on which Japanese life is based."

There have been changes in Japan since Nakane presented her framework, but her concepts remain helpful in explaining much of Japanese behavior, which appears contradictory unless placed in such a perspective. For example, the rudeness of Japanese to strangers when contrasted to their treatment of people within their own social circles, the loyalty to the company and the deference to those in authority, and the emphasis on cleanliness in the home and the incredible filth one finds in public places can be understood within the construct of parallel structures, rank, and status. It should also be noted that the "frame" and situational orientation may be very useful for those who emigrate either to urban areas or to foreign countries where there are other Japanese. Alone in these new situations, the chances of becoming a member of a Japanese group are high, which would then include a position, a feeling of belonging, and the framework for values and behavior.

This system encourages high in-group unity and cohesion but a general isolation from other structures. Group traditions, mottoes, and slogans reinforce the "we" so that the tightly knit group, group consensus, and a lack of individuality are common characteristics.

Cultural Continuity: Japan to America

The family unit survived in modified form in the early Issei era. There were no grandparents to serve as reminders of old traditions, and some of the immigrants felt relatively free from the strictures of the Japanese social structure. But there remained the notion of "good" and "less desirable" families brought over from the social class structure of Japan. Certain groups such as the "eta" were pariahs in Japan (the origin of this outcaste group is somewhat obscure but may be related to their occupation of killing and cleaning animals), and Issei discouraged intimate social interaction with them (Ito, 1966). There were prejudiced feelings against immigrants from Okinawa, especially in Hawaii. Interestingly enough, Ito writes that many of these outcast familis responded by teaching their children what "good" *ies* in Japan would have taught, that is, manners, etiquette, the tea ceremony, dances, and the like.

"Good" Issei families provided an enriched cultural background for their children (e.g., Japanese language schools, music lessons) and attempted to teach proper role behavior, homemaking, and other skills that would be a reflection of their ability to socialize desirable Japanese Americans. Others directed their major efforts toward Americanization, while still others concentrated on the day by day efforts toward sheer survival. In spite of these within-group differences, there was an ethnic solidarity when facing the majority group, so that in out-group interaction the reference group became the entire Japanese community. There were appeals to all individuals to behave in a manner that would reflect to the benefit of all Japanese so that the family and the community became important reference groups, just as the *ie* served this purpose in Japan.

47

The emphasis on adapting to a smaller, ethnic world has long been a part of the Japanese American system. Part of the motivation lies in the barriers placed before them when attempting to participate in the larger structure, but much of it stems from the Japanese culture. Japanese American athletic teams, community, and youth groups remain an important part in their organization, and the tendency for Sansei to stick among their own, even at the college level, is a familiar one since the same observation was made of the Nisei and Issei.

One common complaint of the more acculturated Japanese American woman relates to the limited world of her male counterpart. Rather than expanding and trying for new experiences, he is accused of being satisfied with "going to bowling alleys and hanging out in a small clique . . ." even after marriage (Kikumura and Kitano, 1973). Similarly, college recruiters from the East Coast comment on the general hesitancy of Japanese American students to leave the West Coast. (California students in general seem to have the same tendency.) Nor is there a migration to some of the larger Eastern urban centers in which opportunites in certain fields may be more plentiful. The holding power of the ethnic community, the family, and the home state (especially California) appears quite strong.

There are other ramifications in settling for a smaller world. The Japanese American is not generally a risk taker, and previous studies (Kitano, 1969) have emphasized that as a group, they are characterized by low expectations. Rather than risk embarrassment by failing in trying something different, there is general tendency to fall back on old skills and the "tried and true."

The influence of the Japanese culture was especially strong among the Nisei. For example, they were the recipients of the hopes and expectations of their Issei parents, so that, as Nakane (1970) indicates, the feeling that "because I could not go to college or university and I ended up at the bottom of the barrel I wish to have my children succeed" (p. 111) is a direct carryover of sentiments from Japan. The story of the self-sacrifice of Issei parents to send their children through higher education is a common one in the Japanese American community.

ENRYO. Since the majority of Japanese immigrants came from the middle and lower classes, most were aware of their power positions in the Japanese social structure. Immigration to America did not significantly alter their power except to lower it and render them even more powerless. It is from this perspective that we introduce the norm of *enryo* as one that was brought over from Japan and survived in modified form in America.

Enryo was one of the important norms in shaping Japanese behavior. The norm is related to power—how the "inferior" was to behave to the "superior" through deference and obsequiousness. As with many norms, the meaning was expanded in America to cover a wide variety of situations, "from how to behave towards the white man, to what to do in ambiguous situations, to how to cover moments of confusion, embarrassment, and anxiety" (Kitano, 1969: 104).

Enryo helps to explain much of Japanese American behavior. As with other norms, it had both a positive and negative effect on Japanese acculturation. For example, take observations of Japanese in situations as diverse as their hesitancy to speak out at meetings; their refusal of any invitation, especially the first time; their refusal of a second helping; their acceptance of a less desired object when given a free choice; their lack of verbal participation, especially in an integrated group; their refusal to ask questions; and their hesitancy in asking for a raise in salary—these may all be based on *enryo*. The inscrutable face, the noncommital answer, the behavioral reserve, can often be traced to this norm, so that the stereotype of the shy, reserved Japanese in ambiguous social situations is often an accurate one (Kitano, 1969: 104).

Enryo also meant that if one were in a superior or more powerful position, one could behave accordingly. Arrogance, insensitivity, and the trappings of privilege are characteristic outcomes, and Japanese behavior toward "conquered peoples" or nations that were considered "inferior" is remarkably similar to European and American colonialists.

In the family, the paternal position was associated with power and its privileges. Therefore, even if the Japanese father was subject to the humiliation and abuse of whites in the outside world, within his home and community, he played a totally different role. It should be emphasized that for both the superior and inferior positions, there was also the concept of responsibility and obligation, so that it placed a limit on the indiscriminate use of power.

THE MODERN JAPANESE AMERICAN FAMILY

Family Characteristics

A summary of current Japanese American family characteristics can be drawn from the 1970 census (Office of Special Concerns). Eighty-six per cent have both husband and wife, which is the same rate for the country as a whole. The percentage of children under six (27 per cent) is also equivalent to the national rate. Japanese families are slightly above the national average in size (3.7 to 3.5 persons) and in extended family (16 to 12 per cent). In general it appears that Japanese Americans do not differ substantially from America as a whole. This appears to reflect a high degree of acculturation.

One-third of all Japanese women have married out of the group, and the proportion rises to 46 per cent among those in the 16- to 24-year-old group.

The mean family income (male head) was $13,511. Only 7.5 per cent had incomes below the poverty level (as defined by the U.S. Census) with the preponderence of low incomes in the 65 years or older category (U.S. Bureau of the Census, 1973).

Although there were regional differences on variables such as income, housing costs, and the like, the overall picture is one of an ethnic group that has achieved a reasonable degree of economic security and is similar to the majority group on selected demographic variables.

Intermarriage

The most accurate generalization in terms of dating and marriage is that there are as many patterns for the Japanese American as there are patterns for the population at large. Ethnicity, however, remains an important "other" factor, and how this "Japaneseness" (primarily in terms of physical identifiability) is perceived and treated remains a critical one in terms of dating and marriage. Generally, physical identifiability becomes a salient issue during adolescence.

The most striking pattern of current dating and marriage is the high proportion of out-group interaction. From a historically "closed group" in which intermarriage was controlled by both ethnic community preferences and antimiscegenation laws, there now are out-marriage rates of approximately 50 per cent in areas such as San Francisco, Fresno, Los Angeles, and Honolulu. Although the dominant historical pattern was that of the Japanese female marrying out, recent statistics indicate that the Japanese male is also participating in racial amalgamation (Kikumura and Kitano, 1973).

One indication of the generational differences (and also the changing attitudes of the majority group) is seen in marital preferences. Issei intermarriage was about 5 per cent; Nisei rates were about 15 per cent, while Sansei intermarriage rates are at the 50 per cent level (Kikumuru and Kitano, 1973). It is apparent, then, that sex practices, decision making, and the role of the male and female are intimately related to generation and acculturation. The longer the group remains in America, the closer they appear to behave in accordance with relevant American models.

But in spite of our emphasis on the Japanese group by generation and culture, the single most important factor in their adaptation (the same can be said for all other groups) remains their treatment by the dominant group. It is the interaction between the cultures, shaped primarily by the dominant majority, that defines the parameters and provides the major reinforcements and directions.

Family Solidarity

Japanese American marriages until the 1960s were primarily within the ethnic group, and the Issei unions stressed the importance of duty and obligation over that of love and romance. There were clearly pre-scribed sex roles, so that the Issei and early Nisei families were "tradi-tional families." Roles, duties, and responsibilities, rather than personal affection or likes and dislikes, were the motivating factors for interac-tion. Therefore, instead of the prescription "Obey mother because you love her," it was more apt to be "Obey mother because it is expected of you." (It should be noted that in Japanese families we have observed, such expectations are usually prescribed only when the parents feel that their child is ready for it.)

There is also a strong emphasis on filial piety. It was originally a reciprocal obligation, but many Issei have felt that in America its direc-tion has been only from parent to child. The story of Issei parents denying their own needs for their children is common, whereas the converse is less likely to occur. Nevertheless, it is our impression that there are many families that have absorbed grandparents. (The in-law apartment is a popular feature in want ads aimed at the Japanese Ameri-can.)

The extended family is especially important for young families. The doting grandparents, the large family gatherings, the outings and the vacations, often include numerous in-law relationships. Here discus-sions about the "successes and failures" of friends and acquaintances are told and retold so that they become a part of family folklore and possible models for the newer generations. Standards of behavior and acceptable norms are discussed in conjunction with everyday happen-ings, gossip, and jokes.

51

However, as children grow older, there is a tendency to break away from the family. Nevertheless, family unity remains strong during holidays and anniversaries: The New Year is a special occasion. In spite of eating traditional Japanese foods with Japanese utensils and a Japanese ambiance, other activities are typically American. The men watch the bowl games on television, while the kitchen is reserved for the female. But whereas in previous years there was a total separation of sex roles, the current period sees an intermixing of such roles.

Socialization

A unique feature of Japanese American family culture is the method that exists for handling the crucial issues of independence and dependence with respect to the family unit. One goal of socialization in Japan and to some extent in America is to establish a dependency on the family, the group, the company, and the mutual responsibility and reciprocity that goes along with such relationships. Maeda, a Japanese sociologist (personal communication) indicates that in Japan, children sleeping with their mothers (usually the youngest child) and their fathers (the older child) is common, even to relatively older ages. A group of Nisei were asked about their sleeping arrangements, and although the emphasis is presently on separate rooms for each child, in their own upbringing most of them remembered (some with embarrassment) that they slept with their parents and then with other siblings up to the beginning of school and even later.

This push for dependency, when contrasted with the apparent emphasis on independence and autonomy at an early age for most Americans, is often a source of conflict in many Japanese American families.

CONFRONTATION AND INDIRECTION. Many components of Japanese culture are the outcome of the adaptations that Japanese have made to the relative lack of power they possess.

The Japanese have had to adapt to less powerful positions constantly. The size of their country, the lack of natural resources, and their smaller stature has usually meant that direct tactics would invariably end in defeat. One of their martial arts, *aikido*, reflects this insight and uses indirect tactics rather than meeting force head on. *Aikido* stresses relaxation, deflection, and the interaction of mind and body as a source of inner strength in defending against an outside aggressor. It is an appropriate technique for neutralizing the force and power of much larger and aggressive individuals. To meet strength with strength means that both

52

sides will be hurt, and that the stronger will eventually win, whereas *aikido* attempts by deflection to use the strength of the aggressor against himself.

Socialization into the Japanese culture takes into account the art of deflection and the avoidance of direct confrontation. We have observed one consistent technique in their child rearing that encourages deflection and cooperation (Shimamoto, 1973), which has also been noted by Vogel (1965). Rather than the direct confrontation by the more powerful parent against the child ("You do what I say, or else"), the Japanese parent is more apt to use indirect techniques. They may bring a diversionary stimulus or attempt to bring about cooperation by saying, "Let's do it this way," or, "A good child will do it this way."

For example, the differential modes can be illustrated by how a Japanese and an American family might handle the case of an 8-year-old son who is watching television beyond his alloted time when he should be doing his homework. In the American family, there might be the direct statement: "Why don't you turn off that TV and study?" If there is not the desired response, it may escalate into a conflict between the power of the parent and that of the child. Eventually it may be resolved by "showing the child who's boss around here," and power threats such as "turn off that TV or else . . ." are common interactions. In the Japanese family, a different type of interaction (and often just as ineffective) is used. The parent may indicate to the child, "Isn't that a boring program?" Or, "I think Jun-chan (a close friend) must be doing his homework now"; or the mother might say, "I think Father wants to watch his favorite program." There may be an attempt to bring in another member of the family so that the father might ask his daughter to tell her brother to go study. She may be praised as a good girl because she is studying and not watching TV, and this praise and recognition are probably more effective in socializing her rather than bringing about the desired response in her brother. But direct confrontations between parent and child remain rare. One parent may turn to the other and remark how bad children are getting to be, loud enough for the child to hear, but not aimed directly at him.

It is difficult to evaluate the effectiveness of such techniques in isolation, for they are within the context of each of the cultures. One of the ultimate weapons used by Japanese parents to get children to behave is the threat of banishment from the family circle. Children are threatened by putting them outside, in a closet, or in a basement, and it appears to be an effective device, whereas such threats may have little noticeable effects on an American child. In fact, the American technique is often the opposite; rather than the threat of banishment, the threat to "keep in" is often used, so that a child is told, "You can't go out and play," if he has been misbehaving.

Concepts such as losing or saving face, the difficulty of getting clearcut yes or no answers, and the vagueness of the language itself are other manifestations of the use of indirection in the culture. Although these themes exist in all cultures, they appear to be central to the Japanese system. The indirectness can have both healthy and unhealthy consequences. Among Japanese Americans the lack of direct statements often leads to confusion, misinterpretation, and misunderstanding, but it also avoids those direct attacks that often lead to irreconcilable differences. The current therapeutic techniques of confrontation, of expressing honesty and true feelings, will be difficult for many Japanese Americans to handle.

DIRECT CONFRONTATIONS. We have mixed evidence concerning direct confrontations between husband-wife and parent-child. We never witnessed a direct screaming and yelling interaction between husband and wife in Japan. Instead, the anger came out in much subtler forms, such as the wife half jokingly remarking about the ineptness of her husband's driving, he, in turn, making a general remark about how women with a good education could not read a simple road map. In America, we could expect remarks directed squarely at each other. However, Shimamoto (1973) indicates that although such direct confrontations are rarer in Japan, they are not completely absent.

Similarly, we have mixed evidence concerning the direct spanking and beating of children by Japanese parents. Most of the literature on child rearing in Japan emphasizes the tolerance during the early years, and any rider of Japanese trains will vouch for the relatively high degree of tolerance of and permissiveness with Japanese children by their parents. Part of the reason may be the general conforming behavior of most Japanese children, so that few major disciplinary incidents arise in public. But a major proportion arises from a different style of discipline.

The role of the father is central in the disciplinary schema. The mother is forced to handle most of the everyday happenings and in the process loses a degree of social control and effectiveness because of the tiresome repetition. The father, on the other hand, often appears self-indulgent, with a high degree of tolerance for almost any behavior, especially his sons. However, there is also a limit to this tolerance, so that once the boundary is crossed, discipline may be immediate, severe, and demanding. We have been surprised by the sudden change in tone and behavior of a previously tolerant father when his children finally strain the limits, and one of the childhood skills is to sense when the mood changes will occur.

Perhaps the major difference between the Japanese way and the American way (controlling for the within-group differences based on social class, generation, and the like) is that there may be constant verbal reminders to the American child, including spanking, at a relatively early stage, whereas there is a higher initial tolerance in the Japanese family. However, once the limits are surpassed, Japanese discipline may be quite severe.

AMAE. Another technique used by the Japanese to handle the love-power-dependency relationships between parent and child is *amae*. Doi (1962) and Meredith (1966) write that *amae* is critical in understanding the basic dependency built into the Japanese socialization structure.

> The term refers to the need to be loved and cherished, but is difficult to translate accurately into English. It was frequently used by the Issei mother to describe the behavior of her children—sometimes with impatience. From the child's side, it was a technique of interaction asking for love, for attention, for approval, and for recognition. It was one of the few acceptable ways that individuals had to cope with the *enryo* norm. (Kitano, 1969: 105)

Perhaps the critical part of *amae* is the way it is perceived and responded to in the Japanese culture. If the parent sees the behavior of her child as *amae,* she may not have to respond by spanking or screaming or yelling since it is understood as an important factor in a relationship, whereas if she defines it in some other way, a different interaction may be involved. Probably in the more acculturated areas of the Japanese community in America, the term is probably equated with "being spoiled" and is therefore considered an undesirable action to be restricted or eliminated. But it may also deprive the child of a "soft" technique for gaining attention or asking for a favor.

VISIBILITY AND INVISIBILITY. An important variable related to the low power position of the Japanese American concerns his visibility and identifiability in America. It is closely related to Japanese culture and power and helps to explain Japanese socialization patterns and practices.

Because of the nature of American racism (Daniels and Kitano, 1970) and the problems faced by the Japanese, one important adaptation of the group was through invisibility. The dictum was "don't bring attention to us," and if public attention were warranted, the phrase was then expanded to "only for good deeds and not one that would embarrass the community." The same prescription held for families.

The Issei choice of being less visible was shaped by their culture (one knew his place in the Japanese social structure and conducted himself accordingly) and reinforced through their interaction with the American social structure. Competing on equal terms with the white man usually meant additional discriminatory treatment, so that one strategy for survival was the "low posture," staying in the background so as not to bring undue negative attention on themselves. Therefore, life styles were conservative, and those visible behaviors that would reflect on the community were discouraged (e.g., crime, delinquency, mental illness, flashy clothes, ostentatious spending), whereas behaviors such as good grades in school and membership in scholarship, honor, and good citizenship groups were strongly reinforced.

As a result, it was unusual to see Issei and Nisei riding in Cadillacs, purchasing large, expensive homes in exclusive districts (even if such were available), and using money in a way to draw public attention. Clothes were often dated and conservative in style, and for many the less expensive was chosen with the inference that the "best" was reserved for the Caucasian. The unstated inference "Who does he think he is, a ha-ku-jin (Caucasian)" was often strong enough to discourage those who violated the norms. However, for many of the new generation, there has developed a reaction in the opposite direction to some of the Issei prescriptions. Many demand the "best" (translated into the most expensive) from the most prestigious stores, so that labels have become extremely important.

The desire for invisibility is related to a number of other socialization goals. Japanese are expected to be quiet, conforming, to obey rules and regulations, and to avoid loud, attention-getting behavior, especially in public places. And Japanese students in class, whether in Tokyo, Honolulu, or Los Angeles, retain much of their invisibility by their lack of overt participation.

It is our general hypothesis that although the Japanese American looks successful because he has risen above the lowest levels of our social system, he is currently caught in a middleman minority position (Kitano, 1974). The cohesiveness of the group and the emphasis on hard work and educational mobility have provided the impetus to rise in the American structure. But a combination of discrimination, past experiences, and cultural background (which limits complete upward mobility) have also prevented a rise to the top. The role of permanent middlemen minority, such as that faced by the Jews in Europe and the Chinese in Southeast Asia, is an extremely difficult one and may be the role of this ethnic group for some period of time.

CHANGE AND ADAPTATION

The Japanese American family over the course of the generations has undergone, through acculturation, many changes, bringing it more into line with the family system of the dominant Anglo groups. However, the Japanese culture, in combination with the low power and high visibility of this group, have acted as brakes on total acculturation and assimilation.

In general we can summarize our view of the Japanese American family and the major directions in which it appears to be going:

1. It has remained an intact family unit with low rates of separation and divorce, although there are changes toward a more American model. The low past rates of separation and divorce are probably rising (1.3 per cent in 1960; 4 to 6 per cent in 1970).
2. The structure of the family was initially vertical, with father and males on top. It could be likened to a traditional family model, in contrast to the modern urban American family. Entertainment and recreation often took place in the family and extended family units. Families were larger; problems were often handled within the unit, and the use of outside professionals was a last resort.
3. The *ie* unit was adopted in America to include larger units, including village, *ken,* and even the entire Japanese community. It served as an effective social control device; it provided socialization opportunities through ethnic language schools, cultural and recreational opportunities. The Japanese community became a reference group; the functions were similar to those of an *ie*.
4. Socialization and child rearing took into account minority-group position, power, and the carrying on of the Japanese culture. Those values, norms, and behaviors most likely to persist were those of the Japanese culture that interacted with the power position of the Japanese in America and their visibility in a race-conscious society. Many of these behaviors have also been reinforced by the majority group, so that they have become stereotypes of the Japanese. These include quietness, conformity, loyalty, diligence, maximum effort, good citizenship, high school achievement, and a group orientation.

5. The situational orientation has been an important part of Japanese American behavior. Learning how to behave to those above, below, and equal has meant learning appropriate styles. As we say,

> There are elements of a "schizophrenic adaptation" on the part of the Japanese to life in the United States. But most physically identifiable groups are also faced with the same problem—the how-to-behave problem when interacting with the majority and the behaviors when with one's own group. Therefore, within one individual there is often the many personalities—the "Uncle Tom" to the white man, deferential and humble; the "good son" to his parents, dutiful, and obedient; and the "swinger" to his peers, wise-cracking, loud, and irreverent. And all of these behaviors are real so that none can be said to give a truer picture except in terms of time, place, and situation. (Kitano, 1969: 106–107)

The situational approach is intimately related to power. The less powerful have to learn many adaptations; those with power can afford to use one style. Americans expect others to adapt to them, and with their power can often command or buy this recognition. Therefore, we often assume that there are social-science universals—"the personality" and "the truth," whereas our search may be more a reflection of our power position than a social-scientific reality.

6. Acculturation has been the most powerful single influence on Japanese behavior. But it has not been a simple linear movement; the variables of power and visibility have shaped differential styles so that Japanese Americans in Hawaii will be different in many instances from their peers along the Pacific and Atlantic seaboards. There is a current reawakening of an ethnic identity and a militancy among the Sansei (Kitano, 1969) that may slow the trend toward acculturation.

One of the most influential events hastening acculturation was the evacuation of the Japanese during World War II. It broke up the power of the Issei and the ethnic ghettos; altered family life; scattered Japanese throughout America through resettlement; sent many males into the armed forces and overseas; and made many renounce everything Japanese (Kitano, 1969).

7. Social class has always been a factor in the Japanese culture, but it is difficult to transcribe into the American scene. The *ies* tried to make appropriate matches, and "good" families were class conscious. Although most of the immigrants started at the bottom of American class structure, they did not identify with the life style of

the lower classes. Rather, they brought with them many of the values associated with the middleclass: high educational expectation for their children, respect for those in authority, including the police, desire to own property, emphasis on banking and savings, and a future orientation (Kitano, 1969). They seldom fully adopted a lower-class style even though their incomes and housing were clearly in the ghetto areas.

However, there is an increasing heterogeneity in the Japanese American community and development of a more formal social class system (e.g., debutantes, professional organizations). It remains much more open, but with continued differences in education and income, it may soon become much more crystallized.

8. Outside professionals have not been consulted as frequently by the Japanese Americans as might be expected. Psychiatrists, psychologists, social workers, and lawyers note that for a relatively affluent group with many of the concerns of the middle class, the Japanese use of such professional services has been limited. And often when turning for help, many Japanese have turned to members of their own ethnic group.

Finally, it is important to emphasize that there is no one American culture, just as there is no one Japanese or Japanese American culture. Therefore, acculturation means different things to different families, and these will be reflected in their attitudes and behaviors. Perhaps the most appropriate generalization is that the Japanese families in America were different to begin with, and that length of time in America has been just one of the many influences leading to further change. But in spite of these differences there appears to be enough of a thread so that a broad analysis can still be made of the Japanese American subculture.

REFERENCES

Bierstedt, R. 1950. "An Analysis of Social Power." *American Sociological Review* 15 (December):730–38.

Blalock, A. 1967. *Toward a Theory of Minority Group Relations*. New York: Wiley.

Bosworth, B. 1967. *America's Concentration Camps*. New York: Norton.

Daniels, R. 1962. *The Politics of Prejudice: The Anti-Japanese Movement in California, and the Struggle for Japanese Exclusion*. Berkeley: University of California Press.

———. 1971. *Concentration Camps, USA*. New York: Holt, Rinehart and Winston.

——— and Harry H. L. Kitano. 1970. *American Racism: Exploration of the Nature of Prejudice*. Englewood Cliffs, New Jersey: Prentice Hall.

Doi, T. 1962. "Amae—a Key Concept for Understanding Japanese Personality Structure." *Psychologia* 5(March):1–7.

Girdner, A., and A. Loftis. 1969. *The Great Betrayal*. New York: Macmillan.

Hosokawa, W. 1969. *Nisei: The Quiet Americans*. New York: Morrow. Houston, Jeanne Wakatsuki, and James D. Houston. 1973. *Farewell to Manzanar*. Boston: Houghton Mifflin.

Ito, H. 1966. "Japan's Outcasts in the United States." In G. Devos and H. Wagatsuma (eds.): *Japan's Invisible Race*. Berkeley: University of California Press, pp. 220–21.

Japan Times. 1973. Tokyo, Japan p. 3.

Kalish, Richard, and Sharon Moriwaki. 1973. "The World of the Elderly Asian American." *Journal of Social Issues* 29, (2):187–209.

Kikumura, A., and H. H. L. Kitano. 1973. "Interracial Marriage: A Picture of the Japanese-Americans." *Journal of Social Issues* 29, (2):1–9.

Kitano, H. H. L. 1969. *Japanese-Americans: The Evolution of a Subculture*. Englewood Cliffs, N.J.: Prentice-Hall.

———. 1974. "Japanese Americans: A Middleman Minority?" *Pacific Historical Review* XLIII, 4 (November 1974):500–19.

Meredith, G. 1966. "Amae and Acculturation Among Japanese College Students in Hawaii." *Journal of Social Psychology* 70 (December):171–80.

Nakane, Chie. 1970. *Japanese Society*. Berkeley: McCutchan.

Office of Special Concerns. "A Study of Selected Characteristics of Ethnic Minorities based on the 1970 Census. Vol. II: Asian Americans." Department of Health, Education and Welfare, HEW Publication No. (S)75–121. n.d.

Ogawa, Dennis. 1971. *From Japs to Japanese: The Evolution of Japanese American Stereotypes,* Berkeley, California: McCutchan.

Petersen, W. 1971. *Japanese-Americans*. New York: Random House.

Shimamoto, G. 1973. Participant observations and interview in Japan. Unpublished manuscript, International Christian University.

San Francisco Chronicle. 1910. n.d.

Sue, S. and H. H. L. Kitano. 1973. "Asian American Stereotypes." *Journal of Social Issues* 29 (no. 2):83–98.

Tenbroek, J., E. N. Barnhart, and F. W. Matson. 1970. *Prejudice, War and the Constitution*. Berkeley: University of California Press.

U. S. Bureau of the Census. 1973. *Japanese, Chinese and Filipinos in the United States*. 1970 Census of the Population, PC(2)—1G. Washington, D.C.: U.S. Government Printing Office.

Vogel, E. 1965. *Japan's New Middle Class: The Salary Man and His Family in a Tokyo Suburb*. Berkeley: University of California Press.

The Italian American Family

Italian Americans and their family system are a major component of the American ethnic mosaic. The migration of Italians, mostly from southern Italy, was one of the largest in terms of numbers of people and they brought with them a close knit family system that is and to a great extent remains the prototype of the "ethnic family." Important to understanding Italian family life is as authors Femminella and Quadagno point out, that the Italian immigrant only assumed an Italian ethnic identity after he arrived in America. In Italy individuals were not "Italians" as they had regional or village identities with the family ultimately being the most important source of loyalty and identity.

C H A P T E R F O U R

BY

FRANCIS X. FEMMINELLA
and JILL S. QUADAGNO

HISTORICAL BACKGROUND

Italian Villagers

All persons who emigrated from Italy, Sicily, Corsica, and Sardinia at the end of the nineteenth century were referred to as "Italians." The name was applied by members of host societies around the world who perceived and identified them as belonging to or having a single national origin or language. This identity was not, however, a central perception of the emigrants themselves, at least not initially. The unification of Italy (1861–71) could neither easily wipe out centuries of separation, nor could it instantly supply a new mode of identification for those who knew themselves to be different.

The formation of a group cultural identity is a process necessarily continuing over generations.* Through the centuries emigrants from

---

*The notion of "cultural identity" as used here is derived from a concept of "ego-identity" developed by Erik H. Erikson. See his "Identity and the Life Cycle" in George S. Klein (1959:1–171). Some of the data on which this paper is based are taken from research done by Femminella, an early portion of which was included in *Ethnicity and Ego-Identity* (1968).

Italy had learned to define themselves by their association with their parents and their immediate neighbors. They belonged not to Italy but first to their families and then to their villages. For the most part, Neopolitans, Calabrians, Sicilians, Barese, etc., came to America sharing a common identification as southern Italians. When northern Italians came, they considered themselves Romans, Venetians, Piedmontese, and Genoese. From their perspective they were different peoples; they felt no closer in their relationship to one another than an American might feel to an Australian, or to a Scot (Carlyle, 1962:13ff).

Beyond merely feeling that they were different peoples, there was a pervasive prejudice held by northern Italians against southern Italians (Covello, 1967:23–33; Iorizzo and Mondello, 1971:3,4 *passim;* Lopreato, 1970:25; Rolle 1972:112). These prejudices were deeply rooted and "racial" in content. That is, northern Italians considered southern Italians to be an inferior "race" of people. The major characteristics of race prejudice and intolerance with which we are familiar in America existed in Italy also. Southern Italians were thought of as people who at best ought to be disregarded or, worse, cheated, enslaved, spat upon, and generally treated without regard for basic human dignity. In return, southern Italians despised, but, in a reflection of the psychodynamics of identification, simultaneously sought to emulate the *alt Italiani*—the high Italians of the north.

Of course, to imitate behavior requires, first of all, knowledge of the behavior, but in fact most of the inhabitants of southern Italy were financially impoverished and had little direct knowledge of northern manners and ways. What they knew of it had been learned by observing the actions of the wealthy, more educated, and more traveled local barons. These latter were landowners with extensive holdings who occupied the highest position in the stratification system of the southern Italian villages. Disparaged by northern Italians, *baroni* in turn looked down on their fellow villagers of lower caste. Few of these landed gentry were numbered among the immigrants to America.

This differentiation of northern and southern Italians must be neither exaggerated nor ignored if Italians in America are to be understood. Migrants have come to the Americas from all parts of the southern European boot since even before Colonial times, but the great waves of Italian migration to North America in the late nineteenth century consisted for the most part of southern Italians. On arrival, they neither expected nor received a welcoming hand from their northern Italian brothers who were small in numbers and who had arrived much earlier. If anything, they were made to feel unwanted because their presence in many cases was a source of embarrassment to the earlier immigrants who were finally extricating themselves from the prejudices they had themselves experienced upon arrival in America, and who were more securely lodged in the middle range of the work force. (Glazer and Moynihan, 1963:184).

Moreover, just as the landowners in the villages of southern Italy had imitated the northern Italians, so in this country the new *"baroni"* imitated the successful northern Italians already here. That is, northern Italian exploitation of the new immigrants in turn served as a prototype for successful southern Italian immigrant behavior. A second effect of this exploitative behavior was social psychological, reaching beyond both the individuals involved and the action and occurrences themselves. The exploitative relationships that southern Italians met reinforced those earlier sentiments of trust and distrust that have always been characteristic of Italian peasant life.* In a sense, this was socially more significant than the exploitation itself because it retarded the development of different but integrated social structures in the host society.

To explain this point, it is necessary to understand the meaning of the term *campanilismo* (Covello, 1967:135; Lopreato, 1970:103ff; Vecoli, 1964). This interesting word derives from *campanile,* meaning a steeple or belfry. Central to each of the scattered villages of the Italian countryside was the local church with its bell towers. The sound of the bell was unique and familiar to each and every person in the village, and over the centuries the attachment the villagers felt for the bell metamorphosed into a sense of loyalty to the village itself and to one's neighbors. The sound of the bell defined the boundaries of the villages (often quite literally); those who lived beyond were strangers† not to be trusted since the interests of these outsiders too often conflicted with those of the villagers themselves. The focus was not on the group and its values but on the individual and his family.

These village communities in their isolation developed manners and mores, nuances of language and dress, and human struggles and enmities that distinguished one village from another, regardless of geographical proximity. It is not surprising that when Italian villagers migrated to

---

*This notion has significance for understanding the *"Padroni"* relationships of earlier times and the clientele relationships of criminals in later times. Cf. L. V. Iorizzo and S. Mondello (1971:138). See also Francis A. J. Ianni (1972).

†The word "stranger" is itself pregnant with meaning and heavily laden with emotion today and through history. Cf. A. Lacoque and F. R. Vasquez, *The Newcomer and the Bible* (1971).

America, they sought out their *paisani* who had come ahead of them and as soon as possible began to re-establish many of the typical village customs and social relations, including a detachment and personal sense of being apart from the more broadly conceived polity. The centuries of defending against exploitation by northern Italians and foreign governments, and after 1860 the failure of the newly unified Kingdom of Italy to effect the Garibaldi promise of land distribution, generated mechanisms of preservation closely bound up with patterns of authority and control within the family. Clearly, these migrants from the place called Italy were not Italians; nor, for that matter, were they in the first instance "north" or "south" Italians; rather, they were persons from individual families, specific villages, and towns, which Vecoli (1964) calls "rural cities," whose life, and the meaning it held, derived from their attachment to these settings (Covello, 1967:159-168; Dore, 1968:95-122; Lopreato, 1970:101ff).

The Contadino Family in the Mezzogiorno*

Although the first Italian immigrants to arrive in America in the 1870s were from northern Italy, their numbers were small. The impact of the Italian migration, which increased rapidly after 1900, consisted largely of southern Italians from the region known as the Mezzogiorno. Between 1900 and 1930 over five million Italians came to America, and at least 80 per cent were from the southern regions of Italy (Gambino, 1974:3; Lopreato, 1970:34). In order to understand the Italian American family today, it is necessary to understand the kind of people who lived in the Mezzogiorno and the life style they brought with them to this country.

The name Mezzogiorno refers to the six provinces east and south of Rome. It has been called "the land that time forgot." Those Italians who emigrated from the Mezzogiorno were largely of the peasant class of farmers and day laborers called the *contadino* class. The *contadino* included agricultural workers who owned a tiny plot of land and leased additional land from the large landowners, the agricultural proletariat who owned no land but leased it from the *signori,* and the subproletariat consisting of day laborers, the *giornalieri,* whose daily existence depended on the whims of the weather and the nobility (Lopreato, 1970:31).

---

*Most of the following discussion of the southern Italian family is taken from Gambino (1974).

64

L'Ordine della Famiglia. Centuries of exploitation by the landed class and the harsh exigencies of daily life led to a rejection of the social institutions of the larger society, so that the Italian *contadino* came to rely solely on the family. Within the family a complex system of rules regulating one's relations and responsibilities to the members of his family and one's posture toward the outside world was developed.

Family order, which was the only meaningful order in the lives of the *contadino,* was maintained by adhering to the norms surrounding one's responsibilities to other family members. Relationships between individuals were arranged according to a hierarchy. The first category was *la famiglia* and consisted of blood relationships, family members to whom one owed all his loyalty. *La famiglia* was supplemented by *comparaggio,* or godparents, who comprised the second category in the hierarchy. Causal acquaintances and those whose family status demanded respect made up the third category in the hierarchy. Finally, there were *stranieri,* which included all other people, such as shopkeepers and fellow workers who were objects of suspicion and as such kept at a distance (Gambino, 1974:19).

Marital Roles. The *contadino* family has been described as patriarchal, yet this is somewhat misleading since it implies that all the power is held by the male members of the family. It is true that the father was the *capo di famiglia,* or head of the family, and in this role was responsible for arbitrating disputes and making decisions that affected the relations of *la famiglia* with the outside world. He was also responsible for making a living, a feat that involved skills of wit as well as hard labor to protect his family from the threat of *la miseria,* or desperate poverty. However, the mother, as the center of the family in a society in which nonfamilial relationships were not meaningful, had a great deal of power in terms of internal matters. The southern Italian wife and mother kept the home, which was the source of all that gave meaning to life, managed all financial affairs, and arranged the marriages of her children, which were critical for survival of *la via vecchia,* the old way. In a world in which the family status was judged not by the occupation of the father but by the signs of family well-being that emanated from the household, the mother played an important role in securing that status.

In extended family relationships, the patriarchal image of the Italian family is also misleading since the major kinship ties were with the maternal relatives. The nurturing of the children was done by the mother and her female relatives who were her frequent companions, and if the mother became a widow, the responsibility for her and her children was assumed by her own family, not her husband's. "Thus, despite the pre-eminence of the husband, the wife's role in the economics of the family was considerable, comprising both management and insurance . . . Indeed, the father was formal chief executive of the family, but the actual power was shared with the mother in an intricate pattern of interactions . . ." (Gambino, 1974:26).

THE INSTITUTION OF COMPARAGGIO. The term *comparaggio* refers to the selection of outsiders to be admitted into the family circle in the role of godparents. This was an institution of great significance in extending the kinship ties of families in the Mezzogiorno to include individuals who were not blood relatives. It formed further protection against the intrusion of outsiders and formed links between villages that extended the influence of a single family. Because of their importance, great care was taken in the selection of godparents, who could be either one's peers or older people who were to be treated with respect. While the godparents may have participated in the baptism of the child in the church, godparents were frequently selected independent of ties to the church. It was considered an honor to be offered the role of godparent, and to refuse was considered a great insult. The privileges and obligations extended to godparents approached those of kin with blood ties, yet it was known that in a conflict one's blood relatives came first (Gambino, 1974:29).

LA VIA VECCHIA. Within the family a value system was built and maintained that served chiefly to protect the individual from an essentially hostile environment. These values permeated all areas of social life not only within the family itself but in terms of the attitudes of the *contadino* toward work, education, and definitions of social status.

Of singular importance was the necessity of family ties. One's personal identity was derived from his family, and family membership was essential in terms of defining one's place in society. The most shameful condition was to be without a family (Gambino, 1974:31). A man who violated the family code and was outcast from his family was an outcast from the larger society as well. He could only become a day laborer, and even in this he was the last hired. For a female without a family the only options were to become a beggar or a prostitute. However, loyal kin were rewarded by always having a place within the family. The aged were cared for in the family, and "no one went to poorhouses, orphanages, or other institutions of charity in the Mezzogiorno except those few unfortunates without any family intimates" (Gambino, 1974:29).

The strength of familial ties also affected the attitude of the *contadino* toward work. "Work is regarded as moral training for the young. And among adults, it is regarded as a matter of pride. To work is to show evidence that one has become a man or a woman, a full member of the family" (Gambino, 1974:80). Thus work was not defined as abstract but as tangible, something that could be shown to others as a visible result of an individual's skills and efforts. The disdain for intangibles was also related to the *contadino's* attitude toward education.

While the ideal of the *contadino* was to cultivate children who were *ben educato*—well educated—the translation of this phrase is deceptive. Being educated did not refer to formal schooling but to being educated in proper behavior. *"Ben educato* meant raised with the core of one's personality woven of those values and attitudes, habits and skills that perpetuated *l'ordine della famiglia,* and thus one was attuned to the welfare of the family" (Gambino, 1974:225). In this sense, formal schooling was antithetical to proper training for manhood or womanhood, involving the influence of *stranieri* who might interfere with *la via vecchia* as well as keeping young people from the more important lessons they might learn from work.

The concept of *ben educato* was applied differently to male and female children. For a young boy, this meant first and foremost to be *pazienza,* patient. This is not to be confused with fatalism or stoicism, for it meant more than that. According to Gambino (1974:119), "the idea of *pazienza* is an ideal control of life. First and foremost, it is an ideal of inner control, of reserve." Thus, the Italian male was trained to wait and react cautiously, evaluating the events of life rather than actively pursuing a particular course. This value was expressed in a popular game played by men and boys called *morra* or throwing fingers. The game doesn't stress competition or mere chance. "It stresses cleverness in the context of chance situations, a minimodel of life" (Gambino, 1974:139). A boy was also taught to show respect to those older than himself, to acknowledge their wisdom, and to model his behavior after his male relatives. The Italian's attitudes toward the purpose of child rearing can be summarized by the old saying, "only a fool makes his children better than himself."

In the Mezzogiorno, the ideal of womanhood included not only bearing children and knowing household skills but having those supportive qualities that enable a woman to take her place as the center of the family. In raising a daughter, the family's ultimate goal was to see her settled and competent in her role as a woman (Gambino, 1974:151). From the age of 7 girls were apprenticed in learning household skills, developing the qualities of womanhood under constant supervision. Thus, an Italian girl learned manner and style as well as the crucial economic and social roles of womanhood (Gambino, 1974:155).

The Italian Immigrant in America

Most Italian immigrants, as suggested above, came from Southern Italy. Their points of destination were the large cities of the northeastern seaboard, the central states, and, eventually for some, California. By far the largest number came in the years between 1900 and 1914—over three million, and again in 1921 when 222,260 immigrants came to these shores. Since many of the Italian immigrants planned to return home, they sought jobs with ready or immediate wages (Vecoli, 1964) rather than those which required investment of energy to be rewarded over a longer period of time.

Arriving in this country, the emigrants from the villages and cities of Italy, Sicily, Corsica and Sardinia were not respected or known for their local areas of residence but were collectively identified as Italians and Sicilians and later simply as "Italians." For many this was humiliating. In the case of the Italians who migrated to the eastern seaboard, the unkindest cut, from their point of view, was administered by fellow Catholics, the Irish (Tomasi, in Tomasi and Engel, 1970:1963–193; Vecoli, 1969:217–268) who by this time had been in the United States for two, three or more generations and had internalized nativist values, including the xenophobia toward foreigners under which they too had suffered earlier, and who still worked in construction jobs for which Italian immigrants competed.

From the viewpoint of the Irish, however, several factors militated against helping the Italian immigrants. Some had reached middle class status and saw no advantage in being identified with impoverished, illiterate, "foreign" newcomers. Others reacted strongly against the economic competition which the Italians represented. And almost all Irish were dismayed by the religious style of the Italians particularly with respect to liturgical observance, doctrinal matters, and the relationship between priest and people. These differences were sufficient to generate a resentment which often precluded cooperation between the two groups. The subjective reactions of the Italians to Irish Catholicism in the United States have been dealt with more extensively elsewhere (Russo, 1970:195–213; Femminella, 1961:233–241). What must be pointed out here is that from the viewpoint of the newly arrived *contadino* those who might have been considered closest to him outside his family and *paesani* were of little help. But while there was direct antagonism between Irish and Italian immigrants, neither group fared as well in the occupational sphere as other immigrant groups and native born persons until after World War II (Thernstrom, 1973).

In response to lack of acceptance, Italian immigrants reestablished their village life here as far as possible (Dore, 1968:95–122). This meant the creation of a new kind of *campanilismo* along with the usual distrust of strangers that goes with it. If this is confusing to non-Italo Americans who know Italians as warm and friendly people, the paradox is understandable and is explained by Friedman. He describes the peasants' way of dealing with a guest or neighbor by relating to the core of the person as long as that person is not perceived as having a competing interest (Friedman, 1960:118).

Another reaction was patient resignation, exemplified by calling upon God for help through the intercession of His saints. They also re-instituted the local *festa* (festivals on religious holidays). And they established in the early years of this century several hundreds of social and mutual benefit societies (Nelli, 1970:77–107; Vecoli, 1964; Amfitheatrof, 1973:4; Glazer and Moynihan, 1963:194). These latter were usually small groups organized around direct help to one another's families and to those from the same town in Italy but did not develop over time into larger, more complex institutions for defense of all Italians or for philanthropic purposes (Glazer and Moynihan, 1963:193–194; Vecoli, 1964).

Although the wages the immigrants received assured them survival they took equal comfort from the knowledge that there was a higher good than money—the *rispetto* or pride that comes from hard work. They were proud of their accomplishments, the more so when these resulted from toil and effort. One thanked God for talent, but one deserved praise for effort, including physical work. Honest work for the Italian was honorable and was to be performed with a sense of dignity, whatever the type of work. Digging ditches, carrying garbage, sweeping streets, shining shoes, or cleaning toilets—these were jobs that could bring a man money to feed his family here or in Italy. And if his wife and children were here already, he would manage to put some money aside to be sent back home to help his parents or other relatives who had remained in Italy. And they in turn, whenever they could, invested the money in land not only for their own use but for their sons in America in hope and preparation for their return (Vecoli, 1974:31–43).

THE MODERN ITALIAN AMERICAN FAMILY

The Italians came to America with a culture that was in many ways antagonistic to a rapidly developing society, a society that needed their labor but rejected their seemingly incomprehensible customs. The extent to which they were successful in insulating themselves from the larger society can be seen by examining the characteristics of Italian Americans today. While assimilation has certainly occurred, there are remnants of cultural traditions, maintained by strong family ties, that have affected the relationship of the Italian to American society.

Kinship Ties and Social Mobility

The Italians came to this country basically illiterate and with few skills to offer except a willingness to work. Work was valued over education, and this specific orientation has affected their subsequent position in American society. Specifically, Italians have gone into blue-collar work, a pattern that is just beginning to change within the third generation. Table 1 compares the employment patterns of Italian males of first- and second-generation males from the 1950 census and all males from the 1972 census study of the characteristics of the population by ethnic origin (Bureau of the Census, 1973). Since the 1972 study did not differentiate by place of birth but by ethnic origin, all three generations are necessarily included. However, the average age was 32.0, so it can be assumed that a large proportion are third generation. There was very little change between the first and second generations, with men of both generations largely employed in blue-collar work as either craftsmen or operatives. By the third generation there has been a decrease in operatives and a significant shift toward white-collar work, accompanied by an increase in the ranks of professionals.

In terms of education, the Italians have ranked behind other ethnic groups that came to America about the same time. According to the census report based on 1972 data, the greatest change between Italian Americans over 35 and those under 35 was in per cent graduating from high school. As shown in Table 2, although only 31.9 per cent of those over 35 graduated from high school, 51.1 per cent of the younger Italians finished high school, an increase of almost 20 percentage points. While only 16.5 per cent of those under 35 graduated from college, a relatively

TABLE 1

Employment Patterns of Three Generations of Italian American Males

	FIRST-GENERATION MALES (PERCENT) 1950	SECOND-GENERATION MALES (PERCENT) 1950	ALL ITALIAN MALES (PERCENT)* 1972
Professional	3	6	13
Managerial	13	10	14
Clerical and sales	6	17	15
Craftsmen	24	22	22
Operatives	24	29	16
Laborers	14	9	9
Service workers	14	6	10
Private houschold workers	0		0

SOURCE: Gambino, 1974: 83 U.S. Bureau of the Census, Population Characteristics: Characteristics of the Population by Ethnic Origin. Series P-20, No. 249, 1973.

*The census report did not differentiate by place of birth but by ethnic identification, thus all three generations are included in this figure. However, the average age was 32.0 so it can be assumed that a large proportion are third generation.

low figure, this still represents a marked increase over the 6 per cent of college graduates over 35.

OCCUPATIONAL ADAPTATION. In the peasant family in southern Italy the Italian mother usually did not work outside the home, but in confronting American society, many first- and second-generation Italian women found that work was necessary for family survival. While some have interpreted this as a sign of a breakdown of old patterns, a confrontation between the Italian immigrants and their children struggling to become accepted members of American society (Ware, 1935), others have suggested that Italian American women only took jobs that they perceived to be compatible with the family value system. Thus, they were more likely to work in factories with other Italian-American women and did not work as domestics in other people's homes, which was viewed as a usurpation of family loyalty (Gambino, 1974:13). As shown in Table 3, first-generation Italian women were most likely to be operatives. The second generation shifted to clerical work, as did most women, with the expansion of this sector of the labor force after World

TABLE 2
Years of School Completed by Italian Americans by Age

AGE	ELEMENTARY 0-4	5-7	8	HIGH SCHOOL 1-3	4	COLLEGE 1-3	4/MORE	MEDIAN SCH. YRS.
25-34	0.9	2.4	3.3	13.0	51.1	12.8	16.5	12.6
35 & over	8.7	10.5	17.0	19.7	31.9	6.1	6.0	11.1

SOURCE: U.S. Bureau of the Census, Population Characteristics: Characteristics of the Population by Ethnic Origin, Series P-20, No. 249, 1973.

War II, but even so, a relatively high proportion remained operatives as opposed to most other women, who were more likely to be service workers. Further, Italian women are the least likely to be professionals of all ethnic groups with the exception of Spanish, although, like the males, they did show a significant increase in this category by 1972. Since professional occupations require more schooling as well as a stronger career orientation that might interfere with family life, it would appear that there are still strong remnants of *la via vecchia* affecting occupational choice among Italian-American women as well as men.

These work force statistics can partially be explained by examining the meaning attached to work and education by Italian Americans. According to Gambino (1974:82).

> Because of their general distaste for abstractions and abstracted values, their ambivalent attitude toward formal schooling and their desire to remain close to the family roots, Italian-Americans have gone into blue-collar rather than white collar work. And when they have gone into the latter, it is in areas where the individual as such can exercise his skills or just plain labor. . . . In a pattern that perhaps is just now beginning to change, those few Italian-Americans who have gone into white-collar work and the professions have chosen careers again where personal accomplishment, stability, and noninterference with regular family life were perceived as possible.

Several empirical studies confirm Gambino's impressions. An early study by Rosen (1959) found that Italian Americans placed relatively low value on independence and achievement training and had relatively low aspirations in terms of expectations for education and occupational choice. In a more recent study of adult males, Featherman (1971) found that Italian and Mexican Roman Catholics expressed a high "materialistic orientation" toward work, valuing work instrumentally for achieving

TABLE 3
Employment Patterns of Three Generations of Italian American Females

	FIRST-GENERATION FEMALES (PERCENT) 1950	SECOND-GENERATION FEMALES (PERCENT) 1950	ALL ITALIAN FEMALES (PERCENT) 1972
Professional	2	5	12
Managerial	4	2	6
Clerical and sales	8	40	46
Craftsmen	2	2	1
Operatives	77	44	18
Laborers	0	0	1
Service workers	4	4	15
Private household workers	1	0	2

SOURCE: Gambino, 1974: 84 U.S. Bureau of the Census, Population Characteristics: Characteristics of the Population by Ethnic Origin. Series P-20, No. 249, 1973.

other goals rather than regarding work as intrinsically satisfying. However, he cautions against using adult motivation as an explanatory variable for ethnic-group achievement differentials and suggests that motivation to complete school may be the key intervening variable. Finally, in a study of college seniors, Gottlieb and Sibbison (1974) asked students to explain their reasons for attending college. Both male and female Italian American students rated job training as the major reason over more abstract choices such as seeking knowledge.

Characteristics of Italian-American Families

Marriage was essential for the southern Italian as a source of social identity, and family stability still seems to be relatively intact. According to the 1973 census report on ethnicity (Bureau of the Census), "there were 2.6 million families in March 1972 whose head was of Italian origin. Most of these families were composed of husband-wife families, eighty-seven percent, and only about ten percent were families with a female head." This was the smallest percentage of 11 major ethnic groups for women between the ages of 15 and 44.

DIVORCE. The stability of the Italian family is reflected in the low divorce rates for Italian Americans. According to the 1970 census only about 3 per cent of all Italian Americans are divorced, and the divorce rate for younger Italians is not significantly higher than that for those over 45. In a comprehensive study of ethnicity in America using data based on seven National Opinion Research Center (NORC) surveys, Greeley (1974:46) found that Italian American Catholics had the second lowest divorce rate (only 2.0 per cent) of all ethnic groups. The only group with a lower divorce rate were the Irish Catholics (1.8 per cent). While the effects of religion cannot be discounted, the relatively weaker ties of the Italians to the Catholic church* indicate that family influence is certainly playing some role in maintaining a low divorce rate. This can be illustrated by the fact that other Catholic groups that have stronger ties to the Catholic church have higher divorce rates. For example, Polish, Slavic, and French Catholics all have divorce rates over 4 per cent, and it is 6.6 per cent for Spanish-speaking Catholics. Thus, Catholicism cannot be the only explanatory factor for the low divorce rate among Italian Americans. Strong familism is certainly a critical variable.

INTERMARRIAGE. Rates of intermarriage are useful indicators, telling us something about social amalgamation and the disposition to lose ethnic identification. Endogamy among Italian Americans was the subject of two studies, one dealing largely with second-generation Italians, the other including younger Italians as well.

In the first study, Kennedy (1952) investigated intermarriage among seven ethnic groups in New Haven, Connecticut, for the period 1870–1950. She found that after the Jews the Italians had the highest in-group marriage rate of the seven ethnic groups considered. However, the rate of in-group marriage did show a decrease from first-generation to second-generation Italians. In 1900, 97.9 per cent of Italian marriages were strictly endogamous, as they were for most newly arrived ethnic groups. By 1950 this rate had fallen to 76.7, a sizable decrease but still high compared to other ethnic groups.

More recently Abramson (1973) studied endogamy among nine Catholic ethnic groups, using NORC data that sampled the total white Catholic population of America between the ages of 23 and 57. He found

---

*Since the Catholic church in America was initially controlled by the Irish, Italian immigrants did not form strong ties to the church. However, this is a pattern that appears to be changing among third-generation Italians who exhibit higher rates of church attendance and are more likely to send their children to Catholic schools (Greeley, 1974).

74

that the Italians were the only ethnic group of those arriving prior to 1920 that still showed relatively high rates of endogamy. Sixty-six per cent of the Italian Catholics in his sample were endogamous, compared to 56 per cent or less for Polish, Lithuanian, Eastern European, German, Irish, and English. The only groups with higher rates of in-group marriage were the Spanish-speaking Catholics and the French-Canadians. However, these results were tempered by several factors. Among those factors influencing rates of intermarriage was region. Those Italians living in the Middle Atlantic states with high concentrations of Italians had very low rates of intermarriage (only 27 per cent), but this increased to a high of 49 per cent in the North Central portion of America in which Italians are relatively few in number. Even more significant were the different rates of intermarriage when age was used as a control. While only 27 per cent of Abramson's sample of Italian Americans between the ages of 40 and 50 married non-Italians, 42 per cent of those between 20 and 30 intermarried. He also found level of education to have an effect on endogamy, those completing high school having much higher rates of intermarriage than those without a high school diploma. This indicates that education is a powerful influence on assimilation, and that rates of intermarriage for Italians may continue to increase as they obtain college degrees and are increasingly exposed to individuals of other ethnic backgrounds.

FERTILITY. While the impoverished Italian immigrant women had exceptionally large families, their second-generation daughters reversed this pattern completely. As reported by Rosenwaike (1973:272), the 1910 census showed that women of Italian parentage constituted 4.9 per cent of the female population in Boston between the ages of 15 and 44 and accounted for 15.3 per cent of the births for that city. Data from New York indicate a similar pattern. Immigrant women generally had more children, but those from Italy were exceptional. This changed drastically with the second generation. Rosenwaike (1973:275) concludes, "Obviously very strong assimilationist pressures had been at work, for not only did the second generation Italian-American women, on the average, have fewer than half the children of the immigrant generation; they curtailed their childbearing to a level below that of Americans of native parentage." Certainly, assimilationist pressures is one possible explanation for this intergenerational difference in fertility. However, Gambino (1974:163–164) offers an alternate explanation of this same phenomenon.

75

Large families were found in the Mezzogiorno not because the *contadini* confused womanhood with high fertility. Nor did they have large families to satisfy any religious views. They had large families for two reasons. First, they lacked effective birth control technology. Second, a large number of children was an asset to a family in the economic system of old Southern Italy. . . . Italian-American women of the second generation had means of birth control available to them. They were free to exercise only the traditional criterion regarding children—the economic well-being of the family . . . they had children in proportion to their family incomes in America, where economic realities punished families with many children. They and their husbands decided it was better for the family to limit its number of children. And they did so.

Thus, according to Gambino it was not assimilationist pressures that caused second-generation women to limit their family size, but a continuing tradition of concern for family well-being.

The birth rate for third-generation Italians still appears to be decreasing. In a study of three generations of Italians in New York City, Russo (1970:207) found definite generational variation in family size, with third-generation Italians reporting the fewest number of children. In response to the question, "How many children do you have?" 42.2 per cent of third-generation Italians reported two or less. In contrast among first-generation Italians 54.7 per cent came from families of five or more children. This trend is apparent in spite of the fact that most Italians are Catholic. In fact, in a national survey Ryder and Westoff (1971) reported that Italian Catholics were most likely of all Catholic ethnic groups to use contraceptive methods other than rhythm. Thus, it would appear that the stereotype of the Italian woman burdened by large numbers of children due to her religious convictions is certainly not typical of the average second- or third-generation Italian women.

Residential Mobility and Kinship Ties

While many sociologists have been swayed by an assimilationist model of ethnicity, assuming that America's racial and ethnic groups will eventually be incorporated into the mainstream culture, others have challenged this assumption. Researchers have recognized that ethnic diversity may be a meaningful indicator of group differences independent of social class (Greeley, 1974:22; Kantrowitz, 1973). Others argue that it is social class and not ethnicity that is the critical factor in group differences (Gans, 1962; Gordon, 1964; Lopreato, 1970:79). In arguing for pluralism or assimilation, a key indicator used by both sides has been that of residential segregation, that is, to what extent do ethnic groups, regardless of social class, remain ethnically segregated and how lasting are these patterns of residential segregation.

Several studies have examined residential segregation among Italian Americans. From the very beginning of their immigration, Italians settled in what have been called "Little Italy's," and these ethnic communities tended to be concentrated along the Eastern seaboard, particularly New York and the cities of Rhode Island, Connecticut, Massachusetts, and New Jersey (Lieberson, 1963:79; Lopreato, 1970:41). To a large extent these broad patterns of residential settlement have been maintained (Abramson, 1973:29; Lopreato, 1970:53). According to the 1960 census, nearly 70 per cent of Italian Americans are concentrated in the north-eastern portion of America.

While broad patterns of residential segregation have been maintained, a more significant indicator of ethnic pluralism is the maintenance of neighborhoods. There is evidence to suggest that for Italians the meaning of neighborhood transcends the physical characteristics of housing. Italians imbue neighborhoods with a special significance so that they become, in effect, extended families. In an early study of the Italian North End of Boston, Firey (1947) found that second-generation Italians were more inclined to move to the suburbs than the older first-generation Italians. He interpreted this to mean that they were seeking identification with American cultural patterns (Firey, 1947:200–209).

Years later, when assimilationist theories were being challenged, Glazer and Moynihan (1963:187) noted that "while the Jewish map of New York City in 1920 bears almost no relation to that in 1961, the Italian districts, though weakened in some cases and strengthened in others are still in large measure where they were." They also noted two trends among second- and third-generation Italians. One was a tendency to redo old neighborhoods, so that social mobility did not necessarily mean moving to suburbs. They also noted that when Italians did move, it was often a two-generational process, with both children and parents moving to suburban neighborhoods together. Glazer and Moynihan's finding were confirmed by a detailed analysis of residential segregation by ethnicity in New York City based on 1960 census data (Kantrowitz, 1973). Kantrowitz (1973:7) concludes, "that ethnic segregation . . . has declined little over a generation."

The meaning of the maintenance of ethnic neighborhoods, particularly for Italian Americans, has been investigated in a comprehensive study of ethnicity from the NORC (Greeley, 1971). Greeley (1971:77) found that "of all the ethnic groups, Italians most often live in the same neighborhood as their parents and siblings and visit them every week."

Further, he notes that "when the same data are sorted out according to social class and the physical distance that separates the respondents from parents and relatives, Italians are still the most likely to visit both their parents and their siblings." Greeley (1971:78) concludes that among Italians "ethnic differences seem to persist even when different social classes are examined separately." Similar data were reported by Abramson (1970). Studying ethnic communities in four Connecticut cities, Abramson found that more than 50 per cent of Italians and Eastern Europeans had friends and relatives in the immediate neighborhood as compared with 10 to 15 per cent for Jews, German Catholics, and Yankees.

In contrast to these findings, Lopreato reports that his own research of New Haven Italians indicates that middle-class Italians visit relatives only slightly more frequently than the general population, while working-class Italians visit twice as much. Lopreato (1970:51) concludes: "These findings seem to indicate that to a considerable extent the working class still adheres to old world habits and practices. The Italian American middle class, on the other hand, is for all practical purposes indistinguishable from the American middle class as a whole."

Obviously the relationship between social class and ethnicity is complex, and the final answer has certainly not been provided. Whether the upward social mobility of third- and fourth-generation Italians will lead to complete assimilation, or whether they will maintain a distinct ethnic identity, is something to be determined in the future. In a study based on interviews with 100 Irish and Italian Catholics in Providence, Rhode Island, Goering (1971) found that third-generation Italians were more likely to think of themselves ethnically than first or second generation and concluded that ethnic awareness may be increasing among the third-generation Italians.

Family Roles

While the southern Italian family has been termed patriarchal, the limitations of this description have already been discussed. All authority did not rest with the father, and the Italian mother had considerable power and influence on her family's affairs. However, her power, as the father's, was circumscribed, and there was a distinct separation of roles for males and females. This division of labor was largely maintained by the first-generation immigrant to America. The first-generation woman did work outside the home but, as discussed earlier, in occupations that caused as little disruption as possible to family stability. Further, she had large numbers of children that were likely to keep her tied to house and family. Second-generation women curtailed their child-bearing drastically, apparently freeing themselves further from their traditional roles.

Several writers have emphasized this schism between first- and second-generation Italian Americans, describing the Old World peasants as obstacles to the acculturation and success of their children. An early study comparing attitudes of first- and second-generation Italians in Greenwich Village, New York (Ware, 1935), found quite different beliefs between those over 35 and those under 35 in regard to the interpretation of familial roles. Ware (1935:193) found that 64 per cent of the younger Italians disagreed with the statement "the husband's authority should be supreme" as opposed to 35 per cent of the older group. Eighty-six per cent of the younger group did not think large families were a blessing as opposed to 58 per cent of the older group. Finally, 54 per cent of the second generation disagreed that a child should sacrifice his personal ambition to the welfare of the family group as opposed to 31 per cent of the older group.

In a comprehensive study examining changes between the southern Italian peasant and first- and second-generation Italian Americans, Campisi (1948) found major changes. He described the southern Italian peasant as patriarchal, the first generation as fictitiously patriarchal, and the second generation as democratic, with the father sharing high status with the mother and children. He found little in-group solidarity among second-generation Italians and a general weakening of Italian culture, which was no longer transmitted by the family but by the larger society.

Both of the above studies were done during a time when researchers believed that assimilation was inevitable, and thus both were concentrating on differences. Other more recent studies have found more cultural continuity than was originally believed to exist. In a descriptive study of an urban, Italian neighborhood, Gans (1962) found that while some of the outward manifestations of Italian culture had disappeared, many traditional patterns remained. Specific among these was what Gans termed the "segregated conjugal pattern" in which husbands and wives had distinctly separate roles, duties, and obligations and turned to kin of the same sex for advice and companionship so that the society was essentially sex-segregated. According to Gans (1962:52):

> The segregated conjugal pattern is closely associated with the extended family, for the functions that are not performed by husband and wife for each other are handled by other members of the extended family. In a society where male and female roles are sharply distinguished, the man quickly learns that, on many occasions, his brother is a better source of advice and counsel than his wife.

While Gans' findings have been criticized for being applicable only to second-generation working-class Italians and not descriptive of suburban college-educated Italian Americans (Lopreato, 1970), some more recent empirical studies indicate that even among upwardly mobile individuals, traditional patterns remain. In a survey of graduating college seniors in five schools in Pennsylvania, Gottlieb and Sibbison (1974:49) found that Italian Catholic students were more likely to have a traditional conception of sex roles than any other ethnic group, including Irish, Jewish, Polish, or Black. They also found that Italian females were less traditional than the males, although still more so than the other ethnic groups.

Similar findings were reported by Greeley (1974:157), who was attempting to determine "whether ethnic heritage continues to have an influence on the relationships within the contemporary American family despite the process of assimilation and homogenization that was the American context of the immigrant family." In measuring the source of identification for third-generation Italians, Greeley (1974:162) found that the males found their father to be their primary source of identification, while the females were most likely to identify with their mothers. The identification with the mother was stronger for Italian females than any other group except Blacks. However, Italian females tended to reject traditional roles for women and to not consider domestic skills important. In contrast Italian males' acceptance of the traditional role for women was particularly high. It would appear that there are patterns that have been maintained, but that the greatest challenge to *la via vecchia* may be coming from the Italian women.

Socialization of Children

The first-generation Italians who came to America and settled in insulated communities were able to resist encroachments of American culture in their own lives, but the beliefs and customs they valued were more difficult to instill in their second-generation children. The second-generation Italian was not able to maintain the same degree of isolation. They were socialized not only by their parents but also by American institutions, particularly the school system, and what they were taught at home was frequently in conflict with what they learned at school. According to Gambino (1974:33),

It was a rending confrontation. The parents of the typical second generation child ridiculed American institutions and sought to nurture in him *la via*

80

vecchia. The father nurtured in his children (sons especially) a sense of mistrust and cynicism regarding the outside world. And the mother bound her children (not only her daughters) to the home by making any aspirations to go beyond seem somehow disloyal and shameful.

One solution taken by many young Italian men was to identify with peers rather than parents or school, and so for many youth, their friends became an important source of socialization. In Gans' (1962:38) study of the West Enders of Boston, the significance of the peer group is described:

Before or soon after they start going to school, boys and girls form cliques or gangs. In these cliques, which are sexually segregated, they play together and learn the lore of childhood. The clique influence is so strong, in fact, that both parents and school officials complain that their values have difficulty competing with those being taught in the peer group. The sexually segregated clique maintains its hold on the individual until late adolescence or early adulthood.

Among the concerns of the male adolescent peer groups were self-control, independence, and a competitive sort of display involving games of skill, verbal bantering, as well as conspicuous consumption related to clothes or cars (Gans, 1962:83).

In Gans' study the actual responsibility for child rearing belonged to the mother, with formal discipline being provided by the father (Gans, 1962:59). He found the West End family to be adult centered in the sense that the household was run to satisfy adult wishes first. Children were expected to act like adults and not interfere with adult activities. By the age of 7, girls were expected to assist their mothers, while boys were given more freedom to roam (Gans, 1962:56). Punishment tended to be physical but intermingled with verbal and physical signs of affection.

Socialization practices among third-generation Italian American families has not been the subject of empirical research. It is not known to what extent traditional Italian values and patterns of child rearing are being transmitted to fourth-generation children. Some researchers have speculated that there has been a tendency for third-generation Italians to behave in a manner that is more middle-class American than it is Italian, with a few vestiges of Italian culture remaining (Lopreato, 1970:86). In the absence of empirical data, it is impossible to generalize, but this seems to be an area that is rich with possibility for future research projects.

CHANGE AND ADAPTATION

Some distinction should be made between the old family in Italy and the new family in America. The more important family unit among Italian Americans is the nuclear family, but ties to the extended family are retained (Tomasi, 1972:10). The pace of modern urban life and the pressures of our industrial society frequently militate against actively continuing these extended family relationships. However, when residential dispersion precludes daily visiting, kinship ties are maintained symbolically through such devices as regular gatherings at holidays or feasts, scrupulous attendance at wakes and weddings, the remembrance of the birthdays and anniversaries of at least the oldest members of the family, the casual felicity of occasional visits, and finally, the profound certainty of assistance if help is sought. As one third-generation Italian college professor stated, "You can't reject the family. You can't leave it, no matter what you do . . . Your family comes first. No matter what crisis has ever occurred with me, no matter how hostile the conflict, at the end, after the initial explosion is over, the family is there."

Certain traits of Italian Americans' long process of settlement in America affected their relationship to the larger society and the structure of their own communities.

The immigrant community served the function of helping the immigrant "cross the line," and although it may not have happened in the first generation, subsequent generations could assimilate and become "Americanized." At the same time, the immigrant community had an effect on the host society. People would come into these immigrant communities perhaps because they offered good food bargains and a certain life style. Thus, the Italian community in Greenwich Village in New York or the Italian community in the North Beach section of San Francisco afforded the very things needed by certain non-Italians. Sometimes an American with little money and needing to live cheaply goes to a place in which he can do things considered by other Americans to be somewhat strange. For example, he might be an actor and might want to live what at one time was called a more "Bohemian" kind of life. This life style would not be tolerated in the middle class, White Anglo-Saxon Protestant neighborhood, but because the Italians believed that "as long as you don't interfere with the established institutions you can do as you please," outsiders often established homes in their neighborhoods. "Your liberty extends to the tip of my nose. You can do whatever you want, just as long as you don't stop me from doing my thing." Because this was the dominant norm among the Italians, they were very tolerant. Many bohemians moved into Italian neighborhoods in which they could live their "strange" kind of life and have good food at moderate prices. Thus, we find, in part at least, the reason why Greenwich Village developed the way it did. The same thing happened in South Philadelphia, in Boston's North End, and in San Francisco. Interestingly enough, this inclusion of White Anglo-Saxon Protestants and others into the Italian community made Italian communities mixed communities right from the beginning. There never was a Little Italy that was purely and exclusively Italian. Italian immigrant communities were never more than 65 per cent Italian; they were always mixed, and because of this enormous tolerance Italians, who have always had a desire to be with their own kind, found it difficult to do so exclusively.

Adjustment was a two-way process, and while the immigrants affected their host society, it also affected them and their children. Second-generation Italians were placed in the difficult position of being socialized by two different and often conflicting agencies—the family and the larger culture. They responded to this in one of several ways. According to Hansen (1958:139–44), they tended either to overidentify or reject their heritage. This was the marginal generation that was in America but not of it. These were the sons and daughters of immigrants who either preferred the old Italian ways and tried to maintain them or spurned the ways of the past in exchange for what they considered a superior or at least more satisfying way of life—the American way. Often these latter individuals Anglicized their names, moved to non-Italian neighborhoods, and in subtle ways literally and figuratively denied their heritage. There was also the other group of Italian Americans, on the other hand, who overidentified with the past and idealized the old traditional Italian ways.

Child (1943) described the second generation in a similar way, including an additional category that he termed the "apathetic" reaction. Two of his categories, the "rebel" and the "in-group" reaction, conformed roughly to those identified by Hansen. The "apathetic" reaction, which probably described the majority of second-generation Italian Americans (Lopreato 1970:70), was apathetic only in the sense that they did not take the strong position characteristic of either of the other groups. Instead, they attempted to gain acceptance in both cultures, having both Italian and non-Italian friends, most likely marrying neighborhood girls, and in general making the cultural transition rather painlessly. Thus, while the rebel rejected his heritage and the "in-group" Italian immersed himself in the traditional Italian ways, the "apathetic" second-generation individual adapted readily, accepting the best of both worlds.

What is interesting to note is that their parents, the immigrants, were not strictly traditional people themselves. Too often, writers on Italian Americans miss this point. Spiegel (1972), for example, and Kluckhohn and Strodtbeck (1961) contrast Anglo Americans and Italian Americans on their value-orientation preferences. In this relationship to nature, the Anglo American prefers "Mastery over Nature," while the Italian American prefers "Subjugation to Nature." In their relationship to Activity, the Anglo prefers "Doing," the Italian prefers "Being." In their relationship to Other Men, the Anglo prefers "Individualism," the Italian prefers "Collaterality." In their relationship to Time, the Anglo prefers "Future," the Italian prefers "Present."

A different interpretation is suggested by the present authors' perceived reality. The Italian immigrants, like so many other immigrants, were persons who refused to accept their lot in life. They saw their poverty and rejected it and the hopelessness it breeds. They sought to *Overcome* by picking themselves up and moving, thereby *Doing* something about their condition. Not by group decision but most often individually, they decided to seek a better life, if not for themselves, then at least for their progeny in the *Future*.

In the third generation and beyond, the Italian Americans exhibit similar value-orientation preferences. This is predictable on the basis of the Hansen theory of generations (Spiegel, 1972; Kluckhohn and Strodtbeck, 1961) which derives from the Jewish proverb "What the son wishes to forget, the grandson wishes to remember." Having been born in America, and with parents who were born here, the grandchild feels more secure in his "Americanicity" and is consequently more able to assert his "Italianicity." But in identifying with his immigrant grandparents, his value orientations approximate those of middle-class America, which in its turn acquired these preferences from its immigrant forebears.

The modern Italian American is developing a real interest in both the classical as well as the more immediate aspects of his Italian heritage. The pressures of our society and, indeed, its very nature force him to do this. But the American experience has moderated the old *campanilismo*. Italian Americans are more conscious of the need for unity and more aware of the disadvantages of separate village identifications. At the same time, all Americans can profit from a translated *campanilismo* and *familism* that would provide the much needed *gemeinschaft* relationships so lost by others in urban industrial society.

REFERENCES

Abramson, Harold J. 1970. "Ethnic Pluralism in the Central City." Storrs, Conn.: Institute of Urban Research, University of Connecticut.

————. 1973. *Ethnic Diversity in Catholic America*. New York: Wiley.

Amfitheatrof, Erik. 1973. *The Children of Columbus: An Informal History of the Italians in the New World*. Boston: Little, Brown.

Aries, Philippe. 1962. *Centuries of Childhood*. New York: Vintage Books.

Barzini, Luigi. 1964. *The Italians*. New York: Atheneum.

Berrol, Selma. 1974. "Turning Little Aliens into Little Citizens: Italians and Jews in the New York City Public Schools, 1900–1914." In J. Scerpace (ed.): *The Interaction of Italians and Jews in America*. New York: American Italian Historical Association.

Cahnman, Werner Jr. 1974. "Pariahs, Strangers and Court-Jews: a Conceptual Clarification." *Sociological Analysis* 35 (Autumn): 155–66.

Campisi, Paul J. 1948. "Ethnic Family Patterns: The Italian Family in the United States." *American Journal of Sociology* (May): 443–49.

Carlyle, Margaret. 1962. *The Awakening of Southern Italy*. London: Oxford University Press.

Caroli, Betty Boyd. 1973. *Italian Repatriation from the United States, 1900–1914*. New York: Center for Migration Studies.

Catton, William R. Jr. 1961. "The Function and Dysfunctions of Ethnocentrism: A Theory." *Social Problems* 8 (Winter): 201-11.

Cerase, Francesco. 1970. "Nostalgia or Disenchantment: Considerations on Return Migration." In Silvano M. Tomasi and Madeline H. Engel (eds.): *The Italian Experience in the United Sates*. New York: Center for Migration Studies, pp. 217–39.

Chapman, C. G. 1971. *Milocca: A Sicilian Village*. Cambridge, Mass.: Schenkman.

Child, Irvin L. 1943. *Italian or American? The Second Generation in Conflict*. New Haven: Yale University Press.

Covello, Leonard. 1967. *The Social Background of the Italo-American School Child*. Leiden, Netherlands: E. J. Brill.

Dore, Grazia. 1968. "Some Social and Historical Aspects of Italian Emigration to America." *Journal of Social History* 2 (Winter): 95-122.

Erikson, Erik H. 1950. *Childhood and Society*. New York: Norton. 2nd. ed. (1963).

————. 1959. "Identity and the Life Cycle." In George S. Klein (ed.): *Psychological Issues*. New York: International Universities Press, pp. 1–171.

Featherman, David L. 1971. "The Socioeconomic Achievement of White Religio-ethnic Groups." *American Sociological Review* 36 (April): 207–22.

Feldstein, Stanley and Lawrence Costello. 1974. *The Ordeal of Assimilation*. Garden City, N.Y.: Anchor Books.

Femminella, Francis X. 1961. "The Impact of Italian Migration and American Catholicism." *The American Catholic Sociological Review* 22 (Fall): 233-41.

————. 1968. "Ethnicity and Ego-Identity." Ph.D. dissertation, New York University, Department of Sociology.

————. 1970. "The Italian American Family." In Meyer Barash and Alice Scourby (eds.): *Marriage and the Family*. New York: Random House, pp. 126–40.

————. 1973. "The Immigrant and the Melting Pot." In Melvin I. Urofsky (ed.): *Perspectives on Urban America*. New York: Doubleday Anchor Books.

Firey, Walter. 1947. *Land Use in Central Boston*. Cambridge, Mass.: Harvard University Press.

Foerster, Robert L. 1919. *The Italian Emigration of Our Times*. Cambridge, Mass.: Harvard University Press.

Friedmann, Frederick G. 1960. *The Hoe and the Book*. Ithaca, New York: Cornell University Press.

Gambino, Richard. 1974. *Blood of My Blood*. New York: Doubleday and Co.

Gans, Herbert H. 1962. *The Urban Villagers*. Glencoe: The Free Press.

Giacosa, Giuseppe. 1964. "The Natures of Waste." In Oscar Handlin (ed.): *This Was America*. New York: Harper Torchbook, pp. 390–407.

Gioscia, Victor J. 1967. "Adolescence, Addiction and Achrony." *Personality and Social Life,* edited by Robert Endelman, New York: Random House.

Glazer, Nathan and Daniel P. Moynihan. 1963. *Beyond the Melting Pot*. Cambridge, Mass.: M.I.T. Press.

Goering, John. 1971. "The Emergence of Ethnic Interests: A Case of Serendipity." *Social Forces* 50 (March): 379–84.

Gordon, Milton. 1964. *Assimilation in American Life*. New York: Oxford University Press.

Gottlieb, David and Virginia Sibbison. 1974. "Ethnicity and Religiosity: Some Selective Explorations among College Seniors." *International Migration Review* 8 (Spring): 43–58.

Grasso, Pier Giovanni. 1964. *Personalita: Giovanile in Transizione*. Zurich: Pas-Verlag.

Greeley, Andrew M. 1971. *Why Can't They Be Like Us?* New York: Wiley.

————. 1974. *Ethnicity in the United States*. New York: Wiley.

Hansen, Marcus Lee. 1958. "The Third Generation: Search for Continuity." In H. D. Stein and R. A. Cloward (eds.): *Social Perspectives on Behavior*. New York: The Free Press, pp. 139–44.

Hofstadter, Richard. 1964. "The Pseudo-Conservative Revolt Revisited: A Postscript." In Daniel Bell (ed.): *The Radical Right*. Garden City, N.Y.: Doubleday Anchor Books, pp. 96–104.

Ianni, Francis A. J. 1972. *A Family Business*. New York: Russell Sage Foundation.

Iorizzo, Luciano J. and Salvatore Mondello. 1971. *The Italian Americans*. New York: Twayne.

Kantrowitz, Nathan. 1973. *Ethnic and Racial Segregation in the New York Metropolis*. New York: Praeger.

Kennedy, Ruby Jo Reeves. 1952. "Single or Triple Melting Pot? Intermarriage in New Haven, 1870–1950." *American Journal of Sociology* 58 (July: 56–59.

Kluckhohn, Florence R. and Fred L. Strodtbeck. 1961. *Variations in Value Orientations*. Evanston, Ill.: Row, Peterson.

Lacoque, A. and F. R. Vasque. 1971. *The Newcomer and the Bible*. New York: Center for Migration Studies.

LaGumina, Salvatore J. (ed.). 1968. *Ethnicity in American Political Life: The Italian American Experience*. New York: American Italian Historical Association.

LaGumina, Salvatore J. and Frank J. Cavaioli. 1974. *The Ethnic Dimension in American Society*. Boston: Holbrook Press.

Lieberson, Stanley. 1963. *Ethnic Patterns in an American City*. New York: The Free Press.

Lopreato, Joseph. 1967. *Peasants No More*. San Francisco: Chandler.

——. 1970. *Italian Americans*. New York: Random House.

Nelli, Humbert. 1970a. "Italians in Urban America." In Silvano M. Tomasi and Madeline H. Engel (eds.): *The Italian Experience in the United States*. New York: Center for Migration Studies, pp. 77–107.

——. 1970b. *The Italians in Chicago: A Study in Ethnic Mobility*. New York: Oxford University Press.

Peterson, William. 1958. "A General Typology of Migration." *American Sociological Review* 23 (June): 256–66.

Puzo, Mario. 1964. *The Fortunate Pilgrim*. New York: Lancer Books.

Rolle, Andrew F. 1972. *The American Italians*. Belmont, Calif.: Wadsworth.

Rosen, Bernard C. 1959. "Race, Ethnicity and the Achievement Syndrome." American Sociological Review 24 (February): 47–60.

Rosenwaike, Ira. 1973. "Two Generations of Italians in America: Their Fertility Experience." *International Migration Review* 7 (Fall): 271–80.

Russo, Nicholas J. 1970. "Three Generations of Italians in New York City: Their Religious Acculturation." In Silvano M. Tomasi and Madeline H. Engel (eds.): *The Italian Experience in the United States*. New York: Center for Migration Studies, pp. 195–213.

Ryder, Norman B. and Charles F. Westoff. 1971. *Reproduction in the United States, 1965*. Princeton, N.J.: Princeton University Press.

Spiegel, J. 1972. *Transactions: The Interplay Between Individual, Family and Society*. New York: Science House.

Stein, Rita F. 1971. *Disturbed Youth and Ethnic Family Patterns*. Albany, N.Y.: State University of New York Press.

Thernstrom, Stephan. 1964. *Poverty and Progress*. Cambridge, Mass.: Harvard University Press.

Tomasi, Lydio F. 1972. *The Italian American Family: The Southern Italian Family's Process of Adjustment to an Urban America*. New York: Center for Migration Studies.

Tomasi, Silvano M. 1970. "The Ethnic Church and the Integration of Italian Immigrants in the United States." In Silvano M. Tomasi and Madeline H. Engel (eds.): *The Italian Experience in the United States*. New York: Center for Migration Studies, pp. 163–93.

U.S. Bureau of the Census. 1973. *Population Characteristics: Characteristics of the Population by Ethnic Origin*. Series P-20, No. 249. April. Washington, D.C.: Government Printing Office.

Vecoli, Rudolph J. 1964. "Contadini in Chicago: A Critique of *The Uprooted.*" *Journal of American History* 51 (December): 404–17.

——. 1969. "Prelates and Peasants." *Journal of Social History* 2 (Spring): 217–68.

——. 1974. "The Italian Americans." *The Center Magazine* (July/August): 31–43.

Velikonja, Joseph. 1970. "Italian Immigrants in the United States in the Sixties." In Silvano M. Tomasi and Madeline H. Engel (eds.): *The Italian Experience in the United States*. New York: Center for Migration Studies, pp. 23–39.

Vico, Giambattista. 1961. *The New Science of Giambattista Vico*. T. G. Bergin and M. H. Fisch (trans.), Garden City, N.Y.: Doubleday.

Ware, Caroline F. 1935. *Greenwich Village*. New York: Harper & Row.

Williams, Robin M. Jr. 1951. *American Society*. New York: Knopf.

Winch, Robert F., Scott Greer and Rae L. Blumberg. 1967. "Ethnicity and Extended Familism in a Upper Middle Class Suburb." *American Sociological Review* 32: 265–72.

The American Catholic Irish Family

The author of this chapter combines historical research, the sociological eye, and detailed memories of growing up in a Massachusetts Irish parish community to chronicle the dynamics of change and development of new meanings among one of the more successful ethnic groups to come to America. An early arriving group, the Irish immigrants successfully made the shift from living in a disorganized rural setting to that of an adaptive existence in the turbulence of the growing American cities.

In addition to distinctive cultural mannerisms they brought with them to midnineteenth century America a well-structured variant of the stem family that emphasized familism, matched with a modified bilateral extended kinship system in which consanguineality (blood descent) and siblingship were stressed. The role of the church for most was central, and parish organization tended to define the limits of the local community. Following World War II a variety of family life styles emerge to make being Irish a complex human condition and to make the specification of the typical American Irish family difficult indeed.

CHAPTER FIVE

BY

ELLEN HORGAN BIDDLE

The assimilation of the Irish in American life has been extensive. As a consequence, writing of their family life styles is not easy. Consider that the immigration from Ireland to America took place over a period of at least 200 years; and that the heaviest immigration occurred after the middle and throughout the latter decades of the nineteenth century and, somewhat reduced, on into the twentieth. Current books and articles on the American Irish, moreover, have concentrated little on the family per se, and detailed studies of the major cities in which the Irish settled are only now being published. Recent materials indicate that the Irish experience differed, depending on the economic opportunity structure, the characteristics of native-born persons in the area, and the "precise" ethnic and racial composition of the urban centers in which the Irish settled (Thernstrom, 1973:220–61). Finally, there are contradictions within the scholarly literature as well as in more popular works.

HISTORICAL BACKGROUND

The first obvious characteristic of American Irish families is that in matters concerning the history of the immigration and early experiences here, Irish families failed to pass information on much beyond the second generation* except in the case of an important relative or a few startling events. Families, most of whose members were illiterate on arrival, also taught little to their children about the history of Ireland. In consequence, many Irish in America know almost nothing of Ireland. Yet pride in being Irish and of so identifying is characteristic of most American Irish.

The history of Ireland and its people is complex. In terms of the effects on the immigration, the most significant political fact is that Ireland was ruthlessly subjugated by the English, who maintained the country as an agricultural colony acting in its own interest and that of the minority Protestant citizens of Ireland. Ireland was declared under the lordship of Henry II (of England) in 1169, and the Irish have a turbulent history of battle, rebellion, intrigue, settlement, suffering, terrorism, and pauperism. Independence was attained in 1922 as a divided country: the (now) Republic of Ireland, independent of England and populated heavily by Catholics; and Northern Ireland, still tied to the English Parliament and dominated by a majority of Protestants. Since the history is complicated, this portion of the chapter will focus only on the socioeconomic and familial contexts in which the emigrants made their decisions to come to this country.

Stem Family Adapted

The American Irish family today has structural characteristics created from the elements of the traditional rural stem family of Ireland as changed and developed to meet the conditions found in America. Queen and Habenstein (1974:359–62) have used the term "adaptive" to describe a family type in which minority group members cope with new

---

*The numbering system for generations may be confusing. First generation refers to the immigrants; second generation to the children of the immigrants; third generation to the grandchildren of immigrants, and so on.

90

situations or distressing life crises as best they can without holding strong norms about how they *should* act. In the early years of the immigration, the American Irish family could probably be considered adaptive. The data in the dissertation of Mattis (1975), drawn from a study of Buffalo Irish families from 1855 to 1875, may be reinterpreted as documentation of this view. Isolated in urban quasi-ghettos, Irish families met the exigencies of survival as best they could. Over time, they established an amalgam of family elements from their rural past that fitted their situations in this country, a family structure that represented more than the persistence of stem-family traits. The main section of this chapter describes the American Irish parish family in Massachusetts after this blend took place.

Socioeconomic Background to Irish Migrations

The reasons for the Irish emigration were many,* but the interaction of the patterns of rural Irish society with political, economic, and demographic catastrophes were the most important factors. Briefly, England kept Ireland as a rural colony, taking steps to destroy beginning industrialization. The population increased from approximately four and a half million in the last half of the eighteenth century to over eight million by 1845 (Adams, 1932:3–4; Brody, 1974:49). The excess could not be funneled into a growing industrial economy; in fact, urban growth declined from 1851 to 1891 (Kennedy, 1973:156–57). Concomitantly with this large population increase, subdivision of the land became prevalent, facilitated by the widespread use for subsistence of the potato.† From 1695 to 1746 a set of Penal Laws was passed that resulted in legal discrimination against the Catholic majority, forging in the minds of the Irish a belief that their national identity and religion were one. During the eighteenth and nineteenth centuries the peasants tried several times but failed to rid themselves of the oppression both of England and of the Irish Protestant minority. In addition, famines caused by the infamous potato blights occurred in 1800, 1807, 1816, 1822, 1839, 1845–48 (the "Great Famine"), 1863, and 1879 (Kennedy, 1973:27). These exacer-

---

*For details, see Beckett (1966) for a concise history of Ireland, Adams (1932) for the coalescing of reasons for emigration from 1815 to 1845, and Schrier (1958), Kennedy (1973), and Brody (1974) for short summaries of relevant eighteenth- and nineteenth-century history.

†The population increase (aided by a decrease in the age of marriage for men) and the subdivision of land occurred when the use of the potato became widespread, but the cause and effect relationships between these changes are disputed by scholars. See Adams (1923:4) and Brody (1974:49–53) for *brief* discssions of the problem.

bated what was already a situation of declining living standards. In the more difficult economic periods, the peasants turned on their landlords and the landlords' agents. These causes for the emigration were, moreover, inextricably bound up with the ownership and use of land.

LANDLORDISM. By the eighteenth century most of the land in Ireland was owned either by the gentry or by a landlord class, most of whom were Protestant and many of whom lived in England. Another class was made up of small farmers who held long leases and whose holdings were large enough to make a small profit for themselves after paying rent to their landlords. These, too, were primarily Protestant. But about 80 or 90 per cent of the population, most of them Catholic, were peasants who leased land and raised grain to pay the landlords' rent. During the famines the blight of the potato led to the near starvation of the peasantry, who dared not eat the grain for fear of eviction.

In the latter half of the eighteenth century, when the cheap, easily raised potato became the staple food, peasants began living on smaller amounts of land. Laws favoring landowners encouraged further subdivision of holdings. By the early half of the nineteenth century subdivision had gone too far, chronic malnourishment was common, and the huts built to house the increased population were inadequate. By the time landlords and peasants realized that land would have to be consolidated, it was too late to halt overpopulation, economic misery, and the stampede out of Ireland.

STEM-FAMILY CHARACTERISTICS. When peasants attempted to increase their standard of living by increasing the size of their farms, their method was a familial one. Under the Penal Laws, at the death of the owner or tenant, land had to be subdivided so that *all* sons inherited land equally. When these laws were no longer in force, farmers reverted to a stem-family system of impartible—not to be divided—land holdings, with only one son inheriting the land, or if there were no sons, only one daughter.*

---

*Le Play (1871) provided the classic description of the stem family; Zimmerman and Frampton (1935), reprinted in Farber (1966), interpret passages from Le Play on types of families. For description of the Irish stem family after it was revived, the reader is referred to Arensberg (1937 copyright, reprinted 1950), Arensberg and Kimball (copyright 1940, reprinted 1968), Messenger (1969), and Brody (1974). For a study of families that migrated from rural Ireland to Dublin, see Humphreys (published in the United States, 1966; the field work was done from 1949 to 1951). See Kennedy (1973) for a demographic theory based on the Irish stem family. Glazer and Moynihan (1963:226–29) point out parallels between Irish sural society and the American Irish political machine of New York City. Stein (1971) uses materials from descriptions of the Irish stem family to interpret behavior of disturbed young American Irish males.

(The characteristics of the Irish stem family to be described next are so well known that referencing will be minimal.*

Parents ran the farm until they were too old to do so. Since there was no principle of primogeniture (eldest son inherits) nor ultimogeniture (youngest son inherits), fathers were free to designate among their sons the one who would inherit the land and family home. When the parents retired, the heir married and brought his wife to live in the family home, the young couple establishing themselves as the household heads. Residentially, then, the system was patrilocal. The wife brought a dowry usually about equal in value to the worth of the groom's father's farm. The dowry was given to her father-in-law, *not* her husband, as compensation both for the loss of his farm and for his reduced status. The patronym went with the farm. Other children usually had to move out when the heir married. Their father then used the bride's dowry to make provision for these children, sometimes arranging a marriage for a daughter with a neighbor's son, using the dowry from his daughter-in-law. If a daughter were the heiress, the in-marrying son-in-law brought money to the bride's father, in excess usually of the dowries paid by brides, but the name of the farm remained that of the bride's father for a generation.

The father and his successor wrote a contract concerning the rights of the retired couple. These often included space for sleeping, provision of food, land to cultivate, perhaps a cow, depending on the wealth of the farm, and care for the surviving parent when the other died. Fathers understood that the relationship of mother-in-law and daughter-in-law might be strained, and the contract specified that if conflict should occur, the parents would be cared for elsewhere.

---

*The interpretations that are made concerning Irish peasant family life by the five authors differ somewhat. Arensberg (1950) and Arensberg and Kimball (1968) are "functional" theorists who point out the interrelationships of all parts to a smoothly operating whole and thereby understress strain within families. Sibling solidarity expressed under external threat is discussed, but sibling rivalry as an internal threat is somewhat casually mentioned. They did not recognize the growing dissatisfactions of sons and daughters with rural life, but one should remember that they wrote some time before the present decline of the rural Irish family. Brody (1974) lived and worked in rural Ireland from 1966 to 1971 and draws his views of the traditional family from personal reports of what used to be and describes the sad demise of the well-articulated system that Arensberg and Kimball knew. He notes that in recent times sons as well as daughters leave the countryside by preference. Kennedy (1973) is a demographer and analyzes those aspects of the stem family that affected marriage, permanent celibacy, fertility, delayed marriage, and emigration. He points to the dissatisfactions of daughters. Messenger (1969) has done a cultural anthropology study of a closed peasant community on an island, emphasizes the folk culture, and stresses the relationships between religion and puritanism (including sexual) more than other writers. He underscores the difficulties faced by sons whose father delayed the decision concerning which son would inherit the farm.

The two fathers arranged the marriage. There was little time for romantic love to develop, the details of the match often being completed within a week. The most important aspect of the arrangements was that the fathers should agree on the value of the groom's father's farm, a decision that affected the size of the bride's dowry. The status of the groom changed from that of "boy" or "lad" to "adult" when he married.*

There were several negative consequences for family members arising from this system. The successor was sometimes 40, or possibly 50 years old when he inherited the farm, so that delayed marriage, bachelorhood, and spinsterhood became common. Fathers often waited until close to retirement before choosing an heir, increasing the probability of rivalry among the sons. The wife and mother hoped to have a daughter-in-law with whom she would get along, yet her interest in harmony within the household might not coincide with the desires of her husband to receive a large dowry from the heir's bride. Unless there were only two children in the family, an unlikely occurrence, there was no structural way in the system for other children to obtain an inheritance equal to that of the heir. There was, however, a strong norm that the father should make some provision for the other children, however unequal this might be.†
Another consequence was that the heir and his wife were placed in the difficult situation of living with his parents, and that their marriage was more regulated than those of the heir's siblings (Mattis, 1975).

The major effect of the system, however, was to disperse the unmarried siblings of the heir from rural Ireland, a pattern of neolocal residence. At the time of the Great Famine, when land holdings were small, and the stem family was being reinstituted, migration to an industrializing nation became an acceptable solution to poverty and overpopulation. Two other possible solutions were available for the dispersed siblings: a move to an urban area of Ireland, although economic conditions were little better in the cities, and a decision to become a landless laborer with no economic security (Kennedy, 1973:154–55).

Counterbalancing the problematic aspects of the system was a positive strength. Familism developed—a set of beliefs in which members of the family placed the welfare of the family as a unit above the idiosyncratic wishes of any one person. The father accepted responsibility for the

*Messenger (1969:68) reports that male age grading in Ireland is conceptualized as follows: until age 40, a "boy" or "lad"; until age 60, an adult; until age 80, middle-aged, and after that, old age.
†Mattis (1975) sees the role of the bride as crucial since the other children could not be provided for unless the bride brought the dowry to her father-in-law. She terms the bride the "grand liberator."

economic welfare of the members of the family, and children accepted differential treatment in the interest of family loyalty. All family members shared the value that the land or leasehold should remain in the family. Sibling solidarity was a natural outgrowth of familism. And, in fact, both the emigration out of Ireland to this country and the continuing economic stability of the farms from which the migrants came were supported to a large extent from the savings of siblings and relatives in this country who sent money home even though they were partially destitute themselves.

WORK, AUTHORITY, AND THE SEXES. The Irish believed that married women should not work, a church view. This was reinforced by the belief that a working wife diminishes the status of her husband, that women should stay home and rear children, and that jobs in a marginal economy should go to others. But unmarried daughters were permitted to leave home and go to work. In an economic class with rising material aspirations, some daughters remained single all their lives, for if two people married and the wife stayed home, a single income would have to be used for at least two people rather than one. Since the maintenance of an acceptable standard of living had become a dominant value in Ireland, more important than marriage and a family, the numbers of single people increased over time (Kennedy, 1973:159–60).

This increase in single persons was also a function of the low status of women in rural Ireland compared with urban women in America and England. Within the family, the father was dominant. He made decisions, controlled the money, operated the farm, was waited on by his wife and daughters, and did no women's work. The mother, meanwhile, was in charge of all domestic matters, but she was also in charge of the ecological area around the hut (the haggard) and of any animals the family owned. She also did heavy farm work with her husband and sons when needed. Boys worked with their fathers, did no housework, and were treated by their doting mothers in a warm, supportive manner. Daughters helped their mothers, establishing a no-nonsense quasi-instrumental relationship with them. In the evenings fathers and sons relaxed, but mothers and daughters worked. The women were also subservient to the men, caring for their needs before their own. Women, for example, served the fathers and sons first at meals and gave them not only more food but more nutritious food (Kennedy, 1973:52).

Male domination had serious consequences for women. As early as 1841 in rural areas, men had a higher life expectancy than women (Kennedy, 1973:45). After 1870 life expectancy for women in both rural and

95

urban Ireland was only slightly higher than that for men and not as much higher than the same kinds of rates for women in America and England (Kennedy, 1973:55). From 1871 until 1940, moreover, age and sex specific death rates indicate that more Irish females than males died among children over 5 years old and up to 19 (Kennedy, 1973:60). Daughters would have been unaware of these indices, but they were not unaware of their low status vis-à-vis their brothers and of their future low status as wives. Unless dowried and married to a neighbor's heir, daughters left rural Ireland not just for a job but for higher status and independence (Kennedy, 1973:7). The uncommonly high number of single women in the Irish immigration may be seen as an early Women's Liberation Movement.

Migration Periods

There seem to have been three distinct periods in the Irish immigration (Adams, 1932:68).

1. COLONIAL PERIOD TO 1815. By 1790 the U.S. Census listed 44,000 Irish immigrants (Adams, 1932:70), with an estimate of about 150,000 persons of Irish descent (Shannon, 1963:29). After that, the numbers arriving fluctuated (Adams, 1932:69–70) but were few. Migrating were small farmers of an economic class above the peasantry (Adams, 1932:34–35). They were young, often single, and mostly Protestants from northern Ireland who were English and Scottish in descent.

2. 1815 TO THE GREAT FAMINE OF IRELAND IN 1845–48. Although statistics are barely reliable for this period,* numbers arriving were approximately 50,000 to 60,000 through 1819, about 15,000 between 1820 and 1826, around 45,000 to 50,000 from 1827 to 1828, and at least 400,000 between 1829 and 1845. The total for the period was probably over a half million (Adams, 1932).

The kind of immigrants in this transition period changed little at first. Most were small farmers, but others were tradesmen, weavers, spinners, deep-sea fishermen, shopkeepers, domestic servants, and by 1818 and 1819 a number of peasants from southern Ireland, the first large exodus of Catholic Celts (Adams, 1932:104–11). By 1835 these latter had changed the character of the immigration. Fifty to 60 per cent were

*See Adams (1932:410–28) for a discussion of the difficulties of gathering statistics of immigrant arrivals and the kinds of estimates possible from different sources. The figures are taken from Adams. The writer, however, does not endorse Adams' view of the Irish immigration nor his biased reporting of the Irish poor.

Catholics from southern Ireland (Adams, 1932:191–92; 222). And while in the early 1830s women were about 35 per cent of immigrants, the proportion rose to around 48 per cent in 1835. More of these latter were married, for it seems that peasants came first as intact families (Adams, 1932:194–95). Single women continued to migrate, and those who spoke only Irish increased (Adams, 1932:223).

3. IMMIGRATION AFTER 1845, GREAT FAMINE PERIOD. Around 120,000 Irish immigrants arrived in 1845 and 1846. Then in only eight years, 1847 to 1854, about one and a quarter million Irish came (Schrier, 1958:157). Summarized and based on U.S. Census materials: From 1821 to 1850 about a million Irish entered this country; from 1851 to 1900 not quite three million arrived (Schrier, 1958:159); and from 1901 to 1924 at least 700,000 more came (Ferenczi, 1929:432–43). After 1924, the Irish immigration declined.

Those who came in this period were mostly Catholic peasants from the south and west of Ireland. From 1850 to 1877 about 66 per cent were between the ages of 15 and 35; for the rest of the century the proportion aged 15 to 35 was never less than 80 per cent (Schrier, 1958:4). Except for the early Great Famine years, married immigrants were rarely over 16 per cent (Schrier, 1958:4). After the 1870s the number of single women increased (Kennedy, 1973:76–85). The immigration of the twentieth century seems to have followed much the same pattern except that somewhat more women than men arrived (Ferenczi, 1929:432–43).

Social Context of the Life Styles of the American Irish

A report of events marking the arrival of the Irish and their progress would take the reader far from a focus on the family. Readers should be aware, however, of some of the social context in which the Irish settlement and adjustment were embedded, especially their work experiences. The *first* factor of importance is that the Irish went to cities and stayed in cities. They congregated in Boston, New York, Jersey City, Philadelphia, Pittsburgh, Chicago, St. Louis, and San Francisco (Wittke, 1956:23–24; Schrier, 1958:6–7). That a rural people became urban is not the anomaly one might suppose, for the migrants neither entered as intact families to settle on a farm nor as experienced farmers. They were, instead, the young, single children of poor Irish peasants.

Second, the Irish established the Catholic Church as a powerful institution in this country. Protestant native-born persons feared and hated the church for reasons rational and irrational. But regardless of the wisdom of these attacks, the church absorbed some of the hatred directed toward the Irish and provided the immigrants and their children a clear personal-salvation theology to help them with life-cycle crises.

A *third* aspect notable among the Irish was their startling success at building parallel institutions in areas of life in which services or benefits might be provided (Handlin, 1941:156–83). These helped the immigrants and protected them from knowledge of their exclusion from associations of native-born persons. Unfortunately, they also isolated the Irish and impeded rapid acculturation. The Irish, moreover, co-opted urban political machines *and* major power centers in the Democratic Party, in the growing labor movement, and in the police and fire departments in several cities.

Changing reference groups was a *fourth* matter of importance in the Irish experience. Immigrants first compared themselves to their relatives in Ireland and considered themselves fortunate. Later, they compared themselves with other American Irish, congratulating themselves on success or resenting failure. Socially mobile Irish used double-comparison groups—other American Irish and native-born persons—and were vulnerable to an ambivalence engendered thereby, with less successful Irish putting them down and gossiping about them and native-born persons not quite accepting them. Warner and Srole (1945) depict this situation well in their "personal histories" of American Irish in four life-style groups.

The *fifth* social context was the work experience of the Irish. On arrival, they did menial and manual labor, and most of the second generation did, too. They did pick-and-shovel work, building streets and railroads and were, for instance, the main construction workers on every canal in the North up to the Civil War (Adams, 1932:151). In the cities men were, for example, hod carriers, dock workers, stable hands, street cleaners, waiters, bartenders, and porters. Not without reason were they called "Irish niggers," a willing proletariat at the base of the growing economy. Women were servants, cooks, charwomen, laundresses, and aides to the semiskilled (Wittke, 1956:25). Hours were long, pay was lower than that for native-born persons, work was wearying, and employers often unfriendly. The stability of the family was fragile when work was insecure.

A recent occupational study of *male* Bostonians from 1881 to 1970 (Thernstrom, 1973)* indicates that the Irish clustered in low manual jobs

---

*The immigrants studied in the nineteenth century came from Great Britain, Canada (English speaking), Germany, and Scandinavia. For the 1950 comparisons, the immigrants were from England and Wales, Russia (Jewish in background), Italy, Sweden, Germany, Poland, and Canada (French speaking).

and climbed more slowly up the economic ladder than other ethnic groups and native-born persons. Three sets of findings are relevant.

1. In 1890, Irish *immigrants* were found far more often in low manual work, had fewer skilled manual jobs, and few white collar ones compared with the other groups. (p. 131)

   In 1950, Irish *immigrants,* 45 years old or more, were still over-represented in low manual work, had risen into some skilled laboring jobs, but were under-represented in white collar jobs (especially business and professional ones) compared with other groups. (p. 139)

   Irish *immigrants* in both periods worked more for others compared with the other groups.

2. *Second generation* American Irish, born in 1869 to 1879, studied in the last job they held, fared better than Irish immigrants by having more white collar jobs, but compared with the other groups were still concentrated more in manual work. (p. 132)

   In 1950, *second generation* American Irish, aged 25 to 44, were still concentrated in low manual work and somewhat under-represented in skilled manual work. They were somewhat over-represented in clerical and sales work, and under-represented in high white collar jobs compared with other groups. (p. 141)

   Second generation American Irish still worked more for others.

   Some of the relatively slow movement up the occupational ladder of these *second generation* American Irish is accounted for by the small number of these men whose fathers were middle class compared with other groups. (p. 134) Differences also appeared by religion, however.

3. Catholic *blue collar immigrants* (Irish and Italians) had white collar work at the end of their job careers equally with Protestants (upward mobility) but more Catholics than Protestants who began in white collar work skid to blue collar jobs at the end of their careers (downward mobility). (p. 150)

   Catholic *blue collar second generation* men, born from 1840 to 1930, rose to fewer high white collar jobs, were more likely to remain in low manual work, but moved somewhat more into lower white collar positions than Protestant men of the same group (with the exception of those who entered the work force after World War II when Catholics caught up). (p. 157)

   Catholic *white collar second generation* men, born from 1840 to 1930, did not rise as much as Protestants to high white collar jobs although they were as well represented in low white collar work, but they, too, skid into manual work more than Protestants. (p. 158)

Thernstrom (1973:160–75) suggests two likely interpretations of these data. The first is that ethnic groups sometimes carve niches for themselves in an occupational area (politics, for example, among the Irish; see Levine, 1966), and success therein comes at the expense of not entering other kinds of work. The second and main interpretation is that cultural factors generated and perpetuated within ethnic families led to dissimilar occupational patter ns.

With hindsight, Thernstrom now believes that his pessimistic findings about the slow occupational mobility of laboring men in the nineteenth century, based on his Newburyport study (1964), were confounded by the presence of a large number of second-generation Irish male workers in his sample, men who did not rise even from low manual work to a semiskilled level (1973:247). Thernstrom cites a recent study for the period 1850–80 that seems to confirm the Boston and Newburyport data—the Irish in South Bend also began at the lowest levels of work and climbed more slowly than other immigrant groups (Esslinger, 1972).*

Early Adaptation of the American Irish Family

America was ill prepared for the arrival of the Irish; housing became an immediate problem. Squalid living conditions existed in all major cities. Those of Boston described by Handlin (1941:93–127) were more than matched, for instance, by the miseries in New York of which McCague wrote (1968:20–27). The immigrants found housing wherever they could: lodging houses; older, larger, subdivided houses; warehouses; shanties (huts); flats; and cellars and attics of old buildings. Sanitation was inadequate or absent, smells deplorable, and the water

---

*Thernstrom (1973) cites other studies that seem to confirm the Boston data on the Irish. See page 332. The time perspective involved in comparisons of one immigrant group with another and with native-born persons is important. Presenting findings based on the 1950 United States Census, Nam (1959) shows a spectacular rise in socioeconomic status for second-generation Irish that belies the findings of the community studies for the late nineteenth century. Nam may be easily misinterpreted unless one recalls that his data are for the *end* of the Irish immigration.

supply uncertain. Roofs leaked; walls were damp. Garbage rotted. Privacy was limited; cleanliness next to impossible.

Under these conditions, family and community life were often turbulent. Men left for work early and returned late, as did many women; gangs of children and young teen-agers roamed the streets. In the neighborhoods, pawnbrokers thrived, greengrocers (fruit and vegetable shops) often sold more cheap rye whiskey than other items, not exclusively to men; saloons flourished; idle men stood around hoping for work; fights started easily and spread quickly; some prostitution occurred. Handlin (1941) reported that in Boston after the Irish came infant-mortality rates rose, and Irish longevity decreased (p. 119), marriage and fertility rates increased (p. 121), pauperism rose (p. 121), and mental illness increased (p. 126), as did the rate of illegitimate births (p. 126). Norms of rural family living and social forms such as drinking, argumentation, and visitation lost much of their meaning in the social context of high-density urban living.

In Buffalo, from 1855 to 1875, some carry-over of structural elements of the Irish family were found by Mattis (1975). Delayed marriage remained a salient factor in the Irish immigrant community; when both partners were from Ireland, the average age at marriage for males was 35 and for females, 31. The average age for male native-born persons was 26, and for females, 23. Some Irish, females more so than males, remained single throughout their lives. (For 1950, Heer [1961:236–38] reports that both Irish males and females, immigrants and second-generation persons, were more likely to marry late or not at all compared with 12 other ethnic groups and native-born persons. These findings are for the end of the Irish immigration.) These patterns in Buffalo may be seen as consistent with the need for the Irish to establish themselves economically before marriage and with the relatively high number of women who came here seeking increased independence. That Mattis found more Irish men marrying non-Irish women rather than the reverse pattern is consistent with her finding that some Irish women did not marry at all. (But by 1920 Irish immigrant fathers were more likely to have an Ireland-born wife, 71 per cent, than Ireland-born mothers were to have Ireland-born husbands, 61 per cent [Carpenter, 1927:234–35].)

HOUSEHOLDS HEADED BY WOMEN. A significant form of adaptation in family organization appeared in the first decades after arrival of the Irish. Mattis (1975) reports that households headed by women appeared high—18 per cent in 1855, 14 per cent in 1865, and 16 per cent in 1875.

Most of these heads of households were widows, the latter partly a consequence of men marrying younger women than themselves (Mattis, 1975) and partly, one presumes, of the dangerous occupations of men.* As another adaptive aspect, Mattis also notes that *most of the households expanded to include relatives were headed by women,* a finding noticed in other urbanizing minority groups (Pauw, 1963; Rainwater, 1966; Smith and Biddle, 1975). Most of these lived in multiple-family dwellings. At the height of the Irish immigration in 1855 families expanded to include parents, siblings, nieces, nephews, and various affinal kin (in-laws), some of whom had just arrived in this country. By 1875 the added relatives were mostly grandparents of a family, a finding that might be interpreted as a partial return to the traditional stem family or, more simply, as either a reflection of the passage of time during which other relatives found different housing or as a function of the grandparents having aged and needing assistance.

Additionally, in both 1855 and 1875 about one-fifth or one-fourth of the immigrant households had someone *not* related by blood or marriage living in the house (boarders and their relatives). This pattern is one of adaptation to the economic and social exigencies faced by women, who headed most of these households. Women needed money obtained from rent and assistance managing their families. But they also provided a needed service for others who had recently migrated and/or were in similar circumstances to the head of house. Whether or not the adaptive solution of mutual help through female-headed expanded households, which always have the potential for a shift to a more permanent matricentric family type (Queen and Habenstein, 1974:361–73), may be considered a sign of healthy familial organization rather than disorganization remains an issue for sociological evaluation.

Finally, Mattis reports that in 1855 and 1875 the number of Irish married women in the work force was quite low, but that in 1865, when male unemployment was high and the Irish were establishing themselves economically, an impressive one-third of those Irish women who worked were married. If, in general, the Irish practice of married women not working carried over to this country, exceptions in times of economic adversity, and when families were first making their way, were found as part of an early pattern of social adaptation.

---

*Although Mattis considered the possibility that deserted or separated wives or single mothers might have termed themselves "widows," a more acceptable status than the others among the Irish, she accounts for her data by referring to the high number of widows in Ireland and the demographic effect of men marrying younger women.

THE ESTABLISHED AMERICAN IRISH FAMILY
AND PARISH LIFE: 1920–50

Over several decades after the mass migration and the introduction of further Irish immigrants of a slightly more stable background, the structure, values, and behavior of the Irish stem family combined into an amalgam of the old and new. The immigrant quasi-ghetto neighborhoods in the cities tended to disappear and were replaced by the parish as the unit of community living.* Although not a large number were involved, some American Irish families moved as single units into the economically better neighborhoods. But the majority remained ethnically and ecologically nucleated, building community and family solidarity around the parish, which was organized and dominated by the church. The extensive depiction of family life in one mid-Massachusetts parish that follows represents a form of marshaling ethnographic data through the personalized and extended sociological anecdote as experienced by the author of this chapter who grew up in the parish described. No claim is made that this parish was "typical" of all Worcester parishes, but apart from not having a parochial school, there was little to differentiate it from other parishes in Massachusetts.

Little justification need be made for the style of reporting, for there are few sociological sources of information about American Irish family life. Novels, autobiographies, biographies, and works on aspects of the American Irish experience other than the family abound, yet none of these provides the kind of information readers may wish to know about the American Catholic Irish family. In this description, an attempt has been made to portray the usual family life in a parish from approximately 1920 to 1950 and to de-emphasize the idiosyncratic or deviant.

THE PARISH

The parish was an ecological unit, a community of families and an organized church membership. It was an enclave of American Irish families of the

---

*The use of the parish as a neighborhood unit is a common one when writing of the American Irish, for the coalescence of residence, church, and parochial school (or public elementary school) within a small geographically closed area was a feature of the Catholic parish that the church administrators wisely fostered in the first half of the twentieth century. The parish as a unit has been used most recently by Greeley (1972) when he described the neighborhood of "Beverly," but Farrell's *Studs Lonigan* (1938) also took place in a parish and Curran's novel, *The Parish and the Hill* (1948), contrasts a poor Massachusetts Irish parish with a Yankee neighborhood.

103

second, third and sometimes fourth generation living dispersed among native born persons and a few families from other ethnic groups. Church administrators drew boundaries so that families of about the same economic level were included and erected the church near the center. Shops were close to the church and included a drugstore, laundry, two or three proprietor-run grocery stores, a gasoline station, variety store, shoe repair shop, bakery, liquor outlet, and a tavern. Some of the stores had regular delivery service but many women shopped daily. The priests lived near the church and often employed a parish widow, perhaps the mother of one of them, as a helper. The public school and a park were found in the parish but not always contiguous to the parish center. (If there had been a parochial school in the parish, it would have been located near the church.) Not completely self-contained, the parish served during the week as the unit within which social interaction took place.

CONTROLS

The parish was compact enough that some of the children knew almost everyone and at least half the adults knew one another personally and knew more by sight. People with problems and children with handicaps were enveloped in a relatively closed community. Priests were a familiar sight on the streets talking with adults and watching the young. Some men would go to the tavern at night although a few might be there all day. Older teenagers and young adult men would gather at the shops in the evenings and teenage girls in groups would find some reason to shop or visit the church. There were informal cliques among all age groups and, harking back to Ireland, most of these were age and sex graded. The pace of life was not fast, women shopped leisurely, and small talk passed back and forth. Those in need were visited by the priests. Women individually and voluntarily helped other families at times of crisis.

Lest this picture sound like the happy mythical village, strains should be noted. While small talk kept people informed, it also made family happenings public knowledge quickly, it worked to induce conformity of behavior, and it reaffirmed prevailing attitudes. As a result, new ideas, different values or changes in custom were slow to occur. While deviant behavior was censored, constraints on behavior were as much external as internal. If American Irish families seek respectability and worry about what others might think, one source was the ease with which parishioners knew about others' behavior.

The families were, however, quite private, even secretive, about family matters and children were usually sent out to play while family business was discussed. Adult parishioners kept private within the family how they voted, the size of family income, expenditures planned, gossiped-about sexual deviancy, the beliefs of those who left the church, public affairs on which there might be controversy, job changes, and the futures of children. The conversations to which children might listen involved general discussions about politics and politicians, family events being planned, news about relatives and disparaging comments about those persons whose deviancy was public. The common custom of the pastor to list the amounts of donations to the church by the donor's name each year infuriated many families, as did the list of registered voters by name and party affiliation posted at the polling booth several weeks before elections.

The parish was also an organized church membership. The priests knew every family so the possibility of religious deviancy did not exist. The activities of the family revolved around the church calendar as much as the school schedules of children and the work hours of men. Most religious activities and ceremonies took place in the church. Mothers were responsible both for the religious training and the supervision of the religious activities of the children. Boys were expected to serve at mass as altar boys. Girls participated in services on Holy Thursday and Good Friday. Children, if they did not attend parochial school, went to religious instruction on week afternoons and were separated into groups by school grade and sex. Catechisms were memorized and lessons listened to, with nuns as the usual teachers. Children were expected to go to confession on Saturday afternoon and after fasting from midnight to receive communion on Sunday morning. At the children's mass, the same nuns who taught religious classes supervised and, again, children were seated by school grade and sex. High school students went to religious instruction on a week night, were taught by priests, and, by custom now, segregated themselves in groups of boys and girls.

Families were urged to attend mass on weekdays and to make short visits to the church when close by although few persons did. Attendance at Sunday mass and the special holy days was required and those who did not attend committed a mortal sin, serious enough to send one's soul to Hell if one died before confessing. Most parishioners attended these masses. Those who aspired to attend mass as a family, as Protestant families attended their services, were disappointed, for the priests insisted upon the children attending their own mass and parents often went individually to separate masses so that the younger children might be babysat by the other, if no kin lived nearby to watch the children.

The church affected family activities in many ways. Fridays were days of abstinence from meat as were several Wednesdays during Lent. Mothers took this stricture seriously and children were reminded on a weekly basis that they were expected to suffer or sacrifice for their beliefs. During Lent almost everyone "gave up" something (candy, bubble gum or movies for the children) *or* did an extra religious activity (attending mass on weekdays, praying more often, and visiting the church). There were always pious exemplars of women and children who did these superbly and were reacted to by many with a mixture of awe, envy and ridicule.

There were religious activities, in addition, for which indulgences could be obtained if the religious insurance of these appealed. As the *de facto* theology (what the laity thought the church taught)* had it, persons who went to confession and communion at mass on the first Friday of each month for nine months could not die but in the grace of God. Another was the belief that by going to confession and communion on All Soul's Day one would relieve the suffering of a soul in Purgatory with each visit to the church. Moreover,

---

*Osborne (1969:40) uses this term to describe the everyday theology of lay persons.

105

mothers were thought to be rewarded by special grace if one of their sons became a priest (or a daughter a nun but this was not overly stressed). Parish mothers watched altar boys carefully for signs that they might have a priestly calling and often spoke to one another about the holiness of these boys. There was also a punitive aspect. One of the more difficult of these was that mothers were held responsible for children who left the church.

CHURCH AND FAMILY

But the main thrust of the church was the underpinning it gave to the structure of the American Irish family and the clear dogma of personal salvation it gave. Actual Catholic theology aside, the chief points of the doctrine which the American Irish parents and children believed were these: each person had an immortal soul; man was born with original sin which could only be removed by Catholic baptism; God was three persons (the trinity—God the father, God the Son, and God the Holy Ghost)* but was only one; Mary, the mother of Jesus, was a virgin and, when she died, her body went to Heaven; Jesus became man to provide an opportunity for people to reach Heaven and to create a church which would show man the way to live; the Catholic church is the only true church and adherents of other religions, even if they led exemplary lives, could only go to Limbo, a pleasant place but in which God never appeared; all sins committed in one's lifetime had to be suffered for in Purgatory before one's soul went to Heaven; the difficulties of life were to be borne as best they could and unequal talents or socio-economic success or failure were unimportant to God; mortal sins on one's soul prevented one from going to Heaven so that regular confession was necessary; the list of mortal sins was long but included not only those of murder, theft and lying but also disrespect for parents, having sinful (even sexual) thoughts, using contraceptives, participating in adultery, fornication, divorce, or abortion, marrying in a non-Catholic ceremony, committing suicide and missing mass on Sundays or holy days—and many others; if one were a good Catholic and died in the grace of God, one went to Heaven to be with God forever.†

The sinfulness of man was stressed but the way to salvation was clear: follow the teachings of the church, participate in the sacraments and pray to keep your faith. Children were admonished to obey their parents, believe in their church and show their faith even in such simple ways as not saying the Protestant end of the Lord's Prayer at school or by blessing themselves before batting in a ballgame or going swimming, and by wearing a "miraculous" medal. When children misbehaved, mothers suggested they confess their sins and, if they raised questions about Catholic beliefs, to talk to the priest. When children, especially girls, were required to do something they found unpleasant, mothers suggested they offer it up to God.

---

*The Halloween connotations involved in the term "Holy Ghost" were later reduced by the term "Holy Spirit."
†The writer wishes to stress that this is the theology as understood by lay persons in the parish, circa 1920–50, and to remind readers of the extensive literature created by scholars and philosophers who have astutely interpreted Catholic thought through the centuries.

The church affected family life by supporting the traditional Irish family's way of doing things. When the man lost the tangible sign of the farm as a basis for family cohesion, he did not forfeit his authority and status as head of the family responsible for the economic welfare of all. Because the American Irish man's work took long hours, mothers were dominant in the family and even led some women to imagine they had effective or manipulative power. These views notwithstanding, husbands made most major decisions alone or perhaps after a brief discussion with their wives. Most importantly he was in charge of money and provided a set sum to his wife, usually on a weekly basis. Few children had allowances including those in high school , and even some in college.

Men often decided on the children's occupations and educations and, although the children's abilities were taken into account, their wishes were sometimes ignored. The fathers were deeply involved in decisions about children's marriages but mothers' views were often heard that daughters should be socially mobile by making a good marriage and that marriages for both sons and daughters should be delayed as long as possible and certainly until the young couple could establish themselves. In fact, both mothers and fathers emphasized "good" marriages for their children defined in economic terms and as one to a person of good character. This was not spoken about openly,* but done by innuendo. Going steady was definitely discouraged as was dating a non-Catholic, and in this latter case direct intervention often took place. The father's position was recognized by the expectation that an aspiring groom would ask him for his daughter's hand, not always a ritual matter, for some young men were turned down. But, apart from the mother's input concerning marriage, fathers decided when and how the family should move, buy items of furniture, purchase a car, take a vacation (if any) and held sway in minor matters as well. No matter how quiet, inarticulate or unassuming the father might have been, nor how kindly he exercised his authority, he made the decisions.

There were, of course, some women who did dominate their husbands. Some of these were bossy, nagging types whose meek husbands allowed them to run everything. There were also other women who might not have chosen to run the family but whose husbands did not through default of character, overuse of alcohol or desperation in the face of an indomitable woman. But these were relatively rare. The more usual case was the gentle, friendly, hardworking husband who quietly headed the family and a competent, industrious but mild wife who accepted her husband's authority. It is unfortunate that the American Irish family has sometimes been portrayed as woman dominated, in a grim and perhaps cold manner, [Greeley, 1972:110–13] for this view hides the real difficulties of energetic and instrumental American Irish women who accepted a subordinate role within the family. One problem was

---

*See Humphreys (1966) for a discussion of the openness of Dublin families on this issue.

that some men exercised their power at home in an arbitrary or authoritarian manner.*

Women were in charge of domestic activity with some minor assistance from their husbands who might take a small child for a walk on a Sunday or dry a few dishes or more rarely help prepare a meal. Living in tenements and apartments or rented houses, American Irish women no longer were responsible for the haggard and gardening was a rare activity. But they gained independence in spending the family's money. They also had the responsibility of rearing their sons through the teen years, as they were not expected to do on Irish farms. They diligently kept neat and tidy homes (usually) and seldom questioned the family's economic status over which they worried but had little control.

MARITAL MATTERS

As in Ireland, single women were free to work. Despite some stigma, expressed by married women, which attached to remaining single, some women chose not to marry, as did some men.† Widows, too, went to work but not always full time in a regular job. Some became the itinerant helpers of parish families, assisting in whatever way they might when life cycle crises occurred in others' families. Married women did not work usually either in regular jobs or to help their husbands, except in small proprietary businesses at busy times of the year. The exceptions to this were women who helped establish the family economically and then stopped (as in Buffalo, see above) or when their husbands were unemployed during the Great Depression or when the country needed workers during World War II (although, even then, few did). American Irish women behaved very much like their counterparts in Ireland and, out of each cohort of women, some decided to marry and rear a family (having relatively high fertility rates); others delayed marriage or remained single and worked. Widows had little choice; they ran their homes and often worked. Widows were treated deferentially by men, as if they were the elderly mothers of these same-aged men. Widows were not considered eligible as marital partners, perhaps because men feared the responsibility of caring for a wife and children all gained at once. Widowers usually married single women. Motherhood was considered virtuous, and wifehood was rarely mentioned. One need not remind readers that Irish men feel overwhelmingly sentimental on Mother's Day and that men in tender moments often called their wives "mother."

CHILDREN

Children in American Irish homes were treated as children, not small adults. Mothers were stern, righteous and moralistic but also kind, sentimental and active. Children learned to be subordinate, obedient and respectful. Children were also taught to be respectable, that is, to do the right thing, and to be

---

*Studs' father is an example (Farrell, 1938).
†Kennedy (1973:152) points out that in Ireland there was little or no stigma attached to remaining single throughout one's life.

polite. A spoiled, whiny or bold child was unacceptable to mothers. Sanctions for deviance of children were external and expressed by priests, by parishioners and by fathers. Shame and ridicule, appeals to the embarrassment caused one's mother and mocking the child were used interchangeably with guilt-creating controls. Success, on the other hand, was underplayed, was assumed a part of life and, when reported to others, was understated.

Mothers emphasized physical activity for children and often suggested they go outside to play and exercise rather than read or do inside-home hobbies. Participation in sports was stressed, especially for boys. Achievement in school was also encouraged and mothers pushed the children to do well. Since success in the educational and occupational spheres had not been a part of the mothers' experiences, they could only point to persons they admired in the parish and in general terms to encourage their children "to make something of themselves."

In one area fathers *did* step in and help—in respect to teaching sons to fight. Mothers disapproved of boys fighting and hoped that their sons would not become embroiled in neighborhood fracases. Fathers were ambivalent. They, too, did not want the boys to fight but even more they did not want their boys to be beaten up or not to stick up for their rights. As a result, many fathers taught their boys to fight; and the boys went out and fought and often over the issue of whether or not they would do so! But it was also a part of the youth culture for a boy to be known as a good fighter and even the girls knew who would stand up for his rights and who would not.

Differential treatment by mothers of their sons and daughters continued much as in Ireland. Boys were treated more affectionately than girls. The importance of the boys' occupational future was stressed while girls were taught to run households. Children knew from an early age that the resources of the family could not provide for all. If their brothers were older or equally talented, or almost so, daughters knew that the resources of the family would go first to their brothers. In the less well-off families, older sons and daughters went to work and younger brothers, and sometimes their sisters, might benefit from the increased status of the family. In the better-off families, the older sons were provided opportunities, the younger waited their turn, and daughters hoped to be helped.

The concept of equal treatment of each child remained subordinate to the concept of providing as best one could for all within the context of limited resources. However different one might consider such familism by today's standards of the enhancement of each individual, there was the advantage that a family in which each looks out for the others has cohesion. Sibling loyalty is not necessary when there are adequate resources but, when they are scarce, some system of allocation *without* rivalry is needed. Families, who in the usual course of events had a relatively capable father and a responsible mother who was reasonably warm towards her children, were strengthened by the concern of children for one another. When these were absent, problems occurred.* In the parish, adult siblings kept in touch with one another and mutual assistance was given when needed. All cared for elderly parents but in

---

*See Stein (1971) for current problems of American Irish male adolescents.

different ways depending on their resources: by paying bills, by shopping, by visiting and by having the parents live in their homes.

Sons may have been confused by being the recipients of both affective and instrumental behavior from their mothers in a way in which daughters were not. As long as sons could look forward to being heads of families catered to by their wives and children, major problems were avoided. If daughters could find a husband who would head the family and achieve economic viability, few difficulties occurred. Change the admixture slightly or lessen the priests' support of the traditional family, and some sons would remain bachelors, some would become priests, some would marry a less demanding woman from another ethnic group, and some might simply drink too much. Likewise, some women would remain single, some would become nuns, some would marry but have no children, some would try to dominate their husbands, and still others might marry a man from another ethnic group.

KINSHIP

Kinship among the American Irish follows that of Ireland. Kin were persons related by descent (blood) or marriage to whom one owed mutual assistance and among whom some marriages were tabooed. A modified bilateral system prevailed. In Ireland the kinship bond extended, as an example on the paternal side, from a husband to his father's father's father (great grandparent) and all the kin in the descending generations were kin of the husband (ego); thus, kin on the male side of the family were father's father's brother, and father's father's brother's son and the son of the last. But all possible roots were counted, female as well as male, so that the number of consanguineal kinship positions came to thirty-two in ego's generation of first and second cousins. The church but not the people tabooed marriage with third cousins but dispensations for these marriages were evidently easily obtained. Affinality was limited somewhat, as the spouses of the siblings of one's parents were not considered kin, nor were the spouses of father's and mother's parents' siblings.

The importance of kinship to the Irish cannot be overstated. Although the household was both the unit of economic production and of the family (nuclear and husband's parents), farmers needed help from others at times of planting and reaping, especially, and the families needed assistance or support for some events, such as childbirth, illness or death. The help was given by consanguineal kin who by so doing established a "claim" against the household helped and who could expect that when they were in need the household members assisted earlier would reciprocate. Household members were ambivalent about giving and seeking help, however, for household self-sufficiency was a matter of great pride. But knowing that the day would come when the household members could not alone solve some problems, families assisted others and stored up "claims" for the future. For minor matters, the immediate families of the spouses helped one another but, for major crises, the wider extended kindred were on hand.

At marriage, both husband and wife acquired the full consanguineal kindred of the new spouse but only the spouses did so, not their kindred; the wife's parents and the husband's parents, then, did not become kin to one another. After marriage, the immediate families of each spouse were treated by both spouses as if they were consanguineal kin. Members of the immediate family were father-in-law and mother-in-law, brother-in-law and sister-in-law, and son-in-law and daughter-in-law. Again, however, the spouses of one's spouse's siblings (sister-in-law's husband, brother-in-law's wife) were not included as kin although there were often warm relationships between them. The extended kin of one's spouse were less important than the immediate ones, but in times of need mutual help was given, and on ritual occasions kin ties operated more extensively.

Among the families of the parish, the immediate families of both husband and wife were the close kin: for the couple, these included the four parents, siblings of both spouses (brothers-in-law and sisters-in-law) and the children of the siblings (nephews and nieces). The positions of brother-in-law's wife and sister-in-law's husband were ambiguous; a measure of this non-clarity was that if a person in the position were liked, he was overliked; and if not liked, the critical comments were many. For the children of the couple, the relatives were grandparents, aunts and uncles, and cousins. And, although from the viewpoint of one's parents, spouse's siblings' spouses were ambiguously treated, children used the American system and made no such distinction between aunts and uncles in terminology or gift-giving but did know which of these aunts and uncles were relatives by descent and which by marriage. In most matters, kinship relations took place between members of immediate families and more distant relatives attended weddings, wakes and funerals. When godparents were chosen, one usually came from the father's side of the family and one from the mother's, symbolizing the bilaterality of the kin system.

RITUALS AND RITES DE PASSAGE

Marriages in the parish took place at a mass before noon and usually on a Saturday so relatives and friends could attend. They ranged from the simple with only immediate families present to formal with several bridesmaids and ushers. Festivities included a meal before which toasts were made and sometimes dancing after the meal. Because of the expense, the custom arose of sending invitations of two types: one for the church service only and one which also included the reception. Families followed closely the usual American strictures about which family paid for various expenses of the wedding. Those marrying non-Catholics usually had a private service, not always in the parish. The non-Catholic was asked to take instructions in which the tenets of the church were learned and signed a contract with the priest present in which it was agreed that the children of the couple would be reared as Catholics. Almost as often, the non-Catholic was urged to convert to Catholicism. Couples were often engaged for a year or more in order to get to know one another and, as importantly, to get to know one another's families. The wait also permitted the young couple to save money to furnish their home. Premarital sex was absolutely forbidden and so serious was the situation of a pregnant bride, not a usual one, that the marriage took place in great haste, often outside the parish, and usually without announcement from the altar.

111

The American Irish wake is somewhat unusual. In the parish the family waked the dead person at home after the body had been prepared at a funeral home. The body was raised up in a casket with the upper half of the body showing, a rosary entwined in the hands. Flowers were banked around the casket. Usually for one or two afternoons and two evenings the family was home to meet friends and relatives. The rosary was said around ten o'clock. There was sherry or red wines for the women, whiskey for the men, and food for all. The women often stayed in the livingroom or parlor with the casket and the men moved to the kitchen. Much of the talk was of happy or humorous events concerning the dead person and the reminiscing helped families to mourn publicly and without embarrassment. Drunkenness and raucous joking were not as common as alleged; the usual case was that a few women had a little too much sherry or a few men had too much rye. Two male relatives often stayed up all night in the room with the body. For the religious services, the funeral home took over and brought the body in a hearse and the family in limousines to the church for the funeral mass. Burial was at a Catholic cemetery. Afterwards all returned to the family home for a luncheon. Very young children did not attend wakes but by their teen years children in the family were expected to attend. The cars in the funeral procession were assigned by degree of closeness of the kin relationship or of friendship and of children by birth order. Many persons made contributions to the church for the deceased relative or friend. Cremation was taboo. For persons who committed suicide or were apostates, there were no public services and their graves were located in the cemetery in unblessed land.

Baptisms were less ritualized and usually celebrated with a party at the parents' home. The infant was taken to the church by the godparents for baptism by the priest who usually performed the ceremony on a Sunday afternoon. Children had to given one saint's name. But the naming was less important than the sacrament which removed original sin. Guests usually brought small gifts for the baby, sometimes money to start a savings account. Being a godparent carried with it the responsibility to see that the child was not only reared as a Catholic but also remained so until marriage.

INTELLECTUALISM

The epithet of anti-intellectualism has been directed at the Irish; and few American Irish are in academic occupations except at Catholic colleges. Although it appears now that as many American Irish have earned bachelors' degrees as native born persons [Greeley and Rossi, 1966], this is a measure of school accomplishment and not a measure of the quality of the schooling or of the elusive qualities of intellectuality and curiosity which are aspects of the scholarly life. From the viewpoint of the family, one can understand that children who are reared in seclusion from the new ideas of the society and whose mothers stress activity are not in the usual case going to become contemplative. Instead they choose active occupations, such as physician, banker, lawyer, journalist, politician, nurse, dietitian, and teacher. Until more conclusive data are gathered, the criticism that Catholic homes and schools unite in insulating Catholic students from scholarly attitudes and pursuits is well taken [Trent and Golds, 1967].

SEXUAL PURITANISM

Sexual puritanism has often been seen as interrelated with Irish patterns of delayed marriage and permanent celibacy.* It is accurate, of course, to say that talk of sex was taboo, that premarital intercourse was low, and that this puritanism aided in the recruitment of boys for the priesthood. It is also accurate that young people in the parish learned much of what they knew about sex from others as ill-informed as themselves. But when trying to disentangle cause and effect relationships what one sees depends on where one slices the cross sectional view. Delayed marriage and permanent celibacy appear not to be dependent variables on sexual puritanism. The relationship is the other way around. When the land system in Ireland reverted to one heir per holding and the parents did not retire early, delayed marriage and acceptance of the single status as permanent was revived. Sexual puritanism encouraged this behavior. Kennedy [1973: 145–51] presents this view, noting that the Irish did not always accept the church's teachings. Priests left no doubt that the married state was the one they most approved, but, if people chose to do otherwise, then the priests stressed the immorality of premarital sexual relationships.

COMMUNICATION PATTERNS

This discussion leads to another about the American Irish. Parishioners found little trouble with small talk. But when there were emotional components to the conversation, they were non-communicative. If there were problems within the family or a delicate issue to discuss or a conflict about behavior or ideas, the silence was heavy and went on for some time before someone could manage to bring up the subject. In reaction to this behavior, some American Irish developed eloquence in public speaking and in writing.

There were three notable speech patterns of parish families. The first was that the Irish use understatement in personal interactions. The wry comment, the shy rejoinder, the offhand statement, the modest report of success, the quiet expression of satisfaction—these are typical speech patterns. Another characteristic, the "put-down," arose from this value of understatement. The put-down was often used both as a method of control over family members and of putting public personalities in perspective. And with the put-down came ridicule. Were another ethnic, religious or racial group mentioned in conversation, one could count on derision as a response. Name a public personality, an Irish politician, a pious parish member and out came a story from the past about the laughable traits of the person.

FAMILY AND OCCUPATION

The family influenced the wage earner. Recall that the immigration included a large component of women dispersed by the stem family system who were

---

*Messenger (1969) makes the point with the most strength when writing of the Irish in Ireland.

eager to make their own way. Many of them remained single and worked, primarily as household maids, but many married. The concept of economic success did not necessarily match those in this country. Using as their reference group the persons left behind in Ireland, married women encouraged men to seek jobs with regular incomes and regular hours. They favored economic security rather than risk-taking or responsibility, and respectability rather than status. Acutely aware that family stability depended on the income of their husbands, women were satisfied when work was obtained which provided an adequate standard of living. The middle class attitude that manual labor is demeaning or lacks status was slow to arrive for the American Irish, given their poverty on arrival and their need for security.

IRISH AND YANKEES

Another aspect of parish families concerned the relationships between the American Irish and other nationality groups. In the parish everyone knew that Yankees (the New England term for WASPs) thought themselves superior to the Irish and that some discriminated actively (by not hiring Irish) and some more passively (by not talking to Irish neighbors and not allowing their children to play with Irish children). This situation was accepted as a fact of social life and was downplayed by parents. It was also handled by pointing out, but indirectly, that Yankees were not members of the "true" church. Ridicule was also used and conversation on weekends among relatives often turned to gossip about Yankees, particularly politicians and businessmen. On the other hand, people were aware of members of other ethnic groups and, although they felt discriminated against or put down by Yankees, they nevertheless behaved in much the same way themselves toward members of other groups. On the rare occasion when a German, Italian or French Canadian family moved into the parish, there was talk about foreign ways being introduced. The major element of the system, however, was that everyone knew the nationality background of everyone else and much conversation was interlarded with derogatory comments about those in other ethnic or racial groups.

SENTIMENTALITY

Little of the sentimentality and warmth of the American Irish personality or character has been discussed. But within the pattern of mutual help and reciprocation among an extended kinship system, family members enjoyed one another's company and shared both their sorrows and their joys with their relatives. Conversation was sprightly, jokes abounded, and family news and gossip were shared. Reminiscing was a favorite pastime and memories brought out included both the pleasant and the sad. Warmth of feeling and camaraderie generally prevailed at family gatherings. Sentimentality about people, places, things and events was the norm for within-family behavior.

The American Irish family, then, adapted to conditions in this country and succeeded in creating a strong and loyal family unit. Entering as the most inexperienced of the immigrant groups, they moved slowly into solid working-class jobs and the lower levels of bureaucracies, while some members became upper-middle-class professionals. The family of the parish exists in an attenuated degree in enclaves in several of our large cities today. Others who were more successful have made the exodus to the suburbs bringing with them many of the attitudes of the parish. The children who grew up in the parish are the parents of today's young adults and teen-agers. These young people will probably go on to a more complete integration in our society, not knowing or caring much about their ancestors.

THE MODERN AMERICAN CATHOLIC IRISH FAMILY: CHANGE AND ADAPTATION

If one assumes a 30-year period for a generation, then the young people today are the fifth generation descended from the Great Famine immigrants and the fourth generation descended from those who entered this country in the 1870s. Some immigrants arrived later, of course, and there are some young people today whose grandparents came from Ireland but few compared to the total population descended from Irish immigrants. To write about the new generations in general terms is difficult, for there are few data on family life styles of American Irish of different generations and differing social classes. There are, however, a few types that might be briefly described.*

Typical Adaptations: The Enclaved

First, there are those who remain in enclaves in our large cities or in the near-suburbs and work in manual blue-collar jobs or in the lower echelons of government and business bureaucracies. They are still organized in parishes but live side by side with others of the same economic class but who come from other ethnic groups. The family is still highly important to them, as is their religion. The father has a tendency to make decisions for the family, but the participation of their wives and children has increased. Intergenerational mobility aspirations are somewhat less than those in preceding generations. Married women are more likely to work to maintain the economic viability of the family,

---

*The types described here are not Weberian ideal types and cannot be, for the criteria distinguishing them are too many and the data on which to construct them too few. In fact, the difficulties encountered in trying to present even a few types lead the writer to believe that it is time to make an extensive survey of American Catholic Irish families.

115

and the number of women who do not marry has declined. While home ownership is an important aspiration, education of the children is stressed even more. Many of the children attend parochial schools at both the elementary and secondary levels, and some go on to Catholic colleges. The views of the Catholic church are heard about equally with those of the secular society. They identify as Irish, usually vote Democratic, and sometimes ignore the priests, especially in the matter of birth control. In respect to the latter, the married often use contraceptives, although before marriage many accept the stricture of the church that the sin of premarital sexual intercourse committed in passion is a somewhat lesser evil than to plan to sin by using contraceptives. Some young people believe contraception introduces an unnatural aspect to sexual relations. Delayed marriage seems a matter of the past so long as both spouses can obtain work; women now follow the general American pattern in respect to working sometimes before the last child enters school. Marriage to non-Catholics is more common, and church rules permitting this have been relaxed. Family schedules are less rigidly organized by the church than formerly.

Most of the people have settled into being citizens of working-class America but still retain enough Irish identity that they are distinguishable from other ethnic groups. The major structural differences in the families have disappeared, but many of the characteristics of the group have not, such as the lesser amount of overt affection, the understatement, the favoritism toward sons, the use of ridicule, the feelings of chauvinism, the preference for action rather than contemplation, the inarticulateness, the numbers who use alcohol to increase sociability, the obligations of families to care for one another, and the gathering of family members on ritual occasions and holidays.

Although they have not risen high in the economic scale, they form an important part of our industrial and commercial society. But they also remain a slightly unintegrated sector in our national life. The issue of separation of church and state, for instance, is not seen as one of civil liberties but as one of unfair taxation since they pay tuition for their children to attend parochial schools in amounts that are considerable for the size of their incomes. They have a tendency to prefer administrative and perhaps authoritarian solutions to vexatious problems concerning the spread of new ideas in textbooks and magazines and on television by prohibiting them rather than teaching their children how to evaluate them. They are somewhat resistant to alternative life styles for families, and perhaps this might be generalized to some resistance to all nontraditional ways of doing things.

They are loyal and patriotic, as most American Irish have usually been; when convinced that an activity is for the country's good, they enthusiastically go along. But when they believe that they are being wronged by government action, they will stubbornly refuse to obey. One need only recall the vehemence of the opposition of the South Boston Irish to the bussed racial integration of schools to underline the importance of their neighborhoods. A small irony of this event was that the judge who ordered the integration was American Irish, too, and grew up in the parish described.

Middle-Class Irish Family

Among those who have done better economically and socially, there is diversity of life styles. A few distinct groups emerge from the variety. *First*, out of the strength of the parish families, in which mothers stressed economic success and educational advancement, and in which the children grew up during the Great Depression and the strains of World War II, have come professional and business men and women whose life styles vary little from those of other successful urbanites and suburbanites. They, too, are little influenced by the stem-family structural characteristics but maintain some of the aspects of the Irish family. Many have liberal arts degrees from Eastern private Protestant institutions and from the Midwestern and Western state universities. They are integrated into the mainstream of American life, live in neighborhoods of professional and business families, understand well the philosophical underpinnings of our country, have close friends among many groups, and see themselves and their children as American and not Irish.

Their orientations are to their professions or companies first, and their church and neighborhood second. The parish of the past is a pleasant memory. The new Catholic church does not surprise them, and some are satisfied to go along with whatever happens to be introduced into the Americanized Protestant denomination, which the church is fast becoming. They complain about the poor quality of parochial schools, which they are asked to maintain, but which their children usually do not attend. They also criticize the poor education of the young priests who come from a different ethnic background and who ordinarily do not have professional qualifications for their work. The domination of family schedules by the church has disappeared, and religious practice is declining. Although not living and interacting with many Irish persons on a daily basis, they are nevertheless aware of being Irish, the pan-Catholic attitudes of the church are not greatly accepted, and identification of the ethnic backgrounds of those with whom they work are noted, sometimes unfavorably. They are also identified as Irish by others. Some express self-hatred by putting down both the American Irish who have not "made it" and those who have succeeded but maintain close ties and even perhaps professional and business relationships with other American Irish. Their children are often required to remain members of the church as long as they live at home over the protests of the children who sometimes become apostates after departure for college.

This group is mixed with respect to political-party affiliation, with more of the lawyers tending to remain Democrats and more of the bankers, physicians, and businessmen becoming Republicans. There is less favoritism of sons over daughters. Their children, however, appear less interested in striving for achievement or excellence in professions than their parents, and some are obviously downwardly mobile. Affection within the family is more open, especially by mothers, and maternal domination seldom appears. Some of the women work after marraige or return to work when the youngest child enters school.

Among a *second* subgroup of successful middle-class Irish, there are families begun in the 1950s and early 1960s in the era of "togetherness" who have had six or seven or more children by choice. Mothers are affectionate, worry little about their no-nonsense child-rearing styles, identify positively as having traditional Irish families, and receive kudos from older relatives for having done so. In these families, the men are likely to be preoccupied with their work. They take little part in the rearing of their children, express most concern when it is time to choose colleges for and with the children, and having made it themselves, worry little about an improvement in the economic and social welfare of their children.

A *third* identifiable group among the middle-class Irish are those who maintain close ties with the Catholic Church, many having been educated at parochial schools and/or Catholic colleges. They are seriously interested in religion and philosophy and wish to orient their family life around the church, but in a new way. They bring the church into their homes, celebrating church holidays with family rituals or days of special significance for the family with religious rituals. Customs from Catholic countries may be borrowed for these family celebrations. They are active in their churches both with the formal organizations, such as the parish council, and also with small informal groups that join together to discuss issues, perhaps adding a semiritualistic aspect by sharing bread and wine. They are active in the ecumenical movement.

Greeley includes this third group of middle-class Irish in his term "communal" Catholics and reports that these Catholics are committed to their religion as a world view but interpret the church teachings to fit their needs, expecting little guidance from the clergy. He says they feel themselves independent of the institutional church and of the earlier de facto theology and that they are at ease with their Catholic identity (Greeley, 1974). Their comfort as Catholics and their intense concern with religion seem paradoxical when they state that many of the tenets of the church are irrelevant. Communal Catholics sometimes deny the existence of God, often believe in abortion and sterilization, think the celibacy of priests should be discontinued, consider divorce a viable alternative to unhealthy marriages, want women to become priests and their daughters altar girls, read and interpret the Bible in current terms, participate in sacraments and the weekly Mass when in a spiritual mood, talk of "situation ethics" for individuals regardless of any universal system of morality, treat the family as the unit of religion and not the church, and speak of the social gospel as if they had invented it. They have little empathy for or understanding of more traditional Catholics, seem not to know the meaning of heresy, and find it difficult to comprehend why anyone would be an apostate, now or in the past. They see little contradiction in their self-image as good Catholics and their beliefs. Within this group there will probably be few apostates and few who drift away from the church, but whether or not they transmit their religious loyalty to their children remains to be seen.

The family life of communal Catholic Irish is one of togetherness, there are usually only two or three children in the families, women stay out of the work force until the children enter school, although many women work part time, men work hard but are more integrated into family life than some other American Irish, and children are reared with a mixture of American permissiveness and flexibility overlaid with the learning of complex family rules. Fathers in these families are somewhat less successful than those of the first and second middle-class types and place the importance of their families almost equal to their occupations.

Other Irish

There are many other American Irish who do not fit the types described. There are those who are third or fourth generation married to members of other American ethnic groups—some of whom were educated in Catholic colleges and whose pan-Catholicism seems more important than their ethnic identity, and some of whom are working-class persons who live in mixed ethnic enclaves. There are second- and

119

third-generation Irish at all class levels who married descendents of native-born persons, and if not fully integrated into American life styles themselves, have children who neither know much about their Irish past nor consider themselves different from any of their friends. There are those who drifted away from Catholicism and the American Irish parish without much worry about doing so and their descendents who have little feeling for a different ethnic past. There are deeply concerned apostates from the Catholic Church at an earlier time, and, of these, some have joined nondogmatic religious groups such as the Unitarians. There remain still persons of second- and third-generation Irish who never married or who married late and had no children. There are many thousands of American Irish in the Midwest and West who were never reared in ethnic parishes, have little identification with the Irish, and are unfamiliar with the ethnic rivalries of their Eastern kinsmen. And there are others, reared in Midwestern Irish enclaves, who differ not to much from their Eastern counterparts. And more . . .

CONCLUSION

Diversity among descendents of Irish immigrants is great, and for every family characteristic described herein, someone of Irish descent reading the text will find his/her experiences at variance with those depicted. There are, nevertheless, some cultural and structural tendencies that appear to have been passed on to the present American Irish from the stem family of Ireland and the established parish families. Without implying that all of these are found among all or even most American Irish families today, a short recapituation of the more salient of these is in order.

In spite of numerous exceptions, American Irish families are still predominantly Catholic in religion and Democratic in political affiliation. Most are proud of their Irish descent. Fathers remain heads of their families. Mothers continue to work hard, not only doing women's work at home but holding outside jobs, too. Familism is prevalent, and sibling loyalty is little diminished. Extended kinship gatherings occur regularly; the importance of kin cannot be emphasized too much. Children receive no-nonsense rearing, which stresses loyalty to the family unit and less concern about the total enhancement of each child's abilities and talents. Male domination has decreased, but the enthusiasm with which the Women's Liberation Movement has been greeted by some American Irish females indicates that differential treatment within the family in favor of boys has been their experience or that of their spouses. Alcohol is still used to enhance social occasions.

The American Irish are still very much concerned with the economic welfare of the family, and both men and women work diligently to maintain their achieved status or to increase the status of their children. Entry into active rather than contemplative occupations seems the norm. Many continue to seek respectable and secure jobs. Interest in politics and political careers is little abated. Higher education is valued, but there is a tendency to view education as a means to better jobs rather than a value in itself. The marriages of children are less regulated than in the past, but parents still tend to see a marriage in terms of the good character of the new spouse and in terms of the economic viability of the unit being created.

Other tendencies seem to be diminishing. Delayed marriage and permanent celibacy are probably now matters of the past. Concern over respectability has decreased; American Irish worry less now about what others think. The need for privacy concerning family matters appears little different from those of non-Irish families. Sexual puritanism is being replaced by an ideology that stresses naturalness. Affection is more openly expressed. Distinctively Irish speech patterns are dying out among the young. Tolerance of other ethnic groups has grown, but perhaps not as much as one would wish.

It would be facile to predict that the American Irish will be fully integrated in another generation, for the new ethnic assertiveness and the continuing ethnic divisiveness of those who remain in areas in which many American Irish live will go on. In fact, if economic conditions worsen, one might expect a sharp increase in ethnic rivalries. The different customs and family backgrounds of American ethnic groups overlie prejudiced and competitive attitudes in many groups that might become ugly if our affluent, mass society should come to a standstill. For the moment, however, readers might recall that for many decades the American Irish formed the ill-paid and badly treated proletariat at the economic base of our society. And then balance this view with the knowledge that if the immigrants had remained in Ireland, they might have died of starvation.

R E F E R E N C E S

Adams, William Forbes. 1932. *Ireland and Irish Emigration to the New World, from 1815 to the Famine*. New Haven: Yale University Press.

121

Arensberg, Conrad M. 1950. *The Irish Countryman: An Anthropological Study*. New York: Peter Smith.

———, and Solon T. Kimball. 1968. *Family and Community in Ireland*. Cambridge: Harvard University Press.

Beckett, J. C. 1966. *The Making of Modern Ireland, 1603–1923*. New York: Knopf.

Brody, Hugh. 1974. *Inishkillane: Change and Decline in the West of Ireland*. New York: Schocken Books.

Bromwell, William J. 1856. *History of Immigration to the United States, Exhibiting the Number, Sex, Age, Occupation, and Country of Birth, of Passengers Arriving in the United States by Sea from Foreign Countries, from September 30, 1819, to December 31, 1855*. New York: Redfield.

Carpenter, Niles. 1927. *Immigrants and their Children, 1920*. Census Monographs VII. Washington, D.C.: U.S. Government Printing Office.

Curran, Mary Doyle. 1948. *The Parish and the Hill*. Boston: Houghton Mifflin.

Esslinger, Dean R. 1972. *The Urbanization of South Bend's Immigrants, 1850–1880*. Unpublished dissertation, University of Notre Dame.

Farber, Bernard (ed.). 1966. *Kinship and Family Organization*. New York: Wiley.

Farrell, James T. 1938. *Studs Lonigan: A Trilogy Containing Young Lonigan, The Young Manhood of Studs Lonigan and Judgment Day*. New York: Random House.

Ferenczi, Imre. 1929. International Migrations. Vol. I. "Statistics." Compiled on Behalf of the International Labour Office, Geneva. With Introduction and Notes. Edited on Behalf of the National Bureau of Economic Research by Walter F. Willcox. New York: National Bureau of Economic Research, Inc.

Glazer, Nathan, and Daniel Patrick Moynihan. 1963. *Beyond the Melting Pot*. Cambridge: M.I.T. Press.

Greeley, Andrew M. 1972. *That Most Distressful Nation: The Taming of the American Irish*. Chicago: Quadrangle Books.

———. 1974, October 2. "American Catholics and Catholicism." Public Lecture, School of Journalism, University of Missouri-Columbia.

———, and Peter H. Rossi. 1966. *The Education of Catholic Americans*. Chicago: Aldine.

Handlin, Oscar. 1941. *Boston's Immigrants, 1790–1865: A Study in Acculturation*. Cambridge: Harvard University Press.

Heer, David M. 1961. "The Marital Status of Second-Generation Americans." *American Sociological Review* 26, 2:233–41.

Humphreys, Alexander J. 1966. *New Dubliners: Urbanization and the Irish Family*. New York: Fordham University Press.

Kennedy, Robert E., Jr. 1973. *The Irish: Emigration, Marriage, and Fertility*. Berkeley: University of California Press.

Le Play, Frederic. 1871. *L'Organisation de la famille selon le vrai modèle signalè par l'histoire de toutes les races et de tous les temps*. Paris: Tequi.

Levine, Edward M. 1966. *The Irish and Irish Politicians: A Study of Cultural and Social Alienation*. Notre Dame: University of Notre Dame Press.

Mattis, Mary Catherine. 1975. *The Irish Family in Buffalo, New York, 1855–1875: A Socio-Historical Analysis*. Unpublished dissertation, St. Louis, Washington University.

McCague, James. 1968. *The Second Rebellion: The Story of the New York City Draft Riots of 1863*. New York: Dial Press.

Messenger, John C. 1969. *Inis Beag: Isle of Ireland*. New York: Holt, Rinehart and Winston.

Nam, Charles B. 1959. "Nationality Groups and Social Stratification in America," *Social Forces* 37:328–33.

Osborne, William A. 1969. "The Church as a Social Organization: A Sociological Analysis." In Philip Gleason (ed.): *Contemporary Catholicism in the United States*. Notre Dame: University of Notre Dame Press, pp. 33–50.

Pauw, B. A. 1963. *The Second Generation: A Study of the Family Among Urbanized Bantu in East London*. Cape Town: Oxford University Press.

Queen, Stuart A., and Robert W. Habenstein. 1974. *The Family in Various Cultures*. (4th ed.) Philadelphia: Lippincott.

Rainwater, Lee. 1966. "Crucible of Identity: The Negro Lower-Class Family." *Daedalus: The Negro American–2* 95,1:172–216.

Schrier, Arnold. 1958. *Ireland and the American Emigration 1850–1900*. Minneapolis: University of Minnesota Press.

Shannon, William V. 1963. *The American Irish*. New York: MacMillan.

Smith, Hazel M., and Ellen H. Biddle. 1975. *Look Forward, Not Back: Aborigines in Metropolitan Brisbane 1965–1966*. Canberra: Australian National University Press.

Stein, Rita F. 1971. *Disturbed Youth and Ethnic Family Patterns*. Albany: State University of New York Press.

Thernstrom, Stephan. 1964. *Poverty and Progress: Social Mobility in a Nineteenth Century City*. Cambridge: Harvard University Press.

––––––. 1973. *The Other Bostonians: Poverty and Progress in the American Metropolis, 1880–1970*. Cambridge: Harvard University Press.

Trent, James W., with Jenette Golds. 1967. *Catholics in College: Religious Commitment and the Intellectual Life*. Chicago: University of Chicago Press.

Warner, William Lloyd, and Leo Srole. 1945. *The Social Systems of American Ethnic Groups*. New Haven: Yale University Press.

Wittke, Carl. 1956. *The Irish in America*. Baton Rouge: Louisiana State University Press.

Zimmerman, Carle C., and Merle E. Frampton. 1935. *Family and Society*. Princeton: Van Nostrand.

The Chinese American Family

This chapter's title might well have been expanded to read "The Chinese American Family in a Neglected Ethnic Minority Group." Exploitation and intermittent violence, ghettoization, and the development of values for survival have marked the Chinese American experience. Particularly interesting has been the use of the cultural ideal of a familism built around ancestor worship, filial piety, and patriarchal authority while nevertheless developing a closely knit nuclear family as the central agency of socialization.

Buttressed by clan and other forms of community organization plus a solid array of extended kin, the nuclear Chinese American family retains a remarkable viability as an operating agency of socialization, refuge, and as a center for social intercourse. The adaptiveness of Chinese Americans has been tested by adversity and oppression of earlier decades; it now faces the cultural discontinuities produced by a new influx of Hong Kong migrants, opened gates of social and geographic mobility, and the siren call of American mass life style.

CHAPTER SIX

BY

LUCY JEN HUANG

HISTORICAL BACKGROUND

One may surmise that the main motive of the Chinese to enter America is characterized by the nickname they gave to San Francisco, the "Gold Mountain." Opportunities sought were for the most part denied by the host population. The simplest and most effective mechanism of exclusion was achieved by assigning them an opprobrious category, differentiating them from native white Americans. One writer describes the process:

> Colville's Gazeteer of San Francisco, published in 1856 but referring to the year 1851, described the Chinese as "unique." Their appearance seemed devised "to make people wonder"—the writer thus established a dichotomy between *Chinese* on one hand and *people* on the other—"to make people wonder that nature and custom should so combine to manufacture so much

individual ugliness." On the same page he spoke of Chinese women as "the most degraded and beastly of all human creatures." He had apparently not yet made up his mind whether Chinese were or were not of the human condition; but that they were different and "degraded" was beyond question. (Saxton, 1971:18)

According to Saxton the words "assimilable," "white," and the pseudoscientific term "Caucasian" (just then coming into fashion), would be taken as equivalents. Before the end of the 1870s, there were California workingmen, styling themselves brothers in the Order of Caucasians, who would undertake the systematic killing of Chinese in order to preserve their assimilable fellow toilers from total ruin (Saxton, 1971:18).

The arrival of the Chinese laborers came about in a precipitous manner; only 42 were residing in San Francisco in 1853, but two years later there were between 3,000 and 4,000. Prior to the enactment of the exclusion legislation of 1882, Chinese immigration rocketed to 40,000. Kearny, a leader of the anti-Chinese movement in California, estimated the Chinese population in his state at 200,000 in 1876, with 75,000 in San Francisco alone. However, in October of the same year a joint committee of Congress placed the figure at 117,448. Whether or not the figures quoted were accurate, the major point is that the Chinese came in great numbers and aroused the concern, rightly or wrongly, of a large number of Americans (McClellan, 1971:5). The concern of the host group gradually turned into fear and animosity, resulting in atrocities documented in reports of the last century.

Chinese laborers were invited to this country by railroad agents who went to China, promising plentiful work, high wages, and free passage. In 1868 the Chinese merchants of San Francisco were present at a banquet honoring their contributions to the life and well-being of that city. In the same year the Burlingame Treaty was applauded in that city as the keystone of a new era of prosperity based on Chinese immigration. In 1869 the Central Pacific met the Union Pacific in Utah. Nine years later the Nevada mines collapsed. Suddenly the presence of the Chinese had changed from a blessing to a curse in the minds of most Californians (McClellan, 1971:8).

Fiction writers, Christian ministers, and legislators combined forces in depicting the Chinese as "peculiar," "immoral," "criminal," and less than human. They were described as "opium-sodden," full of "fatuous ignorance," "treacherous mendacity," and "heathenish ways." At the time of the Boxer Rebellion the *Rocky Mountain News* announced that the actions of the Chinese against Westerners represented "the most atrocious crime against humanity and civilization that has been committed since the barbarians sacked Rome in the fifth century" (McClellan, 1971:10).

It was during this period that ethnic slurs were given to the unwelcome immigrants. The Chinese were referred to as "Chinamen," "yellow lepers," or "Chinks." On Broadway the Chinese were burlesqued and ridiculed for the amusement of American audiences. *A Trip to Chinatown* played for 650 consecutive performances between November 1891 and August 1893. "Chin-Chin Chinaman" and "Toy Monkey" were two songs from these dramatic efforts that lampooned the Chinese achieving popularity beyond Broadway. Other productions at the end of the century bore titles like *A Night in Chinatown, The King of the Opium Ring, Chop Suey One Lung, Chinatown Charlie*, and *Queen of Chinatown*. In 1899 *The Singing Girl* appeared with a score by Victor Herbert containing the song "Chink! Chink!." A musical comedy entitled *A Chinese Honeymoon* and several more comic operas contributed many popular songs about the Chinese during the next few years (McClellan, 1971:46).

Thomas J. Geary, a congressman from California, submitted additional provisions to the old Chinese Exclusion Act of 1883, requiring all Chinese in the country to register and submit an identification card with a photograph, thus reducing somewhat the confusing phenomenon that "all Chinese look alike." The Geary Law was enacted in 1894 with strong public support, but the reaction of the Chinese was one of unity in refusing to cooperate. The resentment of the Chinese against unfair laws had, for the most part, brought them closer together in joint efforts and cooperation.

The Chinatown Ghetto

"In our American cities the ghetto refers particularly to the area of first settlement; i.e., those sections of the cities where the immigrant finds his home shortly after his arrival in America" (Wirth, 1956:4). It represents a prolonged case of social isolation, a form of accommodation between divergent population groups. It is one historical form of dealing with a minority within a larger population. The ghetto, in general, was not the product of design, rather the unwitting crystallization of needs and practices rooted in the customs and heritages, religious and secular. This was as true in the case of the Chinese as in the case of Jews, which Wirth described.

Faced with racial prejudice and discrimination from the host society, the Chinese immigrants became scapegoats as a consequence of the heated economic competition with white railroad and mine workers, especially when Irish miners began to invade the West Coast. Under hysterical attacks from all sides, the Chinese began to withdraw from competitive labor and entered occupations that other immigrants were not so eager to perform. Table 1 provides a picture of the resultant change of occupations from labor to domestic service and business.

Once Chinese laborers left work at the railroads and the mines, they moved into the low-rent districts of urban centers. The presence of the Chinese was feared because the part of the city or town in which they congregated soon took on the character of a foreign settlement. Many writers and reporters described the Chinese in Chinatown in terms of animal-like inferiority and viciousness. The eccentricities of Chinatown caught the eye of many a visitor. The clothing of the Chinese appeared very peculiar. The written language was odd in appearance. The local apothecary, with its "beetles, snake bones, lizards, toadsblood, and other tonics," highly amused Americans. Funerals were a source of curiosity and amusement, as were the local religious temples or joss houses. The idols, the incense, the corpulent resident priest, strengthened the impressions of the Chinese as heathens (McClellan, 1971:34–35).

In a study of New York's Chinatown, Yuan formulated hypothetical stages of its development. The first stage was *involuntary choice* due to the host society's prejudice and discrimination toward the Chinese. The second stage was *defensive insulation,* for the Chinese needed mutual

TABLE 1
Selected Occupations for the Chinese in the United States
(1870–1920)

OCCUPATION	YEAR	NUMBER OF CHINESE	PERCENTAGE INCREASE OR DECREASE
Miners and laborers	1870	27,045	−99.45
	1920	151	
Domestic workers	1870	9,349	+280.00
	1920	26,440	
Trades and dealers	1870	779	+960.00
	1920	7,477	

SOURCE: Cheng (1949: 59).

127

help and cooperation against the hostile world. The third stage then became *voluntary segregation* in which a strong sense of group identification and we-feeling developed among the Chinese who shared similar cultural background: religion, language, nationalism, and problems of adjustment in a new environment. The fourth stage is then *gradual assimilation,* a process that may not be easy due to voluntary segregation and social isolation from the majority group (Yuan, 1965:277–84). It is against this historical backdrop of discrimination, alienation, and ghettoization that the characters in the drama of Chinese family life must play their parts. We turn now to the substance and processes of Chinese family life in America.

THE MODERN CHINESE AMERICAN FAMILY

Marriage and Intermarriage

THE GHETTO FAMILY. An old Chinese saying that one should marry a spouse whose front door faces his own indicates the traditional emphasis on homogamy. Parents in traditional China often frowned on their children marrying someone out of the province, let alone out of one's country or race. These attitudes have long historical precedent and were transplanted to the new country. However, due to the extremely unbalanced sex ratio and the difficulties of returning to China to obtain a "picture bride," many merchants, restauranteurs, and laundrymen were found to have non-Chinese wives.

In a study of mate selection among New York City's Chinese males, Schwartz (1951:562–68) found that in the years between 1931 and 1938, there was a pronounced difference among various occupation groups in the patterns of mate selection. During the decade between 1930 and 1940, the sex ratio was 80 per cent male to 20 per cent female according to the U.S. Census report. Among 254 Chinese grooms in New York City the most common type of interracial marriage was between restaurant-worker grooms and white brides, numbering 24 cases, and between merchant-group grooms and white brides, numbering 19 cases. Schwartz also reports that 9 restaurant workers and 5 laundry workers married black brides.

However, even Chinese girls are not considered as desirable as wives as those born in the old country. The following sentiment was very typical among Chinatown-based Chinese:

Chinese girl I think very much better than American-born Chinese. No spend so much money. No like go show. All they think about stay home help husband, save money. American-born Chinese girl, my God, spend lots of money, buy all the time, pretty clothes, fancy shoes, American girl no know Chinese custom, no like big family, little family. Yes I think China boy much better marry girl in China. (Hayner and Reynolds, 1957:360)

The Imigration Act of 1924 tightened the enforcement of the earlier regulation that American-born males of Chinese descent could not bring their wives to America after they had gone to China to select a wife. As a result, many husbands and wives were separated on opposite sides of the Pacific Ocean for years even though their minor children could be admitted.

Discriminatory immigration laws were crucial factors in producing sex-ratio imbalance, not to speak of marital and familial dislocations. It was during this period that falsification of birth records of children born in China was widespread. The birth of a daughter was reported as a son; this "slot" on the family tree had salable values to those who would like to enter the country and yet had no derivative citizenship rights. Through the sale of those "slots" many male immigrants arrived in America, taking the family names of the owners of the "slots." Also, in recent years thousands have entered the country illegally since 1956 according to the U.S. Immigration and Naturalization Service.

Thus, the sex-ratio imbalance continued to create problems for the Chinatown-based men who were either single or whose wives were left in China. A relatively typical case was a successful restaurant administrator who had never brought his family to America, living a bachelor's life for over 30 years except for periodic visits to China. Walking on the street one day, he was asked by a friend why he was still up and around, as the doctor had indicated he had cancer. Upon learning the true state of his health, he bought an airplane ticket and headed for home. He died in China after five days, surrounded by his wife and semistranger families.

Chinese women born in China or in America have for many years been in great demand, especially among Chinatown-based men. Informants have revealed many cases of American-born Chinese women capitalizing on the unbalanced sex ratio, exploiting lonely men and young bachelors behind their husband's back. One may say that these women have "secondary husbands" or were "concubines-in-reverse" except that the latter not only provided extramarital sexual opportunities but also gifts and money. In some cases the husbands, usually older than

129

the wives, knew about such arrangements but could or would not do anything about it because a Chinese woman was hard to find.

Interviews by the writer revealed that educated Chinese girls who became citizens in America experienced great difficulties in accepting the attentions of lonely Chinatown-based bachelors. During dating situations there was no common reference for discourse or common interests to share with one another except in enjoying a dinner at a restaurant in Chinatown. "Besides the delicious dishes, which remind me of home, the date was a total disaster," a female informant confided. "All through the dinner he was reading the racing form, and as if that was not enough, he went to the telephone five times to check with his bookie." Since they did not speak the same dialect, they spoke English to each other. Having come from a large cosmopolitan city and therefore speaking fluent English herself, the girl said there was nothing worse than being courted by a man who spoke pidgin English with attitudes and behavior patterns of her grandfather's generation.

Differential degrees of acculturation on either side of the Pacific Ocean thus creates difficulties in heterosexual associations, either before or after marriage. Those who were born in Chinatowns or grew up there do not seem to be more Westernized than individuals born and raised in coastal metropolitan cities of Asia; in fact, they may be less Westernized. As a consequence, documentary evidence strongly suggests that the Chinatown-based husband in America is not always the boss. A product of traditional values, he is characteristically puzzled and disillusioned by the activities of a spouse who often no longer shares those values, but he tries to be reasonable and make the best of a difficult situation (Hayner and Reynolds, 1957:635).

CHINESE PROFESSIONAL FAMILIES. Informants among Chinese professional families confirm that most parents prefer their children to marry Chinese in spite of the fact that many of them are fighting a losing battle. A family with three daughters born in China was very sure that at least the older daughters would marry Chinese, while the youngest, totally Americanized, would probably marry an American. After the marriage of the eldest daughter to an American, the mother lost all hope. "I never expected Number One would marry a foreigner, for she has always been so reserved and quiet. I can't understand it. There are so many nice Chinese boys on campus, and she had to marry a foreigner," the mother complained.

Chinese young people, though born in America, tend to be socially less aggressive and more conservative than their Caucasian counterparts. One may hypothesize that in the future intermarriage between second-generation Chinese and non-Chinese will increase. Since they are socialized in the Chinese household to be relatively inhibited, many young people may find it difficult to initiate emotional expressions in dating situations. A Chinese mother of a Caucasian daughter-in-law informed this writer, "She chased after him for over two years. Every day she would declare that she was going to marry my son, even in front of me." It is possible that most young Chinese in America are socially more subtle and thus less expressive than their American counterparts, who, in the process of courtship, do most of the active pursuing, thus saving the efforts of the Chinese partner. Whether or not it is true as some males contend, "there is a shortage of good-looking Chinese girls," the fact seems to support a Barnard coed's comment that a good many Chinese Americans seem to go for "those short petite blondes" (*The Wall Street Journal*, 1969).

In the 1940s and 1950s, intermarriage among Chinese professionals might still be considered deviant and unconventional. Good friends and relatives of the Chinese partner, in the process of defending such "exceptionally untraditional" behavior or in consoling the "culprit" for entering into such a daring marital contract, would comment, "But he is so Chinese in his behavior." Thus, the parents of today's American-born children still hold the concept that Caucasian Americans are in general wild, flippant, irresponsible, undependable, childishly unsubtle, and worst of all, foreign. On the other hand, their children in the 1960s and 1970s may consider marrying a Caucasian socially sophisticated and "with it." Hsu (1970:338) believes that the Chinese object to interracial marriage because it would be socially inconvenient, that is, communication between the non Chinese spouse and the Chinese family, friends, and relatives would be difficult. However, from the point of view of the young Chinese of the 1960s and 1970s, marrying a Caucasian may turn out to be more convenient and natural than marrying another Chinese.

Lee (1960:251) suggested that the earlier immigrants from Kwangtung objected to intermarriage out of the desire to maintain racial homogeneity and to avoid hostile situations and general feelings of marginality. Gordon (1964:227) attributes low rates of intermarriage among the Chinese in America to the anti-Chinese feeling in the nineteenth century. Social distance and strong adherence to a family-loyalty pattern contributed to the discouragement of intermarriage. On the other hand, Beaudry (1971:59–67) found that the degree of acculturation and assimilation had a great deal to do with whether one would approve of intermarriage. The more assimilated were more likely to approve of intermarriage. His findings showed females less assimilated and less approving of intermarriage; a majority of foreign-born Chinese professionals were undecided or disapproved of intermarriage. However, from this writer's (Huang, 1956) research in the 1950s and her interviews and observations in the 1970s, the female students and professionals from China proved to be more sensitive to acculturation and assimilation processes in America and therefore tended to be more approving of intermarriage. It is assumed that even if both the male and female professionals are equally Americanized, chances are the male may be more hesitant in entering intermarriage due to the tradition of patrilineal descent of the Chinese family and the possible problem of adjustment in case he returns to China with a non-Chinese wife. Barnett (1963:426) reported there was a slight trend in the direction of more intermarriage by females than by males based on his data from 1955 to 1959 in California. Hsu (1971:31) agrees that the rate of intermarriage among Chinatown-based Chinese is much lower than among the children of professional Chinese families. His report also shows that more Chinese females than males marry non-Chinese.

In recent years, however, both male and female Chinese American youths are marrying Caucasians in increasing numbers. As one male Chinese American of the second generation stated:

Certainly one of the most tangible evidences of an individual's assimilation into a culture is for that individual to take a spouse of that culture. The members of our group have until now so unanimously married non-Chinese persons that it was a standing joke among us that fifty-dollar prize would be awarded to the first one to take a Chinese mate. (Chen, 1972:7)

It is our contention that regardless of the degree of acculturation, American-born Chinese of both sexes tend to find it more comfortable in dating situations with non-Chinese. We have observed that in interracial courtship interactions, the Chinese American partner tends to take a more subdued role, at least publicly. The early socialization of the Chinese American makes it inappropriate for him or her to be socially aggressive.

The future of intermarriage among the Chinese in America may be a function of such factors as propinquity, sex ratio, country of origin, and level of education. Increasing dispersal of Chinese away from the Chinatown ghetto and the propinquity of residence of similar social classes (Heer, 1966) may prove to be important facilitative factors.

132

Divorce

Traditionally, the Chinese considered divorce a great shame and tragedy, especially for the woman. Grounds for divorce generally favored the husband, for example, a wife could be divorced if she happened to be disrespectful to her parents-in-law, especially if she were quarrelsome toward her mother-in-law (Hsu, 1970:142). Moreover, if a wife did not give birth to a son, there was a danger of her being divorced unless she was willing to accept concubines for her husband in the hope that secondary wives might bring male offspring to bless the family and thus continue the male line.

The Chinese, in general, disapprove of divorce no matter how open-minded or educated they are. This attitude is not related to any religious convictions (unless they are extremely pious Catholics); rather, it is that few could afford to experience the serious social ostracism that was usually the consequence of this action. Few Chinese young men today, either American born or foreign born, would consider going with a girl who had been engaged or gone steady with another man before, let alone a divorcée. It would be very difficult for the Chinese to understand why an American bachelor would marry a divorcée with several children. From their standpoint, he either had to be mentally deranged or a social misfit. No decent Chinese man would consider marrying "used merchandise."

The divorce rate, therefore, is relatively low in Chinese families. Only very courageous and independent individuals dare accept divorce as a solution to marital difficulties. It is not uncommon for unhappy couples to remain together for fear of public opinion and social disgrace. One often suffers for the sake of appearance or for fear of "loss of face." However, the younger generation born in America may not be as conservative as their foreign-born parents, especially when they are brought up in a culture in which individual love and happiness is more important than what other people would say.

Family Process and Socialization

In general, Chinese children grow up in the midst of adults, not only their parents but also members of the extended family, grandparents, uncles and aunts, cousins, and other members of the kinship group. Chinese children as a rule are seldom left home with babysitters or other adults.

133

Chinese parents take their children with them not only to wedding feasts, funeral breakfasts, and religious celebrations, but also to purely social or business gatherings. A father in business thinks nothing of bringing his boy of six or seven to an executives' conference.

This pattern is still adhered to by the majority of second, third and fourth generation Chinese Americans in Hawaii . . . (Hsu, 1972:84).

This sharing of the world of reality between Chinese children and their parents may be one of the more crucial factors in the process of socialization. Ruth Benedict pointed out some time ago that American children suffered from cultural discontinuity, that whatever they learned from their parents had to be unlearned or relearned later as they reached different stages of their life cylce (Benedict, 1938:161–67). The child-rearing practices of the Chinese may help to facilitate the socialization process and effect a relatively smooth transition from childhood to adulthood.

Having been exposed to the companionship of adults, Chinese children are more aware of what socially approved patterns of behavior should be, as well as what other people think of them. In the process of child rearing, contrary to what some have called an American emphasis on the sense of guilt, Chinese children experience shame, which "supposes that one is completely exposed and conscious of being looked at: in one word, self-conscious" (Erikson, 1963:252). The person involved is much concerned with what he does in the presence of others (Hsu, 1949:223–42). For one living in the Chinatown ghetto, social control may have been derived chiefly from public opinion rather than an inner sense of guilt.

One aspect of socialization is the strict control of aggression. Sollenberger (1968) found that 74 per cent of Chinese parents demanded their children show no aggression under any circumstances. Not one single parent strongly urged their children to defend themselves or punished them for running home for help in case of encountering attacks by other children. Sibling rivalry and aggression wer generally discouraged. Relationships among siblings is seasoned with the Chinese concept of *jang*, in which older children are encouraged to set an example for their siblings in gentleness, manners, and willingness to give up pleasure or comfort in favor of someone else. It is a sentiment encouraging one to give in during a quarrel or a polite refusal in favor of someone else (Sollenberger, 1968:18–19). Chinese children, however, having been conditioned to refrain from behaving aggressively may find life rather frustrating, especially when they encounter aggressive peers outside the home. Having been brought up in a subculture within a heterogeneous and rapidly changing society, the basic personality of Chinese children would have to undergo certain adaptive changes in order to survive in the larger society.

SEX ATTITUDES. Sex education in the Chinese family has been somewhat a mystery. The segregation of the sexes had been practiced for thousands of years. The only members of the opposite set one was able to meet were cousins within the same extended family. The classic novels *Dreams of the Red Chamber* by Chao Shueh Ch'in (1929) and *The Family* by Pa Chin (1972) illustrate many of the secret love affairs among cousins and other members of the same consanguineal family. Informants from China related incidents that may shed some light on the question of sex education. It was reported that whenver there was a bride-to-be, she would invariably be sleeping with some older female members of the family weeks or months before the wedding. It was suspected that certain sex instruction might be going on during these last minutes before the wedding. This writer once came across a Chinese brass mirror on the four corners of which were etched figures of four sexual positions presumably for the benefit of the newlyweds.

Most Chinese families, like the average Anglo family, do not engage in frank discussions of sex with their children, either foreign born or American born. Somehow, it is assumed that as they grow up, the younger generation will automatically learn about such subjects as sexual relations from their peers. Parental instruction in such intimate relations between the sexes is far from adequate. One may assume because of higher educational levels that among professionals there is greater communication between parents and children in this area than among Chinatown-based families.

A distinct characteristic of the Chinese family is the lack of external expression of affection among the members. Many Chinese children have never seen their parents kiss or hug one another. One does not express such emotions in public except with small infants or children who are often hugged or smell-kissed (burying one's nose in a baby's cheek and inhaling) but never directly on the mouth. The average Chinese is seldom seen hugging and kissing at an airport or railroad station, either when seeing relatives off or welcoming them. There is a great deal of smiling and handshaking accompanied by shouts of joy or other verbal expressions of farewell. A good example is an incident recounted by a female college student. "When I went to New York to meet my brother who arrived in the United States two years after I did, all we did was shake hands. I felt awkward, for I thought I wanted to express more in the American fashion, but we are Chinese, so that's what we did." Hsu (1970:10) contrasted the prominence of emotions in the American way of life to the tendency of the Chinese to underplay all matters of the heart. He analyzed it by stating that the American is more individual centered while the Chinese is situation centered. Being situation centered, the Chinese is inclined to be socially or psychologically dependent on others, for he is tied closer to his world and his fellow men. His happiness and his sorrow tend to be mild since they are shared. Regardless of what the reason is, public demonstration of affection tends to embarrass the Chinese, both professionals as well as nonprofessionals, American born or foreign born. When non-Chinese demonstrate their affection publicly, it is accepted with understanding, but when the Chinese do that, it is considered poor taste or unnecessarily childish. Therefore, at times it is relatively awkward for American-born children who have been away to college among non-Chinese peers to return home after a year's absence to merely greet their parents with "Father, Mother," while they would hug and kiss their casual friends after a week's absence. "When I tried to hug my close relatives after years of absence, they behaved very stiffly. Not that they don't care, but it is just not the way they are used to," an Americanized Chinese girl said. The Caucasian spouse of the family soon learns to repress his affectionate expressions in front of Chinese relatives.

EDUCATIONAL AND OCCUPATIONAL ACHIEVEMENTS. The Chinatown-based parents' attitudes toward education for their children is well documented by Sollenberger (1968:19–20). In his research he found that 100 per cent of the mothers in his study thought that doing well in school was fairly important or very important. Further, only 1 per cent of the mothers expected their children to only finish high school; however, 99 per cent of them expected their children to go to college and possibly graduate school, and it is apparent that they are willing to make great sacrifices to further their children's education.

The Coleman survey (1966) provides some interesting information concerning the educational aspirations of "Oriental Americans." For example, with regard to college plans and aspirations, "The Oriental Americans show by far the highest aspirations toward college of *any group* in the entire sample, 64 per cent reporting wanting to finish college or go beyond." They are further reported to plan to have a professional occupation above the overall average of all groups (Coleman, *et al.,* 1966:279–80). Perhaps most revealing is that portion of the Coleman study that reported the child's sense of control of his environment:

136

It is clear that the average child from each of these minority groups feels a considerable lower sense of control of his environment than does the average white child. It appears that the sense of control is lowest among Puerto Ricans, and among Negroes lowest for those outside metropolitan areas, and that *except for the whites it is highest for the Oriental Americans*. (Coleman, 1966:289) [Emphasis mine]

While more evidence is certainly needed, it appears clear that educational aspirations and educational achievement are quite high among youth from Chinese families. It is also clear that this fact sets the Chinese group apart from the educational world of many other minority groups.

Most Chinese parents consider education as one of the most important symbols of success as well as channels for upward social mobility. There is a general belief embraced by the Chinese family in America as well as in Taiwan that one should not date while still in school in order to concentrate one's efforts on education. The pressure for academic achievement is therefore rather strong among Chinese youth. Mabel Liang, outstanding teen-ager of 1972, when asked who had the greatest influence on her academic success, stated, "I've gotten more help from my parents than anyone else" (Murray, 1972:2).

Due to the important role of education and hard work emphasized by the family, Chinese Americans have occupied a relatively high economic position among ethnic groups in America. Table 2 indicates that the proportion of Chinese Americans in professional and other high-status occupations has been increasing over the last 30 years. In 1940 only 2.4 per cent of Chinese American males were in professional positions, whereas in 1970 over 30 per cent of them were.

Chinese parents have at times realized a certain resistance among the children in learning Chinese, a phenomenon strongly motivated by the fear of being different from their Anglo peers. Cultural conformity may serve as one of the means of racial and cultural minorities to ameliorate discrimination and prejudice in the American society. However, parents have continued to insist, at the risk of cultural conflict and a sense of marginality experienced by the younger generation, on educating their children in Chinese language and culture.

In recent years Chinatown-based parents have been registering protests against the massive transfer of Chinese children away from their neighborhood school in San Francisco. They stated that the neighborhood school system gave their children the opportunity to obtain an education in Chinese language, art, and culture through additional

TABLE 2
Major Occupation Groups of the Chinese by Sex, 1940, 1950, 1960, and 1970

OCCUPATION	1940 MALE 33,625 (PER CENT)	1940 FEMALE 2,829	1950 MALE 40,111 (PER CENT)	1950 FEMALE 8,278	1960 MALE 71,445 (PER CENT)	1960 FEMALE 31,961	1970 MALE 113,929	1970 FEMALE 67,261 (PER CENT)
Total Employed								
Professional, technical and kindred workers	2.41	7.6	6.3	11.0	18.4	14.4	30.23	20.1
Farm and farm managers	1.36	.18	1.43	.22	.73	.25	.37	.12
Managers, officials and proprietors, except farm	21.5	8.9	22.2	7.9	15.5	4.7	11.58	4.26
Clerical, sales and kindred workers	10.2	26.5	11.2	38.8	13.7	32.6	12.69	35.56
Craftsmen, foremen, and kindred workers	1.83	.32	3.36	.51	6.9	.71	7.71	1.58
Operatives and kindred workers	22.3	26.5	16.4	20.7	12.6	18.2	8.7	22.34
Private household workers	5.81	10.1	1.6	6.2	.86	3.4	.29	1.65
Service worker (except private household workers)	31.3	10.9	32.4	11.4	22.7	7.4	23.46	.13
Farm laborers and foremen	2.78	.60	1.52	.58	.43	.35	.23	.32
Laborers except farm and mine	.77	.67	1.9	.57	1.7	.29	3.16	.96
Occupation not reported	.20	.84	1.3	2.12	6.62	17.7	1.04	.04

SOURCE: Percentages for 1940 and 1950 were derived from Seventeenth Census of the United States. "Non-White Population by Race: 1950" 3 B-42; and Sixteenth Census of the United States, "Characteristics of the Non-white Population by Race: 1940": 44.

Percentages for 1960 were derived from Table 40, Eighteenth Census of the United States. "Economic Characteristics of the Chinese Population 14 Years Old and over by Age, for the United States, by Region, Urban and Rural, and for Selected States: 1960." (Based on 25 per cent sample. Data shown for States with 25,000 or more Chinese. Median number, shown where base is less than 200): 153.

Percentages for 1970 were derived from a preliminary 15 per cent sample of the Nineteenth Census of the United States.

facilities maintained by the Chinese community with classes beginning at the end of the public school days (*The New York Times,* August 18, 1971:12).

Problems of Aging

One of the traditional values of the Chinese family is the great respect and obedience shown toward elders of the family. One does not have to be very old to command respect; it is enough for one to be slightly older than the other. The high regard the Chinese hold for a teacher can be explained by how they address him, *Shien-Sheng,* meaning one who was "born first." Filial piety, therefore, is one of the values that has united the Chinese family for centuries.

Both the Chinatown-based Chinese and the Chinese in professional groups still show respect to the older members of the family. This is evidenced by the use of appropriate kin terms of address between individuals in different age groups. In the family, for example, one addresses siblings as "Older Brother, Oldest Sister, Second Older Sister, Third Older Sister and Fourth Older Sister" (Wong, 1945:2).

The early Chinese who arrived in America in the nineteenth century did not intend to stay. They came as laborers in order to make enough money to send home and later return to enjoy the fruits of their toils. Many wonder why the Chinese, who came from a rural background in south China, entered such untraditional occupations as restaurateurs and laundrymen. According to Mead (1955:239), they were working for the family they had left behind, either for a sister's dowry, a brother's education, or for additional family land, which gave them a sense of stability and a feeling of personal freedom. Which explains how Chinese immigrants, with the thought of sustained family continuity, as an ever-present value, were able to withstand the hardships of racial prejudice, persecution, and low-status occupations.

Before 1949, when the People's Republic of China assumed control of Mainland China, it was the practice of many older immigrants to return to China after they retired, to enjoy the glorious period of old age surrounded by children and grandchildren, many of whom they had never seen. For those unfortunate enough to die in America before they left for home, the various clan, district, or benevolent associations would see to it that their bodies were shipped home for burial in the family plot, or they would even have their bones dug up and shipped overseas, sometimes even 8 or 10 years after death. Since 1949 this luxury of being buried in their homeland has been taken away from the elders among Chinese immigrants.

America is a youth-oriented country. Being old and poor is one of the greatest fears of many of its people. Many elderly Chinese Americans have retired to room at association headquarters, living on the generosity of friends and relatives. It is an unspoken charitable gesture for Chinese restaurants in Chinatown to offer free meals to the old and deprived. The elderly can frequently be observed walking straight into the kitchen of a restaurant around mealtime to receive a hot bowl of rice from his fellow countrymen.

Most sojourners could not quality for Old Age Assistance or other forms of relief until the 1940s. However, even if they were qualified, many refused to accept public relief and charity, partly due to the loss of "face" or pride, and partly because they were afraid to be deported as public charges. There was a gradual change of attitude, especially with regard to social security, to which many had contributed during the productive years of their lives, as well as the breakdown of the mutual-aid system provided by the clan and family associations and the indifference of kinsmen in times of genuine need. Neurotic and psychotic disorders have been found among the rejected, lonely, and deprived older people in Chinatown (Lee, 1960:329–31).

Retired immigrants appear to have few pleasures unless they are relatively wealthy. The unsuccessful ones may live at the company houses, several to a room, with limited modern conveniences or comfort. They may gamble at a social club or one of the numerous one-room gambling dens. In the early 1950s the New York Community Service Society and the Department of Welfare initiated a Golden Age Club, and attendance exceeded expectations. The membership in 1962 was well over 1,000, which indicated the great need this group had for recreational activities as well as the fact that their respective family-name associations had not made them welcome. The traditional function of the family-name association may be declining, judging from the fact that there are many older Chinese seeking help from the Chinatown nursing office of Community Service of New York and other public social agencies (Cattell, 1962:48).

On the other hand, few immigrant professionals who arrived in this country in the 1940s are at retirement age. Some of them had brought their aged parents to America after they became citizens or received permanent-resident status. Most of their parents and elders, however, are still in Mainland China and are not able to leave the country. By the time this post-1940s professional group reaches retirement age, they may

140

not suffer the same problems of the Chinatown-based retirees due to their higher educational background, greater intellectual and economic resources, and, most important of all, a family of American-born children and grandchildren well rooted in the new society.

Having been socialized in China in the most formative years of their lives, they may encounter some difficulty adjusting to their increasingly Americanized children and grandchildren, whose ways of treating parents and grandparents are not appropriate to the Chinese tradition. Recently a mother confided in this writer that she and her husband were shocked to receive a letter from their son and Caucasian daughter-in-law. They were happy to hear from them, but not to be addressed as "Dear Jeanie and Jack." "At least she could address us as Father Wong and Mother Wong," she stated, meaning that undoubtedly it was the American daughter-in-law who instigated such a big dose of democracy in their new relationship.

Due to rapid social change in the American society, one may assume that it will take several generations before elders from Chinatown-based families and professional suburban families accept the attitude and behavior of the younger generations. The basic central theme of respect for the elders from the traditional Chinese values may linger on in the minds of most members of the older generation regardless of educational background or length of residence in America. One often hears Chinese Americans express that it is better to live in America when one is young. When one grows old, one should return to the old country where age is respected and catered to. The generation gap in the average American family has been a frequent topic of discussion in recent decades, but the gap between generations in the Chinese American family is many times more dramatic, especially between foreign-born parents and American-born offspring. Resignation among the younger generation rather than rebellion has been the pattern as an open confrontation in human relationships is much frowned on in the Chinese culture.

The attitude of Chinese Americans toward their elders may show greater concern and devotion than in the average Anglo family. The lot of the older people in America, however, may compare unfavorably with that traditional China in which age was not regarded as a problem so long as the pattern of continuity between the generations was maintained. In both Chinatown-based families and Chinese suburban families, one usually expects elderly helpless parents to be included in the household, especially when the parent is widowed. The professional group tends to be more resourceful and independent, and the retired

141

group among them have already organized the Chinese Retirement Association of America, an affiliate of Midwest Chinese Student and Alumni Services (*Newsletter* of the Midwest Chinese Student and Alumni Services, 1972). The major function of the association is to promote the welfare of the retired members.

CHANGES AND ADAPTATIONS

The generation gap has been a frequent topic of discussion in the past decades by social scientists as well as by laymen. It may be an understatement to maintain that this problem is much more serious between immigrants and their children, especially among those from an old society.

One major difficulty in the intergeneration adjustment is that the old Chinese family system, which is still dominant in the villages in Kwangtung, and which lives on in the minds of the "old skulls" of American Chinatowns, is strongly patriarchal (Hayner and Reynolds, 1957:663). This trend all through the years has not changed in spite of the fact that certain major revisions have occurred in the old country. It is not only those brought up in the New World of America who experienced difficulties and conflicts with their parents, but also those who were sent back to China for education or those who arrived in this country in their late teens. "Most were better educated and sophisticated than their parents. Accustomed to more westernized Chinese cities, they rebelled against the prescribed life and the conservatism of Chinatown" (Lee, 1960:208).

Writers and journalists also observe the disparity in the life style and culture between generations among the Chinese. They realize that Chinatown is not quite China, nor is it quite America. Within its blocks one civilization is in transition, and another is not as yet acquired. The elders celebrate birth with ancient ceremonies and keep their wives in upstairs seclusion. After funerals they hold banquets at which it is rude to appear sad and go only to Chinese restaurants in which all at a table eat from the same bowl as symbol of fraternity. They read only Chinese papers and periodicals, while their sons who hardly speak or read Chinese, prefer the city tabloids (*The New York Times,* December 15, 1946).

The young Chinese who grew up in a brand-new world, finding that their parental generation is full of obsolescent precedents and out-of-date responses, have had to resort to looking for new models among

142

their peers. "These peers present them with more practical models than those of the elders, whose past is inaccessible to them and whose future it is difficult for them to see as their own" (Mead, 1970:31).

It is without doubt that Americanization tends to produce a distinct generational difference. The older generation from China can be quite cliquish, grouped according to area of origin for the Chinatown-based group or by university or family background for the professional group. Wealthier Chinese have been accused of being very materialistic in some professional groups. The younger generation, on the other hand, has very little patience for this parochialism. They are caught up in a spirit of idealism and restlessness. Some of them are critical of the Nationalists in Taiwan; others join Students for a Democratic Society, involving themselves in campus sit-ins and civil rights protests (*The Wall Street Journal,* 1969).

Concern has recently been shown by Chinese authorities and parents over an increasing incidence of rebellious youth (Lander, 1954). Lee (1960) has stated that the majority of the delinquents in cases she studied had China-born parents, and culture conflicts were cited by many as the basis for their emotional upheavals. Their parents would want them to remain Chinese and to respect their authority, following the tradition of filial piety; at the same time culture conflicts occurred to many as a part of the acculturation, assimilation, and integration process. Culture conflict has been cited as much more important a factor than the economic status of the families. The American-born children crave identification and status with American peers, while their parents attempt to pull them back into the Chinese world, thus alienating their offspring. The marginality is not only in terms of cultural differences of two social worlds but also racial difference from the majority group. A Chinese mother informed this writer that her 6-year-old daughter came home from school one day in a rather agitated manner. Suddenly she blurted out, "Who wants to be Chinese, anyway!"

A newspaper item reported that of 8,714 juveniles in New York City arrested in 1956, only 7 were of Chinese descent. It further stated that due to the strong presence of family discipline there was nothing resembling the juvenile gang (*The New York Times,* October 6, 1957:49). However, by 1965 police sources estimated that about 3 per cent of the Chinese community's teen-agers were known to be juvenile delinquents, though it was still the lowest rate of any racial or national group. Some of the violations included a marked rise in truancy, school misbehavior, and school dropouts, which reached as high as 30 per cent of the school population. Another crucial development that caused a great deal of concern was the formation in New York City of juvenile gangs among Chinese youths, including such gangs as the "White Eagles," "Kwan Ying," "Hong Kong Refugees," "Oriental Sisters," and the "International Brothers" (*The New York Times*, July 11, 1965:43). Furthermore, it has been observed that recent arrivals from Hong Kong have a great number of adjustment difficulties in America. Suddenly uprooted from their familiar surroundings and transplanted in a strange land, many young Chinese have no knowledge of English. Unfamiliar with the language as well as the American culture, these young Chinese could get only the lowliest of all jobs in restaurants and laundries, while their mothers and sisters work in garment factories to help make ends meet. With new immigrants arriving at the rate of 600 per month, housing in Chinatown became overcrowded and slumlike, with no recreational facilities. On hot summer nights, the overcrowded rooms become unbearable; therefore, gangs of disappointed, disgruntled youths roamed the streets. When bullied by other minority groups in the neighborhood, Chinese youths began to organize into gangs in order to protect themselves (*Newsletter of CSAS*, March, 1969).

On the West Coast, San Francisco has not escaped the new surge of delinquent gangs. Being the first port of entry for Hong Kong immigrants, San Francisco is said to have a juvenile gang known as "the Bugs" or "Tong Shan Tsai," which clashes occasionally with a gang of Chinese American youngsters. There seem to be complex factors responsible for recent Chinese delinquent behavior. Even though in traditional Chinese child-rearing practice in China and in Chinatown there is a great deal of continuity of experience (Hsu, 1971:84), the young Chinese born in America or young immigrants newly arrived from Hong Kong in the 1960s and early 1970s may find this cultural continuity inapplicable and impractical in their life in America. Chinese youth suffering the relative lack of continuity in social and cultural experience with reference to Chinese or American society call to mind Block and Niederhoffer's (1958) thesis. Many young people feel that they are neither child nor adult, and that delinquency of gang behavior may serve as a functional alternative to the "rites of passage" and also as a means of filling status and identity needs.

The problems that many Chinese Americans have encountered have inspired attempts at political organization. In 1971 a group of concerned Chinese Americans organized the ad hoc Chinese-American Leadership Council (CALC). The purpose of this organization was to negotiate with the various federal agencies, the Congress, and state and local governments for the improvement of the basic well-being of the Chinese Americans, a neglected group and a silent minority in America.

In May of 1973 the first national meeting was held in Washington, D.C. For the first time Chinese leaders were concerned not only over the neglected plight of some Chinese in Chinatowns but also over the increasing number of Chinese entering America. The Chinese American population had grown from 237,000 in 1960 to 435,000 in 1970. Problems of immigrants, such as language difficulty, unemployment, juvenile delinquency, and family dislocation, have begun to alarm authorities both in and out of Chinatowns. Though these problems may not be new, that Chinese American leaders have begun to demand equality as American citizens reveals a certain psychological shift from a sojourner's status to that of an American citizen.

When American Chinese parents send their children to visit Taiwan, Hong Kong, and lately the People's Republic of China, they no longer say they are returning home but going for a visit to the homeland of their ancestors. Home is here in America, a country in which other ethnic families have also come and settled. It is one of the hopes and dreams of CALC "to promote unity and strength of the United States of America by cultivating understanding and appreciation of both American and Chinese culture heritages" (*Newsletter of the Midwest Chinese Student and Alumni Services,* 1973:10).

R E F E R E N C E S

Barnett, L. D. 1963. "Students' Anticipation of Persons and Arguments Opposing Interracial Dating," *Marriage and Family Living* 25 (August): 355–57.
Beaudry, James. 1971. "Some Observations on Chinese Intermarriage in the United States." *International Journal of Sociology of the Family* Special Issue (May):59–68.
Benedict, Ruth. 1938. "Continuities and Discontinuities in Cultural Conditioning." *Psychiatry* 1 (May):161–67.
Block, Herbert A., and Arthur Niederhoffer. 1958. *The Gang.* New York: Philosophical Library.
Buck, Pearl. 1956. *My Several Worlds.* New York: Pocket Books.
Cattell, Stuart H. 1962. *Health, Welfare, and Social Organization in Chinatown.* New York: Community Service Society.
Chao, Shueh-chin. 1929. *Dreams of the Red Chamber.* New York: Doubleday.
Chen, Clarence. 1972. "Experiences as an American in Disguise." *Newsletter of the Midwest Chinese Student and Alumni Services* 14 (Summer):4–8.

Cheng, David Te-Chao. 1949. *Acculturation of the Chinese in the United States A Philadelphia Study*. China: Fukien Christian University Press.

Coleman, James S., *et al.* 1966. "Pupil Achievement and Motivation." In *Equality of Educational Opportunity*. Washington, D.C.: U.S. Government Printing Office.

Coolidge, Mary Roberts. 1909. *Chinese Immigration*. New York: Henry Holt.

Erikson, Erik H. 1963. *Childhood and Society*. (2nd ed.) New York: Norton.

Gordon, Albert. 1964. *Intermarriage*. Boston: Beacon Press.

Hayner, Norman, and Charles M. Reynolds. 1957. "Chinese Family Life in America." *American Sociological Review* 22 (October):630–37.

Heer, David. 1966. "Negro-White Marriage in the United States." *Journal of Marriage and the Family* 27 (August):262–73.

Hsu, Francis L. K. 1949. "Suppression Versus Repression: A Limited Psychological Interpretation of Four Cultures." *Psychiatry* 12:233–42.

———. 1953. *Americans and Chinese*. New York: Henry Schuman.

———. 1970. *Americans and Chinese*. Garden City, N.Y.: Doubleday Natural History Press.

———. 1971. *The Challenge of American Dream: The Chinese in the United States*. Belmont, California: Wadsworth.

———. 1972. *American Museum Science Book*. (2nd ed.) Garden City, N.Y.: Doubleday Natural History Press.

Huang, Lucy, 1956. "Dating and Courtship Innovations of Chinese Students in America." *Marriage and Family Living* 18 (February): 25–29.

Humana, Charles, and Wang Wu. 1972. "Ying-Yang: The Chinese Way of Love." *Sexual Behavior* 2 (June):20–25.

Lander, B. 1954. *Understanding of Juvenile Delinquency*. New York: Columbia University Press.

Lear, Martha Weinman. 1965. *The Child Worshippers*. New York: Pocket Books.

Lee, Rose Hum. 1952. "Delinquent, Neglected, and Dependent Chinese Boys and Girls of the San Francisco Bay Region." *Journal of Social Psychology* 36 (August):15–34.

———. 1960. *The Chinese in the United States*. Hong Kong: Hong Kong University Press.

McClellan, Robert. 1971. *The Heathen Chinee*. Athens, Ohio: Ohio University Press.

Mead, Margaret. 1955. *Cultural Patterns and Technical Change*. The New American Library. Garden City, N.Y.: Doubleday Natural History Press.

———. 1970. *Culture and Commitment: A Study of the Generation Gap*. Garden City, N.Y.: Doubleday Natural History Press.

Murray, Classie. 1972. "Mabel Liang, America's Top Teen." Reprinted from *Park Forest Reporter, Newsletter of the Midwest Chinese Student and Alumni Services:* 14, 4 (Summer), p. 2.

Newsletter of the Midwest Chinese Student and Alumni Services: 1968, 11 (March, July, and December); 1969, 12 (March); 1972, 14 (Spring); 1973, 15 (Spring).

146

The New York Times: December 15, 1946, Section VI:60; October 6, 1957, Section VI:49; July 11, 1965:43: June 29, 1968:31; August 18, 1971:12.

Pa, Chin. 1972. *The Family*. New York: Anchor Books.

Saxton, Alexander. 1971. *The Indispensable Enemy*. Berkeley: University of California Press.

Schwartz, Shepard. 1951. "Mate-Selection Among New York City's Chinese Mates 1931–38." *American Journal of Sociology* 56 (May):562–68.

Sollenberger, Richard T. 1968. "Chinese-American Child-Rearing Practices and Juvenile Delinquency." *Journal of Social Psychology* 74 (February):13–23.

The Wall Street Journal: January 28, 1969.

Wang, King Lee. 1973. "An Open Letter to All Concerned Chinese-Americans." *Newsletter of the Midwest Chinese Student and Alumni Services* 15 (Spring):10.

Wirth, Louis. 1956. *The Ghetto*. Chicago: University of Chicago Press.

Wong, Jade. 1945. *Fifth Chinese Daughter*. New York: Harper and Brothers.

Yablonsky, Lewis. 1962. *The Violent Gang*. New York: Macmillan.

Yuan, D. Y. 1965. "New York Chinatown." In Arnold M. Rose and Caroline B. Rose (eds.): *Minority Problems*. New York: Harper & Row, pp. 277–84.

RECENT AND CONTINUING
ETHNIC MINORITIES
(circa 1920-present)

The Arab American Family

The Arab world, with its enormous oil reserve, emerged in 1973 as an area of enormous importance to America and the Western world. It may come as a surprise for many Americans to learn that there is a sizable Arab community in America. It is also a fact that very few sociological studies have been conducted on these Arab American communities and their family patterns. Although the chapter to be presented here does suffer from the relatively scant amount of knowledge of this ethnic group, Dr. Elkholy has relied on two field studies separated by 15 years, one conducted in 1957 and the other in 1972. In addition, the participant-observation technique has aided his interpretation of the statistical data gathered on these small but important Arab Moslem communities in America.

Understanding the Arab Americans and their system of family organization may enable us better to comprehend the Middle East from which they came. On the other hand, this chapter provides not only a spectroscopic examination of the family patterns of an old people in a new land but also by inference a picture of an enigmatic people who may nevertheless, through our scientific and sociological probing, provide us with the knowledge requisite to achieve an overall pattern for assimilation of Middle Eastern nations into a world community of peoples.

CHAPTER SEVEN

BY
ABDO A. ELKHOLY

HISTORICAL BACKGROUND

Arab Americans proudly mention their ancestors crossing the Atlantic from Spain and arriving at Brazil in the year 1150 A.D. Before that, in the tenth century A.D. (according to the Arab geographer Al-Sharilf Al-Idrisi), eight adventurous Arabs sailed from Lisbon, Portugal, trying to discover what lay beyond the sea of darkness (the Atlantic Ocean; Audat, 1956:5–17). It is said that they landed in South America. Historians suspect that Al-Idrisi's story inspired Columbus to try to reach the East through the West, which led to the great discovery of America. In 1955, when Italy celebrated the five hundredth anniversary of the birth of Columbus, there was a fair at which many of Columbus's belongings were displayed. Among them was an Arabic book, said to be the Idrisi book, in which the story of the eight adventurers was mentioned. It suffices to state that migration remains one characteristic of the Arabs because of their nomadic history. If that early migration were initiated by personal curiosity, the late ones have been initiated by social causes.

South America captured the attraction and imagination of the early Arab emigrants, who went there in large groups to form sizable and influential ethnic communities. The Arabs started to migrate to America as late as the last quarter of the nineteenth century. Perhaps the Europeanization of America made it less attractive to the early Arabs than South America. One distinct religious feature dominated the early Arab emigrations of the nineteenth century: The great majority were Christians. Fear of losing their religion in the Christian, missionary-minded New World delayed the immigration of the Arab Moslems to America by 25 years, until the start of the twentieth century (Makdisi, 1959: 970). The head-start migration thus achieved by Arab-Christians increased their ratio to the Arab Moslems up to the start of World War II by nine to one.

The Arab migration to America resulted from two causes (Warner and Srole, 1945: 105): "forces of attraction exerted by the expanding American economy and forces of expulsion exerted in the lands of emigration." Prior to 1950, only 2 per cent of Arab Americans left their native land for political reasons and less than 1 per cent for education in America. Driven by poverty and attracted by wealth, most of them came from the peasant sector in Greater Syria, politically recognized now as Lebanon. It is not surprising that with unfavorable demographic characteristics, such as low socioeconomic and educational status, the early waves of immigrants did not fare very well in the New World. One-fourth of them ended their journey in the Southern states in which farm labor was welcomed, and many became successful farmers in Georgia, Texas, Tennessee, Mississippi, New Mexico, and Arizona. About 50 per cent of the early immigrants stayed on the East Coast, in New York, New Jersey, Pennsylvania, and in the New England states. They peddled dry goods and started grocery stores. The remaining 25 per cent moved to the Midwestern states of Ohio, Michigan, Indiana, Illinois, and Iowa to work as unskilled laborers in the railroad, steel, and auto industries in addition to dry-goods peddling and grocery stores. As some pioneers recalled, they often were sponsored by successful business people who had migrated earlier from the same region. Upon their arrival in New York, immigration officials pinned name tags on them, put them on the train, and called the sponsor to announce their arrival at their destination. Most of the time their passage was loaned by either relatives in the old country or the sponsors, who generally assumed responsibility of finding them living quarters and providing them with employment. The sponsors were mainly dry-good wholesalers who relied on the immigrants to sell their goods from door to door. This arrangement was mutually satisfactory in the short run. The immigrant, who lacked funds and knowledge of the English language, found suitable and ready employment in a strange environment, and the wholesaler found squadrons of laborers who contributed to the prosperity of his business.

Whether Moslems or Christians, the Arabs, who formed the first waves of immigrants from the last quarter of the nineteenth century up to World War II, never intended to spend the rest of their lives in America. They only wanted to accumulate the most money possible in the shortest time and then return home. Sixty per cent of those early immigrants came unmarried. Because of economic uncertainty, only 12 per cent of those married came with their families (Elkholy, 1966:83).

Though attracted to America, as reported by 97 per cent of a sample of the early immigrants, they were handicapped by their lack of knowledge of English. "Learning the English language was the most difficult adjustment to make" (Elkholy, 1966:84). Coming from the lower educational class and having acquired no knowledge of English prior to their emigration, those of the earlier waves found everything very strange in America. The majority of the first immigrants had to cluster around pioneers in order to solve the critical linguistic handicap, which has been one of the most influential factors in erecting ethnic clusters all over the world. The less English speaking an ethnic community in America, the more clannish it is, and the more it segregates itself from American life. Such segregation delays the process of acculturation.

The early immigration waves between 1880 and 1939 carried the Arabs to the agricultural Southern states as well as to the large cities of the East Coast, New England, and the Midwestern states, and forced them to congregate in small as well as large communities. The second immigration waves, which started in the 1950s and are still continuing, scattered the educated elites and technicians randomly across the country.

The sharp demographic contrast between the first and second immigration waves is the function of two dramatic episodes in the Middle East: First, the creation of Israel in 1948 resulted in the expulsion of about two

153

million Palestinians to make room for the European Jews, who have been coming to Israel ever since. Most of those Palestinian refugees who had the chance to come to America for one reason or another remained here permanently. Some were professionals and skilled workers. The majority acquired their higher education in American universities when scholarships were plentiful and an unprecedented expansion of higher educational institutions took place. The second dramatic episode was the Egyptian Revolution in 1952, which grew out of the Arab world's frustration over the loss of Palestine, and which instigated a series of similar military coups d'etat and revolutions in other Arab countries and disrupted the status quo in the social structure of the entire Middle East. Those Egyptians with professional and financial means, who did not fare well under the military regime, started to look around for a way out. A great proportion of them have been emigrating to America since 1952; especially after 1956 and 1967, the late arrivals, the intellectual elite of the Arab society, were highly educated and skilled (*Arab Youth*, April 7, 1975, p.6). Seventy-three per cent were educated in America or Europe. This put them in favorable bargaining positions in the expanding educational, research, and technological markets, especially since they had no linguistic barrier to restrict their mobility. They are highly mobile and are scattered across the country, employed as university professors, schoolteachers, engineers, technicians, physicians, and in other professions. Some have already acquired national fame and prominence.

Many new Arab communities have sprung up all over America during the 1950s and 1960s. From Jersey City, New Jersey, to St. Louis, Missouri, and Los Angeles, California, the newly immigrated Arabs settled in either new concentrations or as individuals, depending on their professions. During the so-called "brain-drain" period, which labeled those two decades, 90,915 Arabs, most of them professionals, immigrated to America. Between 1962 and 1972, 68,305, or about 90 per cent of the total immigrants admitted to America from seven Arab countries, were professionals. Again, the majority of them came from Egypt. Added to these 90,915, another 2,080 nonimmigrants were naturalized between 1950 and 1971. Although there is no religious census taken in America of these new waves of Arab immigrants, it is estimated that 78 per cent are Moslems. High professionalism and Moslem majority characterized the second-wave immigration in contrast to the early waves prior to World War II.

To speak of this professional category as a social group or an ethnic community gives a misleading impression, for there was no single institutional organization prior to 1960 under which they could be sheltered. It was only after the creation of Israel that a number of Arab American organizations were started mainly for the purpose of defending themselves against what they considered Zionist propaganda and defamation practices. In 1952 the Federation of Islamic Associations in America and Canada was formed, followed by the American Arab Association in 1961, the Association of Arab American University Graduates in 1967, and the Association of Egyptian American Scholars in 1970. However, these organizations attracted only a small percentage of the Arab elites in America.

The family style of this professional category approximates that of the typical middle-class WASP family style. In the absence of distinct facial characteristics betraying their ethnic origin, the members of this professional category are fully accepted by American society. Their intention to make America a permanent home facilitated the process of adaptation. Continuing the Elkholy sample study, 68 per cent are married to American or European spouses whom they met on university campuses at the time they were studying. The remaining 32 per cent of Arab wives of these professionals belong to the upper-middle socioeconomic class in the Arab world. They are not handicapped by linguistic barriers, compared with the previous waves of less educated wives, and thus have easy access to higher education and employment. The professional, economic, and social prosperity of this category with Arab wives made assimilation to and acceptance by the American society as easy and speedy as it was for those 68 per cent Arabs with Western spouses. The average number of children is 2.27. Birth control and family planning are practiced by 87 per cent of the couples. Their American-born children are typical Americans with only scant knowledge of the Arab World and its problems.

While it is difficult to identify the product of the second waves of immigration as being members of Arab communities (due to their professional commitments and their high rate of mobility), it is quite easy to find concentrated communities that are the product of the early immigration waves.

THE MODERN ARAB AMERICAN FAMILY

The structure as well as the socialization processes of the Arab family in America oscillate generally between preservation of traditional culture and acculturation, depending on a number of variables, one of which is intermarriage with Americans. From the perspective of intergroup relations, the problem can be seen through the eyes of the ethnic minority looking toward the larger society and its various groups. The intergroup relations are affected by the stereotype images that the minority and dominant groups develop toward each other. The stereotype, which creates social distance, is extended to the members of a given group, and thus the interaction becomes biased. Surmounting the mutually unfavorable images of East and West requires strong personal sentimental preference in the face of traditions of both minority and dominant groups. Intermarriage is viewed here from the standpoint of the minority spouse as a strong agent of assimilation, for the spouse, who belongs to the dominant culture, facilitates the cultural transformation of the offspring.

The difference between assimilation and acculturation may be made clear here. Acculturation cannot occur without assimilation. When the minority members assimilate the prevailing values of the host society and prefer them over the traditional values of their cultural background, one of two things takes place: The minority community rejects the assimilated members and makes their presence in the community unwelcome. This forces them to leave, and they become a total loss to the minority community, which, through traditional preservation, resisted the process of acculturation. On the other hand, the minority community still retains its assimilated members, who become a total gain to the overall community acculturation. In the second case, the community may remain distinct, although acculturated. In the first instance, the community has to ultimately dissolve by the time the last member leaves or dies. Intermarriage between Arabs and Westerners is in general neither desired nor encouraged by the Arab communities in America. Nevertheless, there are two variations in the resistance attitudes correlated with religion and education.

Intermarriage and Religion

Although intermarriage with Westerners is desired by neither Arab Moslem nor Christian communities, it is more strongly resisted by the Moslems than by the Christians. Since it was indicated before that intermarriage facilitates the processes of both assimilation and acculturation, it is to be expected that the Arab-Christian communities will be more acculturated than their Moslem counterparts. In either case the process of interreligious marriage is not always smooth. Various cultural barriers intervene, one of which is the Arab family life style, which differs from the Anglo life-style.

Our sample study has shown that more than 68 per cent of the Moslem immigrants came to the New World unmarried. Less than 12 per cent of the married immigrants came with their families. The pattern, then, was for the immigrants to come alone. Aside from the few female students who marry in the New World and decide to remain, the entire stock of the single Moslem immigrants is composed of young men. These young men are faced with a problem: Whom do they marry?

Marital choice differs between the two types of immigrants. The great majority of the unmarried pioneers married within their own ethnic groups by importing their wives fromt he old countries. Approximately 68 per cent of the late arrivals, however, married Europeans, Americans, or Canadians. Thus, despite the relatively short time span the Moslems have been in the New World, they have generally adopted a liberal attitude toward interreligious marriages. This seems to be true for both males and females, and most particularly true for Moslem immigrants coming to this country after World War II. Liberal attitudes toward religious intermarraige are related to education, which is related to professionalism.

Aside from the fear of diluting their communities in the long run via intermarriage, Arabs desire to preserve their young men to marry their young women. Marrying outside the group, even when the wives are brought to the community, means that an equal number of young Arab women will either stay unmarried or marry outside, thus leading to undesirable consequences. Intermarriage always brings to the community unpredictable members whose values, customs, and habits are not in accordance with those of the community. As one member put it to the author:

With our people, we can drop by at any time, day or night, whenever we feel like it. We can go to the kitchen and icebox to help ourselves with no hesitation. We feel welcome and the wives do not resent us. They are our sisters. They understand what we talk about, for there is a common theme which cannot be taught. A lot of things can be taken for granted and do not require the cautions we have whenever we visit one of our unlucky brothers who married outside. We are hesitant to eat at their homes. The wife cannot follow our conversation. She gets frustrated. We feel embarrassed and soon the atmosphere becomes boring. Some of those wives are snobbish and feel superior. I don't know whether they really feel this way or just play it that way to keep a certain distance from the rest of the community. We feel sorry for the children. They do not have the joy our children have. We also feel sorry for those foolish husbands. We suspect that they are not happy at home. They miss our food, our conversation, and gossip, our entire atmosphere.

This might be an exaggerated image reflecting attitudes of some members toward such marriages. However, such an image constrains the social relations and restricts the interactions between the community and the families of intermarriage.

A REVERSE SITUATION: AN AMERICAN WIFE. From the viewpoint of the non-Arab wife, the story might be somewhat different. The pattern of the Western family hardly coincides with that of the Arab one. The wide gulf of hard reality between the immediate family and the extended one is not easy for the Western wife to comprehend. When she has to cross that rugged gulf to the extended family pattern of her husband, she finds herself aggravated and lost in an infinite number of relationships, each of which is traditionally prescribed and requires a set of specific mutual obligations. The following case study reported to the author illustrates the predicament:

An American wife married to an Iraqi professor when interviewed tried to illustrate the sources of her agony in Iraq which led her husband to immigrate to the United States. As is often the case, she met him on the American campus where they were attending the same university. They left the States for Iraq with their 6-month old child, immediately after the husband received his Ph.D. degree. All that she knew about the Middle East came to her mind through the fantasies of the book *One Thousand and One Nights,* plus the Western image of the sleepy, rosy medieval conditions. She did not find Bagdad the golden city she imagined. Rather, she found it in clusters of confusion emanating from social and ecological changes. Although her husband was given a university teaching position, his salary could hardly sustain the life style of their Americanized household.

Her anxieties started as soon as they strove to find a suitable apartment. The landlords did not desire to rent out their nice places to natives like her husband. They preferred foreigners, perhaps to get higher rent, or to be more sure of better maintenance. Her husband, for the first time, felt discriminated against in his own country. It was some time before they acquired a suitable apartment whose rent they could afford. With one car, which they had brought with them, they could hardly manage. The heavy teaching schedule of the husband, the imposed consultations with government circles for very little reward, and the endless favors the husband had to render daily to acquaintances, friends, and relatives in getting them positions or work here and there, to write them letters of recommendation, or to call influential\people in their behalf—all this hardly left any of the husband's time for her or household affairs.

Managing household affairs without a car, she had to use public transportation which she found frustrating. For help, she had to rely on unreliable maids. After she had half-trained the maid, the girl would quite or was attracted elsewhere by higher wages. She found it a losing battle which, however, she could not afford to stop fighting. During the three-year period the couple spent in Iraq, her husband hardly had time to eat dinner with her at the regular time more than a dozen times. Normal family life was quite often interrupted by unscheduled visits of demanding relatives who felt they had an indisputable right to use the house as if it were their own. The concept of hotels and restaurants was alien to them. Gradually, the social burden became unbearable. Finally, the informant said, "we had to quit and return to the States."

The experiences of the Western wife in the native land of her Arab husband are not the most pleasant. She cannot grasp or bear the burden of the complexity of kinship outside the Western world. In the West, for example, there is only one term, cousin, to denote different types of kin relationships. All of them are equal in one respect: remoteness. There are, in the Middle East, eight different categories of cousins. Each category has a definite set of mutual rights and obligations that are legally acknowledged and traditionally carried out and maintained. The following illustrates the eight different categories of cousins.

Ego

Father's side:	Brother of the father	1. Son of brother of the father
		2. Daughter of brother of the father
	Sister of the father	3. Son of sister of the father
		4. Daughter of sister of the father
Mother's side:	Brother of the mother	5. Son of brother of the mother
		6. Daughter of brother of the mother
	Sister of the mother	7. Son of sister of the mother
		8. Daughter of sister of the mother

When these eight categories are considered by age in relation to the Ego's age, that is, younger, same age, older, the net result of the cousin categories alone adds to 24, for each category may contain persons who are older, younger, and equal in age to Ego. If Ego died without leaving a spouse or children, his belongings are legally distributed among some of these categories, not in equal shares but according to a precise legal formula. If members of some of these categories are alive, they prevent some other categories from inheriting. By the same token, if Ego survives some of these categories, he is apt to inherit a prescribed portion of their belongings. The extended kinship relations constitute the principal fabric of the social structure outside the Western world. They have the greatest functions in societies with little bureaucratic experience in which secondary institutions have not yet taken deep roots. The Western wife finds it difficult to function in this complex kinship, which is a comfortable social world for the one reared in it, even in America.

Life Style of the Arab Moslem Family

Arab Moslems bring to the New World certain traditional family life styles that are more closely adhered to by the early immigrants than by the more recent professional immigrants. Four features are identified:

1. The Arab Moslem family was traditionally patriarchal and generally oriented toward older family members. The elders had a controlling voice in family affairs including approval of marriage partners for their children. Screening of possible mates for a suitable one lay in the hands of the mother, the father making the final arrangements. Islam still considers the husband the head of the household, the manager of the affairs of the family.
2. Traditionally, a boy had the privilege—even right—of marrying the daughter of his father's brother. While this practice has declined, it still occasionally may be claimed as a right, or the girl and her parents may feel that she has been slighted if the cousin does not seek her in marraige.
3. Women may not marry non-Moslems unless the non-Moslem becomes converted to Islam prior to marraige. This prohibition was not explicit in the *Quran* but is implied in the *Traditions*. It is felt that almost certainly the woman who marries a non-Moslem, as well as her children, will be lost to Islam.
4. Men may marry non-Moslems provided they are members of either Jewish or Christian faith, both groups being considered of the Heavenly Books and kin to the Moslems. It is anticipated that the wives will enter Islam, and their children will be reared as Moslems.

These traditional policies create many problems in the social situation of the New World and especially for American-born children of Moslems who tend to adopt the romantic-individualistic pattern of mate selection.

There are two general life styles of the Arab family, depending on the degree of education one or both of the Arab parents have acquired. Those below college education, whether Moslems or Christians, are the backbone of the Arab communities whose life style is depicted here.

Through intimate contacts with their playmates and schoolmates, under the compulsory school system, the second-generation members have the chance to compare two different cultures and ways of life. The unfavorable socioeconomic conditions in the old countries at the time their parents came to America leave no doubt in the judgment of the second-generation members: They prefer the American socioeconomic and political structure over that of the old country. In fact, they consider themselves luckier than their parents to have been born in this country. The parents share this view. The first-generation immigrants are proud to hear their children speak English fluently like any American. It is also very common for the first-generation members to give their children American nicknames. In one family there are Mike, Ralph, Ronald, Fred, Dennis, Vicki, Stephen, and Churchill for outside identification, while the Arabic names are kept for the family and community identification.

The second generation plays a transitional role between the old and the new cultures and thus is often the victim of both. The members of the second generation teach the members of the first generation a great deal about the American culture. But it is hard for the first-genreation members, who are dominated by a patriarchal family image, to accept the reversal of roles, which makes them pupils of their own children. This widens the cultural gap between the two generations. Most of the second-generation members, in response to the question, "About what things do you most frequently disagree with your father?" mention that their fathers are slow at making decisions and have a habit of arguing over little things. Among the common complaints against the mothers are that they "interfere" in their children's personal affairs, are too absorbed in the social life of the immigrant women, and engage in too much malicious gossip in the style of the old country.

The two generations, therefore, live in two different social atmospheres with separate outlooks on life. The first-generation members are affected by the memories of their great efforts to make their way in a strange land. Looking forward, they realize that socially as well as religiously they have lost their offspring to America. They admit that they have gained economic wealth, but they doubt whether that wealth compensates for their loss.

Authority Relations in the Family

Most of the first-wave immigrants have had little or no formal education. The family in the old country performed many functions that, in the more complex societies, are performed by specialized separate institutions. Although the school was the formal educational institution, difficult economic conditions prevent that institution from serving as large a group as in the more economically advanced countries. The agrarian family needed the complete participation of all its members. The children simply could not be spared for formal education. Thus, the main education a child could obtain was in the tradition transmitted from one generation to another. The parents functioned in roles of vocational trainer and educator.

Since the emphasis in knowledge and wisdom was on the past, parents achieved status in the family through experiences that were associated with maturity. The traditional admiration for the aged in less literate societies derives from that association between experience and old age, accentuated in folklore. In more literate, industrialized societies, the emphasis in knowledge is on science and technology. Knowledge is not tied to the past. The machine and space era, with its emphasis on scientific achievement for the future, has shifted family status from the aged to the young. The function of traditional education in the home, to solidify the family under the control of the aged, has given way to a new concept of education.

The tradition-oriented first-wave Arab in America was puzzled by the independence and the disobedience of his children. He often expressed his disappointment about the new pattern of family relations by saying, "We lost our children in America," for they still dream of the patriarchal pattern, which they imagine, incorrectly, to be unchanged in the old country. The attitudes of the first generation puzzle the second generation, too. As Warner and Srole (1952: 125) put it,

> Not only does the child resent the fact that his parents do not act after the American behavioral norms; not only does he resent pressure to act after the ethnic behavioral modes; but, infused with American social logics, he implicitly questions the right of his father to dominate and control his behavior.

The demand for freedom by the second generation conflicts with the desire of the first to retain control. This is the cornerstone of generational conflict. The more traditional the first-generation members, the more they demand control over the second generation, and the wider the differences become.

The progeny of the first-wave immigrants is born into two different cultures and grows up under both influences. In time the influence of his family is outweighed by the influence of the American culture. Once he goes out to play with Anglo children, he encounters the fear and fascination of a new language. By the time he goes to school, the English language is dominant. The different symbols of the English language (especially slang concerning dates, girl friends, and boy friends) convey to him lighter, easier values, which differ from the more ponderous values of his family.

Communication among generations in the family is manifested in the language both generations use at home. Linguistically, the family pattern has become heterogeneous; the first generation speaks in Arabic, while the second generation answers in English. Not only in English easier for the second-genration members, it is superior. He sees the struggles of his parents to express themselves in English and use English words in Arabic constructions. Though the children laugh at their efforts, parents learn a great deal of English from their children—and a great deal, as well, about the American way of life. The crucial point comes, as Warner (1953: 126) says, when "the child, not the parent, becomes the transmitting agent of social change."

Education is, therefore, a major reason why the younger generation of the Arab community has become the catalyst for social change. The sharp educational difference among generations, especially between the first and second, is one of the factors responsible for family conflict in the Arab community. The family has become less integrated as each generation views the other from its own position and values.

Also associated with family conflict is the first generation's strong resistance to the social change introduced by the younger generation. Since the new environment continuously strengthens the value standards of the younger American-born generation over those of the first-wave immigrants, the latter group is frustrated in a losing battle. The unbalanced opposite forces between generations in the family relations have resulted in the father's failure to maintain tradition. "He does not know how to control the children" is the common complaint of the Arab wife against her husband. "The children," she continues, "don't listen to us. They spend most of their time out. They just come home to eat and sleep."

New Arab generation members complain about the failure of traditional family structure to interest them and hold their loyalty. The disintegration of the traditional family structure manifests itself in numerous patterns, ranging from conversation to food. The parents' conversation is centered around persons and families, taking the concrete shape of gossip. The children's conversation is centered around cars, nights, pleasures outside the home, and even general social problems. The parents continue to relish Arabic dishes, which the children

163

do not enjoy. Very often, the housewife cooks *mijaddara* or *Kebba nayya* for herself and her husband and something else for her children. A second-generation member summed up in three words the view of his generation toward their parents: "They neglect life," he said. Asked to elaborate, he replied to the writer:

> I don't remember that my parents ever took us out to dinner, movies, or theater. They never invited any American family or accepted any American invitation. The reason is that my mother does not speak English. When I bought my car, they were angry at me. I don't have complete freedom to spend my money. I work for my father. He gives me much less than what I could get working outside. Despite this they watch what I spend as if I were spending their money. Next year I'll be thirty years old but they still deal with me as if I were a child. If I buy a new suit or spend my vacation in Florida with some American friends they cry that I'm spoiled, that I spend too much on my friends, and so on. I'm sick of this life.

Contrary to what might be expected, when the parents retire and cease to be economically productive, they are taken care of by their American-born children. Usually the parents live alone in the homes they usually own, and their married children, if nearby, look after them. The pattern is that they spend Sundays and holidays with their parents. These occasions, when two or three generations meet, make the old folks happy and give them something to look forward to. The "nursing home" is still an unknown institution to senior Arab Americans whose homes are social centers for an extensive network of relatives and friends. Even those who go back to retire in the old country return to the States because they find that they miss their children, friends, and the life style of the New World. They also prefer to be buried here where their funeral will be attended by hundreds of relatives and friends and representatives of the communities. Public aid is virtually unknown in the Arab communities because they take care of their needy people.

Pregnancy out of wedlock, delinquency, and criminal behavior exist, but the rate is quite low because of heavy group pressure. There are no available statistics on illegitimacy. The communities are somewhat careful not to report hearsay pertaining to such a delicate matter. During a six-month period of a field research in one of the American-Arab communities, the author learned of a single case in which an unmarried Arab girl became pregnant. She had an abortion in another state and her parents ostracized her. The only avenue open to her was a religious organization where she could visit old friends.

CHANGE AND ADAPTATION

Arab Americans refer to America as a paradise for women and children because the Arab family has become dominated by the mother and children. This has resulted because parents attempt to provide children with opportunities they never had. Parents desire to care for their children and control every aspect of their present and future lives. It is the wife who often initiates invitations and entertainments at the home, a sharp contrast from tradition. In fact, the community affairs are to a large degree sustained and run by women.

Marriage is no longer arranged. It follows the American pattern of dating, courtship, and romantic love, a totally alien concept and experience for the older members of the community. At colleges, as well as at work, Arab boys and girls meet other young people and start dating. Arab boys generally dislike dating Arab girls or vice versa, for family connections and relationships preclude any misbehavior making for dull dates. Times of togetherness, or dates, might be interpreted by the elders in the community, especially the parents of the girl, as engagement. If marriage does not follow, ill feelings pervade the families involved. Arab Christians and Arab Moslems, as a rule, do not intermarry. Neither the two Moslem sects of Sunni and Shia nor the two Christian sects of Maronites and Melkites encourage intersectarian marriage. If intermarriage takes place, it is between Arabs and non-Arabs. The Arab Christians are more lenient in this respect than the Arab Moslems. This is a factor contributing to the higher rate of acculturation of the Arab Christian communities in comparison to their Moslem counterparts. In the former communities assimilation aids acculturation. In the latter, in which Arab-Moslem girls (who are left without ethnic religious partners as a result of the tendency of the boys to date American girls) marry Americans, they move outside their community. This further delays the process of acculturation among the Arab Moslem communities, which still preserve a great deal of traditional Middle Eastern values. Similar to Jews, who managed to preserve traditional values on the basis of their religion, the Arab Moslems in America have succeeded in perpetuating their religious institution around the mosque, an organization that has flourished and increased tremendously during the last two decades. Surprisingly, the mosque organization is sustained mainly by the third Arab-Moslem generation, a matter that may usher in a pattern of a religiocultural revivalism similar to the pattern that occurred prior to World War II among the German Americans and the Japanese Americans. The response of Arabs in America following the creation of Israel was a revival of pride in their original culture, which they saw being deprecated by a religious minority. Here we find that religion became a utility for politics, and the mosque started to serve new functions to cater to the Sunday-oriented Arab-Moslem American communities, which are gradually shifting from the traditional Friday religious activities in order to adapt to the working conditions of the American environment.

The speed and degree of assimilation of Arab Americans and acculturation of their communities will also depend on the diplomatic and economic relations between America and the Arab World, which is, after all, the homeland of their ancestors and a hidden source of their personal pride.

CONCLUSION

Since the Arab-Israeli October War of 1973, in which the Arabs restored some of their pride and international reputation, and as a result of an embargo that demonstrated the energy dependence of the free world on Arab oil, American foreign policy became less anti-Arab. The American media reflects a changing American attitude toward the Arabs, and thus the Arab Americans are coming to feel less frustrated and more American affiliated. On the other hand, cultural regression or revivalism, which awakened a sense of tradition among the Arab Americans as a self-defensive mechanism, is likely to be enhanced by the new international prestige the Arab world occupies nowadays. The oil bonanza, which spurred economic development and technological progress in the "homeland," seems likely to inspire Arab American youth to learn or perfect their Arabic and direct their professional aspirations toward the Middle East. The hitherto illiterate Arab states, for example, Kuwait, the Gulf States (United Arab Emirates), Libya, and Saudi Arabia, are launching vigorous programs in developing science, technology, education, and every aspect of their societies to catch up to the approaching twenty-first century.

There is a possibility that the Arab recruitment from those with American knowhow with Arab background will strengthen the Arab ethnic solidarity in the New World. A sense of self-redefinition and ethnic reidentification similar to that which swept the heart of the

American Jews and revivified the Jewish family life style in America will emerge among the Arab Americans. The impact of the actual or exaggerated "reversal brain drain" on the Arab American family lies in the amount of inspiration developing among Arab American youth. However, it is too early to assess the psychological impact of the Middle Eastern Arab prosperity and the emerging new international image on either the Arab American personality or the Arab communities in America.

R E F E R E N C E S

Arab Youth. April 7, 1975, p. 6.

Aruri, Naseer H. 1969. "The Arab-American Community of Springfield, Massachusetts." In Hagopian and Paden (eds.): *The Arab-Americans: Studies in Assimilation*. Wilmette, Illinois: Medina University Press International, pp. 50–67.

Audat, Yacub. 1956. *Al-Natigun bil-dad li Amirika al-Ganubiyya*. Beirut: Dar Rihani.

Elkholy, Abdo A. 1966. *The Arab Moslems in the United States: Religion and Assimilation*. New Haven: College and University Press.

———. 1971. "The Moslems and Inter-religious Marriage in the New World." *International Journal of Sociology of the Family: Special Issue* I (May):69–84.

Glazer, Nathan. 1954. "Ethnic Groups in America: From National Culture to Ideology." In Morroe Berger, Theodore Abel, and Charles H. Page (eds.): *Freedom and Control in Modern Society*. Princeton, N.J.: Van Nostrand, pp. 158–76.

Makdisi, Nadin. 1959. "The Moslems of America." *The Christian Century* (August 26): 969–71.

Warner, William Lloyd. 1953. *American Life*. Chicago: University of Chicago Press.

———, and Leo Srole. 1945. *The Social System of American Ethnic Groups*. New Haven: Yale University Press.

———, and Leo Srole. 1952. *Structure of American Life*. Edinburgh: University Press.

The Greek American Family

In the chapter to follow, Professor Kourvetaris discusses the Greek American family in terms of an "ethnic generational frame of reference," covering three chronological generations of Greeks and Greek Americans in America. Within this generational framework he will first present a concise institutional profile of Greeks in America, followed by a discussion of certain normative patterns, life styles, and changes of three generations of the Greek family in America. Finally, he will present a model of transgenerational change with a prognosis for the future of the Greek American family in the context of the larger and changing society.

CHAPTER EIGHT

BY

GEORGE A. KOURVETARIS

HISTORICAL BACKGROUND

Greek immigration to America began at the turn of the present century. Greeks along with other immigrant groups from southeastern and central Europe made up the "late immigrant" vis-à-vis the "early immigrants" from countries of northwestern Europe. While most other European immigration to America has declined and generally ceased, Greek immigration, excluding the interwar years, has never really done so. Continued Greek immigration has given to the larger Greek American community a graduated scale of ethnicity and doses of "Greek cultural transfusion." At one extreme of the continuum are those Greeks who are totally "Americanized," while at the other extreme are those who can hardly speak a word of English. It is only proper that one differentiates between "early" immigrants, or those who came prior to the 1920s, and the "late" Greek immigrants, or those who came in the 1950s and continue to do so. Although no exact figure of either group is known, a reasonable combined estimate of the present population would be somewhere between 2,000,000 to 2,250,000 Greek-born and Greek-descended Americans.

The overwhelming majority of the early Greek immigrants were working class. For example, it has been reported (Fairchild, 1911:3,35; Xenides, 1922:81; Saloutos, 1964) that early Greek immigrants, as a rule, were poor, had limited education and skills, came primarily from agricultural communities, and consisted of young males. Included in this group was a small number of Greek schoolteachers, priests, journalists, and other professionals who became the apostles of ideals and values of Greek culture and society. Like most southern European immigrants, particularly Italians, early Greek immigrants did not come as families because they did not expect to stay in America.

Despite their working-class and rural origins, the early Greek immigrants had a middle-class work ethic. They were industrious, independent, and frugal. They had a sense of determination and cultural pride coupled with a sense of ethnic consciousness and community. Although a substantial number of Greeks came from different parts of Greece, particularly Asia Minor (modern Turkey), in which one million and a half Greeks were uprooted in the 1910s and 1920s, or from the islands, by far the majority of early Greek immigrants to America came from the southern regions of Greece, especially from the peninsula of Peloponnesus, which has a terrain that is more rocky and mountainous than the central and northern parts of Greece. Immigration was and still is looked on as a source of social and economic mobility.

By contrast, the late Greek immigrants were more educated and did not come exclusively from small agricultural communities; many came as families, sponsored by friends and relatives among the early immigrants. Included in this group was a substantial number of students and professionals* who came to America either to practice their profession or pursue an education in American institutions of higher learning.

As a rule, both groups brought with them a life style that was folk oriented, ethnocentric, familistic, and traditional. This provincialism was a carry-over from the village subculture in Greece that was and still is maintained in America. One finds a proliferation of small ethnic associations in America that reflects the values and traditions of agricultural communities and regions in Greece. The functions of these associations were and still continue to be ethnic and benevolent in nature: to maintain

---

*In a study on the 'Greek Brain Drain" this author (1973) found that Greece is among the few countries that lose a considerable number of her talented and professional people annually. For example, in the decade between 1962 and 1971 Greece lost to America alone 4,517 of her professional, technical, and kindred people, or 4.4 per cent of the total professional occupations admitted to America in the same decade were Greek.

the group ideals and raise funds for their respective communities in the homeland. These village subcultures were transplanted to the New World and enabled the immigrant to keep in touch with his home community, find solace and relief from an urban way of life, and facilitate his transition and adjustment to the larger American society.

Unlike the old, northwestern European immigrants who generally settled in small towns and rural areas, most late southeastern European immigrants, including the Greeks, settled in cities in which opportunities for employment and entrepreneurial activities were greater and ethnic communities flourished. These communities became the marketplace in which intra-ethnic, informal, social, cultural, religious, and business transactions took place.

From the very beginning, the early Greek immigrant was ambivalent about his permanent settlement in the New World. His original intention was to amass his fortune and return to his place of birth. Because of indecisiveness, scarcity of Greek women, job insecurity, and the problems of social adjustment and acceptance in the host society, the Greek male was reluctant to commit himself to marriage and to raising a family. While he was physically in America, sentimentally and emotionally he was in his land of birth. (This is also somewhat true of the late Greek immigrants.) Although a substantial number of early Greek immigrants (over 120,000) returned to Greece, the vast majority remained in America. Only when the Greek male felt reasonably secure in his job or business did he decide to settle down, get married, and have a family. Then he found it difficult to return to his native country. In fact, for many immigrants marriage was the turning point that not only provided them with a feeling of permanence but made it more difficult, if not unthinkable, for them to return to Greece (Saloutos, 1964:85).

During the late immigration, feelings of xenophobia, properly cultivated by a prejudiced press and group vested interests, raised questions of contamination of the Anglo-Saxon cultural superiority by the so-called unassimilated and inferior stocks of southeastern European immigrants. Indeed, in 1924 Congress enacted a discriminatory law according to which a quota system based on the 1870 U.S. Census limited sharply the number of southeastern Europeans entering America. The act, which was the official U.S. Immigration and Naturalization policy until 1965, conspicuously favored immigrants from countries of northwestern Europe (Simpson and Yinger, 1972:121). Thus, like other late ethnic groups, Greeks encountered problems of social discrimination. Omaha and Salt Lake City were just two extreme examples in which riots and strikes occurred in which some immigrants, including Greeks, were killed (Saloutos, 1964; Papanikolas, 1970). However, the tough beginnings, coupled with problems of adjustment and ethnic prejudice, galvanized their characters and made them more determined to master and overcome their lowly social and economic origins.

Despite considerable variation between the early and late Greek immigrants and between generations, it has been maintained by a number of students of Greek culture (Tsakonas, 1967; Sanders, 1962; Capanidou Lauquier, 1961) that family and religion seem to be the two social institutions largely responsible for preserving the traditions, values, and ideals of modern Greek culture among the Greeks of the diaspora. For the Greek immigrant, as for other late immigrant groups, religion and family became the differentiating ethnic institutions that set them apart from the early northwestern European immigrant groups.

Moreover, despite the importance of religion and family to the Greek immigrants, these very institutions were challenged by the Greek American younger generations and the larger American society. Ideally, every Greek ethnic community in America was a spiritual community. A Greek church signified the existence of an ethnic colony and that every Greek was potentially a member of his church. To this effect, "the admonition of Athenagoras—Archbishop of the Greek Orthodox Church in the Americas in the 1930s and later the Patriarch of Constantinople—that the Greeks of America should unite around the Church" was clear in the 1920s (Greek Orthodox Archdiocese of North and South America, 1972:12).

In reality, however, and despite a considerable number of Greek Orthodox churches in America (about 425), only a small sustaining number of dues-paying members are actively interested in church affairs. Furthermore, while Greek communities and churches were established early in the present century, 1922 marks the beginning of organized ecclesiastical life of the Greek Orthodox Archdiocese of the Americas. The average Greek, both in Greece proper and in America, does not perceive his church and/or religion in institutional/organizational terms. A parish priest is closer to the Greek immigrant than the hierarchical structure of the church. A Greek church is a personalized extended family system of relationships interwoven with such events of the life cycle as births, baptisms, weddings, and religious and national holidays.

During the 1920s the church, following the political development in Greece proper, was divided along two political lines, the Royalists (supporters of constitutional monarchy) and the Republicans/Liberals (supporters of a Greek Republic; Saloutos, 1964). Although this cleavage is no longer present in the church, it has nevertheless been replaced by

171

cleavages along generational lines (first versus second, early versus late immigrants), social class, and what Gordon call "ethclass"* subcultures (self-employed versus employed, educated versus uneducated, professionals versus small businessmen), and those divided along Greekness (language) versus orthodox (religion) forms of cultural and ethnic identification. While divisions exist along the lines mentioned above, one can detect a basic unity within diversity.

When the Greek Orthodox Church was formally organized, a group of early Greek immigrants met in Atlanta, Georgia (1922), and established the American Hellenic Educational Progressive Association (AHEPA). Its original purpose was to combat ethnic prejudice and discrimination; later, its scope was broadened to include educational, social, political, cultural, and benevolent activities. It endorsed a policy of "Americanization" and urged all its members to become American citizens. Although AHEPA is a secular organization, it maintains close ties with the Greek Orthodox Church in America and has become the formal linkage between the Greek and the larger American communities. Despite a proliferation of Greek American federations and organizations (over 60 in America alone), AHEPA is by far the largest Greek American organization, with an estimated membership of between 28,000 to 30,000 members in America and with chapters in Canada and Australia, in which large Greek colonies have been established following the mass migration after World War II.

Needless to say, Greeks established other ethnic institutions, schools, and ethnic professional societies. It is sufficient to mention the most important—the ethnic mass media (over 100 ethnic radio and TV stations, newspapers, and magazines in both Canada and America) and the Greek Orthodox parochial school system (over 20 Greek American daily elementary schools; Greek Orthodox Archidocese of North and South America, 1972). Usually most of these ethnic institutions are managed by late Greek immigrants and patronized by those who are active in the church affairs and/or other ethnic organizations. The ethnic press is often the spokesman of the businessmen, *les nouveaux riches,* and some professionals of the larger Greek American community.

Three types of Greek American communities can be discerned at the present time: a predominantly post-World War II Greek community made up of late Greek immigrants and their families, a mixed Greek American community of early and late Greek immigrants and their

---

*By "ethclass" Gordon (1964) meant that primary-group relationships tend to be generated within one's social-class segment of one's ethnic group or the intersection between ethnicity and behavioral-class similarities.

progenies, and a Greek American community made up of second- and third-generation American-born Greeks. The first two are by and large ethnic urban communities. Their members are characterized by working- and lower-middle-class life styles, with a substantial number engaged in small service-oriented establishments, particularly restaurants, taverns, and groceries, and low white-collar occupations, especially among second-generation Greeks. As a rule, they reside in close proximity to their churches. The third type, which is increasingly a suburban Greek American community, is characterized primarily by middle- and upper-class life styles, or they are professionals and businessmen. The latter increasingly follow the patterns and life styles of the tripartite Catholic, Protestant, and Jewish suburban ethnoreligious groups. Although most Greek churches are bilingual, in the third type Greek is gradually but steadily being replaced by English, and the priests are exclusively recruited from the second-generation American-born Greeks. In the last analysis, language has become the differentiating issue between first and second generation.

THE MODERN GREEK-AMERICAN FAMILY

First-Generation Greek Family

Although the first-generation Greek family includes both the early (1900–1920s) and late Greek immigrants (1950s to date), in this chapter only the former will be discussed. In analyzing the life styles of the first-generation Greek family, one should keep in mind the sociocultural and economic antecedents in Greece proper and those in America at the time of early Greek immigration.*

---

*Similarly, when one refers to the late first-generation Greek-family life styles, one must consider the changes both in Greece proper and those in America at the time of late and present Greek immigration. On the contemporary Athenian urban family, for example, see studies by Safilios-Rothschild, whose empirical investigations are both methodologically and theoretically grounded. Her repertoire of topics is extensive and includes among others research on fertility and marital satisfaction; social class and family; deviance and mental illness; morality, courtship, and love in Greek folklore; and sex roles. Also, see the study by Vassiliou and Vassiliou (1966) on social attitudes, stereotypes, and mental health in the Greek family.

On the rural and semiurban Greek family, see studies by Lambiri/Dimaki on dowry and the "Impact of Industrial Employment on the Position of Women in a Greek Country Town," *Also*, a study by Friedl (1967) on dowry, kinship and the "Position of Women in Rural Greece." In addition, Bardis, Campbell, and Sanders have also written on various aspects of the rural Greek family.

Coming from agricultural communities in which a large and extended kinship family system was more conducive to an agrarian economy, one would expect that the first-generation family in America would follow patterns similar to those in Greece. However, this author contends that this was not normally the case. There are many reasons for this. First, the socioeconomic conditions of the immigrants and the problems of adjustment and hardships they encountered particularly in the formative years of their settlement in America did not allow them to replicate the Greek village patterns of large households. Second, the presence of many siblings in the immigrants' family of orientation in Greece forced them to migrate originally. Immigrants wanted to see their children succeed and projected their own unfulfilled aspirations to them. Third, the immigrants had many obligations and promises to fulfill in their home communities such as to provide for their sisters' or nieces' dowries.* (Indeed, many never married for this reason.) Finally, the immigrants had to support their own families in America.

A kinship system and extended family relationships similar to that of Greece was not possible in America, although it was maintained indirectly through "nostalgic" memories, exchange of photographs, letters, and holiday cards, and above all by remittances sent by the immigrants to relatives in Greece. Moreover, an extended system of relationships was developed in America based primarily on spiritual kinship.†

As noted above, early Greeks did not come as families but primarily as young males. The scarcity of first-generation women, for example, forced a substantial number of Greek males to marry non-Greek women (Mistaras, 1950). However, the more tradition bound the Greek male

---

*The dowry system is an extension of the arranged type of marriage whereby the bride's family has to provide their future son-in-law a negotiated amount of cash or property in exchange for marrying their daughter. The dowry system is part of the economic and stratification systems in general in which marriage becomes a vehicle of class mobility or immobility for the parties concerned and favors the higher socioeconomic classes. For example, the higher the socioeconomic class or social origins of the groom, the greater the amount of expected dowry. The dowry system has brought tragedy to many poor families in Greece, particularly those with large numbers of girls. In recent years, however, this practice has been challenged, and it is not followed as widely as it used to be in the past, particularly in cities if both of the future spouses are working and are educated. While in America the institutionalized form of dowry as practiced in Greece was discontinued among the Greeks, nevertheless vestiges of this practice continues to exist in more informal ways in terms of gifts and elaborate wedding ceremonies by the bride's parents.

†Spiritual kinship refers to those relationships not ordinarily based on blood relationships; rather, they are derived as a consequence of marriage or contractual-type relationships. For example, in Greece proper the following terms are used: *koumbaros* (wedding sponsor), *nounos* (godfather), *sympetheros* (affines by marriage of one's siblings), *pajanakis* (two or more individuals marrying different sisters). These relationships become meaningful only within the context of Orthodox religious matrimony.

was, the more strongly he felt the need for a mate of his own nationality and religion. In this instance, many of the early Greek males journeyed to Greece in search of a bride. Some had prospective brides arranged and vouched for by relatives and friends waiting for them in Greece or simply had arranged a marriage through an exchange of photographs (Saloutos, 1964:85). The arranged type of marriage should be understood in the context of the Greek kinship system in which mate selection was an affair that goes beyond the immediate parties concerned. It was also a matter of economics, for many early Greek male immigrants could not afford to travel to Greece searching for a bride. Furthermore, many of the prospective grooms knew the girl's family prior to coming to America.

Another important dimension of family organization involves the structural sex-role differences and decision-making processes traditionally vested in different family statuses and occupied by different members of the immediate family. Thus, one can speak of father versus mother, male versus female, husband versus wife relationships. The majority of fiction and nonfiction writers (Bardis, 1955 and 1956; Safilios-Rothschild, 1967; Vlachos, 1968; Saloutos, 1964; Petrakis, 1966; Chamales, 1959; Stephanides, 1972; Koty, 1958; Lambiri-Dimaki, 1965; Capanidou Lauquier, 1961) have suggested that the early Greek family both in America and Greece was a male-dominated, patriarchal, and close-knit social unit. In most of these writings the Greek father is portrayed as an imposing figure whose authority over the rest of the family members, particularly the wife, was absolute. The Greek wife was depicted as a submissive and powerless creature whose major role was homemaking and catering to the rest of the family. This imagery of the Greek family authority and sex-role relationships was a carry-over from Greece, and it was not always replicated in America.

That there is an "ideal" and "real" dimension culturally and socially prescribed for every sex role and family member is well documented. However, one finds the tendency among students of the sociology of the family to describe normative/ideal patterns of sex-role differentiation as empirical/real facts. With the exception of some studies conducted by Safilios-Rothschild and those conducted by Friedl (1967) and Campbell (1964) in Greece proper, no systematic studies have been conducted on the sex-role differentiation and authority relationships in the Greek family at the level of role performance.

A more realistic analysis of role differentiation in the Greek family would entail a network of role complementarity rather than strict differentiation on the basis of widely held beliefs of male-dominated (in-

175

strumental) versus female-subordinate (expressive) roles. In other words, in most cases a Greek husband/father could assume both expressive and instrumental roles simultaneously whenever the primary group (family) interests were served and family contingencies demanded it.

Ideally, the father was the head and authority figure of the family unit, and he expected respect and cooperation from his wife and his children. In reality, however, his authority was contingent upon his ability to prove himself and be a good provider for his family, a compassionate husband, and an understanding father. Masculinity alone, based on arbitrary exercise of authority without considerations of fairness, family unity, and common good, could not sustain the first-generation immigrant family. The Greek father was as compassionate and good-natured as the Greek mother, particularly in times of adversity and life crises. While he was primarily a provider for the entire family and had to work incredibly long hours outside the home, he helped whenever he could in the household chores, in discipline, and socialization of his children.

The discrepancy between the "ideal" and "real" aspects of husband-wife and mother-father roles in also evident if one examines what Friedl (1967) and Campbell (1964) refer to as the "public" versus "private" domains of behavior in the rural family in Greece. In the public/social sphere, both husbands and wives put on a façade and behave according to the prevailing societal cultural norms. These norms depict Greek husbands/fathers as if they were the true masters and dominant figures within the family unit. The wives/mothers, on the other hand, are expected to behave in a modest and submissive manner, particularly in public places when their husbands are present. However, in a more private, *gemeinschaft* family setting husbands/fathers and wives/mothers change considerably and behave more naturally. What seems to the outsider the unequivocal dominance exercised by the husband over his wife is in reality not so in more informal family settings.

To an immigrant husband who left his parents at a young age, his wife was more than the sociological sex-role partner. She was the wife, the adviser, the partner, companion, and the homemaker. She also assisted her husband in his business and the family decision making. Wives/mothers usually exercised their influence in the family decision making indirectly through the processes of socialization of the children because the Greek father had to work incredibly long hours away from the home. Children were attached to the mother, not the father, particularly in the formative years of immigrant life. Later it was the wife/mother who had to approve or disapprove of her daughter's marriage, and then she would convince her husband. Furthermore, it has been reported by Tavuchis

(1968:150) that among his "respondents and a large unknown proportion of second-generation Greek-Americans, the father emerges as a shadowy, distant figure throughout childhood and adolescence but his sociological presence was always felt . . ." In addition, the relatively higher status and freedom enjoyed by the American women vis-à-vis Greek women in Greece benefited the Greek women more than the Greek men in America.

Perhaps one of the most important functions of the Greek family is procreation. A family without the presence of children was, and still is, thought to be incomplete. It is not by accident that the formal ideology of the Greek Orthodox Church (and other religions for that matter) encourages procreation within a marital context. The birth of a child is not only an affair of the family but of the church as well. Motherhood is highly esteemed in the Greek Orthodox religion. Those couples who have children are looked upon by the church as fortunate and blessed.

Ideally, first-generation Greek parents worked and strived to give their children happiness, love, and material comforts. Parents regulated and guided their children's behavior to a certain point. In return, children were expected to respect their parents, develop a sense of responsibility and self-reliance, and become a credit to their family unit and the larger ethnic and American communities. Like their immigrant parents, the children had a minimum of leisure time. They were exposed to the vicissitudes of life at a tender age and were socialized to postpone their immediate gratifications for a future goal. For a majority of the Greek parents that goal was to see their children happily married, maintain certain ethnic traditions, and move up the social scale through the avenue of education, business, and commerce outside the Greek ethnic community.

It has been reported (Stephanides, 1972; Tavuchis, 1968) that first-generation Greek parents tended to overprotect their children even to the extent of wanting to find marriage partners for them. This should be interpreted in the context of the traditional ideal norms of a family and kinship system. Parents underwent personal sacrifices for their children and therefore had placed high expectations and demands on the part of their children even after they reached maturity.

In general, the Greek immigrant family was adult rather than child centered. The child had to learn to respect his parents and the elderly. It has also been reported (Vlachos, 1968; Capanidou Lauquier, 1964) that there was a differential preference for boys over girls in the immigrant family. This pattern is still true to some extent in Greece because of the institution of dowry. One can argue that this preferential treatment is not

177

as pronounced in America for the following reasons: (1) There is no dowry system; (2) girls incorporated the Greek traditional norms and ideals more readily than boys; (3) girls were more attached to their parents, particularly to the mother; and (4) above all it was the daughter, not the son, who would look after her elderly parents even after she was married.

Second-Generation Greek Family

The second-generation Greek family is that social unit in which both parents are American born of Greek extraction or mixed parenthood. As in other ethnic groups, the second-generation Greek family is a transitional-type family. Children were born and raised in two social worlds. One was particularistic, with an ethnic subculture made up of the Greek immigrant parents and relatives, immigrant priests and schoolteachers, and Greek peers. These agents of socialization shared similar experiences and attempted to socialize the children to traditional norms and values of the Greek subculture. The other was a more universalistic world (American) made up of public schools, non-Greek peers and friends, and institutional norms and values of the majority society and culture. The second generation emerged as a product of a Greek subculture and an American culture; a sociocultural hybrid with a dual identity of Greek American. Despite the fact that "Hellenism" and "Americanism" are basically compatible with each other, the latter exerted a greater impact on second-generation Greeks.

In many respects, members of the second generation shared similar experiences and life styles with their immigrant parents throughout their formative and adolescent years. However, pressures from within and from outside the family unit made them somewhat ambivalent and marginal. They were torn between two ways of life. The emphasis on family ties, the Greek language, and the Greek church shaped their attitudes and behavior (Saloutos, 1964:311). These early attitudes and behaviors changed, however, as the children came of age, went to public schools, began to work, moved away from the original settlement, were married, and started a family.

Three types of family life styles seem to be prevalent in second generation Greeks (Vlachos, 1968:150–51). From a somewhat different perspective these family life styles appear to be phases along a continuum of assimilation/acculturation. One type represents a complete abandonment of the traditional Greek way of life. A substantial number in this group Anglicized their names and moved away from the Greek

178

colony, some changed their religion, and many minimized their interaction with their foreign-born parents and relatives. This group was more concerned with social status and acceptability by their peers and other Americans rather than maintaining their Greek nationality and incorporating the ideals and norms of Hellenism as perceived and represented by their parents and relatives in America. Their intent was to assimilate into the values and norms of American culture as soon as possible. In many respects this type of second-generation family passes for an American family, and it was rather atypical.

A second type of the second-generation Greek family is one of "cultural atavism," an inward retrogressive orientation and identification with what are perceived to be, by second-generation Greeks, ethnic Greek life styles. Ideally, this type of family is economically, culturally, socially, and psychologically tied up with the Greek community and its ethnic institutions.

A third type of second generation Greek family is one of marginality at the structural, cultural, and social-psychological levels. Norms and values are of a "hybrid" nature. Social interaction and networks of social relationships are neither genuinely American nor Greek. The family is likely to move out of the original settlement, and its members are less likely to engage in primary-group interaction with members of the first-generation Greeks outside the immediate intergenerational kinship group. In most instances, this type of family finds some midpoint of accommodation between the two worlds by taking what its members perceive to be the best of the two life styles. This type appears to be more representative of the majority of the second-generation Greek families, a contention supported by the existing literature on the second-generation Greek Americans.

Saloutos (1964:378) alludes primarily to the coming of age of second-generation Greeks. He praises their contemporary professional, commercial, and intellectual prominence, which he characterizes as "impressive" and as the beginning of an "era of respectability" for the Greeks. He describes them as follows: "The emergence of a new generation to positions of influence who have carved successful niches in the business and professional world; they are on the way to a new status in American society. The immigrants of yesteryear had established sobriety, industry, and integrity," Although an idealized picture of the second generation Greeks who in many ways share similar experiences and styles of life with their parents, the former, nonetheless, adopted only those Greek life styles that seemed to them compatible with American life styles in general.

As in other ethnic groups, second-generation Greeks had certain family advantages over the first generation. First, they did not have to start from scratch as did their parents. Second, they grew up in a fairly close knit Greek family in which rudiments of Greek ethnic sub-culture were transmitted to them, particularly those pertaining to court-ship, marriage, language, religion, and respect for mother, father, and the elderly. Third, the values of aspiration, hard work, the Greek *philotimo,* and family honor were implanted in them by their parents. Achievement and success were a pride and credit not only to their immediate families and kin but also to the entire Greek community. It is within this frame of reference that the organization of the second-generation Greek family emerged in America. With the exception of the first, these advantages may not distinguish the two generations, but it contributed to the mobility of the second generation.

A number of writers (Saloutos, 1964; Sanders, 1962 and 1967; Friedl, 1962; Vlachos, 1968) have reported that Greeks traditionally display a high degree of family cohesion and extended kinship relationships within and across generational lines. More recently, it has also been reported (Rosen, 1959; Handlin and Handlin, 1956; Kourvetaris, 1971a and b; Tavuchis, 1972; Chock, 1969) that this intergenerational kinship system is coupled with a strong ideological commitment to social mobility and achievement in the American social structure. Tavuchis (1972), in his study of 50 second-generation male family heads, found an elaborate system of kinship and ethnic ties coupled with strong intergenerational patterns of vertical class mobility.

Unlike other social scientists, particularly family sociologists who have lamented the weakening of kinship bonds and the demise of family as a viable institution, Tavuchis found no evidence of such trends among the second-generation Greek family. In fact Tavunhis (1968:296–97) argues that the stronger the kinship ties the more highly mobile its members were found to be. In his words: "Differential class mobility was not found to be a detriment to close ties with parents, siblings, and affines . . ." Tavuchis (1972:296–97) mentions five mechanisms that in his judgment prevented potential strains: a strong commitment to kinship values, a close propinquity to relatives, extraclass criteria of ranking, identification with successful kinsmen, and gross status differences neutralizing invidious distinctions.

Although Tavuchis' finding is not unique among Greek Americans (Jewish Americans display similar patterns), it is somewhat contrary to the prevailing notion among sociologists who believe that extended kin-

180

ship relationships are a detriment to intergenerational social mobility (e.g., the Mexican Americans).

Three trends of authority relations seem to be prevalent in the emerging literature on the second-generation Greek family: (1) the "quasi-patriarchal" model or a trend toward lessening the patriarchal orientation in which ultimate authority in decision making no longer is exercised by the father (Tavuchis, 1972:11); (2) the "equalitarian" model in which the father shares his status and authority with his wife (Capanidou Lauquier, 1961:225); and (3) the "patriarchal" model (Vlachos, 1968: 162) in which the father is still the ultimate authority with final responsibility for providing for his family and for the discipline of his children, partly because that is a father's duty and partly because he is a man and men are economic providers (Chock, 1969:38).

Yet all these authors accept attitudinal/normative statements from their subjects as empirical facts. Perhaps a more realistic perspective of authority relations of the second-generation Greek family would be a tendency toward a "model of convergence," with a greater propensity toward a middle/upper-middle-class family model, depending on the particular family issue and/or contingency. As a rule, members of the second-generation Greeks believe in small families and claim to practice responsible parenthood. In most instances, however, the decision to have children is commensurate to the socioeconomic position of the couple concerned. To accomplish this goal, most second-generation couples favor contraception but not abortion.

Sex roles of the siblings are also viewed in normative terms by most writers and not in actual role performances. For example, the traditional Greek cultural norms and ideals of filial piety and respect for one's parents and the elderly persist in the second-generation Greek family. Unlike the first generation, the father is not perceived as a fearful and distant person, but the father-son relationship is one of mutual understanding and respect (Tavuchis, 1972; Chock, 1969; Capanidou Lauquier, 1961). According to Chock, "Greek children are expected to love their parents, to respect them and to assume some care for them if they need it in their old age. . . ." Ideally, this is expected of all children in most families, but to what extent this is true cannot readily be ascertained. Likewise, girls seem to be closer to their parents, particularly their mothers, but this is not unique to the Greek families.

Second-generation couples do not approve of co-residence with parents and in-laws but, on the other hand, are against their placement in institutions or homes for the aged (Tavuchis, 1972:107–108). In reality, a

181

substantial number of first-generation parents are found in institutions for the aged. There is a pride in the immigrant family, particularly the father, not to live with his children or son-in-law.

In brief, both parents share in the responsibility for the care, education, and well-being of their children. They believe in planned and responsible parenthood. However, parents also tend to spoil and overindulge their children as a compensation for what they as children were deprived of. Mothers, moreover, claim to have ambitions and high aspirations for their children, but it has not been determined to what extent these expectations are realized. As a rule, the father works and provides for his family, and the mother is responsible for the household and the children. As is true in other religions, Greek women are inclined to take a greater interest in Greek Orthodox religion than men and are more responsible for their children's religious education and training. As in Greece, there is the tendency for second-generation males to receive more education than females, in part because the female was often trained for the role of housewife. In recent years, however, these traditional family and sex roles, culturally and socially prescribed, have been drastically changed; even in Greece, for example, occupational options for women are almost analogous to those of men (Safilios-Rothschild, 1971–72).

Third-Generation Greek Family

The third-generation family consists of grandchildren of the first generation or the children of the second-generation Greek family in America. This group also includes the offspring of intermarriages of second-generation Greek American couples. This is a young, emerging family life style, and most members of that generation are of college age or young adulthood. By the third generation, there is a significant decrease in ethnic identification (as measured by language and Greek family norms); but some vestiges of ethnic social behavior remain, particularly those pertaining to politics (Humphrey and Brock, 1972) and Dionysian aspects of modern Greek culture (Kourvetaris, 1971c).

As a rule, members of the third generation have incorporated the values, attitudes, and norms of the American middle- and upper-middle-class subcultures. Social class is more important to them than ethnicity and religion. Despite the lack of empirical studies, both education and professional achievement seem to be highly valued among members of the third generation. In an empirical and comparative study of six ethnic groups, it was found (Rosen, 1959:47–60) that a high level of aspiration and achievement exists among members of third-generation Greeks. The author argued that the cultures of white Protestants, Jews, and Greeks stand out as being more individualistic, activistic, and future oriented than Italians, Blacks, and French Canadians.

Unlike the first and second generations, members of the third generation are not preoccupied with ethnic prejudice and discrimination. Viewed in this way, they can afford to be proud of their ancestry. However, they consider themselves primarily American and only symbolically manifest an interest in and liking for Greek food, music, and dancing. This Dionysian cultural atavism in things Greek was stimulated by the new influx of Greek immigrants following World War II and the popular movies *Zorba the Greek* and *Never on Sunday*, whose theme song became a worldwide favorite. Furthermore, such national and international developments as the military takeover of Greece in 1967, the marriage of Jacqueline Kennedy to Aristotle Onassis, the Nixon-Agnew ticket in 1968 and 1972, the resurgence of ethnic studies and programs, and summer excursions to Greece have further awakened their interest in modern Greek ethnicity and culture. However, one finds little or no interest among members of the third generation in maintaining the ethnic institutional aspects of Greek culture such as language, family traditions, and endogamous marriage (Kourvetaris, 1971c).

It has been argued by some Greek American writers that the new influx of Greeks following World War II would retard the Americanization and assimilation processes of the third generation. However, American-born Greeks (even new Greeks who have been in America for a longer period of time) do not usually associate with the newcomers. This is especially true in the patterns of dating and marriage. For example, in dating patterns on college campuses there is a tendency for members of ethnic groups to seek dates outside their ethnic group. This is primarily because dating outside of one's group does not have a constraining influence on them. It is also a matter of availability of both sexes of the same ethnic group in a college population. In general, the more ethnically oriented the Greek man or woman, the greater the tendency to date someone with similar ethnic background. Furthermore, the more assimilated the Greek, the less likely he is to place importance on dating Greek girls. This is also true in terms of ethnic endogamous patterns of marriage, religion, learning Greek, and the like.

As a rule, members of the third-generation Greek Americans think and act primarily like Americans and expect to be treated as such. Whereas the majority of the second generation learned Greek in order to communicate with immigrant parents, the third generation does not have to learn Greek to communicate with their parents. In fact, most third-generation children resent learning or attending Greek classes sponsored by the church.

If ethnicity (nationality) is the single most important characteristic in the first generation and religion in the second generation, it appears that social class is characteristic of the third generation (Kourvetaris, 1971a and b). Thus, the oncoming of the third generation is followed by a concomitant decline of ethnoreligious factors and the increase in importance of social class as factors in marriage. However, those who maintain their ethnic (nationality/religiosity) identification tend to date and marry within their class segment of their ethnic group (ethclass).

While intermarriage in the first and second generations was looked upon as atypical behavior by the Greek community, in the third generation it is accepted. Unlike the first and second generations, members of the third generation do not seem to be preoccupied with problems of social acceptance by their American peers. In this respect, the latter perceive themselves as American and identify as such with their peers and other Americans. As a rule, this generation is a college- and profession-oriented generation. It is a status-conscious rather than ethnic-conscious generation (Kourvetaris, 1971c).

By the third generation, there is a diminishing role of the Greek American family compared to the first-generation Greek family as an agent of social control and socialization. Life styles and family patterns can best be described as similar with those of the larger American middle-class family system. The third-generation family like the larger American middle-class family is a small nuclear family with an average of two or three children (Vlachos, 1968:162; Capanidou Lauquier, 1961:225). It is basically a family of orientation with no relatives living in the same household; nor is it an extended kinship system.

Family-authority relations tend to follow the larger American middle-class patterns of equalitarian and individualistic orientation (Vlachos, 1968:151). Both wife and children share in the father's status and authority (Vlachos, 1968; Capanidou Lauquier, 1961:225). There is discussion of family issues and joint decision making. There is love with elements of respect, but the father is not obligated to provide for his parents. "The eldest son is nearly equal in position to the father and need not contribute to the family income" (Capanidou Lauquier, 1961:226).

However, those who were raised within a Greek and Greek-American tradition and environment encourage their children to associate with children from Greek American families of similar socioeconomic status. However, as a rule, parents do not interfere with their children or inist that they marry endogamously.

CHANGE AND ADAPTATION

The movement from the early first-generation Greek family life styles to those of the third generation is accompanied by an attenuation of the Old World family ideals and norms (as exemplified in the first-generation Greek family) to those more consonant with the American middle-class family life styles (as exemplified in the third-generation Greek family in America). "Greekness" (nationality) as a form of ethnic identification in the first generation gives way to the "orthodoxy" (religion) iñ the second generation, which in turn gives way to "class" life styles (behavioral identification). The "Greekness" of the first generation is transformed to the philhellenism (friend of Greece) by members of the third generation. This generational transformation might be genuinely conceptualized as following more or less four processes and/or phases of acculturation initially suggested by Park (1950): the *initial* contact phase, the *conflict* phase, the *accommodation* phase, and the *assimilation* phase.

The Initial Contact Phase

In the first decade of Greek immigrant life in America, the organization of the Old World family was still fairly well intact. Due to pressures from within and outside the family structure, the Old World ideal was challenged. Some of the most salient factors were the following: the physical/ecological separation from the parental and kinship system and village subculture in general; the necessity of physical survival and social-psychological adjustment of the immigrant to a different sociocultural and urban ecological environment; the separation of work and residence and the necessity of the housewife and other members of the family to seek employment outside the house; the exposure of the immigrant's children to the life styles of the American community and public schools, which in many ways meant ethnic prejudice and discrimination against those ethnic groups and families that were culturally different from the Anglo-Saxon group. All these made the first-generation immigrant family extremely ethnocentric and highly cohesive

185

as in the Old World. In this phase of initial contact the immigrant family was socially and culturally insulated in the Greek colony and did not seriously feel the pressures of American society. Despite its many problems the first-generation Greek family was stabilized by its strong desire to return to Greece. However, this initial phase gave way to both the conflict and accommodation phases with the coming of the second generation.

The Conflict Phase

With the oncoming of the second generation, the highly ethnocentric, traditional, and folk-oriented outlook of the first-generation subculture was challenged. Although culture conflict between parents and children was not inevitable, in many instances it did take place. Out of this generational conflict two major types of first-generation Greeks emerged, the cultural traditionalists and the social assimilationists.

The cultural traditionalists were faced with major difficulties in carrying out their intent to socialize their children in the Greek ways of life. These difficulties and their fear of losing control over their children were intensified when the children came into contact with the larger American society, particularly when they entered public schools, began working, dating, and came of marital age. This exaggerated fear by the Greek immigrant of losing control over his children was further aggravated by the Greek Orthodox Church and the family kinfolk. Furthermore, it stemmed from the inability of the immigrant himself to adjust more readily to the nonmaterial and subtler aspects of American culture and thus be able to understand his children. The cultural traditionalists attempted to rear their American-born children as though they were Greeks. This group proved unyielding and was usually found in cities with large Greek colonies. They insisted on preserving their ethnic institutions, particularly those pertaining to religion, language, endogamous marriage, and a close-knit family. They attempted to convince their children of the mystique of the Greek ancestry, warned them against the dangers of intermarriage, and made an effort to instill in them a sense of ethnic consciousness and peoplehood.

The social assimilationsts (known also as environmentalists), on the other hand, believed that their children must grow up as Americans but wanted them to retain membership in the Greek Orthodox Church, maintain a Greek name, and learn some Greek (Saloutos, 1964:312). This group felt that the assimilation process could not be stopped but only temporarily delayed. They were more realistic, experienced less

186

conflict with their children, and were more aware that powerful social and cultural forces operate in the American social structure and culture that exert an unprecedented influence on their children toward Anglo conformity and Americanization.

This phase began roughly during the second decade of first-generation family living in America, especially when the first-generation immigrant family abandoned its intent to return to Greece. It was during this period that both the organizational structure of the Orthodox Church and by far the largest ethnic association—AHEPA—launched an all-out effort to organize the Greeks in America, facilitate the transition and Americanization processes, and maintain the ethnic institutions of church and family, which in many ways became complementary to each other. The second-generation family was able to maintain its ethnic identification through the Greek church. Nationality gradually was giving way to religion, particularly during the 1920s when Greeks, along with other southern and eastern European immigrants, were targets of prejudice and discrimination. Second generation Greeks were discovering that to be of Greek ancestry did not particularly indicate high social status. This phase gave way to a new realization and intergenerational relationship.

Accommodation

This phase is marked by a *modus operandi* between first- and second-generation Greek families. An effort was made to broaden the base for continued and meaningful interaction between the two generations (Tavuchis, 1972). On the one hand, the first generation realized that they had to modify the Old World family life styles for the sake of retaining the affection of their children and maintain the unity of the family. On the other hand, the second generation came to the realization that complete repudiation of the parents' way of life would hurt their parents and leave them isolated. Both generations searched for points of compatability, mutual levels of tolerance, and complementarity of life styles.

This period of accommodation and symbiosis between the two generational family types led to a new stability of the family. Furthermore, this phase was reinforced by the realization on the part of the parents that life in America was to be permanent and the recognition that social and economic status and success can come to their offspring as they become more and more socialized into the "old American" patterns and life styles. An effort was also made on the part of the second generation to resocialize the parent generation to its own life styles and values

187

(Tavuchis, 1972). The dependence of parents on their children as interpreters and informants of the American scene led also to the conscious and unconscious willingness on the part of the parents to sacrifice certain norms and ideals of the Old World family for their own happiness and that of their children. The coming of the third generation around the 1940s gave way to a new phase of generational change.

The Assimilation Phase

By the third generation the Greek family life styles became more symmetrical with those of the larger contemporary American middle-class family. Despite the fact that many third-generation Greek American families retain vestiges of ethnic subcultural life styles, the tendency is toward a model convergent with the contemporary American family. Furthermore, assimilation, a multidimensional process itself, does not have to be complete. Nevertheless, there is no evidence that a resurgence of recent ethnic pride as exhibited most particularly by Blacks, Chicanos, and Puerto Ricans will rekindle the ethnic family patterns of the first-generation (both early and late) Greek family in America. Greek Americans by the third generation no longer live with nostalgic memories and experiences of the preceding generation.

Rates of intermarriage, the authority of the parents and elderly, the peer group, the neighborhood, the occupational patterns, the residential patterns, the language, and the family kinship system have been transformed to those more consonant with the majority American family system. That one may find occasional ethnic life styles within clusters of families in Greek ethnic communities (particularly those pertaining to Greek ethnic food, dance, travel to Greece for doses of Dionysian Greek culture) does not mean that there is a renascence of the more subtle and ideal norms of the Greek family subculture. In Greece the traditional Greek family norms have also become challenged and accordingly modified to correspond with Western European and American notions of modernity, particularly among middle-and upper-class urban Greeks. The postwar Greek immigrants will not retard the ongoing processes of assimilation of the third-generation Greeks. The seemingly "graded scale of ethnicity" is by and large a phenomenon of postwar Greek immigration, which continues but develops along paths similar to those of the early first-generation Greeks in America. There is no evidence that a genuine interaction exists between cohorts of second and third generations and those of late Greek immigrants and their offspring.

The future of the Greek family in America by the third generation will retain membership in the church and some ethnic organizations, provided that both modify and adapt to the needs of the third and subsequent generations. By the third-generation the Greek family life styles are quite similar to those of the larger American middle- and upper-middle-class and suburban family.

REFERENCES

Bardis, Panos. 1955. "The Changing Family in Modern Greece." *Sociology and Social Research* 40 (October):19–23.

————. 1956. "Main Features of the Greek Family During the Early Twentieth Century." *Alpha Kappa Delta* 26 (Winter, November):17–21.

————. 1957. "Influences on the Modern Greek Family." *Social Science* 32 (June):155–58.

Campbell, J. K. 1964. *Honor, Family, and Patronage*. Oxford: Clarendon Press.

Campisi, J. Paul. 1948. "Ethnic Family Patterns: The Italian Family in the United States." *American Journal of Sociology* 53 (May):443–49.

Capanidou Lauquier, H. 1961. "Cultural Change Among Three Generations of Greeks." *American Catholic Review* 22 (Fall):223–32.

Chamales, Tom T. 1959. *Go Naked in the World*. New York: Scribner's.

Chock, P. Phyllis. 1969. "Greek-American Ethnicity." Unpublished. Ph.D. dissertation in the University of Chicago Library, Department of Anthropology.

Cutsumbis, N. Michael. 1970. *A Bibliographic Guide to Materials on Greeks in the United States 1890–1968*. New York: Center for Migration Studies.

Fairchild, H. P. 1911. *Greek Immigration to the United States*. New Haven: Yale University Press.

Friedl, Ernestine. 1962. *Vasilika: A Village in Modern Greece*. New York: Holt, Rinehart and Winston.

————. 1967. "The Position of Women: Appearance and Reality." *Anthropological Quarterly* 40 (July):97–108.

Gordon, Milton. 1964. *Assimilation in American Life: The Role of Race, Religion and National Origin*. New York: Oxford University Press.

Greek Orthodox Archdiocese of North and South America. *Yearbook 1972*. New York: Graphic Arts Laboratory.

Handlin, F. Oscar, and Mary F. Handlin. 1956. "Ethnic Factors in Social Mobility." *Explorations in Entrepreneurial History* 9 (October):4–5.

Humphrey, R. Craig, and Helen T. Brock. 1972. "Assimilation, Ethnicity, and Voting Behavior Among Greek-Americans in a Metropolitan Area." Paper presented at the 1972 Annual Meeting of the Southern Sociological Society, April 5–8, New Orleans, Louisiana.

Koty, John. 1958. "Greece." In Arnold M. Rose (ed.): *The Institutions of Advanced Societies*. Minneapolis: University of Minneosta Press, pp. 330–83.

Kourvetaris, A. George. 1971a. *First and Second Generation Greeks in Chicago*. Athens, Greece: National Center of Social Research.

———. 1971b. "First and Second Generation Greeks in Chicago: An Inquiry Into Their Stratification and Mobility Patterns." *International Review of Sociology* 1 (March):37–47.

———. 1971c. "Patterns of Generational Subculture and Intermarriage of the Greeks in the United States." *International Journal of Sociology of the Family* 1 (May):34–48.

———. 1973. "Brain Drain and International Migration of Scientists: The Case of Greece." The Greek Review of Social Research 15–16 (January–June):2–13.

Lagos, Mary. 1962. "A Greek Family in American Society." Unpublished eight-page transcript, Franklin and Marshall College, Lancaster, Pennsylvania.

Lambiri-Dimaki, Ioanna. 1965. *Social Change in a Greek Country Town*. Athens: Center of Planning and Economic Research.

Mistaras, Evangeline. 1950. "A Study of First and Second Generation Greek Outmarriages in Chicago." Unpublished Master's Thesis in the University of Chicago Library, Department of Sociology.

Papajohn, C. Hohn. "The Relation of Intergenerational Value Orientation Change and Mental Health in An American Ethnic Group." A manuscript in the Florence Heller Graduate School for Advanced Studies in Social Welfare, Brandeis University.

Papanikolas, Z. Helen. 1970. *Toil and Rage in a New Land: The Greek Immigrants in Utah*. Salt Lake City: Utah State Historical Society.

Park, Robert E. 1950. *Race and Culture*. Glencoe, Ill. The Free Press.

Petrakis, Harry. 1966. *A Dream of Kings*. New York: McKay.

Plous, F. K., Jr. 1971. "Chicago's Greeks: Pride, Passion, and the Protestant Ethic." *Midwest Sunday Magazine* of the *Chicago Sun Times* (April 25):22–26.

Rosen, Bernard. 1959. "Race, Ethnicity, and the Achievement Syndrome." *American Sociological Review* 24 (February):47–60.

Safilios-Rothschild, Constantina. 1965. "Morality, Courtship, and Love in Greek Folklore." *Southern Folklore Quarterly* 29 (December):297–308.

———. 1967. "Class Position and Success Stereotypes in Greek and American Cultures." *Social Forces* 45 (March):374–83.

———. 1967. "A Comparison of Power Structure and Marital Satisfaction in Urban Greek and French Families." *Journal of Marriage and the Family* 29 (May):345–52.

———. 1969. "Patterns of Familial Power and Influence." *Sociological Focus* 2 (Spring):7–19.

———. 1969. "Family Sociology or Wives' Family Sociology? A Cross-Cultural Examination of Decision-Making." *Journal of Marriage and the Family* 31 (May):290–301.

———. 1971–72. "The Options of Greek Men and Women." *Sociological Focus* 5 (Winter):71–83.

Saloutos, Theodore. 1956. *They Remember America*. Berkeley: University of California Press.

————. 1964. *The Greeks in the United States*. Cambridge: Harvard University Press.

Sanders, Irwin. 1962. *Rainbow in the Rock: The People of Rural Greece*. Cambridge: Harvard University Press.

————. 1967. "Greek Society in Transition." *Balkan Studies* 8:317–32.

Seder, L. Doris. 1966. "The Influence of Cultural Identification on Family Behavior." A Ph.D. Dissertation in Brandeis University Library, Department of Social Work, Boston, Mass.

Simpson, George, and J. Milton Yinger. 1972. *Racial and Cultural Minorities: An Analysis of Prejudice and Discrimination* (4th ed.) New York: Harper & Row.

Stephanides, C. Marios. 1972. "Educational Background, Personality Characteristics, and Value Attitudes Towards Education and Other Ethnic Groups Among the Greeks in Detroit." A Ph.D. Dissertation in Wayne State University Library, Department of Sociology, Detroit, Michigan.

Stycos, J. M. 1948. "The Spartan Greeks of Bridgetown." *Common Ground* (Winter, Spring, Summer):61–70, 24–34, 72–86.

Tavuchis, Nicholas. 1972. "Family and Mobility Among Greek-Americans." Athens, Greece: National Centre of Social Research.

Tsakonas, Demetrios. 1967. *Koinoniologia Tou Neou-Hellenikou Pnevmatos (Sociology of the New Hellenic Spirit)*. Athens: Ellinka Grammata.

Vassiliou, George and Vasso Vassiliou. "A Transactional Approach to Mental Health." Contribution to the International Research Conference on Evaluation of Community Mental Health Programs of N.I.M.H.

Vlchos, C. Evangelos. 1968. *The Assimilation of Greeks in the United States*. Athens: National Center of Social Research.

————. 1969. *Modern Greek Society: Continuity and Change*. Special Monograph Series No. 1, Department of Sociology and Anthropology, Colorado State University.

Xenides, J. P. 1922. *The Greeks in America*. New York: Doran.

The Puerto Rican Family*

Professor Fitzpatrick, a Roman Catholic priest who has studied Puerto Ricans in America and on the island of Puerto Rico for many years, discusses the Puerto Rican family from the perspective of migration from the island to the mainland. Puerto Ricans are a unique group because of the status of Puerto Rico as a commonwealth. An important implication of this fact is that Puerto Ricans are citizens of America and thus can move to and from the island freely. Because of the movement in both directions Professor Fitzpatrick has found it especially imperative to discuss the family as it is found on the island of Puerto Rico. Its continual and reinforcing influence on Puerto Ricans here on the mainland make it the key to understand the Puerto Rican family in America.

CHAPTER NINE
BY
JOSEPH P. FITZPATRICK

The Puerto Ricans now constitute one of the major minority groups in the Eastern part of America. They come from a small island in the Caribbean, one of the Greater Antilles, about a thousand miles southeast of Florida. Puerto Rico was a Spanish colony from the time of its discovery by Columbus on his second voyage, 1493, until 1898 when it was ceded by Spain to America after the Spanish-American war. The indigenous peoples, now generally called Tainos, disappeared soon after the Spanish conquest either by death, flight, or absorption. The first African slaves in the Western world were brought to Puerto Rico in 1511. As a result the population of Puerto Rico is a mixture of Tainos, Caucasoid Europeans, and Blacks.

Puerto Ricans were granted American citizenship in 1917. In 1948 they were granted the right to elect their own island governor. In 1952, the present political status was approved by the U.S. Congress and inaugurated; this is the constitution of the island known as the *Estado*

---

*Joseph P. Fitzpatrick, PUERTO RICAN AMERICANS: The Meaning of Migration to the Mainland. (c)1971. Reprinted (with minor revision and statistical updating) by permission of Prentice-Hall, Inc., Englewood Cliffs, N.J.

Libre Asociado, the Free Associated State of Puerto Rico, officially identified in English as the Commonwealth of Puerto Rico. Puerto Ricans enjoy most of the rights of American citizens, including that of completely free movement between the island and the American mainland. They do not vote for the President, nor do they have elected representatives in Congress. They pay no federal taxes.

A small colony of Puerto Ricans lived in New York City in the last century, mostly political leaders active in the movement for independence for the island. After 1898 a small but steady migration of Puerto Ricans began. This increased during the 1920s, diminished during the Depression of the 1930s and World War II, and increased to sizable proportions in the late 1940s, which has continued to the present. Many Puerto Ricans now return to the island; the migration is a two-way phenomenon of people migrating from the island to the mainland and others migrating back to the island.

The 1970 Census reported 1,454,000 Puerto Ricans living on the American mainland: 811,000 of these were born in Puerto Rico, 636,000 were born on the mainland of Puerto Rican parentage, 7,000 were born elsewhere. Approximately 60 per cent (872,471) reside in New York State, the great majority in New York City; close to 10 per cent (135,676) live in New Jersey, with sizable numbers in Connecticut, Massachusetts, Pennsylvania, and Ohio.

Puerto Ricans are the ethnic minority with the lowest income of all groups in New York City. As a result, many of them must seek public assistance, a source of income but a source of problems that complicate their lives enormously. As a people, they are a mixture of many colors, from completely Negroid to completely Caucasoid and face the difficult problem of adjusting to racial prejudice. Their children find it difficult to achieve well on the standardized English and math tests in the schools; many drop out before finishing high school. There is a high rate of drug addiction among Puerto Rican youths; and the community faces many complicated problems in the area of health and mental health. Although most are baptized Catholics, it is estimated that less than 30 per cent are in effective contact with any religious group in New York City, Catholic or Protestant. Many of them are attracted to the small, neighborhood Pentecostal sects.

Nevertheless, the Puerto Rican community continues to struggle for stability and development. It now has one elected representative in Congress, two in the New York City Council, one member of the New York State Senate, and two in the State General Assembly. Effective agencies are developing strength and influence: Aspira in the area of education, the Puerto Rican Forum in the area of community affairs, the Puerto Rican Family Institute in social service, the Puerto Rican Merchants Association in commerce, the Association of Home Town Clubs in the area of social and community life, and many others. In their migration and adjustment to New York City, they face the experience of millions of newcomers who preceded them into a city that has been formed by the continued migration of people; they face the conflict and collaboration, the strain and satisfaction, the frustration and achievement, that results from stranger meeting stranger in the most complicated city in the world.

In this experience, the family is the institution that faces the most direct shock of cultural change; it is also the institution that provides the greatest strength for its members in the process of change. Puerto Ricans bring with them a style and structure of family life that has been formed by four centuries of tradition on the island. In order to understand this family as it faces the adjustment to the mainland, the family as it exists on the island must be clearly understood. Many features of the family continue as the context of Puerto Rican life on the mainland. The consequences of cultural transition will be explained after a detailed description of the family in the tradition of Puerto Rico.

HISTORICAL BACKGROUND

Four major influences have contributed to the structure of family life, kinship patterns, and the patterns of family living of the Puerto Ricans:*

---

*The literature on the Puerto Rican family is extensive and uneven. Steward (1957) is one of the best presentations of varied types of Puerto Rican families. Mintz (1960) is a life history that is really a study of family life in a small *barrio* on the southern coast of Puerto Rico in an area in which rates of consensual union have been high. It is probably the finest single book on this kind of Puerto Rican family. Landy (1959) is a study of socialization and life cycle among poor families in a town in the northeast section of the island. It is an excellent study of family life and socialization. Roberts and Stefani (1940) is out of date, but it has detailed descriptions of many family habits and practices that are still common among the poor and rural families of the island. Stycos (1955) was part of a study of attitudes toward birth control but actually presents extensive information about the Puerto Rican family, particularly in attitudes toward marriage, children, and sex. Rogler and Hollingshead (1965) is a study of the causes of schizophrenia in Puerto Rico, but it provides an excellent and detailed analysis of family experience, especially among poor Puerto Ricans. Lewis (1965) is a vivid and detailed picture of the day-to-day experiences of a family with a history of prostitution in a slum area of San Juan. The introduction, which presents a lengthy analysis of what Lewis calls the "culture of poverty," is important as a setting for the rest of the book. Fernandez-Marina (1961) is an analysis of a form of hysteria common among Puerto Ricans, but the analysis involves a study of the changes in the values of Puerto Rican families under the influence of the mainland. Hill (1955) and Stanton (1956) are also studies of family change.

194

(1) The culture of the Borinquen Indians, now generally referred to as the Tainos, the natives on the island when it was discovered; (2) the influence of Spanish colonial culture; (3) slavery; (4) the American influence and economic development.

Very little is known about the culture of the Borinquen Indians. Unlike those in other areas of the Spanish empire, the indigenous people in Puerto Rico seem to have disappeared as an identifiable group early in the history of the colony. Some speculations are available about their culture and family life, but little of it is reliable. New studies are now in progress.

Spanish Colonial Culture

The great influence in the past and present on all levels of Puerto Rican family life was the Spanish colonial culture, the important features of which will now be discussed.

PRE-EMINENCE OF THE FAMILY. As in most cultures of the world, the individual in Latin America has a deep consciousness of his membership in a family. He thinks of his importance in terms of his family membership. This is not a matter of prestige (as in belonging to the Ford or Rockefeller family), but a much more elemental thing, and it is as strong among the families of the very poor as it is among those of the very wealthy. The world to a Latin consists of a pattern of intimate personal relationships, and the basic relationships are those of his family. His confidence, his sense of security and identity, are perceived in his relationship to others who are his family.

This is evident in the use of *names,* the *technonomy* of Puerto Rican and Latin families. The man generally uses two family names together with his given name, for example, José Garcia Rivera. Garcia is the name of José's father's father; Rivera is the family name of José's mother's father. Thus, the name indicates that José comes from the family of Garcia in his father's line and from the family of Rivera in his mother's father's line. In Spanish-speaking areas, if the man is to be addressed by only one family name, the first name is used, not the second. José would be called Mr. Garcia, not Mr. Rivera. The mixing of these names by Americans is a source of constant embarrassment to Spanish-speaking people. The former governor of Puerto Rico, Luis Muñoz Marin was regularly referred to in American publications as Governor Marin. It should have been Governor Muñoz. Referring to Muñoz Marin as Governor Marin would be similar to referring to John Fitzgerald Kennedy as President Fitzgerald.

195

On some formal occasions, Puerto Ricans, like other Spanish-speaking people, will use the names of all four families from which they come. If José were announcing his wedding, or an important official appointment, he might write his name: José Garcia Diaz y Rivera Colon. By this he is telling the world that he comes from the families of Garcia and Diaz on his father's side, and Rivera and Colon on his mother's side. The Puerto Ricans are not as familiar and informal with their public figures as Americans are. They may refer to a person as Don* Luis, Señor Muñoz, Señor Muñoz Marin, or as Muñoz, but they would not refer to him with the equivalent of "Louie" the way Americans refer to Ike and Dick and Jack or Harry. Americans are more sensitive to the importance of the individual—it is Harry who is important, or Ike, or Dick—but Puerto Ricans emphasize the importance of presenting themselves in the framework of the family of which they are a part.

The wife of José writes her name Maria Gonzalez de Garcia. She retains the family name of her father's father, Gonzalez, and she adopts, usually with the *"de,"* the fist name of her husband, Garcia. She may use both his names and present herself as Maria Gonzalez de Garcia Rivera. On formal occasions she may retain both her family names and would then present herself as Maria Gonzalez Medina de Garcia Rivera. The children of José and Maria would be Juan Garcia Gonzalez, the daughter Carmen Garcia Gonzalez; in formal situations, they would be Juan or Carmen Garcia Rivera y Gonzalez Medina.

The family is much more involved in the process of courtship than would be the case with an American family. In America boys and girls mingle freely, date each other, fall in love, and by various means ask each other to marry. If they agree to marry, they will advise their parents. If the parents agree, the marriage proceeds happily; if the parents disagree with the couple, they may go ahead and get married regardless. In Puerto Rico, intermingling and dating is much more restricted. A young man interested in a young woman is expected to speak to the parents of the girl, particularly the father, to declare his intentions. A serious courtship may never get started if the families disapprove. As one Puerto Rican sociologist explained personally to the author: In America courtship is a drama with only two actors; in Puerto Rico, it is a drama of two actors, but the families are continually prompting from the

---

*Don is a title of respect used generally in direct speech toward a man (Doña for a woman). It has no class implication. Very poor and humble people use it of their own family members or friends as a sign of respect. It is generally used with the first name (Don Luis or Doña Maria), never without it (Don Luis Muñoz, perhaps, but never Don Muñoz).

wings. Marriage is still considered much more a union of two families than it would be in America.

Finally, Puerto Ricans have a deep sense of family obligation. One's primary responsibilities are to family and friends. If a person advances in public office or succeeds in business enterprises, he has a strong sense of obligation to use his gains for the benefit of his family. Americans also have a sense of family loyalty, but to a much larger degree, they expect to make it on their own. Success does not make them feel obliged to appoint family members to positions, share their wealth with relatives, or use their position for the benefit of the family. They expect selection in business and government to be on the basis of ability and effort, not personal or family relationships. This is an oversimplication, since family influence operates in America and people in Puerto Rico are increasingly chosen on the basis of ability and effort. But in Puerto Rico the sense of family is much deeper. As economic development proceeds on the island, or as its citizens adjust to American life, the need increases to sacrifice family loyalty and obligation to efficiency. The Puerto Rican finds this a very difficult thing to do.

SUPERIOR AUTHORITY OF THE MAN. A second feature of the Puerto Rican family is the role of superior authority exercised by the man. This is not peculiar to Latin cultures; it is the common situation in most cultures of the world. The man expects to exercise the authority in the family; he feels free to make decisions without consulting his wife; he expects to be obeyed when he gives commands. As a larger middle class emerges in Puerto Rico, the role of the woman is in the process of being redefined. But in contrast to the characteristics of cooperation and companionship of American families, the woman in Puerto Rico has a subordinate role.

This must not be interpreted as meaning that women do not have subtle ways of influencing men. The influence of mother over son is particularly strong in the culture of the Puerto Ricans. Furthermore, women have played an unusually important role in public and academic life. In 1962, of the 76 *municipios* in Puerto Rico, 10 had women as mayors, the most famous being Doña Felisa Rincon de Gautier, who was mayoress of the capital city of San Juan for 20 years. Women are department chairmen of many of the departments of the University of Puerto Rico. Oscar Lewis (1965) found the Puerto Rican women among the families he studied to be much more aggressive, outspoken, and even violent than the women in the Mexican families he had studied.

197

Nevertheless, the role is culturally defined and ordinarily maintained as subordinate to the authority of the husband. Until recently, and still to a surprising extent, women will not make such decisions as consultation of a doctor or sending children for medical treatment without seeking permission of the husband.

The superior position of the man is also reflected in what Americans call a double standard of morality in reference to sexual behavior (Stycos, 1955).* In Latin cultures, as in most cultures of the world, a very clear distinction is made between the "good" woman, who will be protected as a virgin until marriage, and then be protected as a wife and mother, and the "bad" woman, who is available for a man's enjoyment. Puerto Ricans are concerned about their girls, and fathers and brothers feel a strong obligation to protect them. On the other hand, a great deal of freedom is granted to the boys. It is rather expected, sometimes encouraged, that a boy have sexual experiences with women before marriage. After marriage he may feel free to engage in what Puerto Ricans sometimes jokingly refer to as "extracurricular activities." These patterns of protection of the woman and freedom for the man are changing, but they are still quite different from patterns of sexual behavior on the mainland. It is also true that patterns of sexual behavior that are going through a revolution to greater sexual freedom in America involve boys and girls equally and thus draw us even further away from the style of life in Puerto Rico.

COMPADRAZGO. Another consequence of the influence of Spain on the Puerto Rican family has been *compadrazgo,*† or the institution of *compadres*. These are people who are companion parents, as it were, with the natural parents of the child; the man is the *compadre,* the woman is the *comadre*. Sponsors at Baptism, for example, become the godparents *(padrinos)* of the child, and the *compadres* of the child's parents; this is also true of sponsors at Confirmation. Witnesses at a marriage become *compadres* of the married couple. Sometimes common interests or the intensification of friendship may lead men or women to consider themselves *compadres* or *comadres*. The *compadres* are sometimes relatives, but often they are not. They constitute a network of ritual kinship,

---

*See references to *machismo* in Stycos (1955).

†There is some evidence that *compadrazgo* may have existed among the indigenous people. Some traces of it have beeen found among the Mayans. But it definitely was a significant Spanish institution that the colonizers either implanted or reinforced when they arrived.

as serious and important as that of natural kinship, around a person or a group. *Compadres* frequently become more formal in their relationships, shifting from the familiar *"Tu"* to the formal *"Usted"* in speech. They have a deep sense of obligation to each other for economic assistance, support, encouragement, and even personal correction. A *compadre* may feel much freer to give advice or correction in regard to family problems than a brother or sister would. A *compadre* is expected to be responsive to all the needs of his *compadre,* and ideally, he supplies assistance without question. When Sidney Mintz was doing his anthropological study of a *barrio* of Santa Isabel, Puerto Rico, his principal informant was a remarkable man, Taso Zayas, a farm worker who cut sugar cane. Mintz reached a degree of close friendship with Taso and later decided to do his life history. Mintz describes the relationship that had developed between himself and Taso. Taso had reached a point at which he felt free to ask Mintz for money. "In his own words he would not 'dare ask' if he were not sure I would respond; and failure to do so, if it were a matter of free choice would end our friendship" (Mintz, 1960). In other words, Mintz and Taso had become *compadres*.

Slavery

Another influence on family life in Puerto Rico was that of slavery. Slavery was a milder institution in Puerto Rico than in America. But slavery in the Western world has had a devastating effect on family life. Little effort was made to provide for the stability and permanence of the slave family; men and women, relatives, children, were bought, sold, exchanged, and shifted with little or no regard for permanent family union. Slave women were defenseless before the advances of free men.

The usual consequences of slavery in the broken family life of Blacks have been as evident in Puerto Rico as elsewhere. A number of features of Spanish culture modified the effects to some extent. Consorting with a woman who was not one's wife was a practice of upper-class men in the Spanish colonial tradition and was not confined to Black women. Therefore, the extramarital relationships of white men and Black women tended to follow a pattern similar to that of white men with white women. Cultural patterns formed around these relationships that provided some advantages to the women and children involved in them. However, the mother-based family—the family with children of a number of fathers and no permanent male consort—has been a common phenomenon in Puerto Rican history.

America and Economic Development

Within recent years, two other major influences have become important: (1) the influence of America has affected the island through the educational system, which for many years after annexation was in the hands of Americans and conducted on the American model; (2) religious influence from the mainland. Most of the Catholic priests, brothers, and nuns working among Puerto Ricans during the past 50 years have come from America. Protestant denominations have been established on the island since the turn of the century, and Pentecostal sects have preached a strong and effective gospel among the poor. Finally, and most important, Puerto Ricans returning from the mainland either to visit or to stay bring with them a strong and direct influence of mainland culture in relation to the family. The consequences, particularly of this last influence, will be indicated later.

THE MODERN PUERTO RICAN FAMILY

As a consequence of the above influences, a fourfold structural typology can be identified among Puerto Rican families.

1. EXTENDED FAMILY SYSTEMS. These are families in which there are strong bonds and frequent interaction among a wide range of natural or ritual kin. Grandparents, parents, and children may live in the same household, or they may have separate households but visit frequently. The extended family is evident regardless of the type of marriage (regularized or consensual), and it is a source of strength and support. Traditionally, this was by far the most common pattern of family life.
2. THE NUCLEAR FAMILY. With the rise of the middle class, the conjugal unit of father, mother, and children, not living close to relatives and with weak bonds to the extended family, is becoming more common. It is difficult to get reliable evidence on the number of these families, but observant Puerto Ricans are noticing that with migration and upward mobility their number is rapidly increasing. This is an expected response to social and economic development.
3. FATHER, MOTHER, THEIR CHILDREN, AND CHILDREN OF ANOTHER UNION OR UNIONS OF HUSBAND OR WIFE. This is not an uncommon phenomenon among Puerto Rican families. New Yorkers have complained

about the difficulty of understanding the differing names of children in some Puerto Rican households. In places on the island in which this phenomenon is common, children will identify themselves accordingly. If a visitor asks a boy if the girl with him is his sister, he may respond: "Yes, on my father's side," or "Yes, on my mother's side."

4. THE MOTHER-BASED FAMILY, WITH CHILDREN OF ONE OR MORE MEN, BUT WITH NO PERMANENT MALE CONSORT IN THE HOME. According to the 1970 census, 18.5 per cent of families in Puerto Rico were of this type. These four types of family structure are evident among Puerto Ricans on the mainland.

Consensual Unions

Important in relation to family structure is the phenomenon of consensual unions,* which in former years have been common on the island but have been rapidly declining. A consensual union is a relatively stable union of a man and a woman who have gone through a religious or civil marriage ceremony. They begin living together and raising their family, and may live this way throughout their lives. At some later date they may regularize the union in a civil or religious ceremony.

This is not the "common law" marriage, which is an institution in English common law. The Roman law tradition, which has prevailed in Puerto Rico, never recognized a union as a marriage unless it was regularized, but Roman law always acknowledged the situation in which two people would live together without getting married. This state was defined as *concubinatus* or *concubinage*. Concubinage has unfavorable connotations in the English language, but it never had these in the Roman law tradition. Puerto Ricans who live consensually, or in concubinage, refer to themselves as *amancebados,* living together without marriage. The U.S. Census reports consensual unions as a recognized "civil status" and consequently asks perople if they are living consensually. According to the decennial census, of all couples "living together" on the island, the following percentages were reported as "living consensually":

---

*The phenomenon of consensual union is widely discussed in the literature. The best insight into this cultural practice is found in Mintz (1960). A broader but less detailed description is found in Mintz's chapter, "Canamelar," in Steward (1957). A more detailed study of different rates of consensual unions in different parts of Puerto Rico is found in Dohen (1967). Some lengthy descriptions are also found in Lewis (1965) and Rogler and Hollingshead (1965).

1899	34.7 per cent of all unions
1920	26.3 per cent of all unions
1950	24.9 per cent of all unions
1960	13.5 per cent of all unions
1970	6.5 per cent of all unions

It is a status, therefore, that has always been culturally and officially acknowledged, and Puerto Ricans, unless they are speaking with strangers who they think may not understand, are very open about admitting that they are living consensually. They do not look on this as an immoral state, as it would be considered in many parts of the Christian world. The partners generally are not well instructed in any religious faith and consequently have no guilt feelings about living without religious marriage.* In addition, they are usually poor people with no property rights related to marriage. These simple people recognize that a man needs a woman, and a woman needs a man, and they begin to live together and bring up the children resulting from their union or from other unions that either one might have led. They judge the moral quality of the union in terms of their relationship to each other. He is a good man if he works to support the woman and children, treats them respectfully, and does not abandon them. She is a good woman if she keeps his house, cooks his meals, keeps his clothes, and raises his children properly. In fact, people in consensual unions are sometimes more concerned about the basic moral relationships than are people preoccupied with the regularization of the union. More important than the percentage of consensual unions for the whole island is the uneven distribution of consensual unions. For example, if one selected a number of representative *municipios* for low, medium, and high percentages of consensual union, it would break down as shown in Table 1. The table indicates that family patterns differ sharply from one section of the island to another. All of the low-percentage *municipios* are in a small corner of the northwest tip, all of the medium-percentage *municipios* are in the central mountains, while all the high-percentage *municipios* are on the southeast corner.

The percentage of existing consensual unions has been declining sharply. It dropped from 25 per cent in 1950 to 13.5 per cent in 1960, and to 6.5 per cent in 1970. A number of factors help to explain the decline. First, the increase in religious and spiritual care has created a wider concern for religious marriage. Second, important economic benefits

---

*This does not mean they do not respect religious marriage. Many of them do not enter religious marriage because they understand its binding character and do not wish to commit themselves this way until they are sure they mean it.

TABLE 1

Percentage of All Existing Unions That Were Consensual, 1930, 1950, for Selected Municipios of Puerto Rico

	1930	1950	1960
LOW RATES:			
Aguada	6.8	8.2	6.2
Aguadilla	11.3	14.3	6.0
Camuy	11.4	10.8	7.0
Isabela	9.6	9.4	9.0
Moca	6.3	6.9	4.0
Quebradilla	8.9	9.0	5.0
Rincon	8.5	8.6	5.0
MEDIUM RATES:			
Barceloneta	22.3	19.8	13.0
Barranquitas	15.3	15.4	7.0
Ciales	20.3	17.6	16.0
Jayuya	21.4	14.5	12.0
Orocovis	23.7	18.8	9.0
HIGH RATES:			
Arroyo	41.	35.6	14.
Cayey	42.2	34.9	20.
Coamo	41.	29.4	20.
Guayama	46.6	32.7	20.
Juana Diaz	40.5	44.5	28.
Maunabo	41.6	29.5	19.
Salinas	55.9	51.7	33.
Santa Isabel	51.6	43.8	19.

SOURCE: U.S. Bureau of the Census, U.S. Census of Population, 1930. Washington, D.C.: U.S. Government Printing Office, 1933. Vol. VI, Puerto Rico, Families, Table 18. U.S. Bureau of the Census, U.S. Census of Population, 1950. Washington, D.C.: U.S. Government Printing Office, 1953, Vol. II, Parts 51-54, Territories and Possessions, Table 39. U.S. Bureau of the Census, U.S. Census of Population, 1960.Washington, D.C.: U.S. Government Printing Office, 1963, Vol. I, Characteristics of the Population, Vol. I, Part 53, Puerto Rico, Table 29.

have come to be associated with regularized unions; for example, widow's pensions, family benefits, social security, and admittance, particularly in New York, to public housing projects. Finally, the rapid emergence of a middle class has been important. Consensual union has always been a phenomenon of the poor population. As persons from the poorer classes advance to middle-class status, they become aware of regularized marriage as a middle-class value, and so they get married.

Increased education and the gainful occupation and changing status of women have also contributed to the decline. In other words, the social conditions in which it was functional have disappeared.

Illegitimacy

Related to consensual unions is illegitimacy, about which at least brief mention must be made. International reports of population use the term "illegitimate" to designate the children of parents who are not married. Children of consensual unions are included in this. This is a misleading designation. In Puerto Rico, as in the Roman law tradition generally, the term "illegitimate" was never used.* A child of a marriage that was legalized, and whose rights before the law were thus protected, was called "legitimate." He was a "legal" child. "Natural" was the term used for all other children. This had a much less pejorative connotation than that associated with the term "illegitimate." A third term has come into use in Puerto Rico, the *hijo reconocido*, the recognized child.† In Puerto Rico, if the father of a child is known, whether he is living consensually with the mother, or whether the child resulted from a casual union, he is required by law to recognize the child. This gives the child a number of rights before the law, including the right to use the father's name, the right to support, and some rights of inheritance. Therefore, in examining statistics on legitimacy from areas like Puerto Rico, it is important to note that many of the children reported as illegitimate may actually be the children of stable consensual unions.

FERTILITY. Fertility has generally been high in Puerto Rico, although it appears to be dropping in recent years.‡ This may be due largely to the

---

*In contrast to English common law, which was concerned with illegitimacy, Roman law always acknowledged that some people would live together without getting married, in a state of concubinage. English common law, however, had the principle of common-law marriage: if a couple lived together long enough, it recognized the union as legal.

†In the late 1960s the vital-statistics reports do not use the category "recognized child" as they once did. As a result, it is difficult to determine how many there are. They had also ceased using the term *hijo natural* and began to use the standard international category "illegitimate" for children of parents not in regularized unions.

‡The problem of population policy and birth control has been a troublesome issue between the government and the Catholic bishops on the island. For an analysis of the problem up to 1950, see Perloff (1950), Chapters 12 and 13. For the more modern period, Vasquez (1964) brings the data up to date. An intensive study of backgrounds of fertility was done during the 1950s in Puerto Rico. The first pubtiction, Hatt (1952), was a survey of public attitudes toward large or small families. This was followed by Stycos (1955), which sought to determine why people said they preferred small families but continued having large ones; the final study was Hill, Stycos, and Back (1959), which reports the results of various methods to bring people to the practice of birth control.

204

migration of large numbers of young people to the mainland during their most fertile years. In any event, the rate of population increase on the island has been declining. Puerto Rico has been one of the classic examples of "population explosion," and efforts to control the population increase have been widespread, well known, and at times very controversial. The estimated natural increase of the population during the period 1887–99 was 14.3 per 1,000 population; the crude birth rate during the same period was 45.7, and the crude death rate was 31.4. The introduction of better hygiene caused the death rate to decline consistently but the birth rate to remain high, so population increase has been rapid. The average annual increase during the period 1930–35 was 18.9 per 1,000; during the period 1940–45 it was 24.9; in 1950 it was 28.6; in 1965 it had declined to 23.4; in 1970 it had declined to 15.7. Crude rates such as these are not very helpful in explaining population changes, but they give a general picture of increases and decreases. Actually, the continuing migration of Puerto Ricans to the mainland has been the safety valve of population increase. Had all the migrants remained in Puerto Rico, the population would be doubling every 20 years, a rate of growth that would have caused major problems on the island.

FAMILY VALUES

Some aspects of the values of Puerto Rican family life have already been mentioned in relation to the influences that have helped to form it. In the following paragraphs, the range of values will be indicated that distinguish the Puerto Rican family from the predominant middle-class family values of the mainland.*

PERSONALISM. The basic value of Puerto Rican culture, as of Latin cultures in general, is a form of individualism that focuses on the inner importance of the person. In contrast to the individualism of America, which values the individual in terms of his ability to compete for higher social and economic status, the culture of Puerto Rico centers attention on those inner qualities that constitute the uniqueness of the person and his goodness or worth in himself. In a two-class society in which little mobility was possible, a man was born into his social and economic

---

*One of the best brief treatments of Latin values that are shared by Puerto Ricans can be found in Gillin (1960). Another good treatment is found in Wells (1969), Chapters 1 and 2.

position. Therefore, he defined his value in terms of the qualities and behavior that made a man good or respected in the social position in which he found himself. A poor farm laborer was a good man when he did those things that made a man good on his social and economic level. He felt an inner dignity *(dignidad)* about which the Puerto Rican is very sensitive; he expected others to have respect *(respeto)* for that *dignidad*. All men have some sense of personal dignity and are sensitive about proper respect being shown them. But this marks the Puerto Rican culture in a particular way. Puerto Ricans are much more sensitive than Americans to anything that appears to be personal insult or disdain; they do not take to practical jokes that are likely to embarrass or to party games in which people "make fools of themselves." They do not "horse around," as Americans would say in an offhand, informal manner; they are unusually responsive to manifestations of personal respect and to styles of personal leadership by men who appeal to the person rather than a program or a platform. Although the old two-class society in which these values developed has been disappearing, the values themselves are still very strong.

PERSONALISM AND EFFICIENCY. It is this personalism that makes it difficult for the Puerto Rican to adjust easily to what Americans call efficiency. For a Puerto Rican, life is a network of personal relationships. He trusts persons; he relies on persons; he knows that at every moment he can fall back on a brother, a cousin, a *compadre*. He does not have that same trust for a system or an organization. The American, on the other hand, expects the system to work; he has confidence in the organization. When something goes wrong, his reaction is: "Somebody ought to do something about this." "Get this system going." Thus, an American becomes impatient and uneasy when syetems do not work. He responds to efficiency. The Latin becomes uneasy and impatient if the system works too well, if he feels himself in a situation in which he must rely on impersonal functions rather than personal relationships.

THE PADRINO. Related to personalism is the role of the *padrino*. The *padrino* is a person, strategically placed in a higher position of the social structure, who has a personal relationship with the poorer person for whom he provides employment, assistance at time of need, and acts as an advocate if the poor person becomes involved in trouble. The *padrino* is really the intermediary between the poor person. who has neither sophistication nor influence, and the larger society of law, governmenı, employment, and service. He is a strategic helper in times of need, but the possibilities of exploitation in this relationship are very great. The poor person can become completely bound to the *padrino* by debt or by obligations to personal service to such an extent that his life is little better than slavery. The role of the *padrino* has decreased in Puerto Rico, but the tendency to seek a personal relationship in one's business affairs is still strong.

MACHISMO. Another aspect of personalism is a combination of qualities associated with masculinity. This is generally referred to as *machismo,* literally, maleness. *Machismo* is a style of personal daring (the great quality of the bullfighter) by which one faces challenge, danger, and threat with calmness and self-possession; this sometimes takes the form of bravado. It is also a quality of personal magnetism that impresses and influences others and prompts them to follow one as a leader—the quality of the *conquistador*. It is associated with sexual prowess, influence, and power over women, reflected in a vigorous romanticism and a jealous guarding of sweetheart or wife, or in premarital and extramarital relationships.

SENSE OF FAMILY OBLIGATION. Personalism is deeply rooted in the individualism that has just been described; it is also rooted in the family. As explained above, the Puerto Rican has a deep sense of that network of primary personal relationships that is his family. To express it another way, he senses the family as an extension of the person, and the network of obligations follows as described above.

SENSE OF THE PRIMARY OF THE SPIRITUAL. The Latin generally refers to American culture as very materialistic, much to the amazement of Americans, who are conscious of human qualities, concerns, and generosity in American culture that are missing in the Latin. What the Latin means is that his fundamental concerns are not with this world or its tangible features. He has a sense of spirit and soul as much more important than the body and as being intimately related to his value as a person; he tends to think in terms of transcendent qualities, such as justice, loyalty, or love, rather than in terms of practical arrangements that spell out justice or loyalty in the conrete. On an intellectual level, he strives to clarify relationships conceptually with a confidence that if they can be made intellectually clear and precise, the relationships will become actualities. He thinks of life very much in terms of ultimate values and ultimate spiritual goals, and expresses a willingness to sacrifice material satisfactions for these. In contrast, the American preoccupation with mastering the world and subjecting it, through technological programs, to man's domination gives him the sense of reversing the system of values, of emphasizing the importance of mastering the physical universe rather than seeking the values of the spirit. It is striking to note how many important political figures are also literary men with a humanistic flair. Former Governor Muñoz Marin is a poet and is affectionately called *El Vate,* the Bard, in Puerto Rico; the former resident commissioner in Washington, Santiago Polanco Abreu, is a literary critic; some of the best known figures in public service in the Puerto Rican community in New York, such as Juan Aviles, Carmen Marrero, and Luis Quero Chiesa, are accomplished writers and artists.

FATALISM. Connected to these spiritual values is a deep sense of fatalism in Puerto Ricans. They have a sense of destiny, partly related to elemental fears of the sacred, partly related to a sense of divine providence governing the world. The popular song, "Que será, será," "Whatever will be, will be," is a simple expression of it, as is the common expression that intersperses so much of Puerto Rican speech: *Sí Dios quiere,* "If God wills it." The term "destiny" recurs frequently in Puerto Rican popular songs. This quality leads to the acceptance of many events as inevitable; it also softens the sense of personal guilt for failure. If, after a vigorous effort, an enterprise does not succeed, the Puerto Rican may shrug his shoulders and remark: "It was not meant to be."

SENSE OF HIERARCHY. The Puerto Ricans, like other Latins, have had a concept of a hierarchical world during the whole of their history. This was partly the result of the two-class system, in which members never conceived of a world in which they could move out of the position of their birth. Thus, they thought of a relationship of higher and lower classes that was fixed somewhat as the various parts of the body were fixed. This concept of hierarchy contributed to their concept of personal worth as distinct from a person's position in the social structure.

The Puerto Rican Family on the Mainland

The institution that faces the most direct shock in the migration to the mainland is the family, and the progress of Puerto Ricans can be measured to a large extent by a study of the family. First, a statistical description of Puerto Rican families can be presented, followed by an analysis of the effect of migration on the family.

It has long been recognized that the migration of Puerto Ricans is a family migration, in the sense that they either come as families or expect to stay and found their families here. This is reflected in the percentage of the population on the mainland that is married. According to the 1960 Census, of all Puerto Rican males over 14 years of age, 70 per cent were married; of females, about 80 per cent (Fitzpatrick, 1966). Age at marriage shows a sharp decline from first generation to second generation, indicating an adaptation to mainland patterns.

One of the most serious differences between Puerto Rican families on the mainland and on the island, revealed in the 1970 Census, is the high rate of "families with female head." On the mainland 28 per cent of Puerto Rican families were reported as having a female head, almost as high as the rate for American blacks; even more surprising is the fact that this high rate continues in the second generation: almost 26 per cent of the families have a female head. This is in contrast to the 18.5 per cent of families in Puerto Rico with a female head. No one has yet found a satisfactory explanation of this phenomenon. It will certainly affect Puerto Rican family life in the future.

The phenomenon of "out-of-wedlock" children is also steadily increasing in New York State. In 1957, only 11 per cent of Puerto Rican births in New York State were out of wedlock; this increased to 22 per cent in 1967 and 30 per cent in 1969. This was considerably higher than the rate of about 20 per cent in Puerto Rico in 1970.

Type of Ceremony

Another indication of change can be found in the type of religious ceremony of Puerto Rican marriages on the mainland. As indicated before, this varies considerably from one area of Puerto Rico to another. Comparison of type of religious ceremony for all marriages in Puerto Rico for 1960 with type of religious ceremony for Puerto Rican marriages in New York City for 1959 brings results as shown in Table 2.

Two things are evident from Table 2. The pattern of marriage ceremony differs considerably between Puerto Rico and New York, and the pattern in New York, as in Puerto Rico, changed greatly between 1949 and 1959. The increase in Catholic ceremonies can be explained by the widespread efforts of the Catholic archdioceses of New York and Brooklyn to develop special programs for the religious care of Puerto Rican people between 1949 and 1959. In addition, ceremonies in Pentecostal and Evangelical churches declined from 1949 to 1959, particularly between first and second generation. If the Protestant marriages

TABLE 2

Type of Religious Ceremony for All Marriages in Puerto Rico and All Puerto Rican Marriages in New York City for Selected Years

	CIVIL (%)	CATHOLIC (%)	PROTESTANT (%)
Puerto Rico, 1949	24.3	61.4	14.3
Puerto Rico, 1960	36.2	45.8	17.6
New York City, 1949 (n. 4514)*	20.0	27.0	50.0
New York City, 1959 (n. 9370)	18.0	41.0	38.0

SOURCE: Fitzpatrick (1966).

*A small number of other types of ceremonies are included in this total.

performed by ministers of Pentecostal and Evangelical sects are taken separately, the decline is very evident. In 1959, 38.4 per cent of first-generation grooms were married by Pentecostal ministers, but only 33.3 per cent of second-generation grooms; among brides, 37 per cent of first generation, but only 30.1 per cent of the second generation were married by Pentecostal ministers (Fitzpatrick, 1966). The consistent drop from first to second generation tends to confirm the theory that association with sects and storefront religious groups is a first-generation phenomenon. When the second generation becomes more familiar with American life, they tend to withdraw from the sects.

Intermarriage

The most significant evidence of adjustment to life on the mainland has been the increase of marriage of Puerto Ricans with non-Puerto Ricans. In his study of New York marriages for the years 1949 and 1959, Fitzpatrick (1966) established that there is a significant increase in the rate of out-group marriage among second-generation Puerto Ricans over the first. The data are presented in Table 3.

The increase in the rate of out-group marriages among Puerto Ricans in both 1949 and 1959 between the first and second generation was as great as was the increase for all immigrants in New York City in the years 1908 to 1912.* It is legitimate to conclude from this that if out-group marriage is accepted as an index of assimilation, the assimilation

---

*The data for marriages of immigrants, 1908–12, which were used in the Fitzpatrick study were taken from Drachsler (1921).

TABLE 3

**Rate of Out Group Marriage of Puerto Ricans
in New York City, 1949 and 1959, by Generation:
and of All Immigrants in New York City, 1908-12**

| | FIRST GENERATION | | SECOND GENERATION | | INCREASE IN SECOND GENERATION |
	%	NO.	%	NO.	%
GROOMS					
Puerto Rican, 1949	5.2	3,079	28.3	378	23.1
Puerto Rican, 1959	3.6	7,078	27.4	638	23.8
1908-12	10.39	64,577	32.4	12,184	22.01
BRIDES					
Puerto Rican, 1949	8.5	3,077	30.0	523	21.5
Puerto Rican, 1959	6.0	7,257	33.1	717	27.1
1908–12	10.1	61,823	30.12	14,611	20.02

SOURCE: Fitzpatrick (1966).

of Puerto Ricans in New York is moving as rapidly as the assimilation of all immigrant groups during the years 1908–12.

Changes in Values

Much more important than the statistical description of the Puerto Rican families in America or in New York City is the study of the changes in values that they face. Probably the most serious is the shift in roles of husband and wife. There is abundant evidence that this is a common experience of immigrants. It is provoked by a number of things. First, it is frequently easier for Puerto Rican women to get jobs in New York than Puerto Rican men. This gives the wife an economic independence that she may never have had before, and if the husband is unemployed while the wife is working, the reversal of roles is severe. Second, the impact of American culture begins to make itself felt more directly in New York than on the island. Puerto Rican women from the poorer classes are much more involved in social, community, and political activities than they are in Puerto Rico. This influences the Puerto Rican wife to adopt gradually the patterns of the mainland.

Even more direct and difficult to cope with is the shift in role of the Puerto Rican child. Puerto Rican families have frequently lamented the patterns of behavior of even good boys in America. Puerto Rican parents consider them to be disrespectful. American children are taught to be self-reliant, aggressive, and competitive, to ask, "Why," and to stand on their own two feet. A Puerto Rican child is generally much more submissive. When the children begin to behave according to the American pattern, the parents cannot understand it. A priest who had worked for many years with migrating Puerto Ricans remarked to the writer: "When these Puerto Rican families come to New York, I give the boys about forty-eight hours on the streets of New York, and the difference between his behavior and what the family expects will have begun to shake the family."

The distance that gradually separates child from family is indicated in much of the literature about Puerto Ricans in New York. In the autobiography of Piri Thomas, *Down These Mean Streets* (1967), it is clear that his family—and it was a good, strong family—had no way of controlling him once he began to associate with his peers on the streets. The sharp contrast of two life histories, *Two Blocks Apart* (Mayerson, 1965), also demonstrates the difficulties of a Puerto Rican family in trying to continue to control the life of a boy growing up in New York. His peers become his significant reference group. A considerable number of scholars and social workers attribute much of the delinquency of Puerto Ricans to the excessive confinement that the Puerto Rican families impose in an effort to protect their children. Once the children can break loose in the early teens, they break completely. When Julio Gonzalez was killed in a gang fight on the Lower East Side in reprisal for the murder of a Black girl, Theresa Gee, in 1959, he was buried from Nativity Church. Julio's father, a poor man from a mountain town in Puerto Rico, was like a pillar of strength during the wake. He was a man of extraordinary dignity and self-possession. After the funeral Mass, he went to the sacristy of the church, embraced each of the priests who had participated, and thanked them. Here was a man who sought to pass on to his son the qualities of loyalty, dignity, and strength. But when the son reached the streets, different definitions of loyalty and dignity took over. As Julio was dying, after the priest had given him the last rites of the Catholic Church, he fell into unconsciousness, mumbling: "Tell the guys they can count me; tell them I'll be there."*

Probably the most severe problem of control is the effort of families to give their unmarried girls the same kind of protection they would have given them in Puerto Rico. When the girls reach the early teens, they wish to do what American girls do: go to dances with boys without a

---

*For a lengthy discussion of this change of values and its relation to delinquency, see Fitzpatrick (1960). This is reprinted in Tyler (1962):415–21.

chaperone and associate freely with girls and boys of the neighborhood or school. For a good Puerto Rican father to permit his daughter to go out unprotected is a serious moral failure. In a Puerto Rican town, when a father has brought his daughters as virgins to marriage, he can hold up his head before his community; he enjoys the esteem and prestige of a good father. To ask the same father to allow his daughters to go free in New York is to ask him to do something that the men of his family have considered immoral. It is psychologically almost impossible for him to do this. The tension between parents and daughter(s) is one of the most difficult for Puerto Rican parents to manage. It is frequently complicated because Americans, including schoolteachers and counselors, who are not aware of the significance of this in the Puerto Rican background, advise the parents to allow the girls to go out freely.*

Finally, the classic tension between the generations takes place. The parents are living in the Puerto Rican culture in their homes. The children are being brought up in an American school where American values are being presented. The parents will never really understand their children; the children will never really understand the parents.

Weakening of Extended Kinship

Apart from the conflict between generations, the experience of migration tends to weaken the family bonds that created a supporting network on which the family could always rely. To a growing extent, the family finds itself alone. This is partly the result of moving from place to place. It is also due to the fact that the way of life in mainland cities is not a convenient environment for the perpetuation of family virtues and values. The Department of Social Services provides assistance in time of need but not with the familiar, informal sense of personal and family respect. Regulations in housing, consumer loans, schools, and courts create a requirement for professional help, and the family is less and less effective.

Replacement of Personalist Values

Closely related to all the above difficulties, and creating difficulties of its own, is the slow and steady substitution of impersonal norms, norms of the system rather than norms of personal relationships. The need to

---

*Protection of the girls generates its own problems in Puerto Rico, a form of "cloister rebellion" that may lead to escape from the home or elopement. It is well described in Stycos (1955), Chapter 5.

adjust to the dominant patterns of American society requires a preparation to seek employment and advancement on the basis of merit or ability. To people for whom the world is an extensive pattern of personal relationships, this is a difficult adjustment.

The process of uprooting has been described before in the extensive literature about immigrants. It leads to three kinds of adjustments. The first involves escape from the immigrant or migrant group and an effort to become as much like the established community as possible in as short a time as possible. These people seek to disassociate themselves from their past. They sometimes change their name, they change their reference groups, and seek to be accepted by the larger society. They are in great danger of becoming marginal. Having abandoned the way of life of their own people, in which they had a sense of "who they were," there is no assurance that they will be accepted by the larger community. They may find themselves in a no man's land of culture. In this stage, the danger of personal frustration is acute.

A second reaction is withdrawal into the old culture, a resistance to the new way of life. These people seek to retain the older identities by locking themselves into their old way of life.

The third reaction is the effort to build a cultural bridge between the culture of the migrants and that of the mainland. These are the people who have confidence and security in their own way of life, but who realize that it cannot continue. Therefore, they seek to establish themselves in the new society but continue to identify themselves with the people from whom they come. These are the ones through whom the process of assimilation moves forward.

CHANGE AND ADAPTATION

In view of the above discussion, it is important to discover at what level of assimilation the Puerto Rican family now stands, and how it is affected by the problem of identity. In terms of intermarriage, the data indicate that the increase in the rate of out-group marriage between first and second generation is as great as it was for all immigrants to New York, 1908–12. Replication of the study for 1969, which is now in progress at Fordham University, New York, will involve many more first- and second-generation marriages and will give a much more reliable indication of the trend. According to the 1970 Census data, in New York State 34 per cent of second-generation Puerto Rican men and 32 per cent of second-generation Puerto Rican women, married and living with their spouses, are married to non-Puerto Ricans. For Puerto Ricans outside New York the rates are much higher: 68 per cent of second-generation Puerto Rican men, 65 per cent of women, married and living with their spouses were married to non-Puerto Ricans. The 1970 census reports do not discriminate between non-Puerto Rican spouses who are Hispanic and those who are not. The Fitzpatrick data include only non-Hispanic spouses among the non-Puerto Ricans. In this regard, Puerto Ricans are simply repeating the consistent pattern of immigrants who preceded them.

Second, in view of the character of the migration from Puerto Rico (i.e., the return of many Puerto Ricans from the mainland and the continuing movement of large numbers of new migrants to the mainland), there continue to be large numbers of Puerto Rican families in the early and difficult stages of adjustment to New York, struggling for a satisfactory cultural adjustment as defined by Gordon (1963) and Eisenstadt (1955).

The increase in the number of second-generation Puerto Ricans indicates that the classical problems of newcomers, the problems of the second generation, are very likely at a serious level and will continue to be so for a considerable length of time. It is not clear just how family difficulties contribute to these larger problems, but it is certain that these problems contribute immeasurably to family difficulties. In the early 1960s, a group of Puerto Rican social workers founded the Puerto Rican Family Institute in an effort to assist Puerto Rican families in New York. The objective of the institute was not simply to provide family casework but to identify well-established Puerto Rican families in New York and match them as *compadres* to newly arrived families that showed signs of suffering from the strains of adjustment to the city. This was an attempt to use the traditional forms of neighborhood and family help that were characteristic of Puerto Rico. When families could be matched, the program has been very helpful. But recently the institute has found that the percentage of families with serious and immediate problems has been increasing. This may reflect the fact that as agencies around the city learn of a Puerto Rican institute, they refer their Puerto Rican problem cases to it; it may also reflect the shock of uprooting upon the newly arriving families or the disruption that occurs as the numbers in the second generation increase. The growth of militancy among the young will be another factor that will increase tension. However, in the demonstrations at City College of New York in the spring of 1969, in which militant Puerto Rican students played a major part, observers commented that the parents of the Puerto Rican students were very much on hand, supporting their sons and daughters, bringing them food, clothing, and supplies.

In the period during which the Puerto Ricans struggle for greater solidarity and identity as a community, the family remains the major psychosocial support for its members. In many cases, it is a broken family; in others, it is hampered by poverty, unemployment, illness; but it remains the source of strength for most Puerto Ricans in the process of transition. In the turbulent action of the musical *West Side Story,* when Bernardo, leader of the Puerto Rican gang, sees Tony, a youth of another ethnic group, approaching his sister Maria, Bernardo pulls Maria away from Tony to take her home; he then turns to Tony in anger and shouts: "You keep away from my sister. Don't you know we are a family people!"

During 1966 the first presentation in New York of *The Ox Cart* took place. This is a play by a Puerto Rican playwright, Rene Marques, which presents a picture of a simple farm family in the mountains of Puerto Rico, struggling to survive but reflecting the deep virtues of family loyalty and strength. Under the influence of the oldest son, the family moves to a slum section of San Juan in order to improve itself. But deterioration sets in as the slum environment begins to attack the solidarity and loyalty of the family members. The family then moves to New York; there the strain of the uprooting becomes worse, the gap between mother and children more painful, and the virtues of the old mountain family seem even more distant. After the violent death of the son, the play ends with the valiant mother setting out to go back to the mountains of Puerto Rico; there she hopes to regain the traditional values of Puerto Rican family life that were destroyed in San Juan and New York.

This is an ancient theme, and it may be as true for Puerto Ricans as it was for earlier newcomers. But if the Puerto Ricans make it on the mainland, it will be through the same source of strength that supported the immigrants of earlier times—the solidarity of the family.

R E F E R E N C E S

Dohen, Dorothy M. 1967. *The Background of Consensual Union in Puerto Rico.* In *Two Puerto Rican Studies.* Cuernavaca, Mexico: Center of Intercultural Documentation.
Drachsler, Julian. 1921. *Intermarriage in New York City.* New York: Columbia University Press.
Eisenstadt, S. N. 1955. *The Absorption of Immigrants.* New York: The Free Press.

Fernandez-Marina, R. 1961. "The Puerto Rican Syndrome: Its Dynamics and Cultural Determinants." *Psychiatry* 24 (February):79–82.

———, E. D. Maldonado Sierra, and R. D. Trent. 1958. "Three Basic Themes in Mexican and Puerto Rican Family Values." *Journal of Social Psychology* 48 (November):167–81.

Fitzpatrick, J. P. 1960. "Crime and Our Puerto Ricans." *Catholic Mind* 58:39–50.

———. 1966. "Intermarriage of Puerto Ricans in New York City." *American Journal of Sociology* 71 (January):401.

———. 1971. *Puerto Rican Americans: The Meaning of Migration to the Mainland*. Englewood Cliffs, N.J.: Prentice-Hall.

Gillin, John. 1960. "Some Signposts for Policy." In Richard N. Adams, *et al.* (ed.): *Social Change in Latin America Today*. New York: Vintage, pp. 28–47.

Gordon, Milton. 1963. *Assimilation in American Life*. New York: Oxford University Press.

Hatt, Paul. 1952. *Background of Human Fertility in Puerto Rico*. Princeton, N.J.: Princeton University Press.

Hill, Reuben. 1955. "Courtship in Puerto Rico: An Institution in Transition." *Marriage and Family Living* 17 (February):26–34.

———, J. Mayone Stycos, and Kurt W. Back. 1959. *The Family and Population Control: A Puerto Rican Experiment in Social Change*. Chapel Hill, N.C.: University of North Carolina Press.

Landy, David. 1959. *Tropical Childhood*. Chapel Hill, N.C.: University of North Carolina Press.

Lewis, Oscar. 1965. *La Vida: A Puerto Rican Family in the Culture of Poverty—San Juan and New York*. New York: Random House.

Mayerson, Charlotte Leon (ed.). 1965. *Two Blocks Apart*. New York: Holt, Rinehart and Winston.

Mintz, Sidney. 1960. *Worker in the Cane*. New Haven: Yale University Press.

Perloff, Harvey S. 1950. *Puerto Rico's Economic Future*. Chicago: University of Chicago Press.

Roberts, Lydia, and Rose Stefani. 1940. *Patterns of Living in Puerto Rican Families*. Rio Piedras: University of Puerto Rico Press.

Rogler, Lloyd, and A. B. Hollinshead, 1965. *Trapped: Families and Schizophrenia*. New York: Wiley.

Steward, Julian. 1957. *People of Puerto Rico*. Champaign-Urbana: University of Illinois Press.

Stycos, J. Mayone. 1955. *Family and Fertility in Puerto Rico*. New York: Columbia University Press.

Thomas, Piri. 1967. *Down These Mean Streets*. New York: Knopf.

Tyler, Gus. 1962. *Organized Crime in America*. Ann Arbor: University of Michigan Press.

Vasquez, Jose L. 1964. *Fertility Trends in Puerto Rico*. Section on Bio Statistics, Department of Preventive Medicine and Public Health, School of Medicine of Puerto Rico, San Juan.

Wells, Henry. 1969. *The Modernization of Puerto Rico*. Cambridge, Mass.: Harvard University Press.

HISTORICALLY SUBJUGATED BUT VOLATILE ETHNIC MINORITIES

The Black American Family *

Robert Staples' chapter on Black families in America is an attempt to introduce a new perspective to this controversial and at times politically explosive subject. Analysis of the Black family has until recently concentrated on the weaknesses and problems of Black people and their families. The "pathological" Black family has received the lion's share of attention.

Concentrating on the strengths of Black families, Dr. Staples emphasizes the historical importance of family and kinship among Black people, first in African society and later in the slavery and postemancipation period. The family, whatever its weaknesses, has been a survival mechanism serving as a refuge for affection, companionship, and self-esteem.

CHAPTER TEN

BY

ROBERT STAPLES

As America's largest visible minority, the Black population has been the subject of extensive study by behavioral scientists. Its family life has been of particular concern because of the unique character of this institution due to a history that is uncharacteristic of other ethnic groups. There are four traits of the Black group that distinguish it from many other immigrants to America. These differences are cultural in the sense that (1) Blacks came from a continent with norms and values that were dissimilar to the American way of life, (2) they were composed of many different tribes, each with its own languages, cultures, and traditions, (3) in the beginning, they came without females, and, most importantly, (4) they came in bondage (Billingsley, 1968).

The study of Black family life has, historically, been problem oriented. While the study of white families has been biased toward the middle-class family, the reverse has been true in the investigation of Black family patterns. Until relatively recently, almost all studies of

*This chapter is also to be published concurrently in Dr. Staple's own book, *Introduction to Black Sociology* (New York: McGraw-Hill).

Black family life have concentrated on the lower-income strata of the group, while ignoring middle-class families or even "stable" poor Black families. Moreover, the deviation of Black families from middle-class norms has led to the definition of them as "pathological." Such labels ignore the possibility that while a group's family forms may not fit into the normative model, it may have its own functional organization that meets the needs of that group (Billingsley, 1970).

One purpose of this description of Black family life styles is to demonstrate how it is organized to meet the functional prerequisites of the Black community. Additionally, the forces that Black families encounter, which create the existence of large numbers of "problem" families, must be carefully examined. Out of this systematic analysis of Black-family adaptations may come a new understanding of the Black family in contemporary American society.

HISTORICAL BACKGROUND

The Preslavery Period

There are several historical periods of interest in determining the evaluation of Black family life in America. One era is the precolonial one on the African continent from which the Black American population originated. The basis of African family life was the kinship group, which was bound together by blood ties and the common interest of corporate functions. Within each village, there were elaborate legal codes and court systems that regulated the marital and family behavior of individual members.

The structure and function of the Black family was to radically change under the system of slavery. What did not change, however, was the importance of the family to African peoples in the New World. While the nature of marriage and family patterns was no longer under the control of the kinship group, it nevertheless managed to sustain the individual in the face of the many destructive forces he was to encounter in American society.

The Slave Family

In attempting to get an accurate description of the family life of slaves, one has to sift through a conflicting array of opinions on the subject. Reliable empirical facts are few, and speculation has been rampant in the absence of data. Certain aspects of the slave's family life are undisputed. Slaves were not allowed to enter into binding contractual relationships. Because marriage is basically a legal relationship that imposes obligations on both parties and exacts penalties for their violation, there was no legal basis to any marriage between two individuals in bondage. Slave marriages were regulated at the discretion of the slave master. As a result, some marriages were initiated by slave owners and just as easily dissolved (Stampp, 1956).

Hence, there were numerous cases in which the slave owner ordered slave women to marry men of his choosing after they reached the age of puberty. They preferred a marriage between slaves on the same plantation since the primary reason for slave unions was the breeding of children who would become future slaves. Children born to a slave woman on a different plantation were looked upon by the slave holder as wasting his man's seed. Yet many slaves who were allowed to get married preferred women from a neighboring plantation. This allowed them to avoid witnessing the many assaults on slave women that occurred. Sometimes the matter was resolved by the sale of one of the parties to the other owner (Blassingame, 1972).

Historians are divided on the question of how many slave families were involuntarily separated from each other by their owners. Despite the slave holder's commitment to maintaining the slave families intact, the intervening events of a slave holder's death, his bankruptcy, or lack of capital made the forcible sale of some slave's spouse or child inevitable. In instances in which the slave master was indifferent to the fate of slave families, he would still keep them together simply to enforce plantation discipline. A married slave who was concerned about his wife and children, it was believed, was less inclined to rebel or escape than would a "single" slave. Whatever their reasoning, the few available records show that slave owners did not separate a majority of the slave couples (Blassingame, 1972).

This does not mean that the slave family had a great deal of stability. While there are examples of some slave families living together for forty years or more, the majority of slave unions were dissolved by personal choice, death, or the sale of one partner by the master. Although individual families may not have remained together for long periods of time, the institution of the family was an important asset in the perilous era of slavery. Despite the prevalent theories about the destruction of the family under slavery, it was one of the most important survival mechanisms for African people held in bondage (Blassingame, 1972).

In the slave quarters, Black families did exist as functioning institutions and as models for others. The slave narratives provide us with some indication of the importance of family relations under slavery. It was in the family that the slave received affection, companionship, love, and empathy with his sufferings under this peculiar institution. Through the family, he learned how to avoid punishment, to cooperate with his fellow slaves, and to retain some semblance of his self-esteem. The socialization of the slave child was another important function for the slave parents. They could cushion the shock of bondage for him, inculcate in him values different from those the masters attempted to teach him, and represent another frame of reference for his self-esteem besides the master (Absug, 1971).

Much has been written about the elimination of the male's traditional functions under the slave system. It is true that he was often relegated to working in the fields and siring children rather than providing economic maintenance or physical protection for his family. But the father's role was not as significant as presumed (Blassingame, 1972). It was the male slave's inability to protect his wife from the physical and sexual abuse of the master that most pained him. As a matter of survival, few tried as the consequences were often fatal. But it is significant that tales of their intervention occur frequently in the slave narratives. There is one story of a slave who could no longer tolerate the humiliation of his wife's sexual abuse by the master before his eyes. He choked him to death with the knowledge that it meant his death. He said he knew it was death, but it was death, anyhow, so he just killed him (Absug, 1971:29).

One aspect of Black family life frequently ignored during the slave era is the free Black family. This group, which numbered about half a million, was primarily composed of the descendants of the original Black indentured servants and the mulatto offspring of slave holders. For this minority of Black families, the assimilation and acculturation process was relatively less difficult. They imitated the white world as closely as possible. Because they had opportunities for education, owning property, and skilled occupations, their family life was quite stable. Some of them even owned slaves, although the majority of Black slave holders were former slaves who had purchased their wives or children. It is among this group that the Black middle class was early formed (Frazier, 1932).

After Emancipation

There has been a prevailing notion that the experience of slavery weakened the value of marriage as an institution among Afro-

224

Americans. The slaves, however, married in record numbers when the right for the freedom to marry was created by governmental decree. A legal marriage was a status symbol, and weddings were events of great gaiety. In a careful examination of census data and marriage licenses for the period after 1860, Gutman (1973) found the typical household everywhere was a simple nuclear family headed by an adult male. Further evidence that Black people were successful in forming a biparental family structure are the data that show 90 per cent of all Black children were born in wedlock by the year 1917 (Bernard, 1966:3).

The strong family orientation of the recently emancipated slaves has been observed by many students of the Reconstruction era. One newspaper reported a Black group's petition to the state of North Carolina asking for the right "to work with the assurance of good faith and fair treatment, to educate their childre 1 t. sanctify the family relation, to reunite scattered families, and to provide for the orphan and infirm" (Absug, 1971:34). Children were of special value to the freed slaves, whose memories were fresh with the history of their offspring being sold away.

It was during the late nineteenth century that the strong role of women emerged. Males preferred their wives to remain at home, since a working woman was considered a mark of slavery. But during a period described as "the most explicitly racist era of American history" (Miller, 1966), Black men found it very difficult to obtain jobs and, in some instances, found work only as strikebreakers. Thus, the official organ of the African Methodist Episcopal Church exhorted Black families to teach their daughters not to avoid work since many of them would marry men that would not make on the average more than 75 cents a day (Absug, 1971:39). In 1900, approximately 41 per cent of Black women were in the labor force, compared to 16 per cent of white women (Logan, 1965).

What was important, then, was not whether the husband or wife worked but the family's will to survive in an era when Blacks were systematically deprived of educational and work opportunities. Despite these obstacles, Black families achieved a level of stability based on role integration. Males shared equally in the rearing of children—women participated in the support of the family. As Nobles (1972) comments, a system in which the family disintegrates due to the loss of one member would be in opposition to the traditional principles of unity that defined the African family. These principles were to be tested during the period of the great Black migration from the rural areas of the South to the cities of the North.

The rise of Black illegitimacy and female-headed households are concomitants of twentieth-century urban ghettos. Drastic increases in these phenomena strongly indicate that the condition of many lower-class Black families is a function of the economic contingencies of industrial America (Anderson, 1971:276). Unlike the European immigrants before them, Blacks were especially disadvantaged by the hard lines of Northern segregation along racial lines. Furthermore, families in cities are more vulnerable to disruptions due to the traumatizing experiences of urbanization, the reduction of family functions, and the loss of extended family supports.

In the transition from Africa to the American continent, there can be no doubt that African culture was not retained in any pure form. Blacks lacked the autonomy to maintain their cultural traditions under the severe pressures to take on American standards of behavior. There are, however, surviving Africanisms that are reflected in Black speech patterns, esthetics, folklore, and religion (Herskovits, 1958). They have preserved aspects of their old culture that have a direct relevance to their new lives. And out of the common experiences they have shared has been forged a new culture that is uniquely Afro-American. The elements of that culture are still to be found in their family life.

THE MODERN BLACK FAMILY

Demographic Characteristics

The majority of Black families adhere to the nuclear-family model. In 1972, approximately two-thirds of Black families had both the husband and wife present. A significantly larger percentage of Black households were headed by a female than in white families. While white families had a woman head in 9 per cent of all such families, 30 per cent of Black families were headed by a woman. Moreover, this was an increase of 38 per cent from the last decade. This large number of female-headed households is mostly a result of socioeconomic forces. As the level of income rises, so does the number of male-headed families. At the upper income level of $15,000 and over, the percentage of male-headed households is comparable to that for white families. If we combine families reconstituted by a second marriage with those never broken, 69 per cent of Black children live in families with both a father and mother present (U.S. Bureau of the Census, 1972).

One of the most significant changes in the period 1960–70 was the decline in the Black fertility rate. In 1968, the Black birth rate reached its lowest level in the past 25 years. However, the white birth rate declined even more rapidly (29 per cent versus 32 per cent), and the total fertility rate of 3.13 children per Black woman is still higher than that of 2.37 for white women. The Black fertility rate is influenced by a number of factors, including regional variations, rural-urban differencs, and, most importantly, socioeconomic levels. In 1967 Black women in the South had more children than those who lived in the North, and the birth rate of urban Black women was lower than that of Black women in rural areas. Significantly, middle-class Blacks have the lowest fertility rate of almost every demographic category in America, whereas middle-class Catholics and Mormons have the highest. College-educated Black women actually have a lower birth rate than college-educated white women (Kiser and Frank, 1967; Westoff and Westoff, 1971).

One of the more significant events of the last decade has been the steady decline in the out-of-wedlock births to Black women, while the illegitimacy rate among whites has shown a steady rise. The illegitimacy rate among whites went from 9.2 to 13.2 (per 1,000 unmarried women 15 to 44 years old) between 1960 and 1968, while the rate among Blacks decreased from 98.3 to 86.6 during the same time span (U.S. Bureau of the Census, 1971). Some of this racial difference in the illegitimacy-rate increase can be attributed to the more frequent and effective use of contraceptives and abortions among Black women. One study found that Black women received about 25 per cent of all the legal abortions performed in hospitals nationwide (U.S. Population Council, 1972). However, the white illegitimacy rate has been underreported in the past through unreported abortions, falsification of medical records, and shot-gun weddings (Ryan, 1971).

As we reported earlier, about 30 per cent of Black families are headed by women. About 60 per cent of these families have incomes below the official "poverty" level. This is true despite the fact that 60 per cent of the women who are heads of Black households work (most on them full time). Slightly less than 50 per cent of them receive welfare assistance (Hill, 1972). These female-headed households include widowed and single women, women whose husbands are in the armed forces or otherwise away from home involuntarily, as well as those apart from their husbands through divorce or separation. The majority of them came about through separation or divorce, while a quarter of them involve widows, and 20 per cent were never married (U.S. Bureau of the Census, 1972).

Social Structure

It is generally acknowledged that the Black kinship network is more extensive and cohesive than kinship bonds among the white population. The validity of this assumption is born out by the census data, which show that a larger proportion of Black families take relatives into their households. Billingsley (1968) divides these families into three general categories. They include (1) the "incipient-extended family," composed of a husband and wife who are childless and take in other relatives, (2) the "simple extended family," a married couple with children who have other relatives living with them, and (3) the "attenuated extended family," a household composed of a single, abandoned, legally separated, divorced, or widowed mother or father living with their own children, who takes into the home additional relatives. According to the 1970 Census, the attenuated family is the most common, with 48 per cent of families headed by elderly women taking in relatives under 18. The proportion of similar white families is only 10 per cent. In the incipient-extended family category, 13 per cent of Black couples took in relatives under 18, compared to only 3 per cent of white couples (U.S. Bureau of the Census, 1970).

There is some disagreement on the reason for the stronger kinship bonds among Black families. Adams (1970) has suggested that minority status tends to strengthen kin ties because of a need for mutual aid and survival in a hostile environment. Others have attributed it to the individual's general distrust of neighbors and neighborhoods, the prevalence of large female-headed households receiving public assistance, and the high rate of residential mobility that makes long-term friendships difficult (Feagin, 1968; Stromberg, 1967). In opposition to the above theories is the argument by Matthews (1972) and Nobles (1972) that contemporary Black kinship patterns are but a variant of the extended family system found in African societies.

Matthews (1972) advances the proposition that Afro-Americans are relating to their African heritage when they function as members of a corporate group. The individual in the Black community, he says, is always relating to the remainder of the total Black community. In fact, Black togetherness is at the heart of Black social organization. The Black extended family is the functional unit of the Black community. Nobles (1972) has argued that the Black family socializes its members to see no real distinction between his personal self and other members of the family. They are both the same. The individual's identity is always the group's identity, and families function according to this philosophical orientation of the Black community.

With the possible exception of elderly parents, Black families rely more heavily on extended kin than white families. The range of the kin network is extensive and includes parents, siblings, cousins, aunts, uncles, etc. A unique feature of the Black kinship network is the inclusion of nonblood relatives who are referred to and regarded as kinsmen. Among lower-class Black males, for instance, males who are unrelated to one another "go for" brothers and interact on that fraternal basis. Usually, this is a special friendship in which the normal claims, obligations, and loyalties of the kin relationship are operative (Liebow, 1966). These para-kinship ties seem to be a facilitating and validating agent of Black life in America.

One finds no special status or authority associated with roles in the Black family. Contrary to theories about the Black matriarchy and the dominance of women, most research supports the fact that an equalitarian pattern typifies most Black families (Hyman and Reed, 1969; Mack, 1971; Middleton and Putney, 1960). In a succinct summary of authority patterns in the Black family, Hill states: "The husbands in most Black families are actively involved in decision making and the performance of household tasks that are expected of them. And, most wives, while strong, are not dominant matriarchs, but share with their husbands the making of family decisions—even in the low-income Black families" (Hill, 1972:20).

The myth of the Black matriarchy has been reinforced by the failure of many students of Black family life to distinguish between the terms dominant and strong. While Black women have needed to be strong in order for the Black family to survive, she has not necessarily been dominant (Ladner, 1971). In fact, she has not had the resources to impose her authority on many Black males in the society. The husband in most Black families is the primary breadwinner. Even in lower-class Black families, the wife's income is only a small part of the total family income. In 85 per cent of low-income Black families, the husband's income is higher than the wife's (Hill, 1972).

Social Class and Style of Life

When it comes to describing social classes and life styles among the Black population, the task is made difficult for a number of reasons. Among them is the fact that social class is an analytical concept that is neither (1) universally accepted in the social sciences, (2) conceived in precisely the same way by all students of social stratification, nor (3) commonly designated by the same label (Hodges, 1964:12–13). This difficulty is magnified when attempting to delineate the Black class structure. Among the difficulties encountered is the massive amount of mobility occurring in the Black class sturcture, with a fairly large number of upwardly mobile Blacks. Another is the number of middle-class Blacks who want to preserve their cultural traditions and thus adopt values and life styles that are commonly associated with the lower class (Kronus, 1971).

If income and educational levels are used, approximately 30 per cent of Black families would be in the middle-class category. The rest would fall in some level of the lower-class stratum, with only a negligible number in the upper-class group. In 1970, about 28 per cent of Black families had an income over $10,000. About 38 per cent of Black families in the North and West had incomes greater than $10,000. Over 50 per cent of Blacks, 25 to 29 years old, had completed high school in 1971. About 20 per cent of young Blacks are presently enrolled in college. Most of these Black members of the middle class will have a very recent origin from the lower-class group (U.S. Bureau of the Census, 1972).

But the concept of social class refers to more than a person's educational and income levels. It is measured just as well by cultural values and behavioral patterns, summed up as a class life style. Bernard (1966) divides Black families into two strands: the "acculturated" and "externally adapted." The former term describes those Blacks who have internalized Western norms, the latter, those Blacks who have adapted to these norms superficially. It is this writer's belief that most middle-class Blacks belong in the externally adapted group. Instead of internalizing white values, most new members of the Black middle-class have adopted certain middle-class practices as a strategy for obtaining a decent life.

The paucity of research on middle-class Black families does not provide many data for this assumption (Kronus 1971). But if one examines the dynamics of middle-class Black behavior, a certain pattern emerges. For example, the sexual behavior of upwardly mobile Black females is more conservative because a premarital pregnancy can mean dropping out of school and ruining one's chances of gaining entrance into the middle class (Ladner, 1971; Staples, 1972). When the middle-class Black female becomes pregnant before marriage, she is more likely to get an abortion than her lower-class counterpart (Gebhard, Pomeroy, Martin, and Christenson, 1958). Middle-class Black families have a significantly lower family size than low-income Black families not because they place less value on children, but because they perceive a very direct link between low income and large families. These class differences in marital and familial behavior among Blacks reflect pragmatic choices, not different values.

Within the lower-class group exists a variety of Black families. One finds a strong belief in hard work and the value of education among them. A recent study revealed that poor Black youth who have grown up in welfare families have a more positive attitude toward the desirability and necessity of work than the children of the white middle class (Goodwin, 1972). In another study, a slightly larger number of Black workers expressed a desire to take a job as a car washer rather than go on welfare even if the pay for the two sources of income was the same (Tausky and Wilson, 1971). A number of studies have documented the strong desire of lower-income Blank families to have their children attain a higher educational level than they have (Cosby, 1971; Harris, 1970; Hindelang, 1970). One result of this parental support is that 75 per cent of Blacks enrolled in college are from families in which the head had no college education (U.S. Bureau of the Census, 1970).

The Family Life Cycle

COURTSHIP AND MARRIAGE. Studies on Black dating and sexual patterns are few and unreliable (Staples, 1971a). As with the research on other aspects of Black family life, the focus has been on problems allegedly resulting from the different dating styles of Afro-Americans. Thus, one rarely finds a study of Black sexuality that does not associate that aspect of Black behavior with the problems of illegitimacy, female-headed households, and welfare dependency. The sexual relationships of Blacks is rarely, if ever, investigated as an element of the normal functioning of Black families. The intricate meaning and emotional dynamics of the Black sexual relationship are seldom captured in most Black family studies (Turner, 1972).

Heterosexual relationships develop at an early age in the communal setting of Black social relationships. Within the Black households exist high life activities of adults in which children participate (Rainwater, 1966). This is a time of feasting, drinking, and dancing. Even very young children are often matched with members of the opposite sex at this time. Males and females learn to interact with one another on the romantic level, usually associated with the postadolescent stage for whites. Hence, one study of Black students aged 10 to 17 found that half or more of the males and females at all ages claimed to have a boy/girl friend, to

231

have participated in kissing games, and to have been in love (Broderick, 1965).

Within the same sex peer group, Black males and females are socialized into their future pattern of sex-role interaction. Males learn the technique of "rapping," a linguistic pattern designed to convince the female that he is worthy of her interest and as a verbal prelude to more intimate activity. The female acquires the ability to discriminate between men who are with it and how to unmask a weak rap. When the male petitions her for sex, she may accept if interested, or if she has other motivations. Whether she agrees to participate in premarital sexual activity will not be founded on the morality of such behavior but on the practical consequences (pregnancy) that may ensue (Ladner, 1971).

This lack of moral emphasis on sexual behavior will be in opposition to the teachings of her parents. Most Black parents (usually the mother) urge their daughters to remain chaste until an adult—not necessarily until marriage. They are rarely told that premarital coitus is sinful but that sex relations before marriage can result in pregnancy. The Black female's reference group, however, is her peers, and they are more supportive of the philosophy that losing one's virginity is a declaration of maturity, of womanhood. Those who refuse to indulge are often subordinating peer-group approval to their desire for upward mobility. They do not, however, condemn others who decide to participate in premarital sex, even when their decision is to refrain (Ladner, 1971; Rainwater, 1970).

Thus, much dating behavior among Blacks is *ipso facto* sexual behavior (Staples, 1972). In fact, among most Black youth, there is no such thing as the dating pattern found among the white middle class. Young people meet in their neighborhoods and schools and soon begin to go out with one another. Sexual involvement may begin shortly afterward (Rosenberg and Bensman, 1968). In their recent investigation of Black females aged 15 to 19, Zelnik and Kantner (1972) reported that by the age of 19 over 80 per cent of their Black subjects had engaged in premarital intercourse. However, while the proportion of comparable white non-virgins was lower, it was that group that had sex more frequently and with more sexual partners.

While Black women have been socialized to appreciate sexual relationships, it is laden with an emotional meaning for them. Once sex has taken place, the intensity of the emotional relationship begins. As her association with her sexual partner becomes routinized, the emotional aspect is increased, and the male is ultimately expected to limit his close relationships with other women (Ladner, 1971). In the Zelnik and Kantner (1972) study, over 60 per cent of their subjects said their relations had been confined to a single partner. Half of the nonvirgins said they intended to marry the male. The Reiss (1964:697) comparison of Black and white premarital sexual standards revealed that although relatively permissive, Blacks are not generally promiscuous. They tend to require affectionate relations as a basis for sexual behavior.

Most Black women desire a stable, enduring relationship—ultimately marriage. This feeling is not always reciprocated by Black males (Broderick, 1965). Many Black men apparently evade the institution altogether, as a fairly large proportion of them (13.8 per cent) never marry at all (U.S. Bureau of the Census, 1972). Males, traditionally, have been less oriented toward marriage and the domestic responsibilities it entails. In the case of many Black males, reluctance to marry is reinforced by the unhappy marriages around them and the abundance of women available for companionship in their environment. For the Black female desirous of marriage, these facts of Black life all work to her disadvantage.

When it comes to finding a compatible mate, she faces a number of obstacles. One of the biggest hurdles is the excess number of Black women vis-à-vis Black men. In the age group over 14, there are approximately a million more Black females than males listed by the U.S. Census (1972). Although the number of Black males is higher due to their underenumeration in the census, the number of Black men available to Black women for marriage is actually fewer than the census figures would indicate. This low number of eligible Black males is due to their higher rate of mortality, incarceration, homosexuality, and intermarriage (Staples, 1970; Jackson, 1971). Once all these factors are considered, there may be as many as two million Black females without a male counterpart. This fact is particularly important when the reasons are sought for the large number of female-headed households in the Black community. There is simply no way of establishing a monogamous, two-parent household for many Black women within a racially endogamous marriage system.

Still, most Black women maintain an ideal concept of the man they would like to marry. These idealistic standards of mate selection, however, must often be subordinated to the realities they encounter. In the lower-class group, they frequently will settle for a man who will work when he is able to find employment, avoid excessive gambling, drinking and extramarital affairs, provide for the children, and treat her with respect. Even these simple desires cannot be met by lower-class Black husbands who are unable to find work and retreat into psychologically destructive behavior such as alcoholism, physical abuse of their wife, etc. (Drake and Cayton, 1945; Rainwater, 1970).

The middle-class Black woman has a slightly better chance of fulfilling her desires for a compatible mate. She is likely to require economic stability, emotional and sexual satisfaction, and male participation in child rearing. Both Black men and women are in agreement that she will work after marriage. And it has been found that the wife's employment does not pose a threat to the Black male's self-image. Black males are more likely to believe that the wife has a right to a career of her own than white males. The dual employment of both spouses is often necessary to approach the living standards of white couples with only the husband working. It also reflects the partnership of Black men and women that has existed for centuries as part of their African heritage (Axelson, 1970).

Marriage, however, has proved to be a fragile institution for Blacks—even in the middle class. The divorce and separation rate for Blacks as a group is quite high. While marriages are dissolving in record numbers for all racial groups, it has been particularly high for Blacks. In the last decade, the annual divorce rate has risen 75 per cent. In 1971, 20 per cent of ever-married Black women were separated or divorced, compared to 6 per cent of similar white women (U.S. Bureau of the Census, 1972).

The problems of being Black in a racist society have their ramifications in the marriage arena. It seems quite evident that whatever difficulties lower-class Black spouses have in their interpersonal relations are compounded by both the problems of poverty and racism. The middle-class Black marriage is threatened less by poverty than by the shortage of Black males, especially males in the same educational bracket as the women. There are approximately 85 college-educated Black males available for marriage to every 100 Black female college graduates. Many Black college women—especially those who attended Black institutions—remain single (Bayer, 1972). Others may marry men with less education, and this type of marriage has a greater statistical probability of ending in divorce (Noble, 1956; Staples, 1973). One result of the male shortage in the Black middle class has been the tendency of women seeking educated, high-status Black professionals to pursue men who are married as fair game. This type of female competition becomes a direct assault on a man's marriage and increases the risk of divorce (Rosnow and Rose, 1972). Such demographic pressures do not pose as great a threat to white marriages.

Another factor decreasing the available supply of educated Black males is the tendency of males in the middle class to date and marry white women, while white males are less involved with Black women (Day, 1972). In the most recent period, there has been a discernible increase in interracial dating and marriage (Porterfield, 1973; Willie and Levy, 1972). Public-opinion polls support the notion that there is a growing tolerance of interracial marriage by both Blacks and whites (Gallup, 1972). The common belief is that most interracial marriages involve a Black male and white female, and some studies document this via an examination of marriage records (Heer, 1966; Monahan, 1970). However, the Bureau of the Census in 1960 reported 51,000 known interracial marriages, and they were about evenly divided between Black men and Black women as the nonwhite spouse. Thus, marrying outside of the race may be a means for Black women to increase their marriage potential.

The growing trend toward interracial marriages has occurred in the midst of a large movement of Black youth toward Black nationalism and separatism. Much of this paradox can be explained by the entrance of many Blacks into previously all-white settings such as the white university in which they meet and associate wth whites as equals. Much larger numbers of Blacks and whites date than enter into a marriage. Most Blacks have other Blacks as their first preference for dating and marriage (Goins, 1960). It is estimated that fewer than 5 per cent of the Black population are interracially married. Although there are studies showing interracial marriages to be more stable than intraracial unions (Golden, 1959; Monahan, 1970), one sees indications that the external pressures against such marriages, along with the difficulties of marriage in general, pose a threat to the continued stability of many such unions.

Whereas certain problems exist in Black marriages, high separation and divorce rates are not necessarily a valid measure of the stability and functionality of Black families. What is important is whether they meet their functional obligations. There are many female-headed households, for instance, that socialize their children into successful adult roles. The biggest problem they face is the economic and employment discrimination against women that hinders their ability to sustain a decent life for them and their children (Pressman, 1970). In this endeavor, they frequently have the support of a Black male who may not be the legal husband/father. Schulz (1969) has reported that the lower-class Black male contributes to the welfare of his woman more than is commonly acknowledged and plays an important role as a substitute father to her children.

235

CHILDHOOD AND CHILD REARING. One of the most popular images of Black women is that of "Mammy," the devoted, affectionate nurse-maids of white children who belonged to their slave master or employer. This motherly image of Black women probably has some basis in fact. Motherhood has historically been an important role for Black women, even more meaningful than their role as wives (Bell, 1971). In the colonial period of America, missionaries often observed and reported the unusual devotion of the African mother to her child. The slave mother also developed a deep love for, and impenetrable bond to, her children (Ladner, 1972). It would appear that the bond between the Black mother and her child is deeply rooted in the African heritage and philosophy, which places a special value on children because they represent the continuity of life (Brown and Forde, 1967).

Many studies have conveyed a negative image of the Black mother because she does not conform to middle-class modes of child rearing. Yet Black mothers have fulfilled the function of socializing their children into the multiple roles they must perform in this society. They prepare them to take on not only the appropriate sex and age roles but a racial role as well. Children must be socialized to deal with the realities of white racism, which they will encounter daily. Black females are encouraged to be independent rather than passive individuals because many of them will carry family and economic responsibilities alone (Iscoe, Williams, and Harvey, 1964). Taking on adult responsibilities is something many Black children learn early. They may be given the care of a younger sibling, and some will have to find work while still in the adolescent stage. The strong character structure of Black children was noted by child psychiatrist Robert Coles (1964) as he observed their comportment under the pressures of school integration in the South during a very volatile era.

The Black mother's child-rearing techniques are geared to prepare her children for the kind of existence that is alien to middle-class white youngsters. Moreover, many white middle-class socialization patterns may not be that desirable for the psychological growth of the child. The casual upbringing of Black children may produce a much healthier personality than the status anxieties associated with some rigid middle-class child-rearing practices (Green, 1946). Using threats of the withdrawal of love if the child fails to measure up to the parent's standards is much more common among white parents than Black parents of any class stratum. One result of the Black child's anxiety-free upbringing is a strong closeness to his parents (Nolles, 1972; Scanzoni, 1971).

While Black parents are more likely to use physical, rather than verbal, punishment to enforce child discipline, this technique is often buttressed by the love they express for their children. Moreover, as Billingsley (1969:567) has noted: "Even among the lowest social classes in the Black community, families give the children better care than is generally recognized, and often the care is better than that given by white families in similar social circumstances." One indication of this care is found in the statistics, which show that child neglect and abuse are much more common in white families than in Black families. Black children, for instance, are underrepresented in institutions for dependent and neglected children (U.S. Bureau of the Census, 1960).

The most undesirable aspect of the Black child's socialization is reputed to be the inculcation of a negative self-identity (Rainwater, 1966). A plethora of studies have found that the Black child has a low self-esteem because of his Blackness and the fact that many grow up in homes without a male model. A number of studies are emerging that are in opposition to the theories of low self-esteem among Blacks. McCarthy and Yancey (1971) reviewed the literature on Black self-esteem, found much of it invalid, and concluded that Blacks are less likely to suffer from low self-esteem because they belong to a solitary group that possesses an ideology that explains their lowly position.

In a replication of some of the earlier studies on Black children's drawings, a pair of researchers reported that the current emphasis on Black culture had led to a significant change in the characteristics of those drawings. When Black children were asked to draw features that they most admired and wished were characteristic of themselves, most of their figures resembled other Black people (Dennis, 1968; Fish and Larr, 1971). In another investigation of Black self-esteem, it was discovered that even Black children from a separated or never-married family did not have a lower self-esteem than Black children from other families, and Black children as a group did not have lower self-esteem than white children as a group (Rosenberg and Simmons, 1971).

THE AGED. Extensive data on the Black elderly are presently not available. Based on what we presently know, the older Black person is not as likely to live with one of his children as are the white aged. In most cases, the grandmothers are more likely to take children into their own households than to be taken into the household of their kinfolk. About half (48 per cent) of elderly Black women have other related children living with them—in contrast to only 10 per cent of similar white families (Hill, 1971). This is but one more indication of the strong cohesiveness within Black families as well as the functional importance of the family in the Black community.

Because they live longer than Black men, widowhood comes at an earlier age for Black women. In 1970, over two-thirds of aged Black women were widows in comparison to 54 per cent of similar white women. They were also more likely to be widowed than were Black males (32 per cent) or white males (17 per cent; Jackson, 1972a). Due to a history of gross discrimination against it, the Black aged family only has a median income of $3,222. Of those elderly Blacks living alone, about 75 per cent had incomes of less than $2,000 in 1969. One result of this overwhelming poverty is that 26 per cent of the elderly wives in Black families continue to work after reaching the age of 65. Only 15 per cent of elderly white wives remain in the labor force past that age (Hill, 1971).

The extended kin structure in the Black community manages to buttress the psychological isolation and poverty of the Black aged. Most of them have a significant amount of interaction with their children, especially an older daughter. Where there is no child present or in the vicinity, they can rely on secondary kin, such as siblings, cousins, and even "make-believe" kin (Jackson, 1972b). In return, many Black grandmothers provide in-kind services, such as babysitting. Most aged Black parents desire to live independently of, but in close contact with, their children. Where their socioeconomic conditions permit, the adult children assist their elderly parents (Jackson, 1969).

CHANGE AND ADAPTATION

One of the most fluid institutions in American life is the family. Probably in no other sphere of our society have such rapid and profound changes taken place. While the changes are most significant for white Americans, Blacks, too, are influenced to some degree by the same forces. Among the most visible trends are the increase in sexual permissiveness, challenges to the traditional concept of women's role, increases in divorce, and reductions in the fertility rate. Although Blacks are part and parcel of these dynamics, their different history and needs preclude any close convergence of their family lifestyle with that of white families.

There is considerable disagreement over whether a revolution is sexual behavior has occurred. Some argue that only the public acknowledgment of sexual behavior has transpired, which gives the appearance of actual changes in what people are doing sexually. Yet it is impossible to refute the fact that the openness of sexual permissiveness reflects a revolution in attitudes. The most significant change is in the sexual liberation of white women. There are many indications that the double standard of sexual conduct is disappearing or being modified. This change in male attitudes about female sexuality has had little effect on Black female sexuality, for they have rarely been subjected to the same sexual restrictions as white women.

Much of the sexual revolution is caused by challenges to the traditional concept of woman's role in society. White women are demanding equality in employment opportunities, legal rights, shared responsibility for raising children, and to be freed of the liabilities only women face in America. Few Black women are involved in the Women's Liberation Movement because many of its demands seem irrelevant to their needs. They, particularly, cannot relate to the desires of white women to enter the labor force, to cease being viewed as sex objects, or to be freed from child-care responsibilities.

These demands of middle-class white women do not relate to the reality of Black women. They, like many lower-class white women, have always been in the labor force, whether they wanted to or not. Black women have not been depicted as sex objects as much as they have been *used* as sex objects. Motherhood and marriage were two institutions that were denied them in the past. Because they had to work, many were deprived of the time to enjoy their children. Marriage was a luxury many could not afford or the conditions of their lives would not provide. To the many Black women who are heading households, a husband would be a welcome figure.

But many of the methods and goals of the Women's Liberation Movement are of importance to Black women. As a result of women declaring their independence from the domination of men, there will be a greater acceptance of women heading families by themselves. Perhaps the society will then make provisions for eliminating some of the problems incurred by female-headed households, for example, child-care facilities. The demand for equal employment opportunities for women and an income parity for women in the same jobs as men is very important to Black women. It is Black women who are the most victimized by employment and income discrimination against women. They are most likely to be heads of households who will earn the low salaries paid women on the assumption that they do not have families to support.

The shortage of Black males available for marriage may force Black women to rethink the idea of a monogamous marriage that will last

239

forever. There are simply not enough Black males around to permit fulfillment of this desire. Perhaps some convergence of white and Black marital patterns is possible. White women, too, face a shortage of five million males due to the higher infant mortality rate for white males. This discrepancy is not nearly as great for individuals in the young marriageable years.

There is some indication of a homogenization of Black family life styles. This mass family pattern may not be based on the white middle-class nuclear family model. Rather, the increasing nativist sentiments among Black youth may culminate in a family system based on a combination of African and Afro-American cultural systems, which will transcend the class and regional variations that now exist. While white Americans are questioning whether the family as an institution can survive, Blacks may decide that it must become stronger and more relevant to their lives. As the Black youth of America, the group most imbued with the spirit of Black nationalism, becomes the majority of the Black population, this process of Africanizing the Black family may be accelerated. Whether this occurs or not will depend on whether the forces of racial integration and movement into the middle-class strata lead Blacks in the direction of assimilation and acculturation or in the development of an Afro-American identity.

Internal Adaptations

The changes in the interior of the Black family, while ideologically in the direction of pan-Africanism, are statistically in the direction of assimilation and acculturation. Examples of this phenomena are seen in the diffusion of Blacks into predominantly white suburbs, the increase in interracial dating and marriage, higher incidences of suicide and mental illness, and a decline in the extended family pattern. But these patterns reflect the variation in the Black community. What is surprising is that, given the pace of racial integration in American society, more Blacks have not become assimilated into the majority population's mode of behavior. The integration of the school systems, desegregation of suburbia, and greater access to knowledge of majority cultural norms through the mass media have provided, opportunities for Black acculturation without precedent.

Instead, we find Blacks demanding separate facilities and organizations on white university campuses. Those Blacks who moved to the suburbs continue their social lives in the inner cities. While the extended family may not exist together in the same household, its functions of providing emotional solidarity and other kinds of assistance are still carried out. Moreover, the concept of the extended family is broadened to include all members of the Black community. These are among some of the internal adaptations made by the Black community to prevent the trend of racial integration from diluting their cultural unity.

In contrast to the demands of white women for emancipation from the passive role ascribed to the female gender, Black women are discussing adopting the subordinate position of African women. Their contention is that the roles of men and women are different, not unequal. In some of the Black nationalist organizations, the women are placed in auxiliary groups, while the men take leadership roles. Much of this behavior is a reaction to the history of Black life in this country when Black women had the leadership of the family thrust upon them. Black men were not allowed to fulfill the ascribed male-role functions. Hence, in some circles, it is now believed that Black women should step back and let Black men emerge as the leader of the family and the race.

Another most important adaptation under consideration is the adoption of polygamy as the Black marriage system. The assumption here is that there are not enough Black males to go around and that the sharing of husbands could stabilize Black marriages and provide certain legal benefits to women now deprived of them. At least two Black nationalist organizations are on record as advocating polygamy for the Black population. The actual number of Black polygamous marriages is infinitesimal. Since such marriages are illegal in this country, no legal benefits can accrue to the second wife. Moreover, in African society, the practice of polygamy is closely related to the economic system, and people are socialized to accept it.

Problems and Prospects

The problems Black people face are essentially the same as for the past century. Those problems are not related to family stability but to the socioeconomic conditions that tear families asunder. In general, the problems are poverty and racism. While the past decade has produced a decline in racial segregation and white stereotypes of Black inferiority, Blacks are still singled out for discriminatory treatment in every sphere of American life. Moreover, while whites are in agreement about the racial discrimination Blacks are subjected to, any national effort to further remedy these racist practices has a low priority among white Americans.

A low socioeconomic status continues to plague many Black families.

241

Whereas some Blacks have achieved a higher standard of living as a result of the civil rights movement, large numbers of Blacks continue to live below the poverty level. A disproportionate number of these Blacks will be female heads of families. They will have more responsibilities and less income than any other group in American society. Yet no effective programs are being proposed to meet the needs of a third of all Black families. The persistence of employment and salary discrimination against women will continue to handicap Black women in their struggle to maintain a decent life for their families.

However, poverty is not the only reason for the high breakup rate of Black marriages. The increase in the Black divorce rate in recent years is due to sociopsychological factors as well. A primary cause is the independence of Black women. Marital stability among whites in the past was based on the subordinate status of women. Once white women were emancipated from the economic domination of men, their divorce rate increased radically. More Black women have been independent— economically and psychologically—for a much longer period of time. There is nothing inherently wrong with the equality of sex roles in the family, but when men are socialized to expect unchallenged leadership in family affairs, conflict is an inevitable result.

The increased rate of interracial marriages will continue because more Blacks and whites will meet as peers. Some Black men will marry white women because the society's standards of beauty are still white. More Black women will marry white men because the latter can provide them with a greater amount of economic security and because some have become disenchanted with Black men. Whatever the reason, these marriages will face many obstacles. In an era of unabated white racism and Black nationalism, many interracial couples will become outcasts in both Black and white communities.

It is difficult to project the future of Black families because there are several parallel trends occurring at the same time. Many Blacks are entering the middle class as a result of higher education and increased opportunities. At the same time the future is dim for those Blacks in the underclass. The forces of automation and cybernation are rendering obsolete the labor of unskilled Black men, who are in danger of becoming a permanent army of the unemployed. The status of Black women is in a state of flux. Some welcome the forthcoming liberation from male control, while others urge a regeneration of Black male leadership. Easier and cheaper access to contraceptives and abortions may mean a considerable decline in the Black fertility rate. Simultaneously, some Blacks express concern with the implications of genocide in Black family limitation. Whatever the future of Black families, it is time to put to rest all the theories about Black family instability and give recognition to the crucial role of this institution in the Black struggle for survival.

R E F E R E N C E S

Absug, Robert H. 1971. "The Black Family During Reconstruction." In Nathan Huggins (ed.): *Key Issues in the Afro-American Experience*. New York: Harcourt, Brace and Jovanovich, pp. 26–39.

Adams, Bert N. 1970. "Isolation, Function and Beyond: American Kinship in the 1960's." *Journal of Marriage and the Family* 32 (November):575–98.

Anderson, Charles H. 1971. *Towards a New Sociology*. Homewood, Illinois: Dorsey Press.

Axelson, Leland J. 1970. "The Working Wife: Differences in Perception among Negro and White Males." *Journal of Marriage and the Fmaily* 32 (August):457–64.

Bayer, Alal E. 1972. "College Impact on Marriage." *Journal of Marriage and the Family* 34 (November):600–10.

Bell, Robert. 1971. "The Relative Importance of Mother and Wife Roles among Negro Lower-Class Women." In Robert Staples (ed.): *The Black Family: Essays and Studies*. Belmont: Wadsworth, pp. 248–56.

Bernard, Jessie. 1966. *Marriage and Family Among Negros*. Englewood Cliffs, N.J.: Prentice-Hall.

Billingsley, Andrew. 1968. *Black Families in White America*. Englewood Cliffs, N.J.: Prentice-Hall.

———. 1969. "Family Functioning in Low-Income Black Community." *Social Casework* 50 (December):563–72.

———. 1970. "Black Families and White Social Science." *Journal of Social Issues* 26 (November):127–42.

Blassingame, John. 1972. *The Slave Community*. New York: Oxford.

Broderick, Carlfred. 1965. "Social Heterosexual Development among Urban Negroes and Whites." *Journal of Marriage and the Family* 27 (May):200–203.

Brown, A. R. Radcliffe, and Darryl Forde. 1967. *African Systems of Kinship and Marriage*. New York: Oxford University Press.

Carter, Lewis F. 1968. "Racial Caste Hypogamy: A Sociological Myth." *Phylon* 29 (Winter):349–52.

Coles, Robert. 1964. "Children and Racial Demonstrations." *The American Scholar* 34 (Winter):349–92.

Cosby, Arthur. 1971. "Black-White Differences in Aspirations among Deep South High School Students." *Journal of Negro Education* 40 (Winter):17–21.

Day, Beth. 1972. *Sexual Life Between Blacks and Whites*. New York: World.

Dennis, Wayne. 1968. "Racial Change in Negro Drawings." *Journal of Psychology* 69 (July):129–30.

Drake, St. Clair, and Horace Cayton. 1945. *Black Metropolis*. Chicago: University of Chicago Press.

Feagin, Joe R. 1968. "The Kinship Ties of Negro Urbanites." *Social Science Quarterly* 49 (December):660–65.

Fish, Jeanne, and Charlotte Larr. 1971. *A Decade of Change in Drawings by Black Children*. Unpublished manuscript.

Franklin, John Hope. 1967. *From Slavery to Freedom*. New York: Knopf.

Frazier, E. Franklin. 1932. *The Free Negro Family*. Nashville, Tenn.: Fisk University Press.

———. 1939. *The Negro Family in the United States*. Chicago: University of Chicago Press.

———. 1962. *Black Bourgeoisie*. New York: Collier Books.

Gallup, George. 1972. "Growing Tolerance Found Regarding Interracial, Interfaith Marriages." *New York Times* (November 19).

Gebhard, Paul, Wardell Pomeroy, Clyde Martin, and Cornelia Christenson. 1958. *Pregnancy, Birth,* and *Abortion*. New York: Harper and Brothers.

Goins, Alvin. 1960. "Ethnic and Class Preferences Among College Negroes." *Journal of Negro Education* 29 (Spring):128–33.

Golden, Joseph. 1959. "Facilitating Factors in Negro-White Intermarriage." *Phylon* 20 (Fall):273–84.

Goodwin, Leonard. 1972. *Do the Poor Want to Work: A Socio-Psychological Study of Work Orientations*. Washington, D.C.: The Brookings Institution.

Green, Arnold. 1946. "The Middle-Class Male Child and Neurosis." *American Sociological Review* 11 (February): 31–41.

Gutman, Herbert. 1976. *The Negro Family*. New York: Pantheon.

Hall, Gwendolyn Midlo. 1970. "The Myth of Benevolent Spanish Slave Law." *Negro Digest* 19 (February):31–38.

Harris, Edward E. 1970. "Personal and Parental Influences in College Attendance: Some Negro-White Differences." *Journal of Negro Education* 39 (Fall):305–13.

Hays, William, and Charles Mindel. 1972. "Extended Kinship Relations in Black and White Families." *Journal of Marriage and the Family* 35 (February):51–57.

Heer, David. 1966. "Negro-White Marriage in the United States." *Journal of Marriage and the Family* 28 (August):262–73.

Herskovits, Melville. 1958. *The Myth of the Negro Past*. Boston: Beacon Press.

Hill, Robert. 1971. "A Profile of the Black Aged." *The Los Angeles Sentinel* (October 7), A14.

———. 1972. *The Strengths of Black Families*. New York: Emerson-Hall.

Hindelang, Michael. 1970. "Educational and Occupational Aspirations among Working Class Negro, Mexican-American and White Elementary School Children." *Journal of Negro Education* 39 (Fall):351–53.

Hobson, Sheila. 1971. "The Black Family: Together in Every Sense." *Tuesday* 6 (April):12–14, 28–32.

Hodges, Harold. 1964. *Social Stratification*. Cambridge, Mass.: Schenkman.

Hyman, Herbert, and John S. Reed. 1969. "Black Matriarchy Reconsidered: Evidence from Secondary Analysis of Sample Surveys." *Public Opinion Quarterly* 33 (Fall):346–54.

Iscoe, Ira, Martha Williams, and Jerry Harvey. 1964. "Age, Intelligence and Sex as Variables in the Conformity Behavior of Negro and White Children." *Child Development* 35 (March-December):451–60.

Jackson, Jacquelyn. 1969. "Negro Aged Parents and Adult Children: Their Affective Relationships." *Varia* 2 (Spring):1–14.

———. 1971. "But Where Are the Men?" *The Black Scholar* 3 (December):30–41.

———. 1972a. "Marital Life Among Older Black Couples." *The Family Coordinator* 21 (January):21–28.

———. 1972b. "Comparative Life Styles and Family and Friend Relationships among Older Black Women." *The Family Coordinator* 21 (October):477–86.

Kiser, Clyde and Myrna Frank. 1967. "Factors Associated with the Low Fertility of Non-White Women of College Attainment." *Milbank Memorial Fund Quarterly* (October):425–29.

Klein, Herbert. 1967. *Slavery in the Americas*. Chicago: University of Chicago.

Kronus, Sidney J. 1971. *The Black Middle Class*. Columbus, Ohio: Merrill.

Ladner, Joyce. 1971. *Tomorrow's Tomorrow: The Black Women*. Garden City, N.Y.: Doubleday.

———. 1972. "The Legacy of Black Womanhood." *Tuesday* 7 (April):4–5, 18–20.

Liebow, Elliot. 1966. *Tally's Corner*. Boston: Little, Brown.

Logan, Rayford. 1965. *The Betrayal of the Negro*. New York: Collier.

Mack, Delores. 1971. "Where the Black Matriarchy Theorists Went Wrong." *Psychology Today* 4 (January):24.

Matthews, Basil. 1972. *Black Perspective, Black Family and Black Community*. A paper delivered to the annual Philosophy Conference, Baltimore, Md.

McCarthy, John, and William Yancey. 1971. "Uncle Tom and Mr. Charlie: Metaphysical Pathos in the Study of Racism and Personal Disorganization." *American Journal of Sociology* 76 (November):648–762.

Middleton, Russell, and Snell Putney. 1960. "Dominance in Decisions in the Family: Race and Class Differences." *American Journal of Sociology* 29 (May):605–609.

Miller, Elizabeth. 1966. *The Negro in America: A Bibliography*. Cambridge, Mass.; Harvard University Press.

Monahan, Thomas. 1970. "Are Interracial Marriages Really Less Stable?" *Social Forces* 48 (June):461–73.

Moynihan, Daniel Patrick. 1965. "Employment, Income, and the Ordeal of the Negro Family." *Daedalus* 94 (Fall):745–70.

Murray, Albert. 1970. *The Omni-Americans*. New York: Outerbridge and Diensterey.

Noble, Jeanne. 1956. *The Negro Woman College Graduate*. New York: Columbia University Press.

Nobles, Wade. 1974. *African Root and American Fruit: The Black Family*. *Journal of Social and Behavioral Sciences* 20 (Spring):52–64.

Nolle, David. 1972. "Changes in Black Sons and Daughters: A Panel Analysis of Black Adolescent's Orientation toward Their Parents." *Journal of Marriage and the Family* 34 (August):443–47.

Podell, Lawrence. 1970. *Families on Welfare in New York City*. New York: The Center for the Study of Urban Problems, pp. 38–39.

Porterfield, Ernest. 1973. "Mixed Marriage." *Psychology Today* 6 (January):71–78.

Pressman, Sonia. 1970. "Job Discrimination and the Black Woman." *The Crisis* (March):103–108.

Purcell, Theodore and Gerald Cavanaugh. 1972. *Blacks in the Industrial World*. New York: The Free Press.

Rainwater, Lee. 1966. "The Crucible of Identity: The Lower-Class Negro Family." *Daedalus* 95 (Winter):258–264.

―――. 1970. *Behind Ghetto Walls: Negro Families in a Federal Slum*. Chicago: Aldine.

Reiss, Ira L. 1964. "Premarital Sexual Permissiveness among Negroes and Whites." *American Sociological Review* 29 (October):688–98.

Rosenberg, Bernard, and Joseph Bensman. 1968. "Sexual Patterns in Three Ethnic Subcultures of an American Underclass." *Annals of the American Academy of Political and Social Science* 376 (March):61–75.

Rosenberg, Morris, and Roberta Simmons. 1971. *Black and White Self-Esteem: The Urban School Child*. Washington, D.C.: American Sociological Association.

Rosnow, Irving, and K. Daniel Rose. 1972. "Divorce among Doctors." *Journal of Marriage and the Family* 34 (November):587–99.

Ryan, William. 171. "Savage Discovery: The Moynihan Report." In Robert Staples (ed.): *The Black Family: Essays and Studies*. Belmont: Wadsworth, pp. 58–65.

Scanzoni, John. 1971. *The Black Family in Modern Society*. Boston: Allyn and Bacon.

Schulz, David. 1969. "Variations in the Father Role in Complete Families of the Negro Lower Class." *Social Science Quarterly* 49 (December):651–59.

Siegel, Paul M. 1965. "On the Cost of Being Negro." *Sociological Inquiry* 35 (Winter):52–55.

Stampp, Kenneth. 1956. *The Peculiar Institution*. New York: Vintage.

Staples, Robert. 1970. "The Myth of the Black Matriarchy." *The Black Scholar* 1 (January-February):9–16.

―――. 1971a. "Towards a Sociology of the Black Family." *Journal of Marriage and the Family* 33 (February):19–38.

――― (ed.). 1971b. *The Black Family: Essays and Studies*. Belmont: Wadsworth.

―――. 1972. "The Sexuality of Black Women." *Sexual Behavior* 2 (June):4–15.

―――. 1973. *The Black Woman in America*. Chicago: Nelson-Hall.

―――. 1974. "The Black Family Revisited: A Review and a Preview." *Journal of Social and Behavioral Sciences* 20 (Spring):65–78.

Stone, Robert, and P. T Schlamp. 1966. *Family Life Styles Below the Poverty Line*. A report to the State Social Welfare Board from the Institute for Social Science Research, San Francisco State College.

Stromberg, Jerome. 1967. *Kinship and Friendship among Lower-Class Negro*

Families. A paper presented to the annual meeting of the Society for the Study of Social Problems. San Francisco, Calif.

Tannenbaum, Frank. 1947. *Slave and Citizen*. New York: Knopf.

Tausky, Curt, and William J. Wilson. 1971. "Work Attachment among Black Men." *Phylon* 32 (Spring):23–30.

Turner, Clarence Rollo. 1972. "Some Theoretical and Conceptual Considerations for Black Family Studies." *Black Lines* 2 (Winter):13–28.

U.S. Bureau of the Census. 1960. *Inmates of Institutions*. P.C. (2), 3A.

———. 1970. "School Enrollment: October, 1970." *Current Population Reports: Population Characteristics Series* p. 20, no. 222.

———. 1971. "Fertility Indicators: 1970." *Current Population Reports,* Special Studies, Series p-23, no. 36. Washington, D.C.: U.S. Government Printing Office.

———. 1972. "The Social and Economic Status of the Black Population in the United States." *Current Population Reports,* Series p -23, no. 42. Washington, D.C.: U.S. Government Printing Office.

U.S. Population Council. 1972. *Report on Abortions by Age and Race*. Washington, D.C.

Westoff, Charles, and Leslie Westoff. 1971. *From Now to Zero*. Boston: Little, Brown.

Willie, Charles, and Joan Levy. 1972. "Black is Lonely." *Psychology Today* 6 (March):50–52.

Yancey, William. 1972. "Going Down Home: Family Structure and the Urban Trap." *Social Science Quarterly* 52 (March):893–906.

Zelnik, Melvin, and John Kantner. 1972. *Sexuality, Contraception, and Pregnancy among Young Unwed Females in the United States*. A paper prepared for The Commission on Population Growth and the American Future (July).

North American Indian Families

As Professor Price makes clear in this chapter on family life styles of North American Indians the large-scale cultural diversity of American Indians prevents us from discussing a single American Indian type. However, the experience of the American Indian since the appearance of the European settlers, which includes the wholesale slaughter of Indians and their movement to reservations, has brought some similarities to their family life styles. The American Indian differs from most other ethnic groups by virtue of their precedence on this continent, their primarily rural residence on reservations, and the historically paternalistic attitude of the American government. The consequences of these factors have produced a group that is highly resistant to assimilation and incorporation into mainstream American society.

CHAPTER ELEVEN
BY

JOHN A. PRICE

HISTORICAL BACKGROUND

American Indians arrived in the New World in waves of migration from northeastern Asia over a period of some 30,000 years. By the time of Columbus they had spread throughout North and South America and evolved cultures that ranged in complexity from such simple hunting bands as the Eskimo to such agricultural states as the Inca empire. At that time there were about two thousand distinct sociocultural units, each with a distinct language. The populations of the advanced agricultural areas of Central America and western South America were comparable to some European areas at the time, each being over several million in size. North of Mexico, however, the aboriginal population counted only about two million, with concentrations in the agricultural south, and along coasts, especially the Pacific Coast with its rich marine resources.

The center of American Indian civilization in North America, and the historical source for many innovations and most cultivated plants, embraced southern Mexico and Central America. The areas of America and Canada were at the far periphery or frontier of this civilization. In the three milennia prior to the arrival of the Europeans, maize agriculture had slowly spread north from Mexico through Southern and Eastern America and reached its ecological limit in southeastern Canada. North and west of the agricultural area, hundreds of diverse primitive tribes carried on their specific cultural adaptations to their ecological niches: gathering plants and shell fish, land-mammal hunting, fishing, or sea-mammal hunting. The famous horseback-riding and buffalo-hunting cultures of the Plains evolved only after the Europeans arrived and introduced the horse to the New World.

The American Indian was racially as differentiated as the Europeans and far more diverse culturally and linguistically. In language, for example, all of the European languages except Basque, Lappish, and Hungarian are historically related in the European family of the Indo-European phylum of languages. In North America alone there were several major language phyla: Eskimo-Aleut, Athabascan, Algonquian, Uto-Aztecan, Hokan, Penutian-Mayan, among others.

In line with this cultural diversity in the New World, almost all of the world's major variants of marriage, incest prohibitions, postmarriage residence customs, and in-law relations were practiced by one native North American society or another (Driver, 1969:265). This wide variation represents great historical depth and diverse adaptations to natural and cultural environments. In comparison, the Europeans who came to North America had almost uniform marriage and family practices deriving from a relatively shallow and common history of an agricultural and then an industrial adaptation in Europe.

The modern "discovery" of kinship systems is closely connected with the Iroquois. Father Lafitau, a French Jesuit missionary, described the Iroquois and Huron classifications of consanguineal kindred in 1724. Then, in 1858, when Lewis Henry Morgan discovered that the Ojibwa had a pattern of grouping relatives that was similar to that which he had previously recorded for the linguistically unrelated Iroquois, he saw the significance of kinship systems and planned his famous large-scale comparative study of kinship.

Before going into this New World diversity, it is useful to make a few broad comparisons between aboriginal North American Indian and European practices. Indian marriages were invariably public and customary, while European marriages could be private, even secret, and werc legal and in the nature of a contract between individuals. Indian marriages were more in the nature of a contract between kin groups. Indian cultures tended to be far more tolerant and accepting of variant forms of marriage. Thus, for example, monogamy, polygyny, and polyandry were all acceptable forms of marriage in most societies. Polyandry was a very rare practice, usually fraternal; it was brought on by special circumstances such as the crippling of an older married brother with the subsequent additional marriage of the younger brother to the older brother's wife. This tolerance of diversity within Indian societies tended to be greater than in European societies, which have a rather limited set of familial rules emphasizing monogamous marriage, independent nuclear or patrilocal extended forms of family, patrilocal postmarital residence, and patrilineal rules of descent and inheritance.

Polygyny was "common" among Indians of the Plains and northwest coast, occurring in more than 20 per cent of the marriages. Monogamy, on the other hand, was almost the exclusive form among certain northeastern agriculturalists, such as the Iroquois and Huron. Matrilocal postmarital residence and matrilineal descent were common among Indian agriculturalists in the Eastern and Southwestern America, where women played a major role in food production. With the intensification of agriculture, such as in Mexico, men were the predominant food producers, and postmarital residence and rules of descent shifted to patrilocal and patrilineal, as in Europe.

Puberty reckoning, particularly related to a girl's first menstruation, was universal among Indian societies and usually associated with some ceremony. At the time of initial menstruation, the girl was held to be in a potentially dangerous state of close contact with supernaturals and therefore had to behave properly. The girl's conduct at this time tended to predetermine her behavior for the rest of her life. Typically, she was secluded, fasted, learned the duties of a wife and mother from an older sponsor, worked for other women, and finally ended her taboo period by bathing and dressing in new clothing.

Premarital sexual relations were less of a problem to Indian societies than to those of Europe. The age of marriage tended to be young, usually between 15 and 20 years of age. Most Indian societies were also more permissive toward premarital relations except when it violated rules of incest, endogamy, or adultery. Premarital pregnancies were accepted, and the child was usually reared by the mother's kinfolk.

Such customs as bride price and bride service were common in the Plains and northwest coast. Interfamilial exchange marriage, when two families exchange daughters to marry a son in another family, existed in areas in which there were few marriage formalities, such as the Great Basin and Sub-Arctic. Adopting a son to marry a daughter, inherit the family property, and carry on a line of descent among sonless families existed in several patrilineal areas. First cross-cousin marriages were permitted or even preferred in some, usually strongly lineal, societies in which the father's brother's daughter or mother's sister's daughter was in a different descent line than the groom. This was common, for example, among such wealthy fishing matrilineal societies as the Tlingit, Tsimshian, and Haida of coastal British Columbia and the Alaskan panhandle.

The Impact of European Cultures

The horse was introduced into the Plains from Spanish settlements in New Mexico in the seventeenth and eighteenth centuries. Many tribes of Indians then migrated into the Plains to take up the highly productive hunting of buffalo. This ecological shift brought on an initial convergence of social structures. Highly integrated societies that had previously been horticultural "regressed" to more flexible hunting bands and emphasized "generational" kinship, while previously very simple gathering societies tended to build up their structures with more decisive military and political organization. Finally, the Plains Indians, defeated by whites and with the demise of the buffalo herds, relocated on reservations and began to acculturate to European forms of social structure.

Missionaries, teachers, and government agents to the Choctaw of Mississippi, concerned that Indian women worked in the fields, the usual practice in horticultural societies, failed to understand that the fathers' disinclination to provide materially for their own children was in accordance with the matrilineal system of inheritance.

New regulations regarding land were introduced that emphasized the position of the man as head of the family. Marriage was regulated by law, widows were entitled to dower rights, and children could inherit the father's estate. The leaders no longer came from the clans but were elected by the adult male members of the district, and the old town rituals were largely replaced by the church and its activities. (Eggan, 1966:29)

These changes broke down if they did not destroy the clan and kinship structures, emphasized nuclear families and territorial ties, and shifted kinship from a matrilineal system to a patrilineally biased bilateral sys-

251

tem. Similar historic shifts occurred among other Southeast societies, such as the Creek and Cherokee.

Indians were forcibly removed from most of American lands east of the Mississippi River except in isolated spots: Cherokees in the North Carolina mountains, the Seminoles of the Florida Everglades, some Iroquois in northern New York, and some Algonquins in the northern woods. Total removal occurred later and was not as complete west of the Mississippi River. As a result, this is where most of the Indians live today, particularly in Oklahoma, the Dakotas, Montana, New Mexico, Arizona, and along the West Coast. The pattern of displacement was similar in Canada, but the European population was much smaller, so that the extent of displacement and deculturation was less. Also, in the long period of fur trapping and northern exploration there was more use and respect for native skills than in America. However, the Beothuk were extinguished by the French and Scotch fishermen of Newfoundland. Wars between Indians were actively promoted by competing French and British interests in the Canadian fur trade, and Indians were generally displaced and enclaved in "reserves" in the east-to-west sweep of European immigrant agriculturalists across Canada.

Differences between Europeans who arrived in the New World played an important role in determining the nature of Indian-European relations. For example, the French, Spanish, and Portuguese were more tolerant of intermarriage with the natives than were northern Europeans. Thus, since early historical times there have been significant populations of Spanish-Indian *mestizos* and French-Indian *metis,* but few British-Indian "half-breeds," considering the size of the British population in North America. A major reason for this seems to be that in the sixteenth and seventeenth centuries the French, Spanish, and Portuguese came largely as single men, while the British tended to come as families. It also appears that southern European discrimination has been largely based on differences of culture and social class, while northern European (Germanic and British) discrimination has been more racial.

Perhaps more important than the foregoing intimate relations are the differences among Europeans in their colonial designs on the land and the people of the New World. Spaniards colonized basically to exploit the New World for gold, exports, and converting the natives to Christianity. French ends seem to have been similar except that the wealth was in the fur trade in their northern territory. Some northern Europeans engaged in this exploitation as well, but large numbers of northern Europeans came looking for land to settle on and to farm themselves. Northern Europeans tended to force the Indians off the farming lands, while the Spaniards kept the natives working on the land, but now under European feudal-style *haciendas* and *encomiendas*.

The kinds of Indian cultures that the Europeans met were also crucial in determining the character of European-Indian relations. Simple band-organized societies were nonagricultural and without tribal-wide political organization or leadership. Thus, the Europeans had no significant military resistance from band-organized peoples, but they were also incapable of using them as agricultural workers. True tribes and chiefdoms often did give military resistance but still were difficult to rule as an internal agricultural peasantry. Thus, there was often bitter warfare between them and the Europeans until the Indians were finally displaced from the land. Where the Europeans conquered Indians from native agricultural-state societies, however, they were far more successful at simply replacing the existing state leadership with Europeans and keeping the natives working the land as agricultural peasants. With this situation, there was then no need for reservations.

The native states existed in the areas of Spanish colonization, particularly in Mexico and Peru. The modern state cultures in these areas have, in turn, been more strongly influenced by the Indian component in their heritages. This is particularly true of Mexico, which looks back with pride to its Indian foundations and to the heroic resistance of the Aztec leaders to Cortez and the Spaniards. Montezuma and Cuhuatemoc are the national heroes, not Cortez.

Europeans imposed their concepts of proper marriage and family relations on the Indians, particularly through the preaching of Christian missionaries and through laws that were applied to Indians. In countless ways Europeans impressed their particular social system on Indians. One example of European bias is that when the Spanish priests contacted the Pima of southern Arizona, they gave bead necklaces to women and tobacco to men, but both men and women wear necklaces and smoke tobacco among the Pima. In more destructive fashion, Christian missionaries usually tried to eliminate plural marriages and matrilineal customs without understanding the crucial roles these practices had in the normal functioning of native societies. In Canada the potlatch ceremonies of the Pacific Coast that were so crucial in validating titles and bringing order to the kinship systems were outlawed because of Protestant concerns about wasteful feasts.

In Canada there are some 275,000 "registered" Indians and about an equal number of persons who are not "registered" but still identify themselves as Indians. The registered Indians belong to 561 "bands" and live primarily on 2,281 separate "reserves." The nonregistered Indians have been historically excluded from government programs, band membership, and residence on reserves largely because of the biases against interracial marriage and against matrilineal systems in the 1906 Indian Act of Canada.

The Indian Act of Canada was written by Euro-Canadians who applied the assumptions that household heads should be male and wives should be dependent on them, that inheritance should be patrilineal, and that families should be nuclear. This act has been destructive of the social structure of matrilineal and bilateral Indian societies and supportive of patrilineal Indian societies. "Indian status" is essential to inclusion in rights to Indian band lands and to programs of the Indian Affairs Branch, but an Indian woman can lose this status if her husband loses his status, or if she ever marries a person without Indian status. A man with Indian status does not lose his status if her marries a nonstatus woman, instead his wife acquires Indian status even if she is Euro-Canadian. If a status woman marries a nonstatus person and thus loses her status, then later divorces that person, she still cannot reacquire status except by marrying a status Indian. The law supports patrilocal and postmarital residence because at marriage a woman becomes a member of her husband's band. In spite of these inequalities, Canadian Indians are generally in favor of retaining the act as it is until the larger questions concerning the historical treaties have been settled. They are also critical of any changes in the act that would allow more whites (husbands in this case) to move onto the reserves.

Cruikshank's (1969) study of the Indians of the Yukon Territory indicated the development of a frequent pattern of matrifocal families as a result of cultural disruption. Because native men have been economically displaced by Euro-Canadian society, and the traditional sexual division of labor has broken down, women may now do economically better for themselves and their children without a permanent male spouse. For example, Indian women's work in the Yukon, such as domestic servants and waitresses, tends to be steady, while the men work more in seasonal jobs. Indian women can easily relate socially and sexually with the Euro-Canadian men who come in the summer and tend to be treated better by them than by Indian men. There are factors, however, that discourage Indian marriage to Euro-Canadians such as the transient nature of Euro-Canadians' visits to the north and Canada's policy of taking official "Indian status" away from Indian women who marry non-Indians.

Acculturation and the Formation of an Ethnic Group

Several acculturation hypotheses have been employed to analyze historical Indian culture continuity and change. Isolation on reservations is seen as a factor supporting their cultural continuity. Some cases of forced acculturation may have led to resistance toward change and the development of effective institutions that have helped to preserve cultural continuity, such as techniques to ward off religious and government agents of social change. This seems to have occurred especially when the native community has had a strongly bonded "corporate" structure, such as among the Cuna and the Hopi. Also, racist attitudes by Europeans against Indians set up a barrier against Indian assimilation, even to the extent of making Indian-European marriages illegal in the early legislation of several Western states.

Another hypothesis holds that material aspects have changed more readily than social and ideological aspects, so that Indians are still able to revitalize some social and ideological dimensions of their cultures. The individual wage employment and entrepreneurship of industrial society tend to disrupt the cooperative, communalistic, pooling kind of economic arrangements that are an integral part of tribal kinship economics. In fact, these mutual ties of rights and obligations are seen as deterrents to economic advancement in an industrial society, that kinfolk claims reduce the individual incentives that bring healthy competition into a capitalist society.

The modern law of state societies is universalistic. It applies to every sociocultural unit within the geographical jurisdictions of the law and thus reduces their diversity to common practices. Not only is the society-by-society diversity that existed among the hundreds of Indian tribes reduced to conform with national and state laws, but the tolerant diversity that existed within single Indian societies must conform as well. Polygyny, for example, was almost universally allowed by Indian societies and is eliminated through the law. Indian children by law must attend school, so traditional education is undermined. Marriages must now be legally registered. Marital differences that were once handled by kinship councils may now come before the courts. However, it is very hard for even the post industrial state society to control the nonempirical or ideological world of its internal subcultures, and it has no reason to control the ineffectual facades of cultural difference. Thus, we are allowed the myth of a legitimately plural society. The customs that survive are those innocuous ones that escape the conforming crush of law, such as religious practices, music, tastes in food, etc. These, then, become the hallmarks of ethnic difference, the stereotypes, remnants of once truly different cultures.

The basic pattern of cultural retention is that as separate sociocultural entities are integrated into expanding nation states, they are converted into ethnic subcultures. Assuming some continuity rather than outright destruction, the first significant changes tend to be material, economic, and some legal elements of integration with the dominant society. Internal adjustments, as well as direct pressures by missionaries and government agents, then tend to produce a variety of social and political changes. Finally, there is typically not only a survival but a creative readjustment of ideology, identity, religion, and other materially unimportant symbols of ethnic uniqueness: tastes in food, ethnic costumes, music, dance, art, etc. Language acculturation takes place over the whole period of acculturation, usually takes the form of bilingualism during the phase of significant social and political changes, and is complete when all that is left of the original language for most people are the ethnic words and phrases that have been incorporated into the dominant language as used by speakers of that ethnic group.

Societies that are native to a country have many differences with those that are migrants to the country. Thus, Indians identify with no other land, while all other immigrant groups have other geographical identities. Indians live more widely scattered across North America than any other sizable ethnic population. In line with this identification with the land, scatter, and predominantly rural residence, Indians are probably the most opposed to assimilation and integration into majority society and culture of any sizable ethnic population.

MODERN INDIAN FAMILIES: FIVE CASE STUDIES

Cultural continuity in the family life styles of Indians has been greater where European influences come later, as in the tropics and the Arctic, or less destructive, as in Mexico and Peru. Certain reservation enclaves have also provided sufficient isolation from European influences to adapt family structures gradually and with continuing social integration. Sketched below are five brief case studies from North America proper to illustrate the changes occurring in modern Indian families in different settings of European contact and ecology: (1) Cuna of Panama, (2) Eskimo of North Alaska, (3) Hopi of northern Arizona, (4) Menomini of Wisconsin, and (5) Indians of Los Angeles, California. The five case studies are presented in an order based on the extent of change from aboriginal family life styles, beginning with the conservative Cuna and ending with the largest urban settlement in North America of people who identify themselves as Indians.

It is only in reference to the more acculturated Indians, such as the Menomini and urban Indians, that we can accurately speak of an active membership in an "American Indian ethnic group" that would be comparable to the European ethnic minorities in North America. That is, the Cuna, Eskimo, and Hopi tend to still be so involved with their own cultures that they do not actively participate in a self-conscious, integrated, Indian ethnic minority even though they may be racially and culturally defined as members by the majority society. In fact, specific tribal identities are almost universally stronger and more important than identity as a native American.

The Cuna or San Blas of Panama

The Indians of the Darien coast were one of first native societies contacted by the Spaniards when Balboa came and attacked them in 1511. Their policy of tribal exclusiveness, their physical isolation along the tropical Caribbean coast and in the San Blas Islands, and their capacity to defend themselves militarily led to a situation of extremely minimal acculturation. They are best known for one of the highest frequencies of albinism in the world, between .75 and 1.0 per cent, and that has led to their being studied. The tribe today has a population of about 20,000. Aboriginally, the Cuna were an agricultural chiefdom with the four social ranks of head chief, nobles, commoners, and slaves, who were tatooed with property marks. The social organization has since become simpler, with less emphasis on the hierarchy, and slave tatooing is no longer practiced (Weyer, 1959:87–100).

Chiefs and nobles used to have several wives, but today the tribe is almost entirely monogamous. Matrilocal postmarital residence is still practiced, and matrilineal extended families are still in predominance. The oldest male in the family household is the formal head of the household even though he marries into it. Women formerly cultivated the gardens, but now men do this. A few men have begun to take wage work in the Canal Zone. Women still weave hammocks and cloth for clothing, as well as doing the cooking and childtending. Aboriginal religious practices seem to have survived rather fully, and this is seen in their distinctive puberty and marriage customs.

The girl's puberty ceremony, called "the flowering," is held for four

257

days following the first menstruation. She is confined in a menstrual hut built inside her regular house in which teams of men pour water over her almost continuously for four days. So much water is used that a trench is built to carry the water out of the house and into the sea. Her future is decided in a search and analysis of a male and female crab. On the fourth day she is painted black over her entire body with a ceremoniously acquired dye to protect her from evil spirits who might be attracted by her beauty. Her hair is trimmed at the sunrise that ends the fourth day, and then the ceremony is concluded with feasting, drinking, ceremonial tobacco smoking, and singing to the accompaniment of panpipes. A year or so later the girl is given a large "coming out" feast and dance, after which she is eligible to marry.

Parents arrange the marriage, and then the groom is forcibly placed in a "marriage hammock" in the bride's house. The bride is placed on top of the groom, a burning log is placed beneath them, and they are rocked back and forth. They are later undressed and bathed. The couple's life is then one of working and raising children in the communalistic setting of a matrilineal extended family and a close-knit village. Attitudes today toward sex and bodily display are rather puritanical, although aboriginal women wore only small aprons, and men usually wore simply a penis sheath.

The Eskimo of North Alaska

Chance's (1966) study of the Eskimo of north Alaska showed that large families are welcomed, that children enjoy much love and affection, and that adoption between kin is easy and widespread. Children are often named after a deceased person, and some of the qualities or even the spirit of the original person continues in the namesake. Children are packed or carried in the back of a parka a great deal until about 2 years old. Weaning may not be completed until the third or even fourth year, while toilet training begins before the first birthday. There is generally no shame or secrecy about excretory functions.

Childhood training emphasizes egalitarian social cooperation and skills of survival. Boys may begin to shoot a rifle as young as 7 years of age, while girls begin to learn the techniques of butchering at a very young age. The sexual division of labor, however, is not extremely rigid. For example, boys may occasionally cook and girls may go fishing or bird hunting. Storytelling, wrestling, and hand games now combine with such Western games as volleyball, Monopoly, and Scrabble. Children from 6 to 16 are required to attend the local Bureau of Indian Affairs

School in which use of the native language is discouraged or even forbidden. Eskimo adolescents become more peer centered in social groups and in many ways emulate Euro-American teen-agers in dress (denims and black leather jackets), slang ("Man, I don't go for parkas"), music, and dance steps.

Whale, seal, and caribou are still the main sources of food. They are now usually served on the Western three-meals-a-day plan. Government control has removed the need for mutual protection of kin during feuds. Individual wage labor has decreased the economic interdependence that operated in the traditional bilaterally extended family. Sharing is now more common in such secondary economic activities as babysitting, butchering meat, and the distribution of household items. Young people today are more free from parental restrictions on selecting marriage partners, but the tradition of first-cousin marriage is still fairly common in some communities. Formal wife exchanges between friends is no longer practiced, but sexual mores are still relatively free. There is very little display of emotions between husband and wife, although the mutual bond may in fact be close, affectionate, and satisfying. Couples rarely go visiting together or entertain friends together and nonkin adult social gatherings are not usually mixed by sex. However, very casual visiting between same-sex friends is a feature of daily family life. A friend may come in, watch the activities of the household for some time, and leave again without anything more being said between the host and visitor than a brief exchange of greetings.

Chance (1966:85–87) writes that in Kaktovik and other new small Eskimo villages relatively smooth adjustments to modern culture have occurred because of such things as (1) their intensive interaction and communication, (2) the kinship system remained stable enough to support individuals in stressful situations, (3) most of the newly defined goals, particularly for material goods, were successfully realized, and (4) traditional leadership and pride were maintained. In larger communities, such as Barrow, there have been more problems related to the residential and social separation of Euro-Americans and Eskimos, that is, a marked lower status of and discrimination against Eskimos.

A Point Hope study (VanStone, 1962) indicated that women prefer only three or four children, but contraceptives are practically unknown and never used. Many traditional beliefs surround childbirth, for example, windstorms are associated with movements of the fetus. Several elderly women act as midwives and attend each birth in the village. Women who have had a few children apparently acquire a rather casual attitude toward childbirth.

One older woman, far advanced in pregnancy, was traveling by skin boat from Jabbertown to Point Hope. She asked to be put ashore "to go to the toilet" and gave birth after the boat had moved on without her. She cut the cord and scraped sand over the afterbirth, put the baby in her parka and ran up the beach to catch up with the boat. (VanStone, 1962:79).

Cloth diapers are used, but the infant is still carried on the back inside the mother's parka. The mother stays near her baby, giving the breast as soon and as often as it desires, but breast feeding is relatively undemonstrative and without much emotion.

There appears to be no stress placed on rapid toilet training . . . A two-year-old boy was heard to say "toilet" and then went toward the can normally used for the purpose but urinated on the floor. The parents were amused by this "near miss" and the child, obviously partially trained, was given credit for taking a step in the right direction."

The importance of naming, the widespread practice of adoption, and a socialization toward cooperation with mild discipline seem to be general Eskimo traits. Premarital sex relations are not uncommon, but it is difficult to find secluded places for love meetings in a small Arctic village. An old-style "partner" relationship of adult men is still important, especially in hunting.

The Canadian Eskimo has many similarities with those of north Alaska. (Willmott (1960) studied the community of Port Harrison, Quebec, on the east coast of Hudson Bay, in which 340 Eskimos lived in 1958. While most of the 60 marriages were monogamous, there were 2 polygynous families and 2 essentially polyandrous families. About two-thirds of the marriages were traditional and one-third under the auspices of the church. Local clusters of 6 to 10 households formed highly cooperative groups so that people could freely eat and young boys could sleep in any convenient tent or snow house in the cluster. Households were highly flexible in membership because of extensive adoption and the addition of relatives and friends to the nuclear family. Willmott claims that this flexibility and an accepting attitude toward changes has led to relationships with Euro-Canadians that are relatively free of conflict. Sixteen per cent of the children under 15 in the community were adopted, usually because the adopting couple wanted a child rather than because the child did not have a home. A concomitant of this passing around of children seems to be that children receive a lot of attention and "mothering" without strong specific mother-child emotional ties.

The Hopi of Northern Arizona

Pueblo cultures have had more continuity and homogeneity in their histories than most Indian cultures in the "lower 48" states of America. The western Pueblos (Hopi, Zuni, Acoma, and Laguna) tend to have matrilineal exogamous clans and extended matrilocal households, while the eastern Pueblos of the Rio Grande are primarily bilateral with moieties. The isolation of the Hopi has particularly shielded them from some of the pressures of change, although they have periodically faced extinction through drought, disease, and warfare. Each Hopi village tends to be endogamous and independent, except for intermarriage with nearby "colony villages." The history of the matrilineal clans in the village according to their order or arrival, occupation of the clan house, ceremonial possessions, and clan lands is important in determining village social relations.

Marriage is monogamous. Men join their wives' households and economically support them but retain ritual, leadership, and disciplinary roles in their natal households. Thus, they discipline their sisters' children and play a passive role in their wife's household. The tension in these contrasting roles contributes to a high divorce rate among the Hopi (Eggan, 1966:126). Another tension exists in the conflict between the basically theocratic organization of the Hopi and the modern demands for decisive political action that have been imposed on them. While community welfare is highly valued, there is competition between clans and villages in terms of such things as ceremonial performances.

Pueblo socialization is permissive, with gradual weaning and toilet training and little explicit discipline of children until they are over 2 years of age (Dozier, 1970). Admonitions then center on such things as hard work, enduring discomforts, and not wasting food. Masked disciplinarians with whips are used to threaten disobedient children. Initiation of girls and boys into a *kiva* or religious society occurs between the ages of 6 and 9 with rigid physical and dietary restrictions. There is little opportunity for privacy, particularly in those villages that are still constructed as compact, adobe, apartmentlike pueblos. Gossip, ridicule, and the discipline of *kiva* societies keep down social deviancy, maintaining a kind of Taoist "wu-wei" or quietistic solution to social relations. In the past, Hopis executed witches and evicted other deviants, but today the rebellious individuals tend to move to the freer life of cities and just visit their villages to renew kinship and ceremonial ties. One example of a semiurban adaptation is that about 600 Hopi live in a suburban type of life at Moenkopi with such appliances as refrigerators, gas ranges, running water, and automobiles. These people often drive into the city of Flagstaff, Arizona, for shopping and visiting.

Religious ceremonialism, with its rich traditions of costuming, dance, music, and theology, is still at the center of Hopi life and is more attractive to the Hopi than the Christian alternatives. Developing within a context of Spanish and then Euro-American curiosity and pressures to change, the Hopi religious societies developed defensive secrecy and theological adjustments that rationalized Hopi religion in relation to Christianity and American culture. Hopi is an Indian society that has had sufficient autonomy from Euro-American pressures to gradually evolve a modern culture with a consistently high level of internal integration. Wage work, Western education, automobiles, electrical appliances, Western dress, weekend supermarket shopping, etc., are now accepted practices, but the aboriginal language is being retained as a second language to English, and the Hopi religion has never been replaced by Christianity.

The Menomini of Wisconsin

Spindler and Spindler (1971) found five social segments along a continuum of sociocultural adaptation among the Menomini living in a Wisconsin reservation: (1) native oriented, (2) Peyotists, (3) transitionals, (4) lower-status acculturated, and (5) elite acculturated. The native-oriented group receives a definition and identity through maintaining the Dream Dance and other formalized dances and rituals. The peyotists are involved in the pan-Indian "Native American Church," a religion that serves to resolve some of the ideological conflicts between the Christian and Indian traditions. The transitionals lack a firm identity and religious affiliation, but individuals in this large category are moving to either native-oriented or "white man" identity and religion. The more acculturated people tend to have a significantly higher economic status and no affiliation with either the aboriginal religious practices or the historical Peyotist movement. The acculturated, especially the elite, are usually Catholic in religion.

The native-oriented group tend to have the personal qualities of equanimity and, under duress, control of overt emotionality and aggression, autonomy, a sense of humor, and hospitality. They believe in having supernatural power, from a guardian spirit through a vision while fasting or simply through a displaying of quiescent receptivity to power, and that dreams can be used to predict the future.

Children in the native-oriented group are received as reincarnated elders and, like old people, are close to the supernatural power that pervades all things. Naming is ceremonious and very important. Children are treated with tolerance and permissiveness, with gradual weaning, casual toilet training, and mild discipline. When a boy kills his first game, he is given a feast, and praises are sung to him. When a girl fills her pail with wild berries, she is praised. Children participate in the important social happenings, such as the dances. They are told stories by the elders, including formalized "preachings" about proper behavior. The group is childoriented because the transmission of traditional culture is a central purpose of the group. This results in a quite different kind of family life than that found among the "acculturated" Menomini. The Spindlers see the native-oriented cultural system as a conscious attempt to maintain a way of life that is dying, a reaffirmation of the traditional way while attempting to exclude the foreign way. This is similar to the Hopi Kivi societies or the Long House Society people among the Iroquois, who follow the Code of Handsome Lake.

The elite acculturated tend to live in a community different from that of the traditionals, in homes like business and professional people in nearby Euro-American communities. They are active in the Catholic Church, often play golf, or bowl, or go snowmobiling; do not speak Menomini; and are consciously oriented toward Euro-American culture, but still derive some pride and identity from their Menomini heritage.

In 1961 the U.S. Bureau of Indian Affairs terminated its relations with the tribe, the reservation became a county of Wisconsin, and Menominee Enterprises, Inc., became the tribal management. The American government had decided that the Menomini were sufficiently acculturated to entirely operate their own affairs. Still, the determination to keep Menomini identity and lands intact was strong, and after years of political action, their termination was partially rescinded in 1974. In early 1975 the Menominee Warrior's Society forcefully "occupied" the vacant Alexian Brothers Monastery in Gresham, Wisconsin. They negotiated the donation of the monastery to their tribe.

The Indians of Los Angeles

Of the approximately 850,000 Indians in America about 500,000 live on or near reservations in rural settings. The remaining 350,000 live in towns and cities largely as a result of a recent urban migration that began as a significant movement after about 1955. Los Angeles today, by all estimates, has the most Indians of any urban area in America or Canada, somewhere around 45,000.* San Francisco, Tulsa, Oklahoma City, Minneapolis, Chicago, and Phoenix all have over 10,000 Indians. Albuquerque, Denver, and Seattle in America and Vancouver, Edmonton, Regina, Winnipeg, Toronto, and Montreal in Canada also each have several thousand Indians.† Research on urban Indians so far has focused on their migrations to cities and on urban ethnic institutions, so that little is known of their day-to-day family life.

Indians came to Los Angeles from all over North America but generally in the same proportions as the U.S. national distributions of Indians by state or by tribe (Price, 1968). Thus, for example, about 15 per cent of the Indians in America live in Arizona, and 15 per cent of the Indians in Los Angeles are from Arizona. Only about 6 per cent of the Indians in Los Angeles were born in California. A similar correlation is found for tribal representation. Individuals from over one hundred tribes live in Los Angeles, but the larger the tribe the more migrants it will tend to have move into Los Angeles. Thus, nationally and in Los Angeles, there are about 14 per cent Navaho, 12 per cent Sioux, and so on to dozens of tribes with less than 1 per cent.

A major force behind the urban migration of Indians in America has been the Employment Assistance Program of the Bureau of Indian Affairs, which has helped about 100,000 Indians relocate from reservations to urban areas and provided urban-oriented vocational training for over 25,000 household heads. Whether supported in their migration by the government or not, whether in America or Canada, the urban migration of Indians has a large number of parallels. The incentive is primarily economic, such as to find a job or higher wages and to improve physical living conditions. They miss the social contacts and activities of the reservation and, when possible, spend weekends or vacations back visiting on their reservation. As the years in the city go by, they tend to withdraw from reservation social contacts, idealize traditional reservation life, and perhaps talk of retiring or otherwise returning to their reservations, in which as members of the tribe they have a right to reside.

In our 1966 study (Price, 1968) we found a significant shift from traditional practices toward marriages outside the tribe to other Indians (about one-third) and outside the race (about one-third). More Indians

---

*Spanish America is excluded from discussion here because its extreme syncretism of European and Indian cultures led to fundamentally different patterns. Also, there is far more continuity of Indian cultures, so that, for example, over 10 million people still speak Indian languages in Spanish America.

†Indians in Canada constitute a higher proportion of the total population (*ca*. 2.5 percent) than in America (*ca*. 0.4 percent), but a higher proportion in Canada live on or near their reserves (*ca*. 78 percent) and retain a native first language (*ca*. 65 percent).

went to church in the city (70 per cent) than did on the reservation (53 per cent). About 20 per cent of the Indians were active in formal Indian associations, such as Indian athletic leagues, one of the 10 Indian Christian churches, Indian dance clubs, and Indian social centers. In informal associations, some 29 per cent of our sample reported their usual association as being only with other Indians, 67 per cent mixed, and 4 per cent exclusively with non-Indians. The vast majority preferred living in mixed neighborhoods and found no housing discrimination. Indians are, in fact, much more widely scattered residentially than Blacks or Mexican Americans. Recent arrivals tend to live first in the central city and then, usually after about two years, move out to the suburbs.

Indians tend to retain reservation attitudes that one should not spend much on clothes or housing, with large proportions of their budgets going toward travel and entertainment. Sports, television, Indian dancing at "powwows," and socializing at Indian bars are major sources of recreation. We found that active involvement with Indian sports leagues and Indian dance groups was correlated with a positive and permanent adaptation to city life. Most urban Indians visit their home reservations so frequently that it has been characterized as a specialized kind of "commuting," but some finally settle in to a fairly permanent commitment to city life and actively work toward creating a new pan-Indian ethnic culture.

In the city, meeting Indians from over one hundred different tribes, the Indian still finds many cultural commonalities and many common problems, as well as a common racial identity that becomes important in a racially sensitive society. This cultural pan-Indianism and a political awareness of the problems of Indians from other tribes flourishes in the city and becomes a stabilizing and integrating force for this new ethnic group. That is, individuals from hundreds of separate bands, tribes, chiefdoms, and states are in the process of creating a North American Indian ethnic group, and the large urban centers, such as Los Angeles, play a key role in that process of creation.

In every city with a large Indian population there is a significant social overlap between the Indian ethnic culture and the skid-row bar culture. In some regions, such as the Canadian prairies, skid-row culture is usually dominated by Indians (Brody, 1971). This is a lower-class culture with its own norms into which the urban migrant Indian can fit easily, and in which he or she is likely to find friends and consolation from urban culture shock and white prejudice. It is a setting of cafés, cheap hotels, and beer taverns with country music. In much of America's West and Canada, Indians have somewhat acculturated to the cowboy life style in dress, music, ranch work, and rodeos, as well as drinking patterns. However, in Indian bars there tends to be more social animation and interaction. People are louder, freer, more accepting of newcomers, and more mobile as they move from table to table and bar to bar. Gangs form easily for such petty crimes as rolling drunks, prostitution, or just "jumping" someone for their money. Jail is a common, shared experience without stigma for virtually every Indian who has been on skid row for a few months. Arrest rates for Indians in America are about 3 times that of Blacks and 10 times that of whites in general and 8 times that of Blacks and 20 times that of whites for drinking-related offenses (Reason, 1972:320).

There is pride among skid-row Indian men in heavy drinking, fighting ability, the ability to "con" outsiders, generosity with insiders, and attractiveness to women. In comfortable situations Indians are vivacious. They may use silence as a shield against outside intrusions, but when together, the defenses come down. They go to bars primarily to mix socially. They are compulsive socializers, not compulsive drinkers. Those few Indians who are compulsive drinkers tend to live on reservations where life is much cheaper. Skid row is a relatively young-oriented place for Indians, so there are virtually no old Indians on skid row. Skid row tends to be only a passing phase, usually no more than two or three years of intensive involvement in the individual Indian's life.

Indians who make a permanent adaptation to city life tend to settle down to semiskilled and skilled jobs, move outside the city center to reside in mixed suburban areas, and support the middle-class Indian ethnic institutions. Cities as a whole can also be seen to evolve in terms of the progressively comprehensive set of institutions that are oriented to and/or staffed by Indians. That is, the first Indian ethnic institutions in the city are usually Indian bars, as well as perhaps certain government agencies for Indians. These are operated by non-Indians for lower-class Indians, but in time the urban-adapted Indians become middle class and develop their own ethnic institutions, such as social centers, churches, powwow clubs, and athletic leagues.

CHANGE AND ADAPTATION

A number of simultaneous processes are at work among native peoples: (1) a high population increase; (2) government programs to bring Indians out of their poverty life style, (3) convergent social adaptations to the dominant society, (4) urbanization, and (5) an ethnic renascence that involves (a) the creation of a general pan-Indian ethnicity, (b) several special political and religious pan-Indian movements, such as Peyotism and the Sun Dance, (c) the cultural revitalization of certain tribal and regional customs, and (d) a renewed interest in native history, literature, crafts, art, dance, foods, etc. Indian family life styles are intimately involved with these processes.

The future of native peoples is first of all one of *population expansion*. They are probably the fastest growing ethnic or racial population (3.2 per cent annual increase rate in Canada and slightly less in America) in spite of high rates of infant mortality (about twice the American average), certain diseases (tuberculosis is seven times more frequent than the American average), and death (average life expectancy is some 10 years less than the American average). Around 1980 the American Indian population of America and Canada will again reach the estimated two million mark, as when Indians were first contacted by Europeans.

Indian life is generally one of *poverty*. Some cultures define a life of poverty as nonmaterialistic, spiritual, noncompetitive, and in tune with the natural environment, but in North America it is defined as a sign of ignorance and without value. Indian life does look terrible in terms of such majority society criteria as employment, income, housing, education, and health standards. "In 1967 the average Indian income was $1,500, 75 per cent below the national average . . . three-fourths of all reservation housing is below minimum standards as defined by the Census Bureau." (Bahr, Chadwick, and Day, 1972:4–5). About one-third of all adult Indians in America are classified as illiterate, and only one adult male in five has a high school education.

We should not, however, project too much misery into our conceptions of the day-to-day life of Indians. Where the non-Indian visitor might suffer cultural shock in perceptions of reservation uncleanliness, drinking, fighting, etc., the person raised there usually looks back with loving warmth to his childhood in a close-knit community. Indian societies have values that, if used as criteria of evaluation of the majority society, could in turn make the style of life of the majority look "poverty stricken." These values differ somewhat from one Indian society to the next, so that Cuna, Eskimo, Hopi, Menomini, and the Indians of Los Angeles would all judge the pathologies in our styles of life in different ways.

The majority North American society in the past received mostly material rather than social or ideological elements of culture from native societies: cultigens such as corn, tomatoes, potatoes, chocolate, pineapple, tobacco, rubber, and artifacts such as the parka, toboggan, hammock, and moccasin. Today, however, there is some evidence that Indian social and ideological culture is influencing the majority society. Vine Deloria, an Indian spokesman, claims that "American society is unconsciously going Indian" in its search for individual freedom within a socially tolerant community that is in ecological harmony with its environment. The evidence of the history of cultural change, however, is that the major direction of influence will be that of drawing Indians out of their "poverty" into the clean, healthy, materialism of the majority society.

We have already examined the process of convergent *social adaptation* through acculturation. In family life we have seen this in the increasingly predominant pattern of the monogamous, bilateral, patrilineal-biased, nuclear family. However, there appear to be some residual differences in family life between even urbanized American Indians and the majority society. Indian families seem to be less child centered and have less emphasis on such things as toilet training, cleanliness, punctuality, competition, and worldly achievement. Another social feature is that, compared with non-Indians, modern Indian political processes tend to work slower and less aggressively, have more consensus, and involve more personal rapport between leaders and their constituency.

We have discussed the process of *urbanization* in reference to the Los Angeles Indians. As the process of urban migration has proceeded, the reservations themselves have been changed. When the urbanization has already become extreme, as in California, many small reservations that are distant from cities have been abandoned, have become retirement communities for the older generation who stayed on while the younger people moved into the cities, or have become summer-vacation areas for their Indian owners. Among the Cupeno and Luiseno Indians of San Diego County, California, we found one reserve that had been essentially abandoned, one isolated reserve with only a few older people left, two other reserves with a moderate population in farming, and a fifth that was increasing in population because it was close enough to surrounding white farms and towns for the residents to commute to wage work (Price, 1971). We can expect to see many of the small tribes become entirely assimilated, while other larger, more isolated, or more well defended tribes survive as distinct sociocultural units. That is, the Hopi should survive indefinitely because they have a relatively large population, they have some physical and social isolation from the majority society, and they have created defenses against assimilation. The Menomini, even though they have a large population and a large territory, have been terminated by federal Indian Affairs, do not have well-developed defenses against assimilation, and do not have good prospects for survival as a distinct socio cultural unit.

The *ethnic renascence* of Indians has had about a century of significant pan-Indian developments but became a major movement only about 10 years ago, after the Chicago Indian Conference in 1961, if one had to pick a time and place. Since then, in addition to existing reservation and band administrations, about one hundred Indian political organizations have developed in America and Canada. Most of these organizations publish periodicals, and collectively these periodicals form an information network because the various editors read and report news from each other's papers (Price, 1972). Thus, an important news item can spread rapidly throughout the network of periodicals. This "common cause" literature in turn fosters the integration of an Indian ethnic group in spite of the great tribal diversity and the isolated, rural, and scattered residence of Indians.

Indian organizations have pressed all levels of government for action on their behalf, bringing changes in everything from the treatment of Indians in history books to support for the economic development of reservations. Even urban Indians are generally involved with the ethnic renascence, although it may mean no more than such things as reading books about Indians; attending a local Indian ceremonial powwow or fair "so that the children will know their heritage"; or engaging in traditional Indian crafts. This latest step in the long history of the native peoples seems to be the creation for the first time in history of an American Indian ethnic group; as with ethnic groups generally, they are sensitive about what they are called. Eskimos want to be called *Inuit,* which means "people" in Eskimo, while *eskimo* is an Athabascan word for "raw meat eaters." Indians do not like being called "after a land in southern Asia because of some stupid mistake of Columbus." Instead, many leaders prefer terms like "native Americans," "native Canadians," or just "native people."

R E F E R E N C E S

Bahr, H. M., B. A. Chadwick, and R. C. Day (eds.). 1972. *Native Americans Today: Sociological Perspectives.* New York: Harper & Row.
Brody, Hugh. 1971. *Indians on Skid Row.* Ottawa: Information Canada.
Chance, Norman A. 1966. *The Eskimo of North Alaska.* New York: Holt, Rinehart and Winston.
Cruikshank, Julie. 1969. *The Role of Northern Canadian Women in Social Change.* M.A. Thesis, University of British Columbia.

Dozier, Edward P. 1970. *The Pueblo Indians of North America*. New York: Holt, Rinehart and Winston.

Driver, Harold E. 1969. *Indians of North America*. Chicago: University of Chicago Press.

Eggan, Fred. 1966. *The American Indian: Perspectives for the Study of Social Change*. Chicago: Aldine.

Murdock, George P. 1949. *Social Structure*. New York: Macmillan.

Price, John A. 1968. "The Migration and Adaptation of American Indians to Los Angeles." *Human Organization* 27 (Summer). 168–75.

————. 1971. *Cultural Divergence Related to Urban Proximity on American Indian Reservations*. Monographs of the Training Center for Community Programs, University of Minnesota, Minneapolis.

————. 1972. "U.S. and Canada Indian Periodicals." *Canadian Review of Sociology and Anthropology* 9 (May). 150–62.

Reason, Charles. 1972. "Crime and the American Indian." In *Native Americans Today*. New York: Harper & Row.

Spindler, George, and Louise Spindler. 1971. *Dreamers without Power: The Menomini Indians*. New York: Holt, Rinehart and Winston.

VanStone, James W. 1962. *Point Hope: An Eskimo Village in Transition*. Seattle: Washington Press.

Weyer, Edward, Jr. 1959. *Primitive Peoples Today*. Garden City, N.Y.: Doubleday.

Willmott, W. E. 1960. "The Flexibility of Eskimo Social Organization." *Anthropologica* 2 (N.S.):48–59.

The Mexican American Family

Authors Alvirez and Bean in their chapter on the Mexican family illustrate the importance of analyzing the ethnic factor in understanding family life styles. Mexican Americans constitute one of the largest ethnic groups in America, and as the authors point out, there are many characteristics of Mexican culture that still carry great weight in family life. The most noticeable feature of the Mexican American family is its size relative to other groups in America. The fertility of Mexican Americans is substantially higher than other groups. However, as the authors indicate, the traditional Mexican family structure is being influenced by the forces of urbanization and social mobility.

CHAPTER TWELVE

BY

DAVID ALVIREZ and FRANK D. BEAN*

HISTORICAL BACKGROUND

More than six million persons of Mexican origin or descent inhabit America, making Mexican Americans the second largest minority group in the country.† The vast majority (more than 85 per cent) live in five southwestern states close to Mexico—California, Texas, New Mexico,

---

*Some of the information in this chapter is from material gathered in the Austin Family Survey, which was conducted with support of a grant from the U.S. Public Health Service, National Institute of Child Health and Human Development (Grant HD 04262) to the University of Texas at Austin. Principle investigators for that survey were Harley L. Browning, Frank D. Bean, and Benjamin S. Bradshaw. David Alvirez was field director and a full participant in the research.

†The more neutral term "Mexican American" will be used throughout this chapter to designate the white population of Mexican origin or descent in America. Included under this term are many who identify themselves as Chicanos, Spanish American, Hispanos, Mexicanos, Californios, and Latin Americans. The term "Anglo" will be used to designate the white population of non-Mexican origin. The actual number of Mexican Americans in this country is actually very hard to determine and could run as high as 10 or 12 million or more if estimates of Leonard F. Chapman, Jr., Commissioner of the Immigration and Naturalization Service, are halfway correct. He estimates there are anywhere from 6 or 7 to 10 or 12 million illegal aliens in America, with over 90 per cent being from Mexico (Chapman, 1974). For discussions of problems in identifying the Mexican American population, see Buechley (1961; 1967), U.S. Bureau of the Census (1963), and Hernandez, Estrada, and Alvarez, (1973).

271

Arizona, and Colorado. Because of continuous immigration and an unusually high birth rate, the size of the Mexican American population relative to the total population in America has been increasing over the last 30 years. This growth has been accompanied by more active and visible efforts on the part of Mexican Americans to improve their civil rights and economic opportunities. In turn, this has brought about the realization throughout the nation as well as in the Southwest that Mexican Americans are a large and important ethnic group in this country.

The historical experience of Mexican Americans in the Southwest has shaped their contemporary social position and to a lesser extent their family patterns. This unique heritage may be divided into several periods. The first, following the Spanish Conquest, is the period of colonization, beginning with the subjugation of the indigenous natives in the sixteenth century and lasting until 1821 when Mexico achieved her political independence. The explorers and settlers of the Southwest during this time were the Spanish and the Indians, and thus are retrospectively referred to as Mexicans even though Mexico did not exist as a sovereign nation before that time.

The principal elements in the system of Spanish colonization were the *presidio*, the town, and the missions, with the latter serving as the primary agency for "converting" the Indians to Christianity. The first settlements were in New Mexico, in which Juan de Onate established 25 missions between 1598 and 1630. Much later, in 1769, a series of missions were established in California and to a much lesser extent in Texas and Arizona. By the end of the Spanish period, McWilliams (1968:26) notes that the Spanish settlements in the Southwest "consisted of a firmly rooted colony in New Mexico; an easily held and fairly prosperous chain of missions in coastal California; and a number of feebly garrisoned, constantly imperiled settlements in Texas and Arizona." No matter what the earlier warring and proselytizing proclivities of the Spanish, it is clear that their contributions to the Southwest and to America are many, including language, names of places, cuisine, systems of irrigation, and methods of raising cattle, to mention only a few.

But there were Mexican and Indian contributions as well. McWilliams (1968:34) writes:

> While the form of model was often Spanish, the ultimate adaptation showed unmistakable Mexican and Indian influences. If the Spanish were the carriers of seeds and plows, Mexicans and Indians were the planters and plow hands. Beyond all doubt the culture of the Southwest was a trinity: a whole consisting of three intricately interwoven, interpenetrated, thoroughly fused elements.

To attempt to unravel any single strand from this pattern and label it "Spanish" is, therefore, to do a serious injustice to the Mexicans and Indians through whom, and only through whom, Spanish cultural influences survived in the region.

Following Spanish colonization, the period from 1821 to 1848 is of interest for events that took place primarily in Texas, though these influenced the lives of all Mexicans in America. After gaining independence from Spain in 1821, Mexico encouraged the colonization of Texas through immigration from other nations. Colonists came in large numbers, mostly from America, but also from Germany, Norway, Czechoslovakia, and other European countries. Mexico tried unsuccessfully to stop the flow in 1830, but by 1834 Anglos outnumbered Mexicans in Texas by six to one, thus setting the stage for Texas' War for Independence. The Texas Revolution, in which incidentally many Mexican Texans fought for independence from the dictatorship of Santa Anna, brought a decade of increasing hardship for the Mexican Texans. During this period there gradually evolved a pattern of conflict that more and more pitted "Mexicans" against "Americans." As relationships between Mexican Texans and Anglos became more strained, they were compounded by language, legal, religious, cultural, and socioeconomic differences.

Hence, the Mexican War of 1846 to 1848, while provoked by the annexation of Texas by America in 1845, was in part the culmination of 25 or 30 years of rising cultural conflict. In summary, the outcome of the war with respect to the social position of Mexican Americans in Texas has been aptly noted by McLemore (1973:667):

The consolidation of the systems within which "Mexicans" were subordinated to "Americans" in Texas was accomplished through the Mexican-American War, 1846–1848. In the Treaty of Guadalupe Hidalgo, Mexico finally recognized the loss of Texas and accepted the Rio Grande as the boundary. Although Mexico displayed great concern for the welfare of her citizens who were left within the territory of the United States, and even though the terms of the treaty made clear that Mexico's former subjects were to enjoy the rights, privileges, and immunities of the other citizens of the United States, the subordination of those of Spanish-Mexican-Indian descent to those of Anglo American descent had been largely achieved in Texas by the middle of the nineteenth century.

The hostility and conflict of the Mexican War continued on a lesser scale during the conquered era from 1848 to around 1900. The prevalent attitude then was one of Anglo supremacy. In Texas, especially between

273

the Nueces and the Rio Grande rivers, conflict between the two groups flared up frequently. Outbreaks of violence and lynchings of Mexican Americans were not uncommon, and not the least among the instigators of such hostilities were the Texas Rangers, who to this day are still feared and hated by many lower-class Mexican Americans. In constant retreat and retrenchment, many Mexican Americans also lost their lands, both legally and illegally, during this time.

New Mexico stood above such conflagrations, with violence never assuming the proportions that prevailed in Texas. Until recently, Mexican Americans constituted a majority of that state's population, and while many were exploited, the exploitation was practiced by wealthy Mexican Americans as well as by Anglos. By contrast, Mexican Americans in California were held in contempt and often became the objects of violence. Only the *"gente de razon,"* the "Californios," enjoyed immunity. In general, it can be said that in the Southwest, this was a period of the birth (or reaffirmation) of the stereotype that Mexican Americans, as a conquered people, were inferior. Since they were subordinate, they were readily exploited, and it is not surprising to find that signs of withdrawal, defeatism, and fatalism developed among them.

Migration to America

The turn of this century marked the advent of mass migrations from Mexico to this country. This influx heightened the visibility of the Mexican Americans already in this country and worsened the conditions of both old and new Mexican American residents. Poverty and political instability in Mexico enhanced the lure of jobs and economic betterment in the North, and these factors acted as a strong magnet (a magnet still operating today) for immigration. It is impossible to ascertain how many persons migrated between 1900 and 1930, but the number was probably well over a million. Those that came were generally the poor and the unskilled who labored primarily in jobs in farming, mining, and railroads. Though faced with considerable discrimination in America, many of the newcomers thought their situation to be quite good in comparison to their previous living conditions in Mexico. However, despite gains in relative material well-being, once they became aware of generally superior conditions among American workers, Mexican Americans were not completely docile and apathetic, as evidenced by the attempts of laborers to organize between 1915 and 1940, efforts that were quickly and effectively crushed by employers and law-enforcement agencies.

274

World War II marked a turning point in the lives of many Mexican Americans and set the stage for much of the variability that may be found among Mexican Americans and their families today. Many opportunities that were previously closed became accessible. For some of the 300,000 to 500,000 men who served in the armed forces, military service provided their first contact with Anglos on other than a subservient basis. The experience among Mexican Americans that they could compete with Anglos on equal terms undoubtedly contributed to their open opposition to discrimination after they returned from the war. Also, exposure to other countries and cultures diminished some of their own ethnocentrism. They became increasingly politically conscious. Furthermore, for those who had served in the armed services, new vocational and educational opportunities also became available. Even those who remained at home benefited in terms of occupational openings created by the labor shortages of a country at war. All those opportunities and new outlooks gave rise to what Alvarez (1973:931) calls the "Mexican American generation," one whose cultural orientations and loyalties are tied to America and who plan to participate fully in American society.

Finally, in the mid-1960s we have the birth of the Chicano generation, a group of more active, militant Mexican Americans who are no longer willing to wait patiently for the rights which they feel are guaranteed to them by the U.S. Constitution. Although it is not known what percentage of the Mexican American population identifies with this movement, there is little doubt that it has created a new pride among Mexican Americans in their own Spanish-Mexican-Indian heritage, a feeling that ultimately may prove to be a factor in preserving some of the traditional patterns of the Mexican American family.

The Traditional Mexican American Family

In speaking of the "traditional" Mexican American family, one must realize that the heterogeneity among Mexican Americans throughout America means that generalizations based on such a label must be made with caution. In other words, the "traditional" family type should not be taken to imply inferiority to a more modern type or to a more Anglo form. Rather, it refers to a family pattern that is different from what may be considered the prevalent or "typical" Anglo pattern, to the extent that such a depiction is possible. Moreover, the presentation of a "typical" Mexican American family in no way implies that such a pattern is "pathological" in the sense of such a family pattern being responsible for many of the problems Mexican Americans face. What is really being presented is an "ideal type" that is partially reflective of the stereotypes held by Anglos as well as some of the ideas held by Mexicans and Mexican Americans.

Several traits are often imputed to Mexican Americans that are also thought to affect and/or reflect their family patterns (Murillo, 1971). These are frequently presumed to be cultural traits, although they may be at least partially derived from the conditions of poverty common among the majority of the people in this population. First, Mexican Americans are more person oriented than goal oriented. A great emphasis is placed on interpersonal relationships, and the roles played therein appear to make Mexican Americans more warm and emotional than Anglos, whom the former often see as cold and unfeeling.

Second, Mexican Americans tend to be less materialistic and competitive than Anglos and as a result probably enjoy greater emotional security. Tied in with this is a present-time orientation for which the Mexican Americans have been criticized. Yet, as Murillo (1971:100) notes, "Today much of our Anglo society's psychotherapy is aimed at developing or rekindling a *here* and *now* time orientation in the client as a means to improved mental health." For the Mexican American material goods are not an end in themselves but only a means to an end. Other activities in life, particularly the interpersonal relationships mentioned earlier, are considered to be much more important. Whereas the Anglo practices openness, frankness, and directness in his relationship with others, the Mexican American is likely to practice manners, politeness, courtesy, and deference, which may cause the Anglo to misinterpret the actions of the Mexican American.

Structural Features of the Traditional Mexican American Family

Turning to the Mexican American family itself, three main characteristics have been emphasized by Mexicans (see Penalosa, 1968, for a review of their ideas), Mexican Americans, and Anglos as especially typical, although the interpretations given to these characteristics have varied. The first is *familism,* the deep importance of the family to all its members, including in many instances members of the extended family (Grebler, Moore, and Guzman, 1970:351). The second is the idea of *male dominance,* in which the males assume superordinate roles. The third characteristic is the *subordination* of *younger* persons *to older*

276

persons, accompanied by a great degree of respect for one's elders. The rest of this section will examine in more detail each of these three main characteristics.

The importance of familism can be seen in many different ways. For one thing, the needs of the family collectively may supersede individual needs (Grebler, Moore, and Guzman, 1970:351). The family is one of the strongest areas of life activities, a closely knit unit in which all members enjoy status and esteem (Ulibarri, 1970:31). It may be the only place of refuge for the individual, providing both emotional and material security. When one needs advice or help, the person he will most often go to is another member of the family.

This importance of the family is reflected in the idealized role given to the extended family among Mexican Americans. Close relationships are not limited to the nuclear family but include aunts and uncles, grandparents, cousins, in-laws, and even *compadres* (godparents). Hence, those on whom one can rely for support form a numerically large group. Although some persons (Grebler, Moore, and Guzman, 1970:351) have criticized such familism as a hindrance to mobility because it cultivates attachments to people, places, and things, it can also be a supportive force in which members help and sustain each other in attaining goals that would be difficult for the individual to achieve by himself. For example, it has been common for Mexican Americans to care for aged parents within their household, a practice that would be otherwise difficult given the economic status of many Mexican Americans. Also, the senior author of this chapter is familiar with several cases in which large, close-knit families have helped each other in achieving such goals as acquiring a car or providing higher education for children. Only a person who has never experienced the warmth of the Mexican American family would tend to see it primarily from a negative perspective. Furthermore, such a view fails to recognize that for Mexican Americans of lower status the family is often the primary source of refuge from what is often seen as a hostile world. Moreover, as some Mexican Americans improve their socioeconomic status, a strong familistic orientation may forestall the development of strong social-class cleavages within the ethnic group (Grebler, Moore, and Guzman, 1970:353).

The idea of male dominance and superiority is probably the characteristic most emphasized in the literature, both in Mexico and in America. The father is seen as the absolute head of the family with full authority over the wife and children. All major decisions are his responsibility, with part of the wife's role involving seeing that the father's

decisions are carried out. Power and prestige are the absolute prerogatives of the male head, and generally delegations of this authority are
through the male line. Hence, when the father is not present, the oldest
son often assumes considerable authority, and the sisters and younger
brothers are expected to carry out his orders.

The concept of *machismo* forms part of the concept of male dominance. The most emphasized aspect of *machismo* has been sexual virility or maleness. From early childhood male children are given much
more freedom than females and are socialized into the male role. In the
adolescent years they are expected to begin to at least verbalize their
sexual prowess, and stories involving the "conquest of women" often
occupy a dominant place in their conversations. According to the narrow interpretation of *machismo,* the pursuit of extramarital sexual relations is condoned and even encouraged. Furthermore, such behavior is
sometimes presumed not to generate husband-wife conflicts nor to interfere with a man's role as a father and provider. Such interpretations fail
to recognize that *machismo* is more than sexual virility and that there
are some inherent contradictions in the idea. Many would argue that it is
difficult to conceive how a man may carry on after marriage the same as
before without "a diminution in the husband's felt responsibility to his
family or a loosening of his firm ties to it" (Hayden, 1966:20). But
machismo also consists of manliness in a broader sense than just sexual
prowess. It includes the elements of courage, honor, and respect for
others, as well as the notion of providing fully for one's family and
maintaining close ties with the extended family. Murillo (1971:103)
points out that an important prescriptive aspect of the *machismo* role
encourages the use of authority within the family in a just and fair manner. The public pursuit of extramarital sex might often conflict with the
fulfillment of these latter forms of *machismo*. The senior author's own
observations lead him to conclude that while some extramarital sexual
behavior (about which so much has been written) is characteristic of
some Mexican American husbands, the majority do not fall into this
pattern.

FEMALE AND SIBLING ROLES. Complementary to the expectation of
male dominance in the Mexican American family is that of female sub-
missiveness. Generally speaking, the woman is supposed to be subservient to the husband, and her primary roles are those of homemaker
and mother (bearer of children). Drawing from other studies, Grebler,
Moore, and Guzman, (1970:366) note that "the bearing and rearing of

278

children continue to be seen as perhaps the most important function of a woman, symbolizing her maturity." This is one explanation for the large families characteristic of Mexican Americans, an explanation that is combined with one that sees large families as evidence of the husband's *machismo*. In a more ideal sense, the mother is depicted as a naîve, rather childlike, saintly women who is very religious (Grebler, Moore, and Guzman, 1970:360). Her personal needs occupy a place secondary to those of her husband and all other family members.

Early in life the female child begins to learn her proper role. She is given much less freedom than boys and begins to play the role of mother and homemaker by helping to care for younger brothers and sisters and by assisting with the housework. As she reaches adolescence, she is carefully chaperoned to protect her from suitors intent on sexual advances. Then, by the time she marries, the young woman is ready to fulfill the same role that was fulfilled by her mother.

In male-female relations within the family children form an important and indispensable part. Early in life children are assigned real responsibilities necessary for the welfare of the family (Murillo, 1971:104). Children are expected to get along with each other, with the older taking care of the younger and the brothers protecting the sisters. Generally speaking, there is probably less sibling rivalry in these homes than in Anglo homes. Children are expected to be models of respect, which indicates why discipline is so important in the family. Each child knows his place in the family scheme and does not trespass in spheres of life in which he has no business. Within this scheme sibling relationships are more important than parent-children relationships, a pattern different from that in Anglo homes and a possible explanation of why two boys and two girls may be considered the minimum ideal family size among Mexican Americans. With such a family composition, children of both sexes would have the desired companionship.

One last characteristic of the traditional Mexican American family that is important is the subordination of the younger to the older. Older people receive more respect from youth and children than is characteristic in Anglo homes. There is even a familiar form of address that older people use with younger ones and that close friends use with each other, while the formal form is used always by children in speaking to their elders. Anglos may oftentimes offend Mexican Americans without realizing it by trying to become intimate with them before the Mexican Americans feel sufficient closeness has been established.

This pattern of subordination of the younger to the older is partially sex differentiated within the family. The older male children have some authority over the younger children *and* over their sisters. During the father's absence the older son assumes authority, and he is expected to be obeyed just as if he were the father. Sometimes the range of authority even includes the mother, particularly when the son is close to manhood.

The description that has been presented to this point portrays a very idealized family form that may be a long way from the real or actual situations in many Mexican American families. It does provide, however, a starting point from which to consider the present Mexican American family. The next section will outline the demographic characteristics of the Mexican American family, comparing it to the American family, in general, or to the Anglo family, in some cases. After that we will turn away from the "typical" family and consider some of the bases of heterogeneity among Mexican American families.

THE MODERN MEXICAN AMERICAN FAMILY

Demographic Characteristics

An examination of certain social, economic, and demographic characteristics of the Mexican American population highlights some of the more apparent differences between the Mexican American and Anglo populations and provides still further indication of the subordinate status that many Mexican Americans occupy in the social structure of America. These characteristics also describe both the Mexican American family and the context with which Mexican American family life occurs.

One of the most distinctive characteristics of Mexican Americans is their unusually high fertility. Census materials on children ever born show that the fertility of the Mexican American population, compared with the total white population, has been high and remains so, and that their fertility is as high or higher than the Black population. The broadest range of comparisons is presented by results of the November 1969 Current Population Survey (Table 1). According to these data the average number of children ever born per 1,000 Mexican-origin women aged 35 to 44 was 4,429, about 47 per cent higher than the number for all women of this age, and 41 per cent and 21 per cent higher, respectively, than for all white and Black women. Fertility of Mexican-origin women was also greater than that of any of the national-origin groups shown.

Put in terms of the number of children per family, the average family size of Mexican Americans (4.4) is about one person per family larger

TABLE 1
Children Ever Born per 1,000 Women Aged 35 to 44 by
Race and Ethnic Origin, for the Noninstitutional
Population, America: November 1969

TOTAL	3,003
RACE	
White	2,923
Black	3,649
Other	3,119
ORIGIN	
English	2,824
German	3,019
Irish	3,122
Italian	2,439
Polish	2,513
Russian	2,386
Spanish, total	3,760
Mexican	4,429
Puerto Rican	3,568
Other Spanish	2,750
Multiple origin, Black and other	3,076
Origin not reported (white)	2,725

Source: U.S. Bureau of the Census, *Current Population Reports*, Series P-20, No. 226. *Fertility Variations by Ethnic Origins*, November 1971.

than that of the total American population (3.5). The larger size of Mexican American families is also indicated by the fact that only 23 per cent of their families have no children of their own under 18 compared to 45 per cent for the total American population and by the fact that 13 per cent of Mexican American families have 5 or more children compared to 4 per cent for America as a whole (U.S. Bureau of the Census, 1972). The higher fertility characteristic of Mexican American women holds at all ages. And, compared to Anglo women, Mexican American females in the course of their child-bearing years will give birth to an average of two more children.

To what extent the differences in fertility between Mexican American and Anglo populations are the result of cultural differences as compared to socioeconomic differences is difficult to judge. While more research is needed, available evidence does not rule out the idea that as education increases, the fertility of Mexican Americans will more closely resemble that of other whites. If, however, larger families act as a hindrance to upward mobility, then a cycle may be operative that makes it difficult for Mexican Americans to escape the poverty in which many of them live.

Other evidence, however, would seem to show a cultural factor among Mexican Americans sustaining their higher fertility. Grebler, Moore, and Guzman (1970:185–96) found that Mexican Americans had larger families than Anglos in every income bracket and hence conclude that differential family size does not seem to be simply a function of low-income status (and, by implication, of low assimilation). Roberts and Lee (1973), in a more detailed analysis, discovered that the relationship between fertility and ethnic status persisted even after controlling socioeconomic status. Thus, to understand Mexican American fertility, further research must be done on factors other than just the socioeconomic ones.

Turning to patterns of marital status, the per cent married with spouse present among persons 25 to 64 years old is nearly the same among Mexican Americans (81 per cent) as among all whites (84 per cent), with Blacks (66 per cent) exhibiting a somewhat different pattern (U.S. Bureau of the Census, 1971). Also, the per cent of families with a female head of household among Mexican Americans (12 per cent) is very similar to that for whites (9 per cent). One can say that the majority of Mexican Americans live in families in which both parents are present, but one cannot say from this evidence that their families are more cohesive than those of Anglos.

Evidence concerning divorce, however, shows somewhat greater stability among Mexican Americans, particularly among men (U.S. Bureau of the Census, 1971). The number of divorced men per 1,000 currently married is 16 for Mexican Americans and 39 for other whites. Among the women the numbers divorced per 1,000 currently married are 50 and 57, respectively, with the level for Mexican American women being only slightly lower than that for all white women. Though perhaps indicative of somewhat greater family stability, the evidence presented here is not sufficiently conclusive to argue that Mexican Americans demonstrate greater family cohesiveness than Anglos. The problem is made further complex, of course, by the indeterminate number of unreported desertions.

An area in which substantial differences between Mexican Americans and Anglos emerge is in socioeconomic status as measured by occupation, income, and education. Family socioeconomic status depends on labor-force participation, and in this regard Mexican American males of working age are just as likely as whites to be in the labor force, the rates of participation being 87 per cent and 86 per cent, respectively, while Mexican American females (39 per cent) are less likely than other White women (50 per cent) to be in the labor force (U.S. Bureau of the Census, 1972a). The greater absence of Mexican American women in the labor force is probably due to a combination of two factors: their traditional preference for staying home, and the larger families characteristic of Mexican Americans, which leave less time for employment outside the home and the back of preparation for gainful employment, given their low educational levels.

It is an examination of the occupational distribution of Mexican American men compared to other whites that clearly demonstrates the disadvantaged position of Mexican American men (and, by extension, of Mexican American families) within the job structure of American society. Mexican Americans are greatly underrepresented in white-collar occupations, particularly at the top levels. Both among professional and technical workers and among managers and administrators Mexican American men have about one-third as many persons in these occupations as do other whites. On the other hand, they are overrepresented among blue-collar, farm, and service workers. This unequal occupational distribution, which is partly a result of lack of education and partly a result of discrimination, results in income disparities that heavily penalize Mexican American families.

In 1970, the median family income for Mexican Americans was $7,117, compared to $10,236 for other whites, a difference of over $3,000 in annual income (U.S. Bureau of the Census, 1971). Furthermore, when one recalls the larger family sizes of Mexican Americans and considers per capita income, it is fairly obvious that Mexican American families and their individual members are seriously handicapped by their low-income levels. This is evident in the number of Mexican Americans living below the poverty level. In the Southwest, in which more than three-fourths of the Mexican Americans live, 30 per cent are below the poverty-income level compared to 11 per cent for whites; in the remainder of America the respective percentages are 19 and 10 (U.S. Bureau of the Census, 1971). Furthermore, among regions in the Southwest there are significant differences. In California, 14.0 per cent of all Mexican American families are below poverty, compared to 7.5 per cent for all white families. The comparable percentages in Texas are 31.4 per cent and 12.4 per cent, respectively (U.S. Bureau of the Census, 1972). Even within states there are large differences, with the greatest amount of poverty being found in south Texas and northern New Mexico. Yet in spite of regional differences Mexican American families are always overrepresented among the population in poverty. Conditions will have to improve considerably before the socioeconomic position of Mexican American families reaches parity with other American families.

INTERMARRIAGE AND ASSIMILATION. Despite socioeconomic differences between Mexican Americans and Anglos the social assimilation of Mexican Americans, as measured by the incidence of intermarriage between them and Anglos, appears to be increasing somewhat (Table 2). Generally speaking, however, the figures indicate fairly strong patterns of in-group marriage, particularly in Texas. In Albuquerque, New Mexico, and in Los Angeles, California, this is changing. In these cities, the latest available figures show more than one in four Mexican Americans marrying an Anglo. Even these rates, however, demonstrate that Mexican Americans are a long way from complete assimilation into the larger society. Furthermore, with cultural pluralism increasingly becoming a viable option, acculturation may increase without a corresponding rise in intermarriage.

Social-Class Differences in Life Styles

In speaking of social-class differences among Mexican Americans, it is well not to forget the complexity in social-class structures created by combinations of ethnicity and class. Gordon's concept of ethclass (1964) has been put to good use in previous chapters. Occupying a given position in the status hierarchy of a society inevitably structures the economic and life-style possibilities of families. Being a family in certain ethnic groups may enhance or diminish such possibilities. That is, Mexican Americans may not reflect all the characteristics of a given socioeconomic status in the larger society due to the fact they are Mexican Americans. This is particularly applicable to Mexican Americans with higher socioeconomic status who may both retain the cultural heritage of their ethnic group and face discrimination from the larger society. At the same time, it should be recognized that a status hierarchy exists as well among Mexican Americans. Hence, a Mexican American family may have relatively higher status within the ethnic group than outside it. Moreover, the status of the Mexican American family may vary according to the length of time the family has been in this country, ranging from families of newly arrived immigrants to those of persons who trace their ancestors back as much as 10 or 15 generations in this country. With

284

TABLE 2

Percent Exogamous Marriages of Mexican Americans, Various Places and Times

	LOS ANGELES			ALBUQUERQUE				SAN ANTONIO		CORPUS CHRISTI		EDINBURG, TEXAS (HIDALGO COUNTY)	
	1924-1933*	1963*	1924-1940*	1953*	1964*	1967†	1971†	1940-1955*	1960‡	1960-1961†	1970-1971†	1961†	1971†
For individuals§	9	25	8	13	19	32	24	10	11	8	9	3	5
For marriages¶	17	40	15	23	33	48	39	17	20	15	16	5	9

*Results from several studies summarized in Grebler, Moore, and Guzman, 1970.

†Unpublished data gathered by David Alvirez and Edward Murguia, Department of Sociology, University of New Mexico, Albuquerque, New Mexico.

‡From Bradsahw and Bean, 1970.

§Refers for the time period to the percentage of individuals marrying exogamously among all individuals marrying.

¶Refers for the time period to the percentage of exogamous marriages among all marriages.

these qualifications in mind, it can be said that social-class differences among Mexican American families are in many instances similar to those of American society in general. The higher the education of the main breadwinner, the better the job and the higher the income, hence the better the living conditions for the family as a whole.

Scarcely any studies have been conducted into the life-style consequences for Mexican Americans of attaining different levels of education or of holding different kinds of occupations. One exception is a study carried out in Austin, Texas, in which 348 Mexican American couples were interviewed to investigate the possible relations of social and cultural factors to family and fertility characteristics (Bradshaw and Bean, 1972). We will present some of the previously unpublished results from this study that pertain to social-class differences in life styles here. As an indicator of social status, the sample is divided into two groups on the basis of education—one in which the husband had at least a high school education (higher socioeconomic status [SES]) and one in which the husband's level of schooling was less than 12 years (lower SES).

As would clearly be expected, SES affects where a family lives. Most importantly, it is of interest to note whether Mexican American families are or are not *barrio* (roughly the equivalent of a Black ghetto) resident. Mexican American families with higher SES are more likely to be living outside the *barrio* than those low in SES. Seventy-four per cent of the better educated Mexican American families lived outside the *barrio*, compared to 27 per cent of the less educated ones. Though impossible to verify, the tendency as SES improves may be to move from the predominantly Mexican American *barrio* to a more mixed neighborhood, and then in turn to a predominantly Anglo, middle-class neighborhood.

Families with higher SES are more likely to have a working wife (52 per cent) than are those with less education (42 per cent). The higher percentage of working wives is probably due to a combination of two factors: the larger family sizes of the poorer Mexican Americans together with a more personally materialistic orientation on the part of women of higher SES. Indirect confirmation of this is provided by the fact that 62 per cent of the working women whose husbands had not completed high school saw themselves as working due to *family* economic needs, compared to 43 per cent of the working wives with better educated husbands.

Such economic conditions are also translated into role expectations. In respect to whether the wife expects her husband to be primarily instrumental (to mow the grass, to keep the home in good repair, etc.) or primarily expressive (to be sensitive to her needs, to be affectionate, etc.), wives with higher education living outside the *barrio* have the lowest rate of predominantly instrumental or materialistic expectations from their husbands (10 per cent), while wives with low education living in the *barrio* have the highest instrumental expectations (35 per cent). The indications are fairly strong that the wives of poor families are very much aware of their economic needs, and that such needs often take precedence over the expressive or socioemotional expectations that are often important to women in marriage, even those who may find themselves in poverty.

Given the better education and income of the higher SES families, one would hypothesize more homeownership among them. Among the Austin families, only 38 per cent of the low SES families owned or were buying their homes, compared to 71 per cent among the higher SES families. These differences, however, should not be interpreted as being due to a lack of interest in homeownership among the poor but should be seen primarily as a reflection of their low SES.

In terms of friendship patterns and relationships with Anglos, greater contact with Anglos occurred among Mexican Americans with higher SES, suggesting more friendships and greater feelings of equality with Anglos among such persons. Several things in the Austin data lend support to this idea. The higher SES families were less likely to have only Mexican Americans among their close friends compared to the lower SES families, 70 per cent compared to 87 per cent, although even among the higher SES males less than 5 per cent had *only* Anglos as their closest friends. Probably the most noteworthy thing is that regardless of SES or where the respondent lived, one's closest friends were likely to be all Mexican Americans. At least in Austin, ethnic ties are still quite strong and should continue to exert strong influences on most Mexican Americans.

The higher SES families are also more likely to have friends or relatives married to Anglos, 86 per cent falling into this category, compared to 58 per cent for lower SES families. This increased experience with intermarriage is probably both a function of SES per se of their place of residence, and of work in which they and those they know have increased contact with Anglos. Hence, to this extent one might say that higher SES does tend to weaken ethnic ties.

Interestingly enough, however, higher SES respondents are just about as likely as lower-status respondents to oppose their children marrying Anglos, 21 per cent and 23 per cent, respectively. In both cases it indicates that less than one-fourth of the respondents would oppose their children marrying Anglos, another factor that might weaken ethnic ties. Whether the militancy among Mexican Americans today will increase the opposition to intermarriage or cause more of one's ethnic heritage to be carried over into a mixed marriage is a matter that cannot be answered definitely.

Retention of the Spanish language is much more likely to occur among lower SES respondents. Forty-two per cent of them used primarily Spanish in the home, compared to 8 per cent among high SES families. The same finding is also reported by Grebler, Moore, and Guzman, (1970:332). Conversely, 24 per cent of lower SES respondents spoke primarily English, compared to 61 per cent of the higher SES respondents. Given the new emphasis on bilingualism, it would appear that children of lower SES stand a better chance of maintaining two languages and the benefits that come with being bilingual.

One last area to be mentioned in which social-class differences may appear is in that of husband-wife relationships. A more egalitarian relationship would be hypothesized (or expected) in the higher SES homes. On the assumption that an important aspect of an egalitarian relationship is open and free communication between spouses, the couples were asked a series of questions about how often they discussed with one another such matters as religion, birth control, child discipline, sex, and the number of children to have. Forty-nine per cent of the higher SES couples indicated they talked frequently with each other about such things versus 38 per cent of the lower SES couples. Overall, the percentage of couples with high levels of communication is below 50 per cent, indicating some adherence to traditional patterns of husband-wife separation of roles. Nevertheless, the higher SES couples are less likely to follow this pattern than the lower SES couples.

The degree to which these findings for Mexican American families in Austin, Texas, can be applied to all Mexican Americans is something that cannot be answered at the present time. One would expect differences according to region of the country and to the percentage of the population that is Mexican American in that particular region. For example, findings would probably vary in California in which Mexican Americans hold a slightly higher socioeconomic status than they do in Texas. They might also vary in border regions with high concentrations of Mexican Americans and a heavy influence from Mexico. We have no reason to feel, however, that results from other regions would be radically changed, rather, different only in degree.

CHANGE AND ADAPTATION

At various points in the discussion above we have mentioned and at times documented that considerable diversity and heterogeneity occurs among Mexican American families. Our attempt to describe the "typical" Mexican American family, of course, inevitably obscured this to some extent. In discussing the variation that occurs around some central pattern, two points in particular need to be emphasized. The first is that Mexican Americans have never perfectly fit the stereotypes assigned to them. As noted in our treatment of the history of Mexican Americans in America, the Mexican American people do not all come from the same sociocultural backgrounds. The Spanish, Mexican, and Indian influences in the sociocultural background of Mexican Americans have always been and continue to be present in varying degrees in different parts of the population. To base descriptions of Mexican American family patterns on observations made only on poor families of predominantly Mexican backgrounds is to ignore cultural strains that perhaps better characterize other segments of the population and thus to risk perpetuating ethnic stereotypes (e.g., Madsen, 1964; Rubel, 1966).

Furthermore, the interpretation of Mexican American family life in terms of monolithic stereotypes implicitly assigns too great a role to the influence of cultural factors in shaping the family patterns of Mexican Americans. It invites the idea that certain patterns are derivative of beliefs and values passed from generation to generation rather than functional adaptations to a difficult environment. For example, the notion that such family patterns as living in extended family households, taking in poor relatives, and doubling up with other families in a single residence are reflections of the importance of familism does not on the face of it recognize that these patterns, as well as familism itself, may at least in part be responses to historical conditions of economic deprivation.

That the latter may have played some role in the evolution of such patterns is evidenced in the results of the survey of Mexican Americans in Los Angeles and San Antonio (Grebler, Moore, and Guzman, 1970), which shows a virtual absence of extended-family living arrangements among the respondents at the time of the survey as well as for quite some time previously. It seemed clear from the responses to the survey questions that many families felt an *obligation* to help others in time of need, and that such times had often occurred, but that their *preference* was to

289

discard such living patterns as material welfare improved. These results suggest that many family patterns are adaptive responses to the social and physical environment in which families find themselves rather than responses to cultural prescriptions.

A second and very important factor increasingly renders it difficult to speak of Mexican American families in all-encompassing terms. In addition to the fact that the "traditional Mexican family" was never uniformly present in the population, family patterns among Mexican Americans have been involved in processes of change related to generation, class differences, and increasing urbanization. An especially relevant indication of the changes impinging on the Mexican American family can be discerned in changing patterns of intermarriage. Based on marriage-license data in Los Angeles County, a recent study indicated that the social distance between generations of Mexican Americans was even greater than that between some Mexican Americans and Anglos. Third-generation Mexican Americans tended to marry out more than first-generation persons, and as Mexican Americans moved into the middle class, they tended to marry more on the basis of class than ethnic consideration (Grebler, Moore, and Guzman, 1970:408–409).

As Mexican American families have become exposed to and participants in the urban middle-class life style and culture, the internal structure of the family has also changed. The brunt of this change seems to have been borne by the husband's role. The traditional patriarchal role of the man was especially suited for life in the rural past when there was plenty of work to be done outside as well as inside the house. Men did the former, and women the latter, and associated with this sexual division of labor was the patriarchal assumption of power, prestige, and prerogatives in decision making. Considerable doubt has been cast on the notion that this pattern has ever been a behvaioral norm (Grebler, Moore, and Guzman, 1970:360). Certainly a sexual division of labor has lost much of its force in an urban milieu in which the ratio of the number of "masculine" tasks outside the house to the number of "feminine" tasks inside the house has declined. The Los Angeles study (Grebler, Moore, and Guzman, 1970:362) found that this and other changes such as the "changing work situation, exposure to new values of both masculinity and feminity, and higher levels of living . . ." have brought about changes in the definitions of the roles of husband and wife, but especially the husband. Comparing the responses of Mexican Americans to questions regarding who performs certain sex-typed household tasks to those of a sample of the general population of Detroit revealed that Mexican Americans are close to "typical Americans" and suggest "that egalitarianism occurs more in the masculine sex-typed tasks than in the feminine, just as there is more loosening in the norms regarding the husband's role than in those regarding the role of the wife." (Grebler, Moore, and Guzman, 1970:362).

Just as the role of the husband in the Mexican American family seems to be changing, the Mexican American family in general is changing in adaptation to new situations and opportunities. Although little research has been done in this area, the change cannot be occurring without some conflict, between new immigrants and "old" Mexican Americans, between members of one class and those of another. Yet vestiges of the more traditional Mexican American family linger on, especially in rural areas and in the more isolated *barrios*. Perhaps these may even become rejuvenated in the wake of the Chicano movement, which emphasizes the positive features in the Mexican American sociocultural heritage. As the Mexican American family becomes subjected to these many different social forces and situations, one thing seems certain. It will become increasingly difficult to speak of *"the"* Mexican American family.

R E F E R E N C E S

Alvarez, R. 1973. "The Psycho-Historical and Socioeconomic Development of the Chicano Community in the United States." *Social Science Quarterly* 53 (March): 920–42.
Bradshaw, B. S., and F. D. Bean. 1970. "Intermarriage between Persons of Spanish and Non-Spanish Surname: Changes from the Mid-Nineteenth to the Mid-twentieth Century," *Social Science Quarterly* 51 (September):389–95.
———, and ———. 1972. "Some Aspects of the Fertility of Mexican Americans." Commission on Population Growth and the American Future. Research Reports, Volume 1. In C. F. Westhoff and R. Parks, Jr. (eds): *Demographic and Social Aspects of Population Growth*. Washington: U.S. Government Printing Office, pp. 139–64.
Buechley, R. W. 1961. "A Reproducible Method of Counting Persons of Spanish Surname." *Journal of the American Statistical Association* 56 (March):88–97.
———, 1967. "Characteristic Name Sets of Spanish Populations." *Names* 15 (March):53–69.
Chapman, Leonard F., Jr. 1974. "Silent Invasion That Takes Millions of American Jobs," *U.S. News and World Report*, Dec. 9, 1974:77–78.
Goldscheider, C. 1971. *Population, Modernization, and Social Structure*. Boston: Little, Brown.
Gordon, M. 1964. *Assimilation in American Life*. New York: Oxford University Press.
Grebler, L., J. W. Moore, and R. C. Guzman. 1970. *The Mexican American People*. New York: The Free Press.

Hayden, R. G. 1966. "Spanish Americans of the Southwest." *Welfare in Review* 4 (April):14–25.

Hernandez, J., L. Estrada, and D. Alvirez. 1973. "Census Data and the Problem of Conceptually Defining the Mexican American Population." *Social Science Quarterly* 53 (March):671–87.

Madsen, W. 1964. *Mexican-Americans of South Texas*. New York: Holt, Rinehart and Winston.

McLemore, S. D. 1973. "The Origins of Mexican American Subordination in Texas." *Social Science Quarterly* 53 (March):656–70.

McWilliams, C. 1968. *North From Mexico*. New York: Greenwood Press.

Montiel, M. 1971. "The Social Science Myth of the Mexican-American Family." In *Voices*. O. Romano (ed.): Berkeley: Quinto Sol, pp. 40–47.

Murillo, N. 1971. "The Mexican American Family." In N. W. Wagner and M. J. Huag (eds.): *Chicanos: Social and Psychological Perspectives*. St. Louis: Mosley, pp. 97–108.

Penalosa, F. 1968. "Mexican Family Roles." *Journal of Marriage and the Family* 30 (Fall):13–27.

Roberts, R., and E. S. Lee. 1973. "Minority Group Status and Fertility Revisited." Paper presented at the annual meetings of the Population Association of America.

Romano, O. 1968. "The Anthropology and Sociology of Mexican Americans." *El Grito* 2 (November):680–89.

Rubel, Arthur J. 1966. *Across the Tracks: Mexican Americans in a Texas City*. Austin: University of Texas Press.

Simirenko, A. 1964. *Pilgrims, Colonists, and Frontiersmen*. New York: The Free Press.

Ulibarri, H. 1970. "Social and Attitudinal Characteristics of Spanish-Speaking Migrants and Ex-Migrant Workers in the Southwest." In J. Burma, (ed.): *Mexican-Americans in the United States*, pp. 29–39. Cambridge: Schenkman.

U.S. Bureau of the Census. 1963. "Persons of Spanish Surname." *United States Census of the Population:* 1960, Subject Reports, Final Report PC(2)-1B. Washington, D.C.: U.S. Government Printing Office.

U.S. Bureau of the Census. 1971. "Selected Characteristics of Persons and Families of Mexican, Puerto Rican, and Other Spanish Origin: March 1971." *Current Population Reports,* Series P-20, no. 224. Washington, D.C.: U.S. Government Printing Office.

U.S. Bureau of the Census. 1972. Census of Population: 1970. *General Social and Economic Characteristics*. Final Reports PC(1)-C6 California and PC(1)-C45 Texas. Washington, D.C.: U.S. Government Printing Office.

U.S. Bureau of the Census. 1972. "Selected Characteristics of Persons and Families of Mexican, Puerto Rican, and Other Spanish Origin: March 1972." *Current Population Reports,* Series P-20, no. 238. Washington, D.C.: U.S. Government Printing Office.

SOCIO-RELIGIOUS
ETHNIC MINORITIES

The Amish Family

The Old Arder Amish, as described by Dr. Huntington, are an example of an ethnoreligious group that has had great success in preserving its traditions and preventing wholesale assimilation. The primarily rural Amish are, as Dr. Huntington points out, probably contrary to popular opinion, a growing population that has managed to resist the onslaught of modern technology and major social change. Their ability to resist change is grounded in their religious commitment, which is expressed in their major social institutions. In this chapter we see how the family institution helps maintain Amish culture and society.

C.H A P T E R   T H I R T E E N

BY

GERTRUDE ENDERS HUNTINGTON

HISTORICAL BACKGROUND

The Old Order Amish Mennonites are direct descendants of the Swiss Anabaptists of the sixteenth century. "Anabaptist" is a historical and theological term used to designate a number of different theologies and social groups (Littell, 1964) representing the left wing of the Reformation (Bainton, 1952). Those Anabaptist groups who survive emerged between 1525 and 1536 and are today represented by the Amish, the Mennonites, and the Hutterites. These churches are characterized by the maintenance of a disciplined community, pacifism, separation from the world, adult rather than infant baptism, and an emphasis on simple living.

The Amish developed between 1693 and 1697 as a dissenting conservative wing of the Swiss Mennonites (Hostetler, 1974:27–35). Their leader, Jacob Amman, introduced shunning (the avoidance of all normal social intercourse with a member who is under the ban), foot washing as a part of the communion service, communion twice a year instead of only once, the excommunication of persons who attend the state church, and greater uniformity of dress and hair style. The Amman group, or Amish, continue to this day to abide by rules established by Jacob Amman and interpreted by each local congregation.

Although the Amish family as we know it is an American phenomenon, its roots go back to the early days in Europe. Persecution was severe in Europe; the Amish were forbidden citizenship and thus could not own land. Therefore, they were generally unable to establish permanent, stable communities in which to develop their distinctive social structure. Their livelihood, their place of residence, often even their lives were subject to the whim of rulers and neighbors. Families often had to live at considerable distance from co-religionists, religious services were held irregularly and unobtrusively in the home of a church member. This mobility, isolation, and limited community interaction placed the emphasis for producing Christians directly on the family. To this day, the family has remained the smallest and strongest unit of Amish culture.

Anabaptist theology, which emphasized adult baptism, also supported the role of the family in child development. Protestant religious leaders such as Martin Luther and Philipp Melanchthon were suspicious of parents' ability to rear their children without the help and intervention of the state (Schwartz, 1973:102–14). In contrast, the Anabaptists never equated child rearing with schooling, nor did they believe that the child or the parent was morally subservient to some outside civil or religious authority. Child rearing was the parents' major responsibility. Menno Simons (1956:950), and early leader in Holland after whom the Mennonites are named, wrote, "For this is the chief and principal care of the saints, that their children may fear, God, do right, and be saved." He also taught that parents were morally responsible for the condition of their children's souls. "Watch over their souls as long as they are under your care, lest you lose also your own salvation on their account" (Simons, 1956:391).

In addition to urging parents to set an unblamable example for their children and to teach, instruct, admonish, correct, and chastise their children as circumstances require, parents were also to protect their children from worldly influences and from wrong companions. "Keep them away from good-for-nothing children, from whom they hear and learn nothing but lying, cursing, swearing, fighting, and mischief" (Simons, 1956:959). Parents were to direct their children to reading and writing, that they might learn from the Scripture what God teaches. They were to instruct them to spin and to earn their bread by the labor of their hands. One example from the *Martyr's Mirror** of practical in-

---

*The Bloody Theater, or Martyr's Mirror, was first published in Dutch in 1660 and has periodically been reprinted in German and in English. It is a large book containing over

struction for child care was written by Jacob the Chandler shortly before he was burned at the stake:

> Furthermore, I pray you, my dear and much beloved wife, that you do the best with my children, to bring them up in the fear of God, with good instruction and chastening, while they are still young. . . . For instruction must accompany chastisement: for chastisement demands obedience, and if one is to obey, he must first be instructed. This instruction does not consist of hard words, or loud yelling; for this the children learn to imitate; but if one conducts himself properly towards them they have a good example, and learn propriety; for by the children the parents are known. And parents must not provoke their children to anger, lest they be discouraged; but must bring them up with admonition and good instruction. (Braght, 1951:798–99)

Banishment enabled the family to remain intact, and the subsequent isolation often required great self-reliance on the part of the family unit. But often the persecution was so severe that even this small unit could not survive. Men were sold as galley slaves, adults were imprisoned and executed, children were placed in orphanages and foster homes.

During their years in Europe the Amish lived in Switzerland, Alsace-Lorraine, the Palatine, France, Holland, Austria, Germany, and Poland. Even though persecution prevented the establishment of discrete communities, effort was made to stay near members of the faith. An old Amish hymn (Ausband, 1564: Hymn No. 44) quotes another martyr writing to his son: "Live, only where the believers live" (Hostetler, 1968:21). Most of the Amish in Europe continued to be renters. Lack of religious toleration meant that families had limited choice as to where they could settle and frequently were forced to move to new locations as political situations changed. Individual Amish families were often physically isolated from co-religionists, so they could not develop and perpetuate a distinctive community with a characteristic social structure. In some areas the Amish continued for many years as a religious sect, but they never formed a self-perpetuating subculture. Today there are no people left in Europe who are distinctly Amish (Hostetler, 1955).

There is some disagreement as to when the first Amish landed in America. A 1709 letter of William Penn's pertaining to the Palatinate

---

1,500 pages and recounting, often with vivid details, the deaths of over 4,000 men and women who remained steadfast to their faith in spite of branding, burning, stoning, sessions on the rack, the severing of tongues, hands and feet, live burials and drowning. No one who recanted is considered a martyr, nor is one a martyr if he survived his torture. The *Martyr's Mirror* helps strengthen members "to make every preparation for steadfastness in our faith," (preface to fifth English Edition, 1950) whether in the face of an inquisition, school officials, or universal conscription.

297

immigrants mentions "diverse Mennonites" (Smith, 1920:214), which could be construed as a reference to the Amish. Many of the Bernese emigrants banished in 1711, and the Alsatian emigrants deported in 1712 later came to America. After 1727 complete passenger lists were kept, and many Amish names have been found among these, especially in the period between 1735 and 1754 (Smith, 1929:183, 205–21). In spite of continued harassment in Europe few of the nonresistant Amish ventured to immigrate to America during the turbulent period of the French and Indian War, the Revolutionary War, and the War of 1812. However, between 1815 and 1860 three thousand Amish immigrated to America (Luthy, 1973:14).

The first Amish to arrive in America settled in Pennsylvania; there they formed discrete clusters, separate from the Mennonites as well as from the "English."* In contrast to their experience in Europe, the Amish immigrants to America found cheap land and religious toleration. They responded by electing to purchase farms near fellow churchmen and away from the influence of cities. This has continued to be the basis of their settlement pattern. The Ohio Amish community was started in 1808; this community in central Ohio is the largest and in many ways the most conservative of the large Amish communities. In 1841 settlers in Indiana formed what was to become the third largest Amish settlement. More than three-fourths of the Amish live in these three states. Smaller settlements are found in Illinois, Iowa, Wisconsin, Missouri, Delaware, Florida, Kansas, Kentucky, Minnesota, Oklahoma, Maryland, New York, Michigan, and Tennessee. At one time, there were Amish settlements in Arkansas, Oregon, North Dakota, California, Colorado, North Carolina, Georgia, Texas, Nebraska, New Mexico, Mississippi, Montana, Alabama, and Mexico.† There is a small Old Order Amish community in Honduras.

Table 1 gives the 1973 Amish population and the dates of the first Amish settlers in each state. In some instances the first settlements were not successful, and present Amish population is the result of later immigrations. In other cases regular church districts were not established until a considerable time after the earliest settlement.

The Old Order Amish are a tradition-oriented, conservative branch of the Mennonite Church. The term Old Order came into usage during the last half of the nineteenth century when more liberal congregations separated from them. The Old Order are also known as "House Amish"

---

*A term used for all non-Mennonites (and sometimes for all non-Amish) even those who are German speaking.
†Personal correspondence, December 21, 1973, David Luthy, Aylmer, Ontario.

TABLE 1
Old Order Amish Population by State and Country (1973)

STATE	DATE OF FIRST AMISH SETTLERS*	NO. OF DISTRICTS	NO. OF BAPTIZED MEMBERS # (ESTIMATED)	TOTAL MEMBERSHIPS # (ESTIMATED) +
Ohio	1808	120	9,480	20,160
Pennsylvania	c. 1720	94	7,426	15,892
Indiana	1839	75	5,925	12,600
Missouri	1856	18	1,422	3,024
Iowa	1840	13	1,027	2,184
Illinois	1829	12	948	2,016
Wisconsin	1908	10	790	1,680
Michigan	1895	7	553	1,176
Delaware	1915	5	395	840
New York	1833	5	395	840
Kansas	1883	4	316	672
Tennessee	1872	4	316	672
Maryland	1772	3	237	504
Kentucky	1958	2	158	336
Virginia	1895	1	79	168
Oklahoma	1892	1	79	168
Florida	1925	1	79	168
Minnesota	c. 1898	1	79	168
Canada	1824	13	1,027	2,184
Honduras	1968	1	79	168
Paraguay	1968	1	79	169
TOTAL		391	30,839	65,688

*Does not necessarily imply continuous settlement; some communities were disbanned and Amish resettled in the state at a later date. Information supplied by David Luthy, Alymer, Ontario.

+Source: J. A. Raber (ed.), *Der Neue Amerikanische Calendar*, 1973. Baltic, Ohio. Additions by David Luthy.

#Data calculated using Hostetler's estimate of 79 baptized members and 168 total Amish individual per church district. (Hostetler 1970:80-81) This estimate is probably conservative although specific church districts are much smaller. Cross, using data from Ohio, determined the number of baptized members to be 86 and the total membership per district to be 199. (1967:42)

because they hold their church services in their homes, or "Horse and Buggy Amish" because they do not own cars. The Old Order Amish are distinguished by prohibitions against owning automobiles, telephones, and high-line electricity. They have strict dress codes and forbid rubber-tired tractors (if tractors are used at all), central heating, and cameras. They speak a German dialect known as Pennsylvania Dutch in their homes, read the Lutheran Bible, and do not permit attendance at state schools beyond the eighth grade. In this chapter the discussion will be limited to the Old Order Amish.

THE MODERN AMISH FAMILY

Demographic Characteristics

FERTILITY. Many people think of the Amish as a shrinking remnant whose days are numbered, but they are in actuality a growing church. Because the Amish do not proselytize, their growth depends primarily on biological increment combined with the ability to hold their children in the faith. The Old Order Amish have increased from a population of about 8,200 in 1905 to 65,000 in 1973; from 43 church districts to 387 districts (Table 2). Household size varies from those married pairs who have no children to those having 15 children or more.

Studies of family size show that for completed families the average number of children born alive is about seven. This greatly exceeds the national average for white rural households. Cross (1967:108) reported the annual natural increase of the Holmes County, Ohio Amish population to be 3.0 per cent, or a potential doubling of the population every 23 years. Assuming this growth rate to be representative, it is interesting to compare the potential population growth of the Amish with the observed population growth. Taking the estimated 1920 population to be 13,900, the 1943 potential population would be 27,800, and the 1966 potential population would be 55,600. Hostetler (1974:81) gives the actual esti-

TABLE 2
Old Order Amish Population and Districts, 1905–1970

YEAR	POPULATION	NUMBER OF DISTRICTS
1905	8,200	43
1920	13,900	83
1930	18,500	110
1940	25,800	154
1950	33,000	197
1960	43,000	258
1970	59,304	353

SOURCE: Hostetler 1970:80; and Raber 1970.

300

mated total population for 1966 as 49,371. This represents a loss to the church of possibly about 6,000 individuals over a 46-year period. These estimates would indicate that the Amish are successful in perpetuating their own subculture.

DIVORCE. The Old Order Amish are strictly monogamous. The individual's first commitment is to God; his second is to his spouse. There is no divorce, and under no circumstances may an Amishman remarry while his spouse is living. Except for widows, the head of the household is always a man. The rare unmarried farmer will have a sister or perhaps a married nephew who lives in his household and helps out. If the head of house is not a full-time farmer, he may work as a carpenter and do some farming on the side, or perhaps teach and raise small fruits such as strawberries or raspberries that have a limited season. Other Amishmen are employed in jobs related to farming or to the Amish way of life. Thus, in each Amish settlement of any size there will be a blacksmith, a harness maker, a buggy repair shop, and one or more construction gangs or building crews. There are also specialized carpenters who do cabinet work and make the Amish coffins. The Amish build or remodel their own homes and barns, and they prefer the work to be supervised by fellow church members. Thus, there are generally Amishmen who can draw up plans, lay brick, and install plumbing. In some Amish communities there are also small sawmills. Due to the increasing cost and scarcity of land, a growing number of Amish are accepting employment in small, nonunion factories that have sprung up in Amish areas: aluminum plants, trailer factories, and brick yards. Farming is still the preferred occupation, but a growing number of Amish are working in other occupations.

SEXUAL TTRANSGRESSION. The Amish are strongly opposed to extramarital coitus, and any transgression must be confessed to the total membership of the church whether or not pregnancy results. The male and female have equal responsibility to confess fornication. However, after a period of punishment, during which the transgressor is under the ban, both repentant individuals are welcomed back into full church membership, and they are completely forgiven. Although pregnancy is not always considered sufficient reason to marry, if the couple decides to get married, an effort is made to have the wedding before the birth of the baby. The degree of community pressure to marry applied to a couple who has fornicated or conceived varies from one settlement to another. If the parents do not marry, the mother may keep the baby, or it

301

may be adopted by an Amish couple. Sterility among Amish women appears to be about the same as among non-Amish; certainly it is no greater. Twinning seems to be high, which may be related to the longer reproductive history of Amish women and the large number of children born—both of which seem to be factors in frequenty of twinning (Enders and Stern, 1948; Cross, 1967).

MATE SELECTION. Amish marry later than the rest of the American white population. Studies of different Amish settlements show a variation in median age of first marriage during the past 50 years from 22.2 to 24.2 for males, and from 20.8 to 22.6 for females (Hostetler, 1974:83), Cross, 1967:66). In 1965, the median age of first marriage for the American population was 22.8 for males and 20.6 for females; for the Ohio Amish it was 24.1 for the males and 23.0 for females. There is some indication that the age of marriage is increasing among the Amish. However, an analysis of the Old Order Amish obituaries, published in *The Budget* for the three years from January 1951 through December of 1953, indicated an average age at first marriage (unrelated to generation or settlement) of 24 years for males and 22 years for females, which might suggest that the age of marriage has been relatively stable over the years (Huntington, 1956:870).

The Amish perceive the family as a religious and a social unit. Therefore, it is not surprising that Amish weddings are community affairs that fit into the general cycle of activity. In Lancaster County, Pennsylvania, and in Ohio the majority of weddings occur during the winter months, after harvest and butchering and before spring planting, with November and December being the most popular months. Very few weddings occur during May, June, July, August, and September. Outside the Lancaster County settlement there seems to be an extension of the wedding season, with more couples being married in late winter and a few weddings occurring in the summer. This change in season of marriage may be related to the trend away from farming as the only acceptable occupation. In addition to holding weddings at specific times of the year, almost all Amish weddings are on Thursday, with a few being held on Tuesday, and occasionally a second marriage may be incorporated into a Sunday church service. Thursday is the most convenient day of the week to hold an elaborate, day-long celebration, considering the prohibition against all unnecessary work on Sunday. Thursday gives the host family four days in which to "set up" for the wedding and two days to clean up afterward without infringing on Sunday. If there is any connection between Donnerstag (Thursday), Donar being a Germanic god of weddings and the hearth, and the day of celebrating weddings, it has long since been forgotten (Fogel, 1915).

The Amish are endogamous; marriage must be "in the Lord," that is, within the church membership. Even within the Old Order Amish Church there are breeding isolates resulting from preferred marriage patterns. Marriage between affiliations is discouraged, and marriages tend to take place within one settlement or between closely related settlements.

In analyzing marriages in central Ohio, Cross (1967:52–62) determined that 86 per cent of these marriages involved partners both of whom were born in the central Ohio settlement, and in more than three-fourths of these instances the "outside" partner came from a settlement founded by Amishmen from central Ohio and with which contact had been maintained by intervisitation. Although first-cousin marriages are forbidden, the Amish population has such a small genetic base that marriage partners are frequently as closely related as second or third cousins.

The Amish have a high standard of living, good medical care, and prohibit birth control. Therefore, except for the relatively late age of marriage, their birth rate resembles that of nonindustrialized countries, while their death rate resembles that of industrialized countries. When plotted by age and sex, the Amish population forms a wide-based pyramid, with over half the Amish under 20 years of age. This is in contrast to the population pyramid of the American rural farm population, which has a relatively narrow base, a "waist" in the 20 to 40 age brackets, reflecting the depressed fertility of the depression years, and then a swelling in the older categories. Within the typical American farm population, there are a disproportionate number of old people in relation to young people. The demographic structure of the Amish makes it relatively easy for the youthful population to carry the burden of supporting their aged; there are many productive young people to care for the relatively few old people.

Social Structure

The Amish in America have developed a community social structure consisting of the settlement, the church districts, the family, and the affiliation. Although these terms describe the social groupings, they do not convey the personal quality of the relationships.

The settlement consists of all the Amish living in a given geographically contiguous area. A single Amish family cannot be considered to form a settlement; even a small group of Amish families is not considered to be a settlement until they organize a church district. There is a minimum size necessary for a settlement to be able to sustain itself. This size is related to the number of church officials in the settlement (there must be at least two) and to the distance from the nearest communing church district, as well as the actual number of families and the size of the families that make up the settlement. Those Amish who are isolated geographically and socially from other Amish for too long a period lose their Amish identify. The Amish realize this, and if a new settlement does not attract other Amish settlers quickly enough, it will disband. History shows that those individuals who remain where there is no organized church become absorbed into the surrounding culture (Umble, 1949).

A church district is composed of a contiguous cluster of Old Order Amish families who worship together. Typically, each church district has a bishop, two ministers, a deacon, and perhaps 40 nuclear families. The number of families is determined by the density of the Amish in the area and the size of the homes; when the group becomes too large to meet in a home or barn for the worship service, the district divides. The geographical area of a single church district is almost never settled exclusively by Amish. The area is crossed by paved roads, perhaps interrupted by a village, and is interspersed with "English" farms and homes. Although there are geographical boundaries, neither the Amish church district nor the Amish community is territorial; it is a cultural, social, and religious grouping. The community is not necessarily made up of one's neighbors but rather of one's fellow church members, who are bound together by an ideology and a way of life.

The family, rather than the individual, is the unit of the church. When one asks an Amishman how big his church district is, he always answers you by stating how many families belong, never by how many individual members there are. The *Ohio Amish Directory* lists the families in each district, with no indication as to which individuals have been baptized into the church; unmarried baptized members are not listed unless they own their own home. Growth of the church is related to number of weddings, not number of baptisms.

Due to the congregational structure and the strict rules of discipline, differences that may seem minor to the outsider often arise within the larger settlements. These differences are the basis of various affiliations. Church districts that are "in fellowship" with one another interpret the *Ordnung* (discipline) similarly and exchange ministers for Sunday services. All those churches whose ministers "help out" one another form a single affiliation. The affiliations are informal, often unknown to non-Amish, and frequently changing. The tendency is to divide into more affiliations rather than to coalesce. This functions to keep the groups small, to limit social interaction, and to protect tradition. In the general Ohio community there are at least seven different Old Order Amish affiliations that are not "in fellowship" with one another. These range along a conservative-liberal continuum from churches whose members will not even ride in a private car (except to attend a funeral or go to the hospital) to churches in which young men drive cars until they actually join the church. Affiliations extend beyond settlement boundaries and, combined with kinship ties, help to bind different geographic Amish settlements together.

Kinship Relations

Kinship ties are maintained throughout the life of the individual. Excerpts from newsletters in *The Budget,* a weekly paper that goes to almost every Amish settlement, illustrate the importance of kinship ties both to the families and to the community.

> The children, grandchildren and great-grandchildren of Levi L. Slabach of Berlin were together for Sunday dinner at Bish. Roy L. Slabachs. All were present but three grandchildren. This was in honor of Levi's birthday which is August 6. (*The Budget,* August 2, 1973)
> Mother and us sisters were together at Benuel Stoltzfous, Jr. (sis. Mary). Mother Fisher is having quiltings this week and next to finish the quilts grandmother Fisher had started. (*The Budget,* August 2, 1973)

Extended families gather to celebrate birthdays and Christmas; brothers and sisters meet to work together, to help one another with church, to sew rags for woven rugs, to put up a milk house. And in the case of illness or any other stress, the extended family, the members of the church district, and other Amish neighbors rally round to help. Members of the Amish settlement are always identified by kinship groups. Husband and wife names are used together, Joe-Annie to signify Annie, the wife of Joe, or Annie-Joe meaning Joe, the husband of Annie; or father's name is used, Menno's Annie or Menno Annie to identify Annie, the daughter of Menno. Traditionally, the Amish children in Ohio were always given their father's first name as a middle initial to help identify them. In some settlements the initial of the mother's first name or maiden name was used for an identifying middle initial. There are generally so few last names in a given settlement that first names are used more frequently than last; thus, families are identified as "the Raymonds" and "the Aiden Js" instead of "the Millers" and "the Detweilers." In the central Ohio Amish settlement 12 names account for 85 per cent of the families. Nicknames are also used to distinguish individuals: "Barefoot Sam" or "Turkey John." Individuals are always identified by their families. Children in the Amish community schools introduce themselves by giving their father's first name. Young people quickly tell who their father and their mother are so that they can be placed genealogically. The signers of some Amish guest books are asked to indicate their date of birth and, if they are unmarried, to add their father's name. Kinship networks function to tie distant settlements together. Families visit married sons and daughters; brothers and sisters visit one another to "help out" or for a family get-together. Marriages, when outside the settlement, tend to take place between settlements that are closely related by kinship ties. Amish both publish and purchase genealogies and family reunions are widely attended. *The Budget* has a section in the classified ads, "#23-Reunions," and in the late summer many of the columns from different communities mention reunions.

Family Roles

Roles are well defined in the Amish family. The man is the head of the woman (I Cor:3) as Christ is the head of the church. Although the wife is to be subject to her husband, her first commitment is to God, and her second is to her husband. Because she has an immortal soul, she is an individual in her own right. She is not a possession of her husband, nor is she merely an extension of her spouse. Husband and wife become one flesh, a single unit separable only by God. She follows her husband, but only in that which is good. At council service before communion she decides, as an individual, if she is ready for communion. Should her husband transgress to the extent that he is placed under the ban, she, too, will shun him, as he will her in a similar situation. For the Amishman, the question of sacrificing his family for his job never comes up. The family comes first. A job is of no intrinsic importance; it is necessary because it supplies the economic basis for the family. The work of the household should provide vocational education for the children and fulfill the biblical standard, "In the sweat of thy face shalt thou eat bread." The wife's relative position is illustrated by her position in church, where she has an equal vote but not an equal voice. Farms are generally in the name of both husband and wife. Important family deci-

306

sions are made jointly. Unlike the corporation wife, the Amish wife participates actively in any decision to move to a different locality.

Parents present a united front to their children and to the community. In dealing with their children, Amish parents should be of one mind, discussing any differences privately and prayerfully. Admonitions to parents in sermons and in Amish writings are directed not to fathers as such, or to mothers alone, but to parents. Couples are never to disagree in public. The wife is expected to support her husband in all things, especially in his relationship with other people, whether it be their children, their parents, or friends and neighbors. The husband, in turn, should be considerate of his wife with respect to her physical, emotional, and spiritual well-being. The ideal is to be individuals to one another but of one mind to all others.

The major community role of Amish adults is child rearing. Parents have no individual rights, only responsibilities and obligations for the correct nurture of their children. They are to be examples to their children in all things, so that the children may become good Amishmen and eventually, through the grace of God, achieve life everlasting.

The role of the children within the family is more closely related to age than to sex. The older children are to care for and help the younger, while the younger are to obey the older in any reasonable demand. Older children do not physically punish younger children but cajole them into obeying. Although there is a division of labor by sex, children help one another and their parents as they are needed rather than strictly dividing the work by sex. Children function as socializing agents for the parents, for as parents strive to be good examples for their children, they become better Amishmen themselves.

Social Class and Style of Life

The Amish are a small, homogeneous group within which social class has no meaning. They are exclusively rural, operating small family farms and, in some instances, working in small nonunion factories or on small carpenter crews. In relation to the outside society, these occupations would probably place them in the rural working class. Within the community, life style is more important than economic income, but family farming is definitely the preferred occupation, and many types of employment are forbidden as incompatible with their way of life.

The Amish style of life is distinctive and consciously maintained. In an effort to build a "church without spot or blemish" and to remain a "peculiar people," strict disciplinary codes have been developed and are observed by members and their children. Most of these rules are unwritten, vary slightly from one church district to another, and are only completely known to participants. Most of the rules are taken for granted, but those pertaining to borderline issues, about which there might possibly be some disagreement, are reviewed twice a year by all baptized members of the church district. This allows for slow, orderly change in details of their life style that is necessary for group survival. Only if consensus on the rules (*Ordnung*) is achieved, and if there is a unanimous expression of peace and good will toward every fellow member, is communion celebrated. Most church districts reach this degree of integration twice a year.

The Old Order Amish style of life is characterized by the following focal concerns: separation from the world, voluntary acceptance of high social obligation symbolized by adult baptism, the practice of exclusion and shunning of transgressing members, and a life in harmony with nature. The Amish interpret separation from the world quite literally. Physically, they prefer to have some distance between themselves and non-Amish, between their households and non-Amish households. "Be ye not unequally yoked together with unbelievers; for what fellowship hath righteousness with unrighteousness? and what communion hath light with darkness?" (II Cor. 6:14). The Amish may not be union members or form partnerships with non-Amish, for both would join the believer with the unbeliever. In spite of this created distance, the Amish are not self-righteous nor judgmental in their relations with outsiders, whom they consider to be so different that the same criterion of conduct does not apply to them as it would to a fellow Amishman. "My kingdom is not of this world; if my kingdom were of this world, then would my servants fight." (John 18:36). Observing this teaching, the Amish may not serve in the military. Formerly, if they were called, they paid fines or served prison sentences; now they perform alternative service as conscientious objectors. All forms of retaliation to hostility are forbidden. An Amishman may not physically defend himself or his family even when attacked. He may not defend himself legally even when his civil rights have been violated. He is taught to follow the New Testament teaching of the Sermon on the Mount and the biblical example of Isaac. After the warring Philistines had stopped up all the wells of his father Abraham, Isaac moved to new lands and dug new wells (Genesis, 26:15–18). The Amish take this advice, and when they cannot remain separate from the world according to their own definition of separate, they move to new locations.

The adult Amishman voluntarily accepts a high degree of social obligation. His willingness to take on this responsibility is symbolized by the rite of baptism. Prior to baptism the future communicant renounces the world, the devil, his own flesh and blood, and acknowledges Christ as the Son of God and the Lord and Savior. He accepts a personal willingness to suffer persecution or death in order to maintain the faith. In addition, he promises to abide by the *Ordnung* and not to depart from the discipline in life or death. Each young man promises to accept the duties of minister should the lot ever fall on him. Applicants are warned not to make these promises if they cannot keep them, for once made, there is no turning back. It is not unusual for young people, during the period of instruction, to drop out. Generally they join a year or two later. No one may be married in the Amish church without first being baptized.

When deemed necessary, the Amish use excommunication and shunning (*Bann und Meidung*) to enforce the discipline and to keep the church pure and separate from the world. The full church membership participates in the decision and in the ceremony, in which the erring one is rebuked before all and purged out as a leaven. An Amishman in good standing may receive no favors from an excommunicated person; he may neither buy from nor sell to him, nor may he eat at the same table with the excommunicated person. The ban applies also between husband and wife, who may neither eat at the same table nor sleep in the same bed. The *Bann und Meidung* is used both to protect the individual and to protect the church. An erring member is shunned in order to help him realize the gravity of his sin and his need to return to the church. It is also used as a necessary step in the process of forgiveness, and thus helps the individual deal with guilt. The *Bann und Meidung* serves to protect the church by removing, both from ceremonial and social participation in the community, those individuals who will not follow the *Ordnung,* thus protecting the true believers from disruptive influence and temptations to modify their life style.

The Amish style of life is in harmony with nature. The prohibition against electricity helps to keep the Amish work day related to the solar day. The Amish home has neither air conditioning nor central heating, yet by modifying their daily routine, they manage to live comfortably with the changing seasons, relatively oblivious of energy crises. They do not exploit their environment, but care for it. The pea pods are put back on the garden, not thrown down a garbage disposal. There is a human scale to all of Amish life. Within the settlement distances are not too great, social groups are not too big, farms can be managed by a single family, and Amish schools have one or, at the most, two rooms. People know one another and identify with the physical environment in which they worship, live, and work. After a day visiting in a large city, an Amish farmer commented as we turned off the highway onto an unpaved road in his home county, "I know myself around here." He is the very antithesis of alienation.

By exercising a personal and a community discipline that excludes those who will not follow the dictates of the group and that stresses a voluntary commitment to a life in harmony with nature and separated from the outside culture, the Amish have been able to determine to a remarkable extent the style of their lives.

Family Life Cycle and the Socialization Process

The goal of the Amish family is the achievement of eternal life for each member. On an existential level, the goal is to teach children right from wrong, to be socially responsible as defined by the Amish community, to join the Amish church, and to remain faithful in the *Ordnung* until death.

In Amish society, a person passes through a series of six distinct age categories or stages of socialization as he progresses through life. Different behavior is demanded of him at each stage. The stages are: infancy, preschool children, schoolchildren, young people, adulthood, and old folks. (For a more detailed treatment of socialization, see Hostetler and Huntington, 1971). Infancy covers the period from birth until the child walks. Children of this age are generally referred to as "babies." Preschool children are referred to as "little children;" they know how to walk but have not yet started school, which is generally entered at age 6 or 7. Schoolchildren are called "scholars" by the Amish. They are fulfilling the eight years of elementary schooling required by the state. They attend either public schools or Amish schools and are between the ages of 6 and 16.

INFANCY. Babies are enjoyed by the Amish; they are believed to be gentle, responsive, and secure within the home and the Amish community, but vulnerable when out in the world. Babies are not scolded or punished, and there is no such thing as a bad baby, although there may be a difficult baby. A baby may be enjoyed without fear of self-pride, for he is a gift from God and not primarily an extension of the parents. If he cries, he is in need of comfort, not discipline. It is believed that a baby can be spoiled by wrong handling, especially by nervous, tense handling, but the resultant irritability is the fault of the environment, not the baby; he remains blameless. Old Order Amish parents give generous attention to their babies' needs, both physical and social. An Amish baby is born into a family and into a community. He is never spoken of as "a little stranger" but is welcomed as a "new woodchopper" or a "little dishwasher." Each baby is greeted happily as a contribution to the security of the family and the church.

CHILDHOOD. Amish children are taught to respect authority, and respect is shown by obedience. The Amish do not strive for blind obedience but for obedience based on love and on the belief that those in authority have deep concern for one's welfare and know what is best. Most traditional Amish parents teach obedience by being firm and consistent rather than by violent confrontations or single instances of breaking the child's will. The switch is used freely but not harshly. The prevailing attitude is matter-of-fact rather than moralistic in dealing with their children. Not only is the child taught to respect and obey those in authority, but he also learns to care for those younger and less able than he, to share with others, to do what he is taught is right and to avoid that which is wrong, to enjoy work, and to fulfill his work responsibilities pleasantly. The parents create a safe environment for their children. They live separated from the world, maintaining the boundary for their children that protects them from malevolent influence. The parent has the responsibility to punish transgressions but also the power to forgive. Punishment is used primarily to ensure the safety of the child; for his physical safety ("stay away from that nervous horse"), for his cultural safety ("be respectful to older people"), for his legal safety ("don't fish without a fishing license"), for his moral safety ("be obedient"). Rewards are used to develop the right attitudes in the child: humility, forgiveness, admission of error, sympathy, responsibility, and appreciation of work. Children are motivated primarily by concern for other people and not by fear of punishment.

Although children are primarily the responsibility of their parents, the community plays an important part in their socialization. Families attend church as a unit every other Sunday. The chidren sit through the long service, learning to be considerate of others, quiet, and patient. Until they are about 9 years old, the girls sit with the mothers or grandmothers, and the boys with their fathers. After the service, the children share in the community meal, and the youngest may nap on a big bed with other babies. The rest of the time the children play freely and vigorously about the house and yard, safe in the presence of many adults who care for them and guide them. If a small child suddenly feels lost, someone quickly returns him to a member of his family. The Amish child experiences the community as being composed of people like his parents, all of whom know him and direct him. He is comfortable and secure within the encompassing community. In many settlements the community also participates in the socialization of the child through the Amish "parochial" school, which supports the teaching of the home.

Throughout his childhood the Amish child spends the greatest part of his time interacting with members of his family. Unlike the typical suburban school child, the Amish child is usually in a mixed age group rather than isolated with his peers (Bronfenbrenner, 1970:96–102). The Amish child's parents and siblings play a central role in his development. Although the Amish generally consider childhood to end with the graduation of the child from the eighth grade or on his sixteenth birthday, they do not feel that their task as parents is even near completion. The desired end product will not be achieved until much later.

Young People. The age category known by the Amish as "young people" covers the years between 14 or 16 and marriage. It corresponds roughly to adolescence. This is the most individualistic period in the life of an Amishman and is considered to be the most dangerous. If an individual is to become Amish, he must be kept within the Amish community, physically and emotionally, during his crucial adolescent years. Yet at this time the family's control of the young person is somewhat limited, the community's control is informal, and the lure of the world is most strong.

During adolescence the peer group is of supreme importance, for during these years more of the Amish young person's socialization takes place within this group than within the family or the church. If the young person's peer group remains Amish, he has a reference point, a buffer, and a support. Even though as an individual or as a member of this Amish peer group he trangresses many rules and crosses most of the boundaries between the Amish community and the world, he will eventually return to the church to become a lifelong Amishman. However, if during this stage he makes "English" friends and identifies with an alien peer group, even though he is well behaved, he will probably leave the Amish church, never to return.

A certain degree of adolescent rebellion has become institutionalized among the Amish. The Amish child is raised in a carefully protected environment by relatively authoritarian parents. However, during this stage, the young Amish person will make the two most important commitments of his life: He will decide if and when to join the church and whom to marry. Both of these commitments he must make as an individual, albeit an individual who has the help of God, the concern of his parents, and the support of the community. In order to make such important decisions, he must establish a degree of independence from his family, and to some extent from his community, in order to develop his own identity. This is done in many ways, most of them carefully institutionalized. The family relaxes some of its tight control over the young person. He goes to social gatherings of his peers rather than having all of his social life with the family. The young person is learning what it means to be Amish. He may test some of the boundaries of the Amish community, sampling the world by such means as owning a radio, having his photograph taken, attending a movie, and occasionally wearing clothes that are outside the *Ordnung*. As long as these forays into wordliness remain discreet, they are ignored by the parents and the community, for it is believed that the young person should have some idea of the world he is voluntarily rejecting. One of the reasons courtship is secretive is that it is a means of achieving privacy in a closely knit community and within a large family. The young person is protected by a degree of institutionalized blindness on the part of adults, who thereby give him freedom—within safe boundaries.

The community indirectly counteracts youthful rebelliousness by providing social activities and vocational training for the adolescents. The Sunday-evening singing is an important social event in most Amish settlements. Young people generally begin attending when they have finished day school and are about 16 years old. The family that "has church" has "a singing" for the young people in the evening. Generally brothers and sisters go together to the singing, although they frequently return home in couples. In some of the larger settlements there will be Saturday night singing, or the young man may visit his girl friend in her home. Weddings, wiener roasts, work bees, and pound suppers will provide occasions for the young people to gather.

Proper vocational training is essential if the young person is to become an Amish Christian. Both the young Amishman and young Amish woman work for a variety of different people during these years, learning various acceptable vocational roles and, through their jobs, gaining a knowledge of other Amish families and other Amish settlements, and sometimes even a glimpse of the world by working for "English" people. The skills the Amish need are best learned by doing, and they have worked out an informal community apprentice system that serves the needs of the individual and the culture.

The relative freedom to test the boundaries of his culture, to make mistakes, to become aware of human weakness, counterbalanced by the individual's growing ability to be economically productive, and perhaps his interest in marriage, all function to make him think seriously about joining the church. When he finally makes this commitment in his late teens or early twenties, the parents have fulfilled their moral duty to the child, to the church, and to God. However, although in a theological sense they have completed their task as parents, in practice the parent-child relationship continues. Marriage, which even more than baptism is considered the beginning of adulthood, modifies the parent-child relationship but does not basically change it.

ADULTHOOD. Marriage is the beginning of social adulthood, but full adulthood is attained with parenthood. The adult Amish are responsible for the maintenance of their culture. They produce the children, who are expected to become Amish, they raise them in such a way that they want to become Amish, and they teach them the skills and attitudes that will enable them to remain Amish. The adult Amish watch over the boundaries of their culture, participating in the selective acculturation that is necessary for their survival as "a visible church of God" in twentieth-century America. Economically they must be sufficiently successful to support a large family and to help their children become economically independent after a few years of marriage. The Old Order Amish community is economically self-sufficient, and church members do not accept social security or welfare. Socially they are also self-sufficient, caring for those who are ill and old within the community. The adult Amish man or woman has no set retirement age. Retirement is voluntary, usually gradual, and related to the individual's health and the needs of his family. It generally takes place some time after the youngest child is married and has started to raise a family.

OLD FOLKS. Old folks normally signify their retirement by moving into the grandfather house adjacent to the main farmhouse. Their role as parents is rather modified but still continues, for the old people remain physically and emotionally close to their children and grandchildren. The young farmer discusses problems of farm management and sales prices with his father, the young mother asks advice about the children. The old people have an increased obligation to attend funerals, to visit the sick and bereaved. And when they are ill, members of the community visit them. As long as health permits, old folks spend a considerable amount of time visiting children, nieces, nephews, and friends in different parts of the settlement and in other settlements. They form an important link the network of informal communication that ties the larger Amish community together. They are often reliable sources of news, as well as of local history and of genealogical relationships. They exert a conservative influence as they fulfill their accepted roles of admonishing the young. As they grow older, and perhaps become senile or bedridden, they are still cared for at home. Typically, dying takes place in the home, surrounded by family and friends, not in the lonely, impersonal, and mechanical environment of a hospital.

> On June 19th she . . . was admitted and put under oxygen . . . She seemed to be losing out fast, as she had to labor to breathe even with oxygen. On Fri. we pleaded to go home. So arrangements were made with an ambulance to take her home, she being under oxygen all the while.
>   . . . At daybreak in the mornings for the last 3 mornings were her hardest and on the morning at 4:45 of the 26th of June she easily and peacefully faded away. (*The Budget*, August 2, 1973)

When death occurs, neighbors and nonrelatives relieve the family of all work responsibility, leaving the relatives free for meditation and conversation with the guests who come to see their departed friend and to talk to the bereaved family. Funerals, especially of elderly people, are large, and often 500 mourners may be present. After burial in an Amish graveyard, the mourners return to the house of the deceased for a meal. With this meal, normal relationships and responsibilities are restored. The family circle has been broken by death, but the strong belief in eternal life indicates that the break is only temporary. Another member of the family has achieved life everlasting.

CHANGE AND ADAPTATION

The rapid social changes since the Depression have broken down the isolation of the Amish. Specific threats to their community structure and family organization have been posed by (1) social security, (2) consolidation of elementary and junior high schools, (3) lengthening of the compulsory-attendance period and consequent required high school attendance, and (4) conscription. More subtle threats are the availability of motorcycles and cars, the cheapness and small size of transistor radios and phonographs, televisions blaring in every store, the ease of travel, and the use of telephones. These are all dangers inherent in our technologically sophisticated mass culture. A specific threat to the

315

Amish young people is variants of the Billy Graham type of religious fundamentalism. Fundamentalist radio programs are one of the means for introducing these dissident ideas into the community; local revival meetings are another. The more liberal branches of the Mennonite Church also offer a ladder to those who want to climb into "higher" churches step by step, changing their life style more than their theology. Finally, the greatest problem in the immediately foreseeable future is the scarcity and expense of land, the resultant trend to factory work as acceptable employment for household heads, and the consequent change in the Amish patterns of child rearing.

SOCIAL SECURITY. The four specific threats to the Amish culture have all been somewhat resolved during the past few years, but in every instance certain Amishmen bore the brunt of the encroachment by the state and paid fines, spent time in prison, and moved to other localities. The Amish do not believe in life insurance or old-age insurance. They live separate from the state, which they will support with taxes but not with their vote or with their lives. They believe that the Christian brotherhood should care for its own, and they are forbidden by the *Ordnung* to accept any form of survivors' insurance. Because they do not and will not accept social security payments from the state, they refuse to pay the social security tax to the state. After years of conflict, during which some Amish witnessed the sale of their horses and farms at public auction, the Amish were finally granted an exemption from the self-employment social security tax. This was a crucial issue for the Amish because both their family and their church structure, with the strong emphasis on social responsibility, would be weakened by reliance on outside funds.

ELEMENTARY SCHOOLING. The Amish in many settlements have responded to school consolidation and to rapid changes in the rural American culture by withdrawing further from the mainstream. It is not that they want to be more different from their non-Amish neighbors; it is that they do not want to change so rapidly; they want to keep the old ways. Large, modern consolidated schools are not suitable agents of socialization for the Amish child. Almost half of the Amish children still attend public schools. Some of these are rural schools that were not caught in the net of consolidation, some are relatively small village schools, and some are large, sprawling elementary schools. When their children attend public school, the parents attempt to isolate its influence and to counteract the disruption it may cause. Over half of the Amish

316

children attend community schools designed, built, and staffed by members of their own church. In 1973–74, there were 326 parochial schools with an enrollment of over 11,000 children. These schools were located in 13 states and in Canada and Honduras *(Blackboard Bulletin,* December 1973). In the community schools the Amish children learn the three Rs in an environment in which they are protected from the assumptions of twentieth-century America, in which they can learn discipline, humility, simple living, and cooperation. The Amish schools emphasize shared knowledge rather than individual knowledge, the dignity of tradition rather than the importance of progress. The Amish schools do not teach religion, rather a style of living. The school's task is to cooperate with the parents to preserve the faith taught by the parents, for it is the role of the family, not of the school or even the church, to make Amish Christians of the children. The Amish family constellation will change if the school-age children cannot participate in the ongoing work of the home and farm. When the children are removed from the home for many hours each day, as is the case when they must spend long hours on the bus in addition to the hours spent in class, when the school year interferes with the agricultural season, and when the children are physically and ideologically removed from their community, they cannot be taught the skills and attitudes needed to become Amish.

COMPULSORY HIGH SCHOOL ATTENDANCE. High school attendance is no longer a problem for the Old Order Amish because the Supreme Court ruling of May 15, 1972, protects the religious freedom of the Amish be permitting Amish children who have graduated from the eighth grade to particpate in community-based vocational programs in lieu of attending high school. The students spend half a day a week in school under the direction of a teacher and four and a half days working in a modified apprentice system, generally under the direction of their parents. They learn technological skills in a social context as participants in the economy of the community. While working on a family farm, Amish children of high school age learn not only how to perform a task, such as how to harrow, but also when to harrow, and how to integrate harrowing into all the other work that is required of the vocation "farmer." They also learn wider community work roles by helping in threshing rings and at barn raisings, getting ready for church, and helping care for neighbors' children. Of great importance to the success of the Amish vocational training is the fact that the vocational expectations of the young people coincide with the vocational opportunities available to them.

CONSCRIPTION. Since the beginning of World War II the draft has taken young men outside of the Amish community at a most vulnerable stage in their development. The I-W program which provided an alternative to military service functioned in such a manner that young Amishmen spent two years outside the community, often alone in a city, perhaps wearing non-Amish clothing while at work. These measures separate the young men from community control and to a limited extent made them non-Amish. The draft was never incorporated into the Amish life style. It interfered with two of the most important *rites de passage* among the Amish: baptism and marriage. Baptism signifies total commitment to the believing church-community, physically and spiritually separated from the world. If the drafted young man were baptized before his alternative service, he could not live physically separated from the world as he was pledged to do. If he were not baptized before his service, he had not committed himself to the church-community and so was more vulnerable to outside influence. Was it best for a young man to marry before, during, or after his alternative service? If he went into the world without a wife, he might form friendships with non-Amish girls, and because marriage must be with a co-religionist, such friendships were dangerous. If he had a wife, she helped protect him from worldly influences, but they started their married life with modern conveniences, electricity, and telephones, which are hard to give up when they return to an Amish way of life. During I-W service, both the Amish men and their wives learned non-Amish work patterns, and many received training they could never use on an Amish farm.

The most traditional Amish refuse I-W service when it requires them to live in a city or to wear non-Amish garb. As one Amish father explained, "God did not mean for the Amish to take the way of I-W service. It is better for the Amish to go to prison, though it is hard. God is with them there." At the time of writing, young men are not being drafted, but the selective service act is still in effect, so it is a moot point whether or not the draft will continue to disrupt the lives of young men. Certainly the Amish community will continue to be affected by the experiences of those young men who have already spent two years outside the protective boundaries of their culture.

OTHER AREAS OF CHANGE AND ADAPTATION. The *Ordnung* protects the Amish from the encroachment of technology, from a throwaway mentality, and from the overstimulation of the individual (Toffler, 1970). The *Ordnung* further specifically forbids members to have high-line electricity, which means that all electrical conveniences, from clothes dryers to vacuum cleaners to toasters, are unavailable. All musical instruments are forbidden, and radios and television sets can come under this prohibition. Telephones connect one with the outside world and "cause women to waste time," because "you can work and talk when you are both in the same room, but neither of you can work while talking on the telephone." Cars, and to a lesser degree motorcycles, are threatening because they enable people to travel too far, too fast, and to go beyond the face-to-face community in which everyone is known and everyone is watched. Movies are forbidden but offer little threat to the community because there is no interest in them; they are too far from the individual's experience and value system to do more than elicit passing curiosity. In many ways the Amish culture is oral rather than literary, and though they have kept out the medium, and along with it the message (McLuhan, 1962), they are not really threatened by the printed word, by radio, or even by television. Consistent with the oral tradition, the Amish stress shared knowledge and the importance of meaningful social interaction. They are so far outside the mainstream of American culture that they have little shared knowledge with the average American citizen and little reason to interact socially with him. The area in which they may be the most vulnerable is that of religious fundamentalism, for here the familiarity with the Bible gives a degree of shared knowledge that may open the way for outside influence. Although the Amish are relatively immune to changes in their world view and basic thought patterns, they are more open to change in the area of economics. They know they must survive economically in order to survive culturally, but they also believe that it is better to suffer economic and physical hardship than to lose their unique religious orientation. There is more pressure to accept telephones and electricity than to permit radios and movie attendance. Those aspects of the outside culture than can enhance Amish family life and can reinforce community ties and community economic strength are tempting and will continue to be accepted if they can be incorporated without changing the family roles or the social structure and without permitting encroachment of worldly ideas and worldly ways.

Perhaps the greatest problem facing the Amish today is the above noted scarcity of good farming land and the availability of factory work. As it becomes more expensive to get established on a farm, more family heads look for other types of suitable employment. In many Amish settlements small factories have been built to take advantage of the cheap (nonunion), skilled, reliable labor the Amish supply. The trend from farming to nonfarming occupations may have a profound effect on the Amish culture. The Amish family and Amish patterns of child rearing are built on the concept of shared parental responsibility, on the expectation that both parents work together caring for the farm and the children, that both parents are almost always in the home and available to support one another and to guide and teach their children. For example, family devotions are led by the father, but it is difficult to have these when the father has to punch a time clock rather than being able to adjust his farm chores to the sleeping patterns of his growing family. The authority patterns within the family change when the father is absent during most of the day. A sick baby, a fussy 3 year old, are minor inconveniences when both parents are available. On an Amish farm the boys spend most of the time, when they are awake and not in school, working with or under the direction of their father. In no other occupation can the father so consistently teach, instruct, admonish, and correct his children.

The social structure of the Amish community is based on the availability of brethren and sisters to gather for work bees, for barn raisings, for day-long weddings, and day-long funerals. The Amish share labor within the family, between families and among church members whenever there is extra or special work to be done. This combination of mutual aid and social interaction keeps the community strong and of one mind. This interaction can be relatively easily achieved in a church district in which most of the household heads are farmers; it is almost impossible when most of the men work in factories or on construction crews. The traditional Amish culture is dependent on both parents working in the home, that is, being available to each other and to the children and to the community any hour of the day, on any day of the week. Although the Amish are tied to the American market system, their culture mitigates these ties and functions to isolate the Amishman by circumscribing his economic options in such a way that the Amish family-centered culture can be perpetuated both socially and physically.

During the 250 years the Amish have been in America, they have successfully resisted the lures of mass consumption and mass communication, they have maintained their emphasis on limited gratification and limited consumption, stressing economy, savings, and cash payments. While the urban villagers of Boston argue that money earned should be spent immediately to make daily life more pleasant, because "life is too short for any other way of behavior" (Gans, 1962:187), the Amish argue that "no one would want such a beautiful home here on this earth if they hoped for heavenly home after this time" (*Family Life*, June 1973:11).

Life is too short to risk losing one's soul just for comfort or pleasure. "Only one life, t'will soon be past; Only what's done for Christ will last."

The Amish stress on the individual's total commitment to God, thus his responsibility to live according to the Amish *Ordnung,* has enabled the Amish culture to survive, sometimes at tremendous personal expense to the individual. In the early years of their history, some individuals were martyred, and the total group was strengthened by the payment of the few. In recent times certain individuals have lost their farms and savings; they were in a sense economically martyred, and again the total group profited by the payment of the few. The steadfastness of the Amish as individuals finally resulted in changes in and the enforcement of various laws, for example, social security, high school attendance, non-certified teachers in Amish schools, and alternative forms to military service. The Amish culture will continue to change as it adjusts to economic, technological, and social changes in the surrounding culture, but as long as the Amish are able to maintain their basic cultural figuration, their unique world view, and their own social structure, they will persist even though the details of their lives change.

R E F E R E N C E S

Ausband, Das ist: Etliche schöne christliche Lieder. First edition, 1564.

Bainton, Roland H. 1952. *The Reformation of the Sixteenth Century.* Boston: Beacon Press.

Blackboard Bulletin. Aylmer, Ontario: Pathway Publishing Corporation. A monthly published "in the interests of Amish parochial schools."

Bronfenbrenner, Urie, 1970. *Two Worlds of Childhood: U.S. and U.S.S.R.* New York: Russell Sage.

Budget, The. Sugarcreek, Ohio. "A Weekly Newspaper Serving The Sugarcreek Area And Amish-Mennonite Communities Throughout The Americas."

Braght, Thieleman J. van 1951. *The Bloody Theatre or Martyr's Mirror of the Defenseless Christians Who Baptized Only Upon Confession of Faith, and Who Suffered and Died for the Testimony of Jesus, Their Saviour, From the Time of Christ to the Year A.D. 1660.* Scottdale, Pa.: Mennonite Publishing House.

Cross, Harold E. 1967. *Genetic Studies in an Amish Isolate.* Ph.D. dissertation, The Johns Hopkins University.

Enders, Trudy and Curt Stern. 1948. "The Frequency of Twins, Relative to Age of Mothers, in American populations." *Genetics* 35:(May),263–72.

Family Life. Aylmer, Ontario: Pathway Publishing Corporation. A monthly "dedicated to the promotion of Christian living among the plain people, with special emphasis on the appreciation of our heritage."

Fogel, Edwin Miller. 1915. *Beliefs and Superstitions of the Pennsylvania Germans*. Philadelphia: American Germanica Press.

Gans, Herbert J. 1962. *The Urban Villagers*. New York: The Free Press.

Hostetler, John A. 1955. "Old World Extinction and New World Survival of the Amish." *Rural Sociology* 20 (September-December):212–19.

Hostetler, John A. 1968. *Anabaptist Conceptions of Child Nurture and Schooling; A Collection of Source Materials Used by the Old Order Amish*. Philadelphia (mimeographed).

Hostetler, John A. 1974. *Amish Society*. Baltimore, Md.: Johns Hopkins Press.

Hostetler, J.A., and G. E. Huntington. 1971. *Children in Amish Society: Socialization and Community Education*. New York: Holt, Rinehart and Winston.

Huntington, Gertrude Enders. 1956. *Dove at the Window: A Study of an Old Order Amish Community in Ohio*. Ph.D. dissertation, Yale University.

Littell, Franklin H. 1964. *The Origins of Sectarian Protestantism*. New York: Macmillan.

Luthy, David. 1973. "The Amish in Europe." *Family Life* (March):10–14. Aylmer, Ontario: Pathway.

McLuhan, Marshall. 1962. *The Gutenberg Galaxy*. Toronto: The University of Toronto Press.

Mennonite Encyclopedia. 1955. Scottdale, Pa.: Mennonite Publishing House; Newton, Kan.: Mennonite Publication Office; Hillsboro, Kan.: Mennonite Brethren Publishing House.

Ohio Amish Directory. Millersburg, Ohio.

Raber, J. A. (ed.). 1971, 1973. *Der Neue Amerikanische Calendar*. Baltic, Ohio.

Schwartz, Hillell. 1973. *"Early Anabaptist Ideas About the Nature of Children." Mennonite Quarterly Review* 47 (April):102–14.

Simons, Menno. 1956. *The Complete Writings of Menno Simons*. Scottdale, Pa.: Herald Press.

Smith, C. Henry. 1920. *The Mennonites: A Brief History of Their Origin and Later Development in Both Europe and America*. Berne, Indiana: Mennonite Book Concern.

Smith, C. Henry. 1929. *The Mennonite Immigration to Pennsylvania in the Eighteenth Century*. Norristown, Pa.: Proceedings of the Pennsylvania German Society.

Toffler, Alvin. 1970. *Future Shock*. New York: Random House.

Umble, John. 1949. "Factors Explaining the Disintegration of Mennonite Communities." *Proceedings of the Seventh Annual Conference on Mennonite Cultural Problems*. North Newton, Kansas: Bethel College. Published under the auspices of the Council of Mennonite and Affiliated Colleges.

The Franco American Working Class Family

Professor Laurence French has written an analysis of the Franco-American family that follows the "critical sociology" approach. Since parts are perhaps controversial we are happy to present his scholarly and research credentials.

"I am of French Canadian descent," writes Professor French, and was born and raised in French Canadian mill towns, I lived seventeen years in Suncook, New Hampshire (Saint John the Baptist Parish). Our family was a typical working class one with both parents working in the mills. We had nine children during a thirteen year span and my mother left school at 12, which was quite common then, and my father never finished high school. In fact, I was the first in my extended family network to finish high school, and this was against their wishes. I left in 1959 to join the Marine Corps and when I returned eight years later I was now a college student. For the next six years (1966–72) I lived, visited and worked among the French Canadians as part of an ethnomethological research of my people. This took me to both Canada and other Northern New England communities: Sherbrooke, Coaticook, St. Marie, Quebec city and the Gaspé in Canada as well as mill towns in northern Massachusetts, New Hampshire, Maine and Vermont."

CHAPTER FOURTEEN
BY
LAURENCE FRENCH

INTRODUCTION

The French Canadians have had a long tenure in the New World and currently share minority status in two North American countries—Canada and America. The French Canadians are unique for several reasons. First, they have retained their minority status for nearly 400 years, and second they have done this without the aid of any visible racial or physical stigma. Many who have studied the French Canadians would argue that the main reason for their minority status is due more to internal resistance than to external hostilities. The universal presence of the Catholic Church in French Canadian culture is more than just an added consideration.

This selection looks at the French Canadian as an ethnic entity, tracing its traditional culture historically through both Canada and New England. The family and the parish (French Canadian community) are the most important aspects of both the traditional and contemporary French Canadian culture. One type of family, that of the working-class mill worker, is focused upon. Granted not all French Canadians fall into this category, but it is these people nonetheless who seem most responsible for the continuation of the traditional French Canadian culture among the numerous mill towns scattered throughout northern New England.

HISTORICAL BACKGROUND

The French in the New World

Unlike most minority groups discussed in the volume, the French Canadians initially settled in Canada, and it is there they first established their minority status. In this respect French Canadian culture in America actually reflects a sub-subculture in that the Canadian French are themselves a subculture of seventeenth- and eighteenth-century France. Relevant parallel developments in both French subcultures will be discussed since open lines of communication and influence continue to facilitate the cultural development and identity of French Canadians in both countries.

The French Canadians represent a unique minority in that their cultural heritage in the New World equals that of the English dominant group. A French colony, New France, was established in eastern Canada in 1534, 86 years before the pilgrims landed at Plymouth and two centuries prior to American independence. One might ask why they are still ascribed a minority status in both Canada and America when most other Caucasian ethnic groups have overcome this stigma, integrating into the larger dominant culture. The answer to this perplexing question rests in part on the religious ideals and those of the dominant Protestant ethnic. This, coupled with the unusual circumstances surrounding the transfer of French Canada from French to British control, accounts for the unique phenomenon concerning the French Canadian's minority status. Relevant to these circumstances are numerous historical occurrences that further solidified and polarized the two cultures (French and English). It is in the context of these unique situations that the French Canadian family and social life have emerged.

The major attributes that distinguish the French Canadians as a minority group are: (1) They have the longest tenure of any Caucasian minority group in the New World; (2) They hold minority status in two countries in the New World, Canada and America; and (3) The communication channels with the mother country (Canada) are still strong. The general historical background is especially important in that it provides the framework on which the French Canadian family style emerged.

The family is the basic economic and socializing unit, while the parish is the religious and civil community in which the family functions. The original French in Canada were affiliated with the trading companies, which more or less isolated them from the influence of the European industrial revolution. This enabled them to retain the medieval and feudal life style they brought with them to the New World. The quasi-feudal system that emerged in colonial Canada was patterned after the agrarian family system in France and consisted of: (1) government officials; (2) landlords (*seigneurs*); (3) the priesthood (*curé*); and (4) the peasants (*habitants*).

The wars with England during the eighteenth century greatly altered the status of the French colonies in the New World. This in turn had an effect on the life style of those French Canadians stranded on the American continent. The 1713 Treaty of Utrecht ended the War of the Spanish Succession, granting England important colonies that were previously owned by France (to become Nova Scotia, Newfoundland, and the Hudson Bay territory). A consequence of this treaty was the dispersion of the Acadian French, who previously populated these areas. And in 1755 the English authorities finally expelled the remaining Acadians (some 7,000) from Nova Scotia. The Catholic church refers to this incident as "one of the greatest crimes against civilization known in the annals of America" (Byrne, 1899). According to church sources families were separated in the most cruel manner, and many were forced to migrate to the French territory in America, later known as the "Louisiana Territory," while others fled to the 13 colonies. Only 500 escaped removal, illegally residing in their Canadian homeland. The hostility between the French and English reached such intensity at this time that a major manhunt occurred throughout the 13 colonies during the years 1755–66 in an attempt to rid the colonies of French Canadians.

In 1763, the Treaty of Paris ended the Seven Years War, more commonly known as the French and Indian War. This document provided for French cession to England of Canada and all the territory east of the Mississippi River. After the defeat of 1760, French government officials left for France, leaving the leadership role to the Catholic church. The French outnumbered the British 14 to one (70,000 French Canadians and only 5,000 British) at this time, forcing the British to delegate French Canadian control to the Catholic Church. With the departure of both government officials and many *seigneurs* (landowners), the Catholic Church conveniently filled the ensuing power vacuum. This endowed the Catholic Church with both sacred and secular powers—a situation closely resembling that of medieval France. With ties of communication severed with France and a lack of British concern, the French Canadians continued to maintain their traditional preindustrial life style.

From the beginning, conflict emerged between the normative values of these two Canadian groups. The French Canadians spoke French, were Catholics, and belonged to an agrarian economic system. The British spoke English, were Protestant, and developed a progressive industrialized society. What resulted was a communication and cultural lag between the French majority and the ruling British government. This situation is reflected in French Canadians' dissatisfaction over their political impotence, which began in the early 1700s and continues today.

Local autonomy was established, however, when the Treaty of Paris temporarily united North America under the British flag. The British authorities, faced with growing unrest in the 13 colonies, gave up an early attempt to assimilate the French Canadians. Instead, they established the Quebec Act of 1774, recognizing the major institutions of the French-speaking community, especially the church and the French language. By doing such, the efforts of the rebelling colonies to ally the French Canadians to their cause failed. Again, in 1791, the Canada Act was enacted to divide Canada for better representation by ethnic background. Yet, by 1834, the French Canadians, comprising three-quarters of the total population, still held less than one-quarter of the public offices. In 1837 a series of small-scale revolts were staged by the French Canadians in reaction to the Ex-Quebec Act, which advocated forcible assimilation. The Ex-Quebec Act attacked the Catholic Church indirectly by outlawing the use of the French language and curtailing the parochial education system. This act also encouraged migration to other areas of Canada in an attempt to disperse the French and weaken their solidarity. In 1840 the Union Bill, which established the Province of

326

Canada, proved to be the main vehicle of forced assimilation. In 1867, the British North American Act created the Dominion of Canada. This act reduced some of the harshness of the Ex-Quebec Act by recognizing the French language and allowed each province certain powers of its own, such as educational control.

Migration to America

Meanwhile, during and immediately after the Civil War, the textile industry's rapid growth in New England provided the impetus for French Canadian immigration to America. In the mid-nineteenth century hundreds of mills were built along New England's many rivers. The Civil War, low status associated with mill work, and westward migration caused a shortage of indigenous laborers. The mill owners desired a readily available, docile, easily controlled, low-salaried work force. Southern Blacks, Filipinos, and other "minority" groups were under consideration, but initial cost of transportation and sensitive racial issues made these groups less desirable to the mill owners than the Caucasian French Canadians. The French Canadians met all the ideal prerequisites, while remaining racially invisible.

The motive for migrating was economic, for in Canada the French Canadians' traditional values and mores kept them out of commercial and industrial activities, and at the same time, their own economic system of farming, lumbering, and trapping began to decline. The large stem family could no longer absorb and support the excess labor force ushered in by the depression of 1873. The New England textile industry's manpower needs seemed at the time to offer the best solution to this crisis. The French Canadians proved to be an ideal labor source, with their large available work force, their willingness to work for low wages, and the relatively short distance necessary to migrate. The French Canadians proved to be docile laborers, submissive to authority, with families, following tradition, often working together in the mills.

The French Canadians' migration and the development of a new Franco-American subculture had an adverse effect on both the prevailing Quebec and New England cultures. The French Canadian family system in Canada was, and still is, predominantly large and patriarchal, constituting a strong influence on the roles of the individual members. When the French Canadians came to New England to work in the factories, they did not originally intend to make the host state their permanent residence. Their main intent was that of economic exploitation with plans eventually to return to Canada. Their initial purpose was to work in New England during the Canadian depression in an attempt to alleviate the economic strain on their families left in Canada. While many did not plan to remain, only 10 per cent returned to Canada. The peak influx of the French Canadians into New England was the decade 1890–1900. The rate dropped off thereafter, and in 1930, during our own Depression, the border was closed.

The French Canadians' ethnocentricity in New England was strong. While they tried to retain their total ethnic background, they succeeded only in producing a subculture apart from their mother Canadian culture. One reason for this occurrence was that the ethnic code was supported by three diverse classes of people with different motivations: (1) the priesthood; (2) the businessmen, and (3) the bulk of the French Canadian laborers. The clergy knew from previous experience in Canada that when the French identity was separated from the Catholic Church, the people were prone to reject Catholicism. A case in point was the French Canadians who had migrated to Canada's western provinces. The businessmen, on the other hand, backed ethnic unity because it was profitable. They virtually held a monopoly on the business in the French Canadian ghetto communities in the mill towns. Most of the businessmen sent their children back to Canada for their education so they would be properly exposed to and supportive of the Quebec culture. Consequently, because they tended to gain from the situation, the French Canadian business group as a whole supported the church's doctrine advocating cultural separatism. The third group, the mass of the French Canadian laborers and mill hands, nourished nostalgic ties with their mother country through frequent contact with relatives and friends from Quebec and (until 1930) by contact with the renewed supply of immigrants from Quebec.

Ethnic identification was also kept alive by various organizations and institutions that were established to provide for the needs of the immigrants. The organizations took the form of mutual-aid corporations and ethnic activities such as drama clubs and credit unions. The first French Canadian credit union in America, for example, was established in Manchester, New Hampshire, in 1907. The French newspaper was another medium by which ethnic unity was preserved. The major institutions promoting ethnic identification was the Catholic Church with its parishes and parochial schools. The church was the focal point of all organizations, and the priest had influence in both religious and secular matters. Many organizations were established in conjunction with the local parish, since the church's approval often determined their success or failure. French Canadian parochial education was and still is closely related with the Catholic Church. Most parishes provided at least primary-school facilities. The purpose of the parochial school has been to educate the children within the context of the ethnic culture, hence providing a major vehicle for the preserving and perpetuating of that culture.

In spite of numerous attempts to preserve the French Canadian culture, the system has undergone change. The old rural family system was threatened by the mechanisms of rational capitalist enterprise and economic organization. The mills were situated in towns and cities, and some 80 per cent of the French Canadians migrated to urban areas in New England. The people who retained their old traditions were those who kept their old occupations, such as farmers and lumberjacks. Thus, it is ironic that the French Canadians should be one of the last groups of Western European heritage to be exposed to industrialism, capitalism, and urbanization. After all, it was the French who initially influenced the rest of the world with their own capitalistic and democratic ideas.

The Early French Family in North America

Extended families combining into small parish communities provided the nucleus of an early French Canadian society, which to a large extent still exists in rural Quebec province and in the Gaspé Peninsula. These families consisted of the ruling patriarch, his immediate family of procreation, and those of his married sons. In this respect the early French Canadian extended family was both patriarchal and patrilocal. Not only did the eldest male dominate the family, but married sons were expected to take up residence with their fathers. The patriarchs, in turn, were answerable to the parish priest and the priest to the bishop.

A general characteristic of these extended families was their large constituent families of procreation. Incentives were provided by the French crown to stimulate large families, thus strongly supporting the Catholic doctrines regarding procreation and providing a strong cultural value that still persists among French Canadians. Women were sent from France to become the wives of settlers, while incentive bounties were allotted males who married prior to age 16. Special compensations were given families with 10 or more children, and, *au contraire*, patriarchs who failed to marry off their children at the prescribed ages were fined.

329

The parish community, which as noted was comprised of extended families, approached an autonomous socioeconomic unit. In such a community the priest, not the landlord, became the center of community life, and the church pervaded all aspects of French Canadian life from birth to death. Miner (1967:91) writes:

> The philosophy of this religion is ingrained in the people from childhood. Emulation of the socially powerful individuals in the community means the acceptance of Catholic ideology and behavior patterns. All methods of orienting the child in the society are employed to develop in him emotional attachment to this particular set of beliefs. Lack of contact with persons of other convictions and the relative lack of functional problems in the mode of living mean that the particular native belief is seldom questioned.

Religious ritual became an indispensable part of community and family life. All records were kept by the parish priests, and all decisions awaited their approval. Until British rule the only taxes the peasants paid were tithings to the church. Religion and education were inseparable. The only formal education (primary school) was and still is parochial. In short, the church both defined and provided the French Canadians with their social, cultural, and normative systems.

The family provided the real basis of rural life in the parish. In the early extended family all members, regardless of sex and age, shared in the family enterprise. The females did the spinning, weaving, knitting, sewing, cooking and serving of meals, washing, gardening, milking, and housekeeping, while the males tended the farm. All profit, whether it be capital gain or material objects, was received and handled by the family patriarch. When the patriarch died, the management of the family holdings was transferred to the next eldest male, while the moral leadership of the clan remained entrenched in the patriarch's wife. Daily prayers and compulsory church attendance helped weld the family into a sacred unit. Mores and folkways provided effective informal modes of control both within the family and the larger parish community. Marriages were arranged with the payment of dowries and were closely controlled so as not to disrupt the community balance. The church, in turn, exerted considerable control over the family not only morally but economically. The upkeep of the parish was paid by a yearly *dime* or tithe by which every twenty-sixth minot of grain belonged to the church.

High occupational, political, and social aspirations were not emphasized. Sons took on the occupation of their fathers, such as farming, logging, trapping, or fishing. The women and children held subservient positions in the family scheme. In a hierarchy of control and dominance within the parish community, the priest ranked highest, the extended family patriarch second, his married sons next, while women and children ranked last, playing submissive, subordinate roles. The Catholic Church itself provided the highest aspirations for the French Canadians. Nearly every family had at least one member in the church, occupying the role of priest, brother, or nun. All this helped strengthen the inter-relatedness and autonomy of the parish community. But even in the church women played subservient roles. Nuns or sisters either performed servitude roles for the priest and brothers or taught in the parish parochial schools.

Mill-Town Subculture of Early Franco-Americans

The migration of French Canadians to New England had a tremendous influence not only on those who migrated but on the lift style of their countrymen who remained in French Canada. The open American-Canadian border from the 1860s to 1930 allowed cultural dissemination not only from Canada to New England but also vice versa. The areas most resistent to these influences were the small farm parishes along the lower St. Lawrence, both in Quebec province and in the Gaspé. In the rest of French Canada there was a trend toward urbanization and industrialization, which eventually replaced the archaic agrarian life style. The new Franco-American life style became the focal point of social change among French Canadians. By the same token it provided a new French Canadian subculture. The mill ghettos became autonomous social units, bringing with them their own parish priest, and while the migrants did succeed in retaining a distinct ethnic identity, their life style nevertheless changed considerably. The new economic life style, the exposure to other types of social institutions, and the relatively higher standard of living altered the French Canadian's social system such that it eventually emerged into a distinct New England, Franco-American subculture.

In the early Franco-American family, French was still the primary language, but contrary to the Canadian situation English was often learned as a second language. Education still consisted of primary parochial education provided by the church. The priest and church still had a strong influence, but the patriarch's dominance diminished as the extended family often broke into conjugal units and no longer remained patrilocal. The male head of the conjugal but usually large family became the dominant figure, while women and children still played subservient roles and often spent long hours in the mills themselves.

THE MODERN FRANCO-AMERICAN FAMILY

Once the French Canadian immigration to America began, an interesting social phenomenon occurred that altered the life style of French Canadian families in both countries. The new family structure created in the New England mill communities soon had a reverse effect on the life style of French Canada, providing impetus for Quebec province to industrialize and urbanize, something the British Canadians had tried in vain to initiate for decades. The irony of this situation is that the lines of communication between Franco-Americans and French Canadians were better established than were those between the dominant British Canadians' culture and the subordinate French Canadians. What has emerged is a dual French Canadian subculture along rural-urban lines, with similar characteristics in each subculture in both countries.

The older, rural subculture still exists virtually unchanged in the farm parishes along both banks of the St. Lawrence, while in northern New England (Vermont, New Hampshire, and Maine) Franco-American farmers and loggers still maintain a rural existence. Today, however, the rural French Canadians represent a distinct minority of the French population in both areas. It is estimated that less than a quarter of the residents of both Quebec province and northern New England reside in rural areas. The major difference in the population composition between the two areas is that in Quebec 90 per cent of the population is French Canadian, while it is estimated that approximately 30 to 40 per cent of northern New England's population is of French Canadian descent. In southern New England the proportion is somewhat smaller, comprising 15 to 20 per cent of the population. Most of the French Canadian population, in both areas, reside in urban, industrialized settings. This does not necessarily imply large urban settings, for relatively small mill towns with populations varying from 2,000 to 10,000 fall into this category. Interestingly enough, northern New England, which is considered to be an industrialized area, has no cities with a population exceeding 100,000. It is the French family living in these mill-town industrial areas in both Canada and New England that represents the new French Canadian subculture that has emerged within the last hundred years and that remains the focus of this chapter.

Social characteristics now to be discussed (family structure, education, occupation, social and physical mobility, and community organization) refer to those Franco-American ghetto mill communities throughout New England that have physically and culturally insulated themselves, effectively resisting outside influences. The communities most susceptible to this life style are those that have managed to retain both French Catholicism and the French Canadian language while at the same time remaining isolated from divergent cultures.

Family Structure

Today's Franco-American family is basically a conjugal unit, although strong intergenerational kinship ties are maintained. The family hierarchy of social positions and responsibilities still focuses on the "earthly trinity" analogy, whereby the father, like God, dominates, controls, and protects the family interests, while the mother's role, like that of the Virgin Mary, is to be compassionate to the family while remaining subordinate and submissive to the father. Her specific role is to provide moral support for the family. The religious aura encompassing and binding the family together through the use of daily ritual is analogous to the binding effect of the "holy spirit."

In the Franco-American family model the dominant socioeconomic role is ascribed to the father, while the role of socialization agent is left to the mother. However, unlike the normative conjugal family model, which portrays small family units, the Franco-American family is often large. A generation ago it was not uncommon for there to be 10 members within a Franco-American family unit. Currently, family sizes seem to be decreasing. This phenomenon can be attributed to trying economic conditions and new child-labor and minimum-educational laws that place excessive children as economic liabilities. Nevertheless, children seek to help the family economy, often leaving school as early as possible, seeking employment, and contributing to the household until they themselves marry and set up their own family unit. This system functions because of the unique socialization process and kinship structure of the Franco-American family. Franco-Americans, like their French Canadian cousins, establish complex primary relationships within their parish communities, whereby reciprocal family, kinship, and religious obligations still supersede the individual's self-interest.

This phenomenon is best explained within the context of French Canadian kinship. Piddington (1971) noted that French Canadian kinship patterns more closely resemble those of folk cultures than they do Western societies. The French Canadians have a wide range of priority kin, coupled with a large number of prescribed social relationships, while in most Western societies the priority of kin are fewer, most being restricted to the closed conjugal family unit. The French Canadian family is distinguished as a discrete residential and economic unit through its constellation of kinship relationships. And through these kinship networks parish communities in both Quebec and New England are closely linked. The interparish linkage serves to provide acceptable mates and does much to offset the disruptive effects of migration. It also provides facilities for social contacts and economic opportunity. From the standpoint of religious organization, the kinship network has long been the handmaiden of a French Canadian Catholicism that has managed to easily transcend international boundaries in the maintenance of its Quebec and New England parishes.

Male dominance in the Franco-American family and community is readily evident in both Canada and New England. Family status and identity is transferred through the male lineage. Informal nicknames, passed down from father to son for generations, play an important role in the preservation of family status, while at the same time providing a secure identity for the male child. Females assume their husbands' status upon marriage. In this fashion, family and community status is preserved through the male lineage. Even children born out of wedlock trace their status and identity to the biological father if his identity is known.

Early marriages are common among the Franco-Americans mainly because they lack the restraints their Canadian relatives employ, such as matched marriages and dowries. The absence of these controls and the church's continued opposition to birth control have produced a situation among the lower-class Franco-American families in which pregnancy is often the determining criterion for a decision to marry. Accordingly, early marriages, while frequent, are not met with any noticeable reaction from the Franco-American community other than mild token resistance from the Catholic Church. Nevertheless, the practice does contribute to the negative stigma of the ethnic group held by the dominant Yankee culture and fosters further resistance to interaction and eventual assimilation of the two groups. The impact of such resistance manifests itself in interreligious and ethnic marriage taboos, imposed by both the Franco-Americans and the dominant culture. Catholicism, especially French Canadian Catholicism, has traditionally opposed interreligious marriages. On the other hand, Protestant Yankees are opposed to marriages with Franco-Americans on the grounds that it would lower one's social status. Franco-Americans are also opposed to most types of interracial marriages, the exception being between French Canadian and

American Indians, since intermarriage between these two groups has existed for over 400 years.

Premarital sexual behavior likewise plays an important part in the mate selection process. It is prevalent among French Canadians in both New England and Quebec and seems to provide one of the few outlets to an otherwise restrictive French-Canadian life style. Illicit sexual behavior, officially condemned by the Catholic Church, has nevertheless emerged as a somewhat expectable mode of behavior in French Canadian communities in both countries. And, as matched marriages decrease in popularity, mate selection among French Canadians will become more contingent on chance and correspond more closely to the prevailing American patterns.

The substantial incidence of premarital sex without the safeguards of birth control make illegitimacy a common threat to the working-class French Canadian community. However, the situation is usually handled without much conflict. Both abortions and adoptions are frowned upon, so in most cases the unwed mother keeps her child, and if she later marries, the child is generally accepted, taking an unheralded place in the new family. Until she finds a spouse, the participating conjugal family units, comprising the unwed mother's larger extended family, help the mother and child secure a position in the community. Their aid is subtle, so that the unwed mother and her child may appear to be a self-sufficing autonomous social unit, thus improving her chances at marriage. The same holds true when a divorce occurs. Deprived of her husband's status, the estranged wife must revert to her family lineage for social support and identity.

When a couple marries, the new conjugal family unit seeks to establish its own neolocal household. Quite often the family resides in an apartment that belongs to either the husband's or wife's lineal kin. When this situation occurs, it is preferable to reside with the husband's lineage (patrilocal) rather than the wife's (matrilocal), since living with the wife's relative implies dependency on the wife by the husband. Franco-American communities consist physically of mostly tenements and private homes. A family unit generally starts in a rented apartment, with all eligible family members working and saving so that, if successful, they later will be able to buy their own tenement to live in and rent or to purchase a private home.

The tenements are old, plain, two- or three-story wood-frame units, housing from 4 to 12 families. These were popular housing units for previous Franco-American generations because they provided a convenient residence for the entire extended family. Large brick or wood apartment complexes, known as "cooperations," still provide housing for the immigrant French Canadian families. Regardless of the nature of the Franco-American family residence, most are adorned with religious objects, personifying the crucifix, child Jesus, and the Virgin Mary. Holy-water receptacles, blessed palms, pictures, and statues are found in most homes. The most affluent families adorn their lawns with larger statues, usually of the Virgin Mary. The function of religious objects in Franco-American families is twofold, providing both religious continuity to their everyday life and relative community status.

Peer Grouping

Another interesting and relevant attribute of the Franco-American family structure is also shared by their Canadian relatives, that of like-sex peer-group association. These relationships are fostered early in the primary family setting and endure into adulthood. It is within these peer-group associations that males and females encounter each other, with the success of the relationship often being dependent on the approval of either participant's peer group. The female, once married, most likely forsakes her peer-group interests for that of her new marital role. The male, however, continues his peer-group membership all through his adult life, with peer-group interests often superseding those of his immediate family. Membership clubs, licensed to serve hard liquor as well as beer and wine, consist of numerous ethnic and national organizations, including the Knights of Columbus, and American Legion, and the Veterans of Foreign Wars. These drinking establishments are the central social meeting place for the adult males in the Franco-American community. Many men frequent these establishments daily in a more or less ritualistic pattern. In the winter months the clubs and bars are filled with the seasonal construction workers who draw unemployment during the off season. On weekend evenings group socials highlight the community's weekly festivities. Consequently, the relatively autonomous Franco-American community is organized to provide two opposite but complementary social functions. The church, through its manifold social and religious activities, provides the moralistic and ideological support for the community members, while the clubs and bars provide acceptable avenues of tension and frustration release. Both functions seem crucial to the maintenance and preservation of the Franco-American subculture.

Education

As noted above, the French Canadians who originally immigrated to the New England mill communities brought with them their church and parochial educational system. The French Catholic Church, parochial schools, and the French Canadian language, all closely interrelated, provide the three most crucial cultural institutions responsible for the preservation and perpetuation of the Franco-American subculture. Parochial schools, although currently under considerable economic pressure in New England, still provide the basic educational needs of the Canadian French in both countries. French Canadians have traditionally been opposed to the public educational system, viewing it as an instrument of the dominant Protestant culture. Public schools are viewed, in both countries, as really being "Protestant schools." The French Canadian parochial educational system, through the preservation of its language, culture and church doctrines, provides the Franco-Americans with their strong sense of ethnocentrism, which in turn keeps them isolated from the larger dominant culture and forestalls assimilation.

Occupation

When the original French Canadians emigrated to New England, their occupational status changed from that of peasant farmers to factory laborers. The occupational transformation was successful due to the minimal degree of specialization and training required for either occupational role. Correspondingly, the low value placed on formal education provided a socioeconomic situation whereby the French Canadians were unprepared to occupy the more specialized and prestigious occupational roles available in the commercial and industrial economy of New England. Lacking the necessary managerial and technical skills, and having failed to attain the educational prerequisites required of these occupations, the Franco-Americans find themselves, for the most part, relegated to marginal occupational roles.

The traditional occupation of Franco-American families has been employment in textile mills. During the early 1950s, after nearly a century of operation, the larger textile industries moved South, seeking lower operational costs. Shoe shops, fiber glass and electronic industries, among others, replaced the departed textile industries in the mill

337

towns throughout New England. In northern New England (Maine, New Hampshire, and Vermont) woodcutting and other lumber and pulp-related occupations provide employment for Franco-Americans. A third major source of employment is provided through seasonal construction work related to highway, bridge, and building construction.

The above-mentioned occupations account for the employment of the majority of the working-class Franco-Americans. Other occupational specialties range from small-business proprietors to professional occupations. Each Franco-American community has its own small ethnic businesses: clothing and shoe stores, small grocery and variety stores, plus an array of other small community enterprises. Other Franco-American families own and operate their own dairy farms, truck gardens, or small-scale logging operations. Professionals of Franco-American heritage provide the necessary medical, dental, and legal services for the community.

The factories, seasonal construction, and lumber-related industries are not high-paying occupations, yet they seem abundant enough to provide the Franco-American families with a somewhat stable and sufficient source of economic support to sustain their life style. Ironically, the areas of northern New England bordering Canada are those with the highest rate of unemployment (at least a percentage point higher than the states' average), and out-migration of young adults. This creates a fluctuating manpower shortage, and subsequently bonded and visaed French Canadians have to be imported to rectify the situation. They are needed on a yearly basis as cutters in the lumber industries and on a seasonal basis in the harvesting of apples. This action requires permission from the U.S. Department of Labor, and although extensive efforts are made to recruit native laborers, each year the effort seems in vain. This fresh source of French Canadian contact through the imported laborers reinforces the communication lines between the two French subcultures.

Social and Physical Mobility

Social and physical mobility or the lack thereof reflect the degree of internal cohesion within Franco-American working-class communities throughout New England. Both phenomena are closely related to the high degree of ethnocentrism and the resulting process of "resistance within." Social mobility implies vertical mobility, that is, moving through the various social strata that comprise the larger dominant culture. Physical mobility, on the other hand, represents the degree of out-migration from the Franco-American communities to other more integrated communities within the larger culture. As a consequence of their basic value system Franco-Americans are restricted in both forms of mobility. As previously mentioned, the Franco-American socialization process occurs through a cooperative relationship between the parish church and the primary family situation. Education is a quality that facilitates vertical social mobility in our society by preparing its members to enact occupational roles that are highly valued in themselves. It seems apparent that the low level of education among the Franco-Americans can only serve to restrict vertical, social mobility as they compete both socially and economically within the American system. A result of this situation, and in turn contributing to it, is low-achievement motivation among Franco-Americans. In one such study they ranked lowest among ethnic groups, with Blacks being the only minority group below them (Secord and Backman, 1964:570).

That the most salient criterion for determining high social status among the Franco-Americans, that is, church-related roles, has little relevance to the vertical social-occupational structure of the dominant culture reinforces and intensifies the ecological boundaries surrounding the Franco-American communities. As a result, the Franco-American communities evolved into psychological ghettos that perpetuate the same values that restrict their social and physical mobility, consequently the assimilation of their members into the larger culture. The selective socialization that occurs among the families and institutions within the context of these protective ghetto communities creates in its members both a psychological and sociological dependency on the community for fulfillment of the basic human needs, while at the same time instilling behavioral patterns and mannerisms that account for the negative image of the Franco-Americans in the eyes of the dominant culture. As a result, encounters with the larger culture are often viewed as being negativistic and undesirable and reinforce the desirability of the Franco-American community, whether it be the home community or an adopted one. Voluntary physical mobility among working-class Franco-Americans is mostly restricted to movements to other Franco-American communities or to communities in Canada in which relatives reside. When involuntary physical mobility occurs, such as military conscription, many return to the relative security of their home community, remaining there for the duration of their lives. Hence, low social and restricted physical mobility among Franco-Americans results from a unique socialization process that creates the member's community dependency while instilling those social characteristics that make the Franco-Americans visible as a minority group.

Family Life Cycle and Socialization

CHILDHOOD. The birth of a child, since it brings additional social and religious status to both parents, is a significant factor within the working-class family. For the female, childbirth, especially the first born, signifies her *rite de passage* into adulthood. And while both children of either sex are welcomed, male children are more indulged by both parents. Fathers, as noted above, often give their first-born son their nickname along with the responsibility for continuing the male lineage and tradition. The result may well be rather heavy pressures brought on the son to excel in the same activities as the father, such as hockey, pool, street fighting, and hunting.

Pregnancy, also discussed above, often precipitates marriages between young couples, or when not followed by marriage, the infant is usually accepted by the girl's family. A third arrangement is to have an unmarried couple live together with their children. After a number of years these arrangements become recognized as common-law marriages subject to the same church and community expectations as are church and civil marriages.

Regardless of the father/mother relationship, the child, in order to secure its appropriate position in the hereafter, is baptized as soon as possible. Prebaptismal deaths bring great sorrow to Franco-Americans, mainly due to the belief that the infant's soul will remain in limbo and be denied access to heaven. Considerable affect, attention, and liberties are showered on and made available to surviving children, especially by the mother, grandmothers, and other female relatives. The concern about children, which in its intensity is a relatively new phenomenon, is associated with the smaller Franco-American families and such other factors as pregnancy leaves from work and the greater accessibility to modern conveniences, such as laundromats, diaper services, and the like, which permit more time for the mother to nurture her children.

The preschool child learns both French and English, with its distinctive Franco-American accent, in the home during the first six years. Preschool institutions such as kindergarten, nursery schools, and the like are rare occurrences among this group. Early family socialization is supplemented by the church activities and involvements, with most young children attending church with their mothers on a weekly basis. In all but the high mass, it is not unusual to see numerous mothers holding infants in their arms as well as all other preschool children attending church. School-age children attend church by class and sit in a special section up front accompanied by their teacher-nuns.

Franco-American children learn quite early the norms of sex peer-group separation. The division is maintained even within the family setting, and early-founded peer groups continue to be maintained during the school years. This was especially the case when the parochial school system flourished in New England. The nuns themselves reinforced sexual separation in the classroom, the girls setting on one side and boys on the other. Similar seating arrangements were made for morning Mass, a compulsory daily activity in the parochial school system. Associated with the primary educational process is the child's first communion, which is the first conscious formal activity for the child, and much is still made of it. A new dress or suit for the child and a well-attended ceremony by family, relatives, and friends highlight this activity. In fact, religious ceremonies such as baptism, first communion, confraternity, and marriage have a seemingly far greater significance than civil ceremonies such as convocations and graduation exercises. All in all, the working-class Franco-American child is allowed considerable latitide in his or her behavior within the family, with its patriarchal overtones, and in most community settings. The church, notably through the parochial school, on the other hand, is more the strict disciplinarian. These contravening behavioral expectations sometimes lead to conflict situations, but when this does occur, the person in these days is more likely to reject the proscriptions of the church.

ADOLESCENCE AND YOUNG ADULTHOOD. Puberty, as a biological phenomenon and confraternity, the social recognition of puberty through a religious *rite de passage,* highlight adolescence in the Franco-American community. Simultaneously, the church, family, and peer group compete for the youth's attention and devotion. The six peer groups become all the more significant during this period, especially for the males. Within them they find themselves pressured to live up to their father's image. Family expectations are more or less consonant with those of the peer group. To accommodate these demands, the school and church often become less crucial to the adolescent male. The days of complete integration of all local institutions and associations, if they ever existed, are apparently over.

Dating as well as the establishment of sociability patterns emerge during this period. Although many Franco-American youth have been drinking beer and smoking cigarettes for a few years, the social significance of these activities becomes internalized during adolescence. In fact, most activities, whether they be related to sports, religion, or social events (dating, drinking), are closely tied to the peer-group structure. In this sense, then, the peer group and not the family or church is the ultimate influence in mate selection. Female youth, however, rely less on the influence of their peer group during this period than do their male counterparts. The family, school, and church still play an important role for many Franco-American girls; this is evident for one thing in their higher-educational achievements. Yet the female peer group is an important instrumentality for dating and for determining one's social standing at this time. The main difference, then, between the male and female adolescent peer-group structures is that the former is somewhat more salient and enduring than the latter.

Since it is not unusual for working-class Franco-Americans to marry during their teens, the male's occupational status is often determined during this period. And while the father's occupation is an important consideration, certain occupations are held to be more prestigious than others. Iron workers, truck drivers, machine operators, and construction and mill foremen have considerably more status than laborers or some white-collar workers. The female's occupational status is less crucial since her paramount role is to raise the children and maintain the household. Many females do work, but sporadically, and the primary consideration is her pay rather than the job itself.

The young married couple often lives in an apartment in a tenement owned by one of their relatives. Their children are indulged by the relatives on both sides, again with the first-born male child shown special attention. The young father continues to associate with his peer group, spending considerable leisure time with them. This is important since the peer group specifies and evaluates his social success. Ritualistic drinking, card and pool playing, along with an avid interest in sports such as hockey, baseball, boxing, hunting, wrestling, and horse racing are all important aspects of the lives of young adults. And while most still attend church during this period, it is more of a formality than a devotion. Adolescent and young adult males can be seen standing in the back of the church during mass—the last in and the first out. The female, in comparison, establishes a new interaction network, one based on her own and her husband's family and relatives, as well as a new cluster of girl friends who share a life situation similar to hers.

MIDDLE AND OLD AGE. As the male gets older, he comes increasingly to incorporate into his personality his peer group's perception of him. If this is a positive reflection and is reinforced by his family, community, and church, then the person usually develops a good self-image, at least within the Franco-American subcultural setting. But not all adult males find themselves in this situation. Numerous interaction confrontations are discernible, the most notable occurring between the peer group and the family. When this situation occurs, the peer group usually emerges the victor, and a breaking of the marital bond results. Dependent children normally remain with their mother, and she continues to receive support from both her family and her estranged husband's family, as well as from the community and church.

The middle years are a particularly important period for those who have adequately adjusted to the working-class Franco-American life style. This is the time when their years of working and saving finally bring their reward. Unlike their middle-class counterparts, these Franco-Americans seldom get involved in long-term loans and mortgages. Instead, they save their money, rent an apartment, and drive used cars until the time when they can afford to buy their own home, new car, and boat. Such affluence as they enjoy is possible also because Franco-Americans are not traditionally burdened with financing their children through an extended and expensive period of adolescence. They help their children with emotional concern and support but do not see the wisdom or need for mortgaging their own future to assure that of their offspring.

Old age, unlike in the larger dominant American society, brings considerable status on both the Franco-American male and female. If both grandparents survive, it is the female who has the higher status. Most social and religious events as well as Sunday-after-mass visits require a stay with *grand-mere*. When both grandmothers are alive they share this status. Considerable reverence is also associated with the grandmother's status, and she is the repository of knowledge concerning the entire family kinship network.

Death to the Franco-Americans carries both religious and social significance. The person has borne his or her cross and now awaits God's judgment. With the exception of death prior to baptism (infant death) death is viewed somewhat philosophically by the Franco-Americans. As with baptism, first communion, confraternity, and marriage, it is a time for formality and social interaction. It is often said that the dead are better off now. This refers to passage of the trial of life and the ultimate

343

reward of everlasting peace or punishment, depending on the final judgment. An interesting social ritual associated with the death of veterans who occupy an important male peer-group membership is a military or paramilitary representation at the funeral, accompanied with a rifle salute and an American flag draped over the coffin. After the burial those participating in the burial ceremony go to the local American Legion Hall, VFW, or Lions Club to drink to the deceased. In any event there is little alienation from the dead. Like birth, it is a phenomenon too mystifying to be dealt with rationally and expeditiously. The knitting up of torn social and personal fabric and the re-establishment of social solidarity require ritualization and for some period of time ceremonial remembrance.

CHANGE AND ADAPTATION

The current situation in Canada has been turbulent. Distinct polar, political, and social boundaries have been drawn and reinforced between the English and French Canadians. French radicals view themselves as being oppressed "white niggers," while a substantial proportion of the less radical French strongly support the separatist policy (Vallieves, 1971). The current political and social indicators seem to imply more chaos and conflict between the French Canadian subculture and the dominant English Canadian culture.

These turns of events minimize the chances for assimilation, convergence, or homogenization of Canada into one mass life style. Yet some feel that French Canada will long resist assimilation and will remain a strong separatist Canadian subculture. Wagley and Harris (1964:200–201) drew this conclusion from their UNESCO study:

What will be the future of the French Canadian minority in Canada? It is obviously not a group that will be assimilated into English-Canada society rapidly or easily. It is composed of a large population with an exceedingly high birthrate. It has political power in the nation and political control over Quebec. It has its own schools from the primary level to great universities. It takes pride in its French traditions and cultures. . . . French Canada has its national sport and its sporting heroes in ice hockey. The French Canadians as a group have all the elements in a vigorous social unit which cannot easily be overwhelmed even by the more rapidly expanding English-Canadian group.

And as long as these conditions continue to prevail in Canada, their ramifications will be felt among the Franco-Americans residing below the border in New England. The French Canadian parent culture has numerous life lines to its New England relatives, and these continue to nourish the Franco-American subculture.

The Franco-American problem, inasmuch as New England is not engaged in any overt political and social conflict with the French minority group, is not as severe. Discrimination is subtle and different in New England. Some states, especially those with other minority populations, openly attempt to accommodate the French much in the same manner they do other minorities. In northern New England, in which the dichotomy between the French and Yankees is more vivid and distinct, the degree of discrimination intensifies. It manifests itself particularly in political, occupational, educational, and residential discrimination. However, some changes are slowly coming about. Maine has recognized it has a French minority problem and has recently implemented Franco-American programs such as workshops for public schoolteachers and university and college faculty. Attempts are being made by some academic institutions to provide Franco-American awareness programs, while other institutions are engaged in collecting and preserving the historical and cultural development of the Franco-Americans.

Another contributing factor that could reduce the isolation of future generations of Franco-Americans is the rapid disappearance of the parochial school system. Due to the rising costs of maintaining these institutions, many are earmarked for closing within the next decade. This changing situation could mean a reduction in the use of the French Canadian language and a loosening of church control over the primary socialization of young Franco-Americans. However, the successful accommodation and assimilation of the new generations will depend considerably on how well the public-school system facilitates and supports the family socialization of the Franco-Americans. A total disregard for, or a negative perception of, the Franco-American family life style by the middle-class-dominated public-school system could very well increase the conflict and differences between the minority group and the host culture.

R E F E R E N C E S

Anderson, E. L. 1957. "The French-Canadians in Burlington, Vermont." In M. L. Barron (ed.): *American Minorities*. New York: Knopf.
Beattie, Christopher, and Byron G. Spenser. 1971. "Career Attainment in Canadian Bureaucracies: Unscrambling the Effects of Age, Seniority, Education, and Ethnolinguistic Factors on Salary." *American Journal of Sociology* 77 (November): 372–490.

Byrne, William D. D. 1899. *History of the Catholic Church in the New England States*. Vol. I. Boston: Hurd and Everts.

Darroch, Gordon A., and Wilfred G. Marston. 1971. "The Social Class Basis of Ethnic Residential Segregation: The Canadian Case." *American Journal of Sociology* 77 (November): 491–510.

Department of Forestry and Rural Development. 1967. *Development Plan for Pilot Region Lower St. Lawrence, Gaspe, and Iles-de-la-Madeleine*. Ottawa.

Grayson, L. M. and Michael Bliss (eds.). 1971. *The Wretched of Canada*. Toronto: University of Toronto Press.

Grochmal, Bernard, Jr. 1969. "An Analysis of the Social Stratification of the French-Canadian Community of Newmarket, New Hampshire." Unpublished Master's Thesis, University of New Hampshire.

Hughes, Everett. 1943. *French Canada in Transition*. Chicago: University of Chicago Press.

Kramer, Judith R. 1970. *The American Minority Community*. New York: Thomas Y. Crowell.

Lieberson, Stanley. 1970. *Language and Ethnic Relations in Canada*. New York: Wiley.

Metalious, Grace. 1964. *No Adam in Eden*. New York: Pocket Books.

Miner, Horace. 1967. *St. Denis: A French-Canadian Parish*. Chicago: University of Chicago Press.

Ministry of Industry, Trade and Commerce. 1972. *Canada 1972: The Annual Handbook of Present Conditions and Recent Progress*. Ottawa.

Ministry of Industry, Trade and Commerce. 1971. *Canada Year Book—1970–1971*. Ottawa.

Newsweek. 1972. (November 13):53.

Ong, Walter J. 1961. *Frontiers in American Catholicism: Essays on Ideology and Culture*. New York: Macmillan.

Piddington, Ralph. 1971. "A Study of French-Canadian Kinship." In K. Ishwaran (ed.): *The Canadian Family*. Toronto: Holt, Rinehart and Winston of Canada.

Rose, Peter I. 1968. *They & We*. New York: Random House.

Ryerson, Stanley B. 1968. *Unequal Union*. New York: International Publishers.

Second, Paul, and Carl Backman. 1964. *Social Psychology*. New York: McGraw-Hill.

Urguhart, M. C. 1965. *Historical Statistic of Canada*. Toronto: Macmillan Company of Canada.

Vallieves, Pierre. 1971. *White Niggers of America: The Precocious Autobiography of a Quebec "Terrorist."* Translated by Joan Pinklam. New York: Monthly Review Press.

Wagley, Charles and Marvin Harris. 1964. *Minorities in the New World*. New York: Columbia University Press.

The Jewish American Family

The crucial question pursued by the authors in this chapter on the American Jewish family concerns the movement of Jews away from the traditions they brought with them from the European continent. The analysis takes a look at the Jewish family from a generational perspective, pointing out the increasing rates of change and movement away from Jewish tradition in each subsequent generation. In spite of the emphasis on loss of tradition, however, it becomes clear that the Jewish family is still an important unit, and Jewish identity still ha$ an impact for individual behavior.

CHAPTER FIFTEEN

BY

BERNARD FARBER, CHARLES H. MINDEL and BERNARD LAZERWITZ

HISTORICAL BACKGROUND

From the earliest days of the Exodus, Jews have been a people on the move. Their settlements may have at times seemed permanent, but time and again forces or events, political, social, or religious have conspired to make them a nomadic people. The most remarkable characteristic of these people has been that in spite of the oppressions and persecutions, or perhaps because of them, Jews have retained to a remarkable degree a distinct religious and cultural identity.

Judaism, a worldwide religion, embraces about 14 million constituents, tending to be concentrated in a few key areas throughout the world. Until the time of Hitler, the largest concentration of Jews lived in Europe. Now, approximately 43 per cent of the world's Jews, or about 6 million, live in America.

Jews in America

The settlement of Jews in America is an old one. Jews have been in America since the colonial period, though they have only arrived in large numbers relatively recently. It has been agreed that the immigration of

Jews to America occurred in three historical waves involving people from three national locations: Sephardic Jews from Spain and Portugal, German Jews from the Germanic states, and East European Jews, largely from Poland and Russia but also from Rumania, Hungary, and Lithuania. It would be inaccurate to assume that there has been no overlap among these three waves of immigration because there was immigration from Germany at the same time as immigration from Poland and Russia. These three waves of immigration are important, though, because they define three distinct cultural patterns that tended to differentiate Jews in America.

The Sephardic, German, and East European Jews differ for a variety of historical, cultural, and economic reasons. Those immigrating from Eastern Europe, though the last to arrive, comprise by far the largest number of America's Jews, probably over 90 per cent. The Sephardic Jews and the German Jews are and have been important not for their numbers but largely due to their social position and influence.

The Sephardic Jews

The earliest Jewish settlement in America occurred in 1654 in what was then New Amsterdam, a colony of the Dutch West Indies Company. The Jews who settled there followed a circuitous route, ultimately traceable to the Iberian peninsula of Spain and Portugal. However, the Jews were not particularly welcome in New Amsterdam, Peter Stuyvesant the governor resisted and argued that "none of the deceitful race be permitted to infest and trouble this new colony" (Golden and Rywell, 1950:13). However, the Dutch West Indies Company decided to allow the Portuguese Jews to live in New Netherland "provided the poor among them shall not become a burden to the Company or to the community but be supported by their own nation" (Golden and Rywell, 1950:14).

A religious community was quickly established, although it was to be 30 years before the first Jewish synagogue, *Shearith Israel* (remnant of Israel), was built in what was by then New York. This synagogue was a Sephardic synagogue in which Portuguese was spoken and the *marrano*** ritual was used. By the end of the American revolution there were more than 3,000 Jews, mostly *marranos,* from Spain, Portugal, Brazil, Jamaica, Barbados, Curacao, South America, Holland, and England.

---

*Marranos were Spanish Jews who had converted to Christianity during the period of the Inquisition. Many of these *marranos* secretly kept their Jewish faith, using modified religious ritual which enabled them from being detected as practicing Jews.

From this beginning there continued a steady flow of immigration of largely Sephardic Jews, who numbered in 1840 around 15,000.

The German Jews

The middle of the nineteenth century, from approximately 1840 to approximately 1880 saw a second "wave" of Jewish immigration, mostly German Jews. Conditions in Germany, or to be more accurate the collection of Germanic states, at midcentury were quite inhospitable for Jews and non-Jews alike. Anti-Jewish medieval laws of oppression were enacted, especially in Bavaria, which among other things provided for heavy discriminatory taxation, designated areas to live in, restricted occupations, and restrictions on the number of Jewish marriages. These conditions led to many German Jewish single men leaving for America to seek opportunity. Later on, in the latter part of the nineteenth century when these laws were relaxed, immigration of these German Jews slowed down to a trickle (Glazer, 1957; Weinryb, 1958).

Many German immigrants started out as peddlers, an occupation that did not require great skill or large capital investment. They spread out all over America and gave many non-Jews their first glimpse of a Jewish face. Originally starting out with a pack carried on their back, they traversed the countryside. If they were reasonably successful, they would graduate to a horse and wagon. If they were able to accumulate a little money, they might open a dry goods store in one of the many small towns and cities in which they traded. These were the origins of what later became the great clothing and department stores in America, such as Altmans, Bloomingdales, Bambergers, Gimbels, Goldblatt, Nieman-Marcus, Macys, Mays, Maison Blanche, Stix, Bare & Fuller, and others.

The importance and influence of the German Jews is linked crucially to their spectacular financial success. While certainly not all German Jews became wealthy, the rise of one group of families, many of whom started out as peddlers, had enormous implications for the status of Jews in America. They became important figures in banking and finance in a period of American history when the industrialization of America was just beginning and there was a need for large amounts of capital to feed the growing industrial base.

The German Jewish influx into America was great enough to overwhelm in number the Sephardim. By 1848 there were 50,000 Jews in America, and by 1880 there were an estimated 230,000, largely German Jews, here in America (Sklare, 1958).

349

Eastern European Jews

It was, however, the arrival of the Jews from Eastern Europe that has had the greatest impact on Jewish American life. Beginning around 1888 and largely ending by 1930, almost 3,000,000 Jews immigrated to America.

These individuals and families, though Jewish, like their American counterparts, were in fact of another world. Whereas the Germans came from an "enlightened" modern society in which Jews were more often than not integrated into German culture, the Eastern European Jews came from a milieu in which the feeling of homogeneity was strongly entrenched, where a set of Jewish values and attitudes prevailed, including religious devotion and observance.

Most of the 5 million Jews of Russia and Poland had been restricted, from the time of Catherine the Great, to an area established for them known as the Pale of Settlement. The Pale extended from the shores of the Baltic south to the Black Sea. Jews were generally not allowed to settle in the interior of Russia and were limited to this area. The Pale has been described, except for the Crimea, as a 313,000 square-mile, monotonously flat, sand-arid prison (Manners, 1972:30). Within this area, about the size of Texas, 808 *shtetlach* (townlets), each of which was perhaps two-thirds Jewish and 94 per cent poor, Jews lived, survived and "attained the highest degree of inwardness . . . the golden period in Jewish history, in the history of the Jewish soul" (Manners, 1872:31).

The concentration of Jews in these areas for hundreds of years led to the development of a culture and civilization grounded in biblical and talmudic teachings that remained to a remarkable degree unchanged until the twentieth century. Those who migrated from this society to America and elsewhere have on the whole been prosperous; those millions who remained, including most of the devout were for the most part, destroyed.

The mass migration of East European Jews began in the 1880s and continued at a high level until the passage of the restrictive immigration laws in 1924. The chief instigating factors that started the massive flow were the governmentally inspired *pogroms* of the Imperial Russian Government in 1881. *Pogroms* (Russian: devastation and destruction) consisted of ransacking, burning, rape, and assorted violence committed on Jews in the towns and villages of Russia. The government, driven by an overwhelming fear of revolution, used *pogroms* as a form of diversion and weapon against dissenting minorities (Manners, 1972).

Beginning in 1882, new laws, the so-called "May laws," were issued by the Czar, which severely restricted Jewish rights, such as they were. Thousands were forced to leave their homes, especially those who resided within interior Russia. These laws and the extensions of them left most Jews no choice but to emigrate.

Most emigrants came to America. Some went to Palestine, and some others went to other parts of Europe. Forty thousand came in 1881–82, another 62,000 came in 1888, and by 1906 the number was up to 153,000 per year (Manners, 1972:57).

The *pogroms* and restrictive laws that forced the migration of these Jews were but the final chapter of a long process of disintegration of Jewish communities that had been going on for more than a century. Antagonisms and tensions had been developing within for a long period of time. More importantly were the effects from the world outside the *shtetl*. Industrialization and the decline of the feudal system of relations came late to Eastern Europe, but by the nineteenth century its effects were being felt there as well. Thus, by the time of the *pogroms* in the late nineteenth century and early twentieth century social change and social disintegration had already come to this traditional society.

German Jews Versus Eastern European Jews

The arrival of this mass of people was not an unmixed blessing to the already established, especially to the German American Jews who feared for their recently achieved middle-class status. However, native Jews and Americans, in general, took a compassionate though largely condescending view toward poverty-stricken immigrants (at least until 1924 when the American government, in the throes of a xenophobic isolationist wave, passed a racist and restrictive immigration law).

Relations between the older established, primarily German American Jews and the newly arrived Eastern European Jews were nevertheless difficult. The German Jews were interested in helping the immigrants in order to "Americanize" them so they would not be a source of embarrassment. They saw the strange dress and speech and the poverty as reflecting poorly on themselves, feeling that the quicker they became indistinguishable from the rest of America the better. Americanization was made more difficult by the fact that the Eastern European Jewish immigrants clustered together in distinct urban neighborhoods, especially in the American Northeast and particularly in New York City.

The Eastern European Jewish immigrants also introduced Orthodox Judaism to America. Though the immigrants tended to be less observant and traditional than their counterparts who remained in Europe, the religious institutions established by them in America were traditional and Orthodox recreations of the institutions that existed in Eastern Europe. The immigrants did not recognize the Reform Judaism as it was practiced by the native, predominately German Jews. To them it was unacceptable. "They are Jews," declared Rabbi Dr. Issac Meyer Wise, the leading light of Reform Judaism. "We are Israelites." And the Russian Jews said with equal assurance, "We are Jews." They are *goyim* (gentiles)" (Manners, 1972:76).

One important ingredient in the continuing vigor of Orthodox Judaism in America was the immigration during the Hitler and post-World War II years of numbers of Orthodox *Chassidic* Jews. The *Chassidic* groups, organized around a particular charismatic leader, the *rebbe,* or *Tzaddik,* are identified by the location in Europe from which they originated. These groups stress a communal life and close-knit group cohesion. They are found generally in New York and Brooklyn, often in old neighborhoods. One group, however, the Skverer *chassidim,* has established their own town, New Square in the suburbs of New York City, in which they have attempted to recreate the traditional life of the Eastern European Jew. The impact of these groups has been to bring new life into what was a disappearing branch of Judaism. The close ties of the members and the emotionalism of the religion as they practice it are attractive to many young people who have been seeking more emotion in their religious practices. Others who have not become members of Chassidic groups have borrowed much of the emotional content of this movement and put it into their own observance.

The Traditional Family of the East European Shtetl Community*

It has been estimated that today over ninety percent of America's Jewish population are or descend from immigrants from Eastern Europe. Since their arrival has been relatively recent, family patterns which existed in Europe and were brought to the United States can still be expected to have an impact on present day family life styles. In the following paragraphs family life in the small Eastern European town— the *shtetl*—where most Jews lived will be described.

> The *shtetl* was a poor place, a place of unpaved streets and decrepit wooden buildings. It is said that there was no "Jewish" architecture, rather the most noticeable features of the dwellings were their age and their shabbiness (Zborowski and Herzog, 1952:61) Occupationally the Jews were generally tradesmen—dairymen, cobblers, tailors, butchers, fishmongers, peddlers and shopkeepers.

---

*Much of this discussion of shtetl family structure comes from Landes and Zborowski (1968) and Zborowski and Herzog (1952).

Social Organization

The marketplace was the economic center of the *shtetl,* however, the synagogue was the heart and soul of the community. The values of the religion infiltrated all aspects of life; every detail of life was infused with some religious or ritual significance. It was impossible to escape and to separate the religious from the secular.

Chief among the values of the *shtetl* and of Jewish culture was the value of learning. One of the most important obligations of a devout Jew is to study and learn. In order to obey the commandments of the scriptures one must know them. And one must study them in order to know them. Studying and learning *Torah** became the most important activity in which a man could involve himself, even more important than earning a good living. Every *shtetl* of reasonable size would contain schools of various levels including the *cheder* for boys as young as three and four years of age. A learned young man was considered the most highly prized future son-in-law. In fact it was considered prestigious for a father-in-law to support his new son-in-law for the first few years of marriage if the son-in-law was bright, so that he could devote himself to full-time study.

The stratification of the *shtetl* was based in large measure on learning and on the tradition of learning in one's family. *Shtetl* Jews were either *sheyneh yidn* (beautiful Jews) or *prosteh yidn* (common Jews). The position of a person in this status hierarchy was dependent ideally on learning but wealth played an important part in determining the *sheyneh.* A third quality, *yikhus,* a combination of family heritage with respect to learning and wealth was also an important criteria in determining social position. A person with great *yikhus* was able to claim many ancestors of great worth particularly with respect to learning and philanthropy. To have *yikhus* was very prestigious.

Life in the *shtetl* was guided by written codes of behavior that derived from the Talmud and other religious sources. These standards ideally had the effect of regulating behavior of all Jewish residents of the *shtetl, sheyneh* and *prosteh* alike. It is in these codes of behavior and the folklore, folksayings and other customs that grew up around the *shtetl* that we find the unique cultural basis for Jewish family life, important aspects of which still have an impact today.

Marriage

Duties and roles for men and women were carefully detailed by traditional writings and chief among these was the injunction that a man and woman marry. For it was said that "It is not good for man to be alone."

---

*Torah literally refers to the Pentateuch, the five books of Moses, or the written scriptures. However, *Torah* has come to mean much more. It has come to include remaining portions of the Old Testament as well as the whole of the commentaries and interpretations on the Pentateuch which was known as the oral law or the *Talmud.* In addition, the numerous condifications and newer commentaries that appeared during the middle ages such as the works of Maimonides in Spain have also come to be included under this rubric. In essence, *Torah* means all the religious learning and literature including and surrounding the holy scriptures.

Marriage in the shtetl was traditionally arranged by the parents of the young couple frequently through the use of a matchmaker (*shadchen*). It was assumed that the "parents always want the best for their children" (Zborowski and Herzog, 1952:275) and the children went along with the match.

Since marriage was considered such an important institution, indeed a commandment (*mitzvah*), there was great pressure for marriage and families to remain united. . . . In fact, because divorce reflected badly on one's family and stigmatized the individuals involved it was a relatively rare occurrence. Marital stability was related to a dominant orientation in Jewish family life, *sholem bayis* (domestic harmony or peace). Only when maintaining a satisfactory family equilibrium became impossible and the *sholem bayis* was broken was divorce considered. The relative infrequency of divorce indicates that adaptations of many kinds occurred with some frequency.

Marital Roles

The injunction that a man should study, learn and promote the book learning tradition had important implications for the functioning of the husband in the family. The husband/father was often remote from most domestic concerns. If he was a scholar much of the economic responsibility of the home was left to the wife. The husband's primary responsibility was in the spiritual and intellectual sphere; only the males were taught to read, speak and write Hebrew, the sacred language, women who were literate spoke and read *Yiddish*.*

In reality, women often played a dominant role in family life and in the world outside. There was a high degree of interchangeability in family roles and wives were trained to be ready to assume the economic burdens of supporting the family. She often had wide latitude and opportunity for movement to conduct business or seek employment and in time of emergency or need women were able to partake in any number of "male" activities. It has been argued that women as a consequence of their subordinate status were less regulated than men and therefore they were able to partake in all activities that were not expressly forbidden to them. As a result they quite often had greater freedom than men who were bound up very tightly in a highly regulated way of life (Landes and Zborowski, 1968:81).

THE JEWISH MOTHER. Basic to the Jewish family with its wide range of rights and obligations is parental love. Seldom demonstrated verbally or physically after the child is four or five, parental affection, especially from the mother was felt to be an unbreakable bond. "No matter what you do, no matter what happens your mother will love you always. She may have odd and sometimes irritating ways of showing it, but in a hazardous and unstable world the belief about the mother's love is strong and unshakable" (Zborowski and Herzog,

---

*Yiddish a middle high German dialect written in Hebrew characters was the common *mamaloshen* (mother tongue) of most Eastern European Jews. Its use can be traced back 1000 years and though Yiddish varied in form and pronunciation in different parts of western and eastern Europe it provided a common language for Jews across all national boundaries and was a crucial factor in maintaining the unity of the Jewish people.

1952:293). The Jewish mother's love was expressed by and large in two ways: "by constant and solicitous overfeeding and by unremitting solicitude about every aspect of her child's welfare" (Zborowski and Herzog, 1952:293). Both paternal and maternal love contain the notions of suffering and sacrifice for the sake of the children. It is said that "she kills herself" in order to bring up her children. She is always worrying, nagging, scolding and sacrificing for her children and for her husband as well, who also becomes like a child in the family. Her conduct is understood and tolerated by her children who nostalgically idealize it when they get older, she is remembered as a "loving despot."

Affection amongst the shtetl Jews as mentioned was not expressed with kisses and caresses after a child reached four or five and especially in public. However, a mother was more likely to be demonstrative to her son and a father more demonstrative to his daughter. Furthermore, though much contact between members of the opposite sex was restricted by avoidance etiquette, such as between brother and sister there is virtually no avoidance between mother and son. It has been claimed that "though marital obligations are fulfilled with the husband, the romance exists with the son" and that "when the son marries, he gives the wife a contract and the mother a divorce" (Landes and Zborowski, 1968:80–88).

The father relates to his daughter like the mother to her son only not with quite the same intensity. With his daughter he is undemanding and indulgent. A father, however, is a distant figure for the most part, one to whom great respect is owned. He is a particularly remote, authoritarian figure for the boy whose growth into a "Jew" and a *mensch* (a "whole person" or adult) was his responsibility.

FAMILY OBLIGATIONS. The *shtetl* was viewed as an extended family, at the very least Jews consider themselves as ultimately related as the "Children of Israel" and often because of extensive intermarriage within the shtetl they were closer than that. In any case there were strong obligations and pressure to maintain close ties to kin. Particularly strong was the obligation to take care of elderly parents although there is great reluctance on the part of the elderly parent especially the father to accept aid.

THE MODERN JEWISH FAMILY

Characteristics of Jewish Families

Because of the apparent impact of European social structure on the Jewish family, it seems useful to analyze the American Jewish family in terms of distance from its European stem. Table 1 shows personal and family characteristics of three age cohorts of household heads in the National Jewish Population Study of 1971. The first age cohort refers to household heads who were roughly 60 years of age or older in 1971. These are persons who generally married prior to the European

355

TABLE 1

Family Characteristics of Three Generation Cohorts of Household Heads
in the National Jewish Population Study[1]

PERSONAL AND FAMILY CHARACTERISTICS	COHORT 1: PRE- HOLOCAUST GENERATION	COHORT 2: THE HOLOCAUST GENERATION	COHORT 3: POST- HOLOCAUST GENERATION
Household composition			
Lives alone	+	−	=
Lives with spouse only	+	−	+
Lives with spouse and children	−	+	−
Percentage married	−	+	=
Percentage divorced or separated	=	−	+
Percentage female household heads	+	−	−
Percentage foreign born	+	−	−
Percentage first-generation native born	−	+	−
Percentage second or earlier generation native born	−	−	+
Religious membership			
No synagogue or temple affiliation	=	−	+
Reform	−	+	−
Conservative	=	+	−
Orthodox	+	−	−
Married to non-Jewish spouse	−		+
Graduate education			
Male household heads	−	=	+
Female household heads	−	+	+

*Based on tables in Massarik and Chenkin 1973. The symbols in this table refer to comparisons with percentages for total household heads in National Jewish Population Study, so that:

+refers to category percentage at least 10% greater than percentage for total sample

=refers to category percentage within 10% of percentage for total

−refers to category percentage at least 10% smaller than the percentage for the total sample

Holocaust that began with the Nazi regime in Germany. Some of the personal and familial characteristics of Cohort 1 derive from its family life-cycle stage and others from its origins. By the 1970s, Cohort 1 reached the point in its family life cycle in which a sizable percentage of household heads live alone or with spouse only. Through widowhood, many household heads are now unmarried. In origin, a majority of household heads are foreign born; there is an overrepresentation of Cohort 1 with Orthodox religious affiliation and an underrepresentation of persons with non-Jewish spouses or with graduate education.

Cohort 2 in Table 1 is referred to as the Holocaust Generation. This cohort generally spent its formative years (or at least its youth) during the tenure of the Nazi regime, which roughly coincided with the Depression in America. By 1971, this cohort was in the family life-cycle stage during which virtually all households consist of married couples and their children. This cohort has a low rate of divorce or separation. In origin, Cohort 2 is comprised mainly of first-generation, native-born household heads, who tend more often than other Jews to join Reform or Conservative synagogues; they also tend to marry a Jewish spouse. As for graduate education, the men are representative of the Jewish population as a whole, while the women household heads are overrepresented, even in the Jewish population.

Cohort 3 in Table 1 is called here the Postholocaust Generation. The household heads in this cohort are below 30 years of age. For the most part, this cohort of families had not yet (in 1971) begun to have children, although there was no deficiency then in percentage married. Cohort 3 did, however, have a greater than expected number of divorces and intermarriages with non-Jews. This generation was generally far removed from its European origins, with most persons having native-born parents. Perhaps as a result of its liberation from European conceptions of the Jewish community and family, this generation is low in religious affiliation, and it is unusually high in graduate education for both men and women. The third cohort grew up in a world in which: (a) the Holocaust had erased most kinship ties in Europe; (b) Israel had been established as a Jewish state; and (c) except for the aged, probably less than 10 percent of Jewish households consisting of a married couple and their children had incomes of under $10,000 (at least in 1971); (Massarik and Chenik, 1973).

Jewish Identification

The three cohorts described in Table 1 reveal not only changes in personal and familial characteristics with temporal distance from the European setting, but they also reflect dramatic modifications that have occurred in Jewish communal life. Lazerwitz (1970) has developed a series of indices of involvement in Jewish community affairs, which he calls indices of Jewish identification, and he has examined scores on these indices by generations for a probability sample in Chicago. Although his definitions of generations do not correspond precisely to the cohorts in Table 1, there is a sufficient overlap (because of the particular waves of immigration) to regard them as approximately congruent.

Roughly, Lazerwitz's (1970:55) "first generation" fits Cohort 1 in age, his "second generation," Cohort 2, and his "third generation," Cohort 3.

Table 2 presents the percentages of Jewish men and women who rank *low* on the indices developed by Lazerwitz (1970). For example, whereas only 14 per cent of the first-generation men rank *low* in religious behavior, more than one-third, 35 per cent, rank low in the third generation. In ratings on ethnicity, a mere 10 per cent of the first generation women are low, but the percentage increases to 38 per cent by the third generation.

The general trends in Jewish identification from the foreign-born cohort to the second generation of native Americans indicate that:

1. There is a definite trend in the dissipation of Jewish organizational participation and of informal involvement with other Jews. This trend is slower for men than for women. This trend is apparent also in the marked increase in marriage to non-Jews for the Post-holocaust generation;
2. There is a decline in sex differences in religious identity. The reduction of involvement by men in distinctly religious aspects of

TABLE 2

Percent Ranking Low by Sex on the Nine Jewish Identification Indices across Three Generations, Chicago Metro Area, 1967

| | PERCENT RANKING LOW BY SEX IN: | | | | | |
| | 1ST GEN. | | 2ND GEN. | | 3RD GEN. | |
IDENTITY INDICES	M	W	M	W	M	W
Religious behavior	14	26	22	33	35	29
Pietism	6	30	14	22	35	32
Jewish education	17	46	25	54	30	29
Jewish organization activities	25	28	20	37	33	54
Traditional Jewish beliefs	25	33	34	40	51	21
Zionism	45	33	29	38	51	37
Jewishness of childhood home	7	7	21	12	57	54
Jewish education for children	32	30	22	27	22	17
Ethnicity	12	10	13	26	20	38
Overall Jewish identity index	12	27	24	32	49	36
Sample base size	52	63	101	171	80	105

SOURCE: Lazerwitz, 1970.

358

Jewish life is partly compensated for by an increase in involvement by women.

3. There is a growth across the generations in interest in providing for some Jewish education for children. Other investigations have indicated that parents increasingly affiliate with synagogues and temples primarily for the sake of providing their children with a Jewish identity and education (Gans, 1958; Sklare and Greenblum, 1967). Possibly, that most married couples in the Postholocaust generation do not yet have children partly explains their low rate of synagogue or temple membership

In general, whatever increase has occurred in Jewish identification over the generations, integration into American society has taken place in distinctly *religious* matters. Communal interests, which might more directly influence family organization, appear to be waning. The emphasis on religious education of children can be interpreted as the resultant of a desire for instilling a Jewish identity in one's progeny while the parents continue to withdraw from Jewish communal activities.

Fertility

As Jewish families have become involved in urban, industrial societies, they have rapidly lowered their fertility levels. Indeed, the first birth-control clinic opened by Margaret Sanger was in the then New York City Jewish immigrant neighborhood of Brownsville.

Freedman, Whelpton, and Campbell (1959:110) report that the 83 percent of American Jewish women employing contraception start such use before their first pregnancy, while only 52 per cent of Protestants start contraception as early in married life. Several national fertility studies (Freedman, Whelpton, and Campbell, 1959; Whelpton, Campbell, and Patterson, 1966; and Freedman, Whelpton, and Campbell, 1961) report that American Jews are the most successful of American major ethnic groups with regard to family planning and birth spacing. Estimates are that from about 1920 to 1940, the Jewish birth rate in America fell almost 40 per cent (Seligman, 1950:42).

Reduction in the Jewish birth rate derives not only from effective use of contraceptives but also from late marriage. In the 1957 U.S. Census survey, the median age at first marriage for Jewish women was 21.3 as compared with 19.9 for Protestants and 20.8 for Catholics. Goldstein (1971:24) indicates that "later age of marriage has characterized Jewish women since at least 1920." For Jewish men as well, marriage has been later than it has for Protestants and Catholics. However, the data also indicate that the discrepancies in age at first marriage for Jews and non-Jews are disappearing. Although the high educational levels may be a factor in this tendency for Jews to marry later than others, it is unlikely the only one.

The shift from families characterized by large numbers of children in Eastern Europe, North Africa, or the Middle East to families having two to four children may have been a major factor permitting Jewish women to increase their involvement in Jewish communal life, to extend and enlarge their participation in the labor force, and to have less rigid sex work tasks within the home. Furthermore, the rapid fertility reduction characteristic of all the world's Jews who have entered to any extent in modern life seems to reflect extensive communication and decision making with regard to their husband-wife, father-mother roles within the Jewish family (Lazerwitz, 1971a). Rapid fertility reduction has also permitted Jewish parents to support the educational desires of their fewer offspring and, thereby, give strong support to the rapid socioeconomic mobility that has been the outstanding achievement of American Jews (Lazerwitz, 1971a).

Intermarriage

The characteristics and consequences of intermarriage and conversion have been long-standing major concerns and "scare" topics among both Jews and Christians. In turn, these concerns have stimulated a large number of research endeavors, particularly in the past decade or so. Among the recently published works are the studies by Goldstein (1968) of Springfield, Massachusetts, and, Goldstein and Goldscheider (1968), of the Providence, Rhode Island, Jewish communities; Axelrod, Fowler, and Gurin (1967) on Boston Jewry; Sklare and Greenblum's (1967) study of a contemporary Jewish suburb, Gordon's (1967) case studies of conversion; and Rosenthal's (1963) investigation into intermarriages in Washington, D.C., and the small Jewish communities of Iowa. Elsewhere, intermarriage data have been developed for the Jews of Australia by Lippmann (1969), for Italy by Pergola (1969), for Canada's Jews and Christians by Heer (1962), and even for Israel by Cohen (1969). The characteristics of intermarriages and conversions among American Protestants and Catholics have been recently investigated by Greeley (1964); Croog and Teele (1967); and Salisbury (1964 and 1969).

Collectively, the studies of Jewish intermarriages have revealed the following demographic information:

RATES. Initially low, but definitely increasing, intermarriage levels. The U.S. Census Bureau's (1958) Current Population Survey, taken in March 1957, reported that 7 per cent of existing Jewish marriages were with non-Jews. However, all researchers agree that in this century the percentage of Jews married to non-Jews rose considerably with the number of generations in an industrial diaspora country. For example, the Springfield and Providence surveys by Goldstein (1968:145–48) and Goldstein and Goldscheider (1968:155–57) report that 4.4 and 4.5 per cent of Jewish households were based on intermarriages, but that the children of respondents have intermarriage rates of 9 and 6 per cent, respectively. The National Jewish Population Study reports even higher rates of intermarriage (Massarik and Chenkin, 1973).

SIZE OF COMMUNITY. Intermarriage rates appear to be highest in large growing Jewish communities and in the very small ones. For instance, Rosenthal (1963:16) reports that a substantial (for America) 13 per cent of Washington, D.C. Jewish marriages were intermarriages, and that the small Jewish communities of the state of Iowa averaged a 42 per cent intermarriage rate between 1953 and 1959.

REMARRIAGE. The intermarried have a higher proportion who are in their second, or more, marriage. For example, Goldstein and Goldscheider (1968:164–64) report an intermarriage rate of 24 per cent among those 40 to 59 years old who have married more than once but one of only 4 per cent among those of this same age group married just once.

CONVERSION. The typical convert to Judaism is a non-Jewish woman marrying a Jewish man. Furthermore, according to Goldstein and Goldscheider (1968:157) the conversion rate is on the increase. Among their intermarried couples 60 years old or older, none of the non-Jews had been converted to Judaism. Among those intermarried couples under 40 years, 70 per cent of the non-Jews had been so converted. Conversely, all students of intermarriage agree that very few Jews are converted to other faiths.

RELIGIOUS EDUCATION. Goldstein and Goldscheider (1968:164), Goldstein (1968:150), and Rosenthal (1963:30) report less intermarriage with increasing amounts of *Jewish* education. The reverse seems true with regard to the amount of *secular* education.

In addition, Berman (1968:548) reports that:

Jews who intermarry—compared with those who inmarry—are more likely to have a history of broken homes and lack of contact with extended family (cousins, aunts, uncles, grandparents) than the inmarrying majority. . . . Jews attending a prestige private university hold more favorable attitudes toward intermarriage than Jews attending urban state universities. . . . Intermarrying Jews marry later in life than inmarrying Jews. Oldest children are *least* likely to intermarry; youngest children and only children are most likely to intermarry. Personality traits favoring intermarriage seem to be related to birth order: intermarrieds are venturesome, slightly unconventional persons who see themselves as "exceptions" to the normal rules of society—shading into the hypomanic and manic personality types. . . . Intermarriage seems to appeal to Jews whose socioeconomic position places them at the periphery of the Jewish community, or outside of it. Intermarriage is therefore likely to occur among the highly upward mobile members of the *salaried* professions; Jewish professors and government experts are more likely to intermarry than Jewish physicians, dentists, lawyers, and business owners.

The continued movement of the Postholocaust generation to the periphery of the Jewish community, to salaried professions, and away from the parental home suggests that the rate of intermarriage with non-Jews will continue to increase in the future.

GENDER. Jewish women for a long time have had about half the inter-marriage rate of Jewish men. Despite their greatly increased equality with men, they still are more restricted to, and undoubtedly prefer, dating and courtship within the Jewish community. Furthermore, there is some evidence, though it is far from conclusive, suggesting that a considerably larger percentage of intermarrying Jewish women wear their ethnic backgrounds more lightly, or deliberately reject it, than do intermarrying Jewish men.

Family Solidarity

Writers on the Jewish family have assumed that "solidarity" is a hallmark of Jewish domestic life throughout history. Brav (1940:7) notes, for example, that in the Biblical period "strong family solidarity was a matter of course," and he goes on to state (p.20) that "observers of the modern scene claim to note the existence in the Jewish family of a solidarity or cohesiveness that appears to be unique in degree as well as in quality. Among Jewish writers this is generally admitted as axiomatic." Brav ends by questioning whether this assumption about Jewish family solidarity has "sufficient factual support." This questioning appears to have reflected the concern of those whose family values had been nourished in a European setting but who now found themselves in a society in which less emphasis was placed on family obligations.

The research findings reported by Balswick (1966:167) in his review of studies suggest that although indices of solidarity indicate a greater cohesiveness on the part of Jewish than other families, "it seems obvious that the change has been from the closely knit European Jewish family to the less closely knit American Jewish family." Beginning with Brav's (1940) investigation, there has been little effort by researchers to distinguish between family organization of foreign-born household heads and native-born heads. Many of the findings, however, seem to refer to families of the Preholocaust generation (Cohort 1). Landis (1960) found, for example, that in families of Jewish college students in the 1950s (as compared with Catholic and Protestant families), the divorce rates of the parents was lowest and the relationship of respondents to their parents was closest. W. I. Thomas's analysis of the *Bintl Brief* in the *Daily Forward* (Bressler, 1952) again focused on the immigrant generation. Thomas, too, regarded "the key motif expressed in Jewish family patterns (to be) . . . an effort to preserve the solidarity of the family" (Balswick 1966:165). Brav's own conclusions in comparing indices of solidarity among Jewish and non-Jewish families in pre-World War II Vicksburg, Mississippi, were that Jewish solidarity is not markedly stronger than that in non-Jewish families.

But such concepts as solidarity or cohesiveness by which earlier writers sought to explain personal loyalties and the acceptance of familial obligations are vague, and the indicators chosen to measure then do confound various motives, pressures, and meanings. For example, merely because couples do not divorce does not suggest a high degree of "solidarity"; and because people live together or visit or assist one another is not a definite indicator of personal affinity. Be that as it may, disorganizing effects of migration eventually wore off, and family "cohesiveness" ceased to be a primary concern; the next cohort of Jewish families no longer could make a direct comparison between the "solidarity" of the European family and the "individuality" of the Americans.

Kinship and Mobility: Diaspora Upon Diaspora

One can also observe trends in the American Jewish family by charting the migration patterns of Jews over generations. As in the case of problems facing the Jewish family in different periods of adaptation to the American society, population movements are not confined to clearly delineated eras but to general shifts in migration.

Table 3 presents data on trends in the distribution of the American Jewish population from 1900 to 1972. The following movements seem to be occurring:

1. Prior to 1900, the existing Jewish population had spread westward and southward to the East North Central and South Atlantic states.
2. Immigration during the first part of the twentieth century, however, reconcentrated the bulk of the Jewish population in the Northeast. Relative to the Middle Atlantic states in particular, by 1928 all other regions showed a smaller percentage of the total Jewish American population.
3. Since World War I, there has been a steady redistribution of the Jewish population, with the major losses in the Northeastern and North Central states.
4. Dramatic shifts occurred between 1930 and 1972 in the movement of population to the South Atlantic and Pacific states. For the most part, this movement represents large Jewish migrations to more salubrious, warmer climates—to Florida (particularly to Miami) and to California. Writing in 1950, Seligman (1950:45) notes that Miami and Tucson, Arizona, showed "tremendously rapid growth in the last decade."

Most of the recent data pertaining to ties among Jewish kinsmen, however, pertain to the Holocaust generation in relation to their parents. For the most part, then, these studies refer to Cohort 1, which is mainly foreign born, and Cohort 2, the families of their first-generation children. The Holocaust generation was molded in an era of extermination camps, economic depression, aspirations for founding a homeland in Palestine, and war. One generation removed from the factionalist conception of Jewish community sustained by law, one would expect this cohort of families to sustain many traditional norms in family life.

A study of Jewish kinship ties in New York showed the persistence of traditional norms in the Holocaust generation. Leichter and Mitchell (1967) found that a majority of men and women each feel closer to their own relatives than to their spouse's. In general, women interact more often with their kin and have a wider variety of kinds of assistance that they exchange with relatives, much of which involves child care. Yet men interact more often with their own relatives when matters arise pertaining to business or to help in household repairs.

TABLE 3

Distribution of the Jewish Population, by Regions, 1900, 1918, 1930, 1963, and 1972 and Total U.S. Population for 1972

REGION	1900	1918	1930	1963	1972	TOTAL U.S. POPULATION 1972
Northeast	**56.6**	**69.9**	**68.3**	**65.9**	**62.6**	23.9
New England	7.4	8.6	8.4	6.7	6.8	5.8
Middle Atlantic	49.2	61.3	59.9	59.2	55.8	18.1
North Central	**23.7**	**20.2**	**19.6**	**13.7**	**12.2**	27.7
East North Central	18.3	15.7	15.7	11.2	9.8	19.7
West North Central	5.4	4.5	3.9	2.5	2.4	8.0
South	**14.2**	**6.9**	**7.6**	**9.1**	**11.8**	31.9
South Atlantic	8.0	4.0	4.3	6.7	9.4	15.3
East South Central	3.3	1.3	1.4	0.8	0.7	6.3
West South Central	2.9	1.6	1.9	1.6	1.6	9.6
West	**5.5**	**3.1**	**4.6**	**11.5**	**13.3**	17.3
Mountain	2.3	0.7	1.0	0.9	1.1	4.2
Pacific	3.2	2.4	3.6	10.6	12.2	13.1
TOTAL: PER CENT	**100.0**	**100.0**	**100.0**	**100.0**	**100.0**	**100.0**
NUMBER (in 1,000's)	**1,058**	**3,389**	**4,228**	**5,599**	**6,115**	**208.232**

Data on distribution of Jewish population from *American Jewish Year Book*, 1 (1900), pp. 623-624; 21 (1919), p. 606; 33 (1931), p. 276; 65 (1964), p. 14; 74 (1973), p. 309. The 1972 U.S. data from the U.S. Department of Commerce, *Population Estimates and Projections*, Series P-25, No. 200 (cited in *American Jewish Year Book*, 1973, 74: 309). Data for 1900 and 1930 cited in Goldstein, 1971.

The husband's kindred, like the instrumental leader in small groups, attempts to dominate his family, offering criticisms and demanding loyalty (Parsons and Bales, 1955). Indeed, Leichter and Mitchell (1967:177–81) did find that there was greater conflict with the husband's kin over interference in internal family affairs.

Research in a Chicago suburb indicated that Jewish families during the 1960s showed the greater amount of "familism," that is, more than Protestant and Catholic families: (a) Jewish families had more households of kin in the same metropolitan area; (b) more often the related households of Jewish families consisted of close relatives (often parents or siblings); (c) there was a greater amount of interaction among the related Jewish families; and (d) the Jewish families were more likely to give or receive assistance from these relatives. Holding migratory status constant statistically, the investigators reported that "familism" was more a *basis* for reluctance to migrate than a *result* of residential stability (Winch, Greer, and Blumberg, 1967).

The findings of families in other cities are comparable (see Leichter and Mitchell, 1967.) Lenski (1961) found, for example, that in Detroit during the 1950s Jews, much more often than Protestants or Catholics, had relatives living in Detroit and visited with them weekly. Lenski found also that Jewish respondents, more often than Christians, reported that their spouse, children, and parents influenced their religious beliefs. Croog, Lipson, and Levine (1972) found, however, that Jews did not differ from non-Jews in assistance given to relatives stricken with heart attacks. On the other hand, Wake and Sporakowski (1972) reported Jews are more willing to support aged parents.

Gordon (1959) suggests that movement to the suburbs by Jews during the 1950s did little to damage strong kinship ties. About 60 per cent of his respondents reported visiting with parents and other relatives as often as they did while the whole *mishpokheh* (extended kin group) lived in the central city. Most of those who see their relatives less frequently still observe festival and holy days together. In these respects, the move to the suburbs has perhaps had a less disruptive effect than that found in England among lower-middle-class non-Jewish families (Young and Willmot, 1962); findings reported by Gordon are, however, consistent with those that indicate that in highly industrialized societies, when relatives see one another with less frequency, feast days and holy days, for Christians as well, become special days for visiting and celebrating (Luschen, *et al.*, 1971).

Despite the findings on the stability of kinship ties, the recent shifts in population to the South and to the Southwest may contribute much to the decline in social relationships among family and relatives. In the Lakeville study (Sklare and Greenblum, 1967:252) there was a sharp decline in the amount of time spent with relatives from one generation to the next. Although almost 40 per cent of the respondents reported that when they had been children their parents spent more time with relatives than with friends, only 5 per cent of the respondents indicated that they themselves spend more time with relatives than with friends. Moreover, while almost 60 per cent saw their cousins at least monthly when they were children, only 40 per cent of their own children now visit with cousins.

There is also a significant decline in extended family households as families move to the suburbs or migrate to warmer climates. In their study of Providence, Rhode Island, Goldstein and Goldscheider (1968) reported that 85 per cent of the Jewish households consisted of husband, wife, and their children, and a mere 8 per cent held other relatives as well. The effect of generation on household composition was considerable. When age was held constant statistically, the percentage of nuclear-family households headed by third-generation persons was considerably greater than that for first-generation heads. Since generation is related to religious orthodoxy, one would expect to find more households augmented by relatives among the more orthodox than among the more liberal or among nominal Jewish families.

The Jewish population movement to the South and the Southwest has included not only young families but also the elderly. Young families may see in this migration an opportunity to live a more desirable existence away from familial obligations, only to find that their relatives, perhaps now old and retired, wend their way southward and westward. It is difficult to assess fully the implications of this movement. Undoubtedly, it will act to deconcentrate the Jewish community and will likely decompose family obligations still further.

Family Roles

Household division of labor in traditional European non-Jewish families is often associated with an ideology of patriarchial authority and the subordination of women. Yet writers about the Jewish family generally agree that the subordination found in some European systems (e.g., the Italian) has been absent among Jews. Gordon (1959:58), for example, suggests that:

> Historically, the entire responsibility for the support as well as the care of the family often rested on the woman's shoulders. Jewish women, through the centuries, often carried on the business or earned the family's livelihood in order that the husband might devote himself to the intensive study of Torah. Her influence with respect to her children and her husband was extraordinary.

Even among immigrant families (in the Preholocaust generation), Gordon notes (p. 59) "there was a far greater degree of equality between husband and wife than is generally assumed. . . . The mother was the homemaker, but it was she whose personal piety and example within the home was expected to influence her children, while winning their love and veneration."

Gordon (1959:59) suggests further that as the Jewish families moved to the suburbs following World War II, "the wife, by virtue of her increased duties and responsibilities within the family, has become the modern matriarch of Jewish suburbia. Her ideas, opinions and values clearly dominate."

The movement by women toward increased labor-force participation (especially in professional and managerial positions) is leading to a growing ambivalence toward maternal roles. (See, for example, Luria, 1974.)

367

One would expect women in traditional homemaking roles to have a strong investment in their children's behavior. In a study of Westchester County, New York, concern over possible deviance in children's behavior was greatest among the more traditional groups. As one might anticipate on the basis of the Jewish mother stereotype, "More Jewish than non-Jewish mothers reported worrying, though their children were no more impaired than those of other religious groups" (Lurie, 1974:113). Probably, the farther we move from the Holocaust generation, the more committed will young Jewish women be to work and career, and the greater will be their ambivalence toward motherhood—especially toward being a "Jewish mother."

Traditionally, the father has had a priestly role in the household. Since the husband had been the link between the family and the religious community, he was responsible for the piety, morality, and ethical standards of the family members. In the contemporary American context, the priestly status of the father is translated into his occupational dedication and his retention of achievement values for his children, especially sons (Strodtbeck, 1958). For whatever reason, Jews have traditionally gone into occupations that require long hours and energy demands—self-employed in business, the free professions—and even in blue-collar occupations they have exerted much dedication toward achieving unionization and increased social welfare. In many instances, participation in social movements apparently substituted for the *shtetl* synagogue. Yet in suburban America, "few mothers or fathers accept easily the role of religious director in the family" (Seeley, Sim, and Loosely (1956:214). In fact, in religious organizations, Jewish "women are much more in evidence than men and more frequently represent the family" (Seeley, Sim, and Loosely, 1956:215). Thus, insofar as men have retained their traditional priestly status in the family, they have, for the most part, shifted their dedication to the mundane.

Sklare (1971:87) points out that in the traditional Jewish family, a child is never considered as truly emancipated from his parents. He suggests that children are seen as extensions of their parents rather than as distinct entities. One of the basic forms of exchange for parent and child is for the parents to provide a basis for their children's own success in family and community, while the child has an obligation to supply *nakhus* (Hebrew: pleasure or gratification) for his parents. In providing the conditions for *nakhus,* the parent creates a lifelong obligation for the child.

The decline of the special structure of the Jewish parent-child relationship emanates, according to Sklare (1971:89) from two sources. The first source is the high level of secular educational attainment of Jews, which stresses urbanity and cosmopolitanism. The second source is the affinity of Jews toward those schools of modern psychology that "stress the reduction of dependence (whether on the part of parents or children) [and in doing so] they are necessarily critical of the structure of the Jewish family and of its special culture" (Sklare, 1971:90). Sklare thus sees an escalating estrangement that is destroying traditional family commitments.

Socialization of Children

The parent-child relationship described by Sklare (1971) of creating in the child an obligation to be successful by bringing *nakhus* to the parents, makes certain assumptions about the nature of conduct. These assumptions provide a basis for the kinds of socialization practices found in Jewish families. Essentially, one channels behavior rather than "shaping" it. The person is seen not as a responding mechanism or a *tabula rasa* but as someone who has a drive to act requiring controls and outlets. The psychoanalytic perspective is quite congenial to this conception of socialization.

Viewing socialization of children as channelization suggests that personal behavior is the outpouring of a substance (such as water or vital matter) that demands expression in its flow. One can guide the flow or dig new channels, but one cannot dam up the flow indefinitely. Punishment does not inhibit behavior, but only diverts it to other channels.

In the European *shtetl,* the aim of socialization was to make each child a *mensch,* that is, one who does the appropriate things at the appropriate time and place with appropriate persons. For example:

> Weeping is accepted as a normal means of expression and, on occasion, a legitimate weapon. . . . Grown men are not expected to weep as often or as freely as women and children, but for them too tears are in order during certain rituals, or as an accompaniment to pleas for help, either for themselves or for their community" (Zborowski and Herzog, 1952:335).

Channelization of behavior, as found in Jewish families, implies that "each year adds new responsibilities in the child's life" (Zborowski and Herzog, 1952:350) but also fresh forms of tension release. With each special responsibility, the child is seen as becoming more of a *mensch.* "Despite the persisting, but steadily contracting, areas of indulgence, from the moment a child is able to help with the younger ones or with the family *parnosseh* (earning a living), or to go to *cheder* (religious school),

369

it becomes a responsible and functioning member of a group" (Zborowski and Herzog, 1952:331). Especially strong is the separation of male and female worlds in the *shtetl*. As boys and girls mature, they "become more and more aware of the rules against intermingling of sexes" (Zborowski and Herzog, 1952:352). Bit by bit, the individual assumes the "yoke of Jewishness," *ol fun Yiddishkeit,* the discipline imposed by Judaic ritual.

The channeling of behavior in terms of division of labor seems to give rise to a heightened intensity of behavior in specific roles. Indeed, the father is not merely head of the house; ideally, he is also its "priest," responsible for its living according to ritual and Jewish law and ideally dedicated to prayer and study. One is not merely a mother, one is instead a *Yiddisheh mahmeh,* with all of the stereotypical nurturance, overprotection, and domineering that the "Jewish mother" implies. The mother-child relationship is "complementary rather than reciprocal. Parents are donors and should not receive from children. The children can make return by passing benefits to their children" (Mandelbaum, 1958:512). In illness, a Jew does not suppress pain; instead, concerned with its symptomatic meaning, he makes the most of it, expressing its intensity at every opportunity (Zborowski, 1969:240–42). In family conflict, one is forbidden to use physical violence; but he may still curse, and Jewish curses contain imaginative invective in their expression—for example, oxen should grow in your belly, or your father's godfather should get a kick. Children are often imbued with the "Protestant ethic," often to a greater extent than Protestants (Slater, 1969). Findings indicate that high-achievement motivation is related to parental praise and expression of parental pride (Rehberg, Sinclair, and Schafer, 1970). Participation thus tends to be unbalanced—perhaps even caricatured— in different spheres of the social world. Complete dedication to work, to home, or to piety seems to flow from the conception of socialization as the channelizing of energy.

Some balance in behavior is achieved, however, through the ritualization of the rhythms of living. There are religious injunctions covering daily, weekly, monthly, and seasonal rhythms. The daily prayers, the celebration of the Sabbath, and the periodic holidays during which one must turn from the tension of the workaday world, all act as regularized forms of tension release. Ritualization of tension release requires (a) the development of delayed gratification patterns since time and place of rituals are fixed, (b) deflection and sublimation as socialization techniques as opposed to inhibition and negation, and (c) reliance on authority and benefice as justifying conduct rather than seeking reciprocity in all behavioral exchanges. The heavy reliance on ritual thus does not leave even tension release to chance.

The research on drinking supports this conception of child socialization. Without exception, studies of drinking patterns indicate a low rate of heavy drinking among Jews, especially in Orthodox homes (Snyder, 1958). At the same time, cross-cultural analysis of drinking shows that societies that are highly indulgent to their children in the preadolescent years tend to be high in drunkenness, and where there is a general pressure for obedience and responsibility in children, drunkenness tends to be low (Field, 1962). Thus, Jewish families seem to fall into the latter category, characterized by highly controlled tension release, permitting and even encouraging the ritual use of alcohol.

Psychoanalytic concepts seem appropriate to describe what happens when the channelized expression of behavior exceeds acceptable limits or when channels are blocked. Given general socialization data, it does not seem surprising that, in types of mental illness, Jews tend to specialize in neurotic or mild or moderate symptoms of mental illness, whereas Catholic and Protestant populations are more prone to severe mental impairments (Rose and Stub, 1955:112; Srole, Langer, Michael, Opler, and Rennie, 1962:304; Roberts and Myers, 1954). Moreover, unlike Catholics and Protestants, parental religiosity is unrelated to degree of impairment among Jews (Srole, Langer, Michael, Opler, and Rennie, 1962:310). The qualitative difference between Jews, Protestants, and Catholics is expressed further in attitudes toward psychotherapy and psychoanalysis. Among psychiatrists, there is a marked tendency for Jews to hold a psychoanalytic orientation (Hollingshead and Redlich, 1958). In general, Jewish individuals are more favorably inclined toward psychotherapy as an effective mode of treatment and are more often outpatients in psychiatric services than are Catholics or Protestants (Srole, Langer, Michael, Opler, and Rennie, 1962:125–318).

As the Postholocaust generation matures, one finds a waning of the modes of socialization that have characterized earlier generations. Boroff (1961) reports that Jewish youth are losing their sense of uniqueness. He finds that the younger teen-agers identify strongly with other teen-agers as a generation, but that older Jewish teen-agers are more college oriented than their peers. In the Postholocaust generation, when parents differ with friends of their children over such things as the use of Kosher meat, the children agree more often with their peers than their parents (Rosen, 1955). The youth seem to have developed a strong bond to the broad American community, with its emphasis on the insulation of youth from family influence.

CHANGE AND ADAPTATION

Forecasts of the future of the American Jewish family generally fall into three groups: the pessimists, the ambivalent, and the optimists. Each group has its fervent proponents, and each group establishes it case on different grounds.

THE PESSIMISTS. The pessimists view trends in Jewish family organization as mirroring those of the American middle class. According to this position, the same forces that are weakening traditional family bonds in middle-class society are destroying the Jewish family. This group sees the steady increase in mobility and migration, the continued growth of individualism, and the heightening of cosmopolitanism in American society as undermining the basis for strong family life in American society. For example, Gordon (1959:83) writes:

> It is my belief that, if our suburban communities continue to change internally as they have since 1950 . . . Jewish residents will inevitably feel that they are a rootless community. They will not feel "at home" or at ease within any given area. To regard the suburb in which one lives as a *temporary* home is to destroy the sense of permanence that all families need . . . Jewish family relations, which to date have remained excellent, may not be able to survive another decade of extreme mobility without showing signs of great stress and strain.

Focusing on the role of the family in establishing Jewish identification in children, Sklare also presents a pessimistic stance. He regards the very social and economic success of American Jews as contributing to the downfall of the traditional *mishpokheh,* which long has acted as a bedrock of Jewish community institutions. Sklare proposes (1971:89–100):

> The changing significance of the family, and particularly the fairly recent declines in the frequency and intensity of interaction with the kinship group, means that identity can no longer be acquired through this traditional institution. . . . American Jewry has a highly developed communal structure as well as a firmly established network of Jewish schools. . . . But however significant the communal network and the school system are as building blocks, they are a kind of super-structure resting upon the foundation of the family—for it is the family that has been the prime mechanism for transmitting Jewish identity. This system of identity-formation is currently on the decline. The emerg-

372

ing crisis of the Jewish family in identity-formation is in part due to the newer limitations on the family as a socialization agent—limitations that affect all other Americans as well. But it is traceable to . . . the high acculturation of many Jewish parents, the diminished interaction with relatives, and the presence of Gentiles in the Jewish kinship network. . . . It is the shrinking contribution of the family to Jewish identity transmission that constitutes its essential weakness.

In summary, the view of the pessimists is mainly that the American family itself is becoming ineffective as a socialization agent, and that by becoming assimilated into the mainstream of American life, the Jewish family has lost its crucial role in identity transmission.

THE AMBIVALENT. Whereas the pessimists emphasize the decreasing differentiation between Jewish and non-Jewish family life in the American middle class, the ambivalent observers regard the survival of the Jewish family as a personal decision. The risk taken by relegating choices in social issues to personal decisions is that many individuals will choose *against* the perpetuation of traditional norms and values.

Charles Liebman (1973:151–52) expresses a pessimism over preference for interaction with other Jews or affiliation with formal organizations in the Jewish community to be effective in the survival of Jewish institutions. He notes, for example, that preferred association with other Jews—as ubiquitous as it is—is uncorrelated with any other index of Jewish identification. Affiliation with Jewish formal organization is of limited interest; Jewish communal organizations are experiencing difficulty in attracting talented and highly educated persons. Liebman thus expresses doubt that communal motives can be induced to strengthen Jewish identification and Jewish family life. His solution rests solely on personal decision.

Jewish peoplehood is threatened by the growing impulse toward cosmopolitanism and universalism; in a society which increasingly stresses the primacy of conscience and individual freedom against even society's own law, *Torah* and the study of sacred texts become increasingly absurd. The very notion of sacred text is antiquarian, and there is no room for a tradition of study in a culture which affirms the values of sensation and of the individual as the final arbiter of right and wrong. It is, therefore, my strong belief that, at least until we enter a postmodern world, the Jew who wishes to remain in the United States, but who is also committed to the survival of Judaism, has no alternative but to retreat into a far more sectarian posture than has up to this time characterized American Jewish life.

The personal decision to adopt traditional Jewish norms and, by implication, Jewish family norms in particular necessarily assumes the risk that a significant proportion of Jews will make this decision. Otherwise, there can be no survival of the idea of peoplehood, of religious community, or of communal life according to biblical injunctions. Liebman's position thus implies a faith that others will also make a "moral" decision as a resolution of personal ambivalence.

Perhaps the survival of a remnant living according to norms of Jewish family life is all that can be hoped for in modern society. Berman (1968:560) suggests:

> An open society where ethnic boundaries survive because they serve the individual's needs for variety, for belongingness, for continuity of identity, for authenticity—where ethnic boundaries are not prison walls—where those Jews who would rather be Gentiles and Gentiles who would rather be Jews are equally free to cross the boundary and find a more congenial ethnic home—that, in this writer's opinion, is a good society.

THE OPTIMISTS. The optimists believe that modern society sustains ethnic differences by its very composition, and that this persistence of ethnicity will act to sustain traditional Jewish family organization. The argument presented by Glazer and Moynihan (1974) is as follows: (a) More and more modern societies are becoming multiethnic states; (b) diverse ethnic groups occupy different and conflicting positions in modern social structures; (c) because of their opposing positions, ethnic groups become rallying points in the identification of interest groups in the society; (d) in becoming rallying points in relation to political, social, and economic interest, ethnic groups tend to stress those features that define their uniqueness; (e) features that ethnic groups claim as unique thus tend to survive. One of the features that Jews have claimed as unique is their family life—the *Yiddisheh mahmeh,* the term *nakhus,* etc.; hence, the optimist would see a conscious effort to sustain Jewish family norms growing ultimately out of a need to defend Jewish interests (e.g., support of Soviet Jewry, backing of Israel, opposition to quota systems in occupations).

The view expressed by Glazer and Moynihan presupposes that there will always be a series of significant issues to provide for the constant revitalization of ethnic identification. At best, however, one can expect the flow of issues as rallying points to mobilize only segments of the Jewish community, and despite the optimism of Glazer and Moynihan, people tire of mobilization. Thus, without coercive constraints, one

374

would anticipate a general waning in volunteristic mobilization. Without institutionalized factionalism, one would anticipate a slow languishing of the norms and values traditionally associated with Jewish family life.

R E F E R E N C E S

Axelrod, Morris, Floyd Fowler, and Arnold Gurin. 1967. *A Community Survey for Long Range Planning: A Study of the Jewish Population of Greater Boston*. Boston: Combined Jewish Philanthropies of Greater Boston.

Bales, Robert F. 1962. "Attitudes toward Drinking in the Irish Culture." In David J. Pittman and Charles R. Snyder (eds.): *Society, Culture, and Drinking Patterns*. New York: Wiley, pp. 157–87.

Balswick, Jack. 1966. "Are American-Jewish Families Closely Knit?" *Jewish Social Studies* 28:159–67.

Baron, Salo W. 1945. *The Jewish Community: Its History and Structure to the American Revolution*. Philadelphia: The Jewish Publication Society of America.

Berman, Louis. 1968. *Jews and Intermarriage: A Study in Personality and Culture*. New York: Thomas Yoseloff.

Birmingham, Stephen. 1971. *The Grandees*. New York: Harper & Row.

Boroff, David. 1961. "Jewish Teenage Culture." *The Annals of the American Academy of Political Science* 338:79–90.

Brav, Stanley R. 1940. *Jewish Family Solidarity, Myth or Fact?* Vicksburg, Miss.: Nogales Press.

Bressler, Marvin. 1952. "Selected Family Patterns in W. I. Thomas' Unfinished Study of the Bintl Brief." *American Sociological Review* 17:563–71.

Cohen, Erik. 1969. "Mixed Marriage in an Israeli Town." *The Jewish Journal of Sociology"* 11:41–50.

Croog, Sidney, Alberta Lipson, and Sol Levine. 1972. "Help Patterns in Severe Illness: The Roles of Kin Network, Non-Family Resources, and Institutions." *Journal of Marriage and the Family* 34:32–41.

Croog, Sidney, and James Teele. 1967. "Religious Identity and Church Attendance of Sons of Religious Intermarriages." *American Sociological Review* 32:93–103.

Elazar, Daniel J., and Stephen R. Goldstein. 1972. "The Legal Status of the American Jewish Community." *American Jewish Year Book* 73:3–94.

Farber, Bernard, 1971. *Kinship and Class: A Midwestern Study*. New York: Basic Books.

———. 1975. "Bilateral Kinship: Centripetal and Centrifugal Types of Organization." *Journal of Marriage and the Family* 37.

Farine, Avigdor. 1973. "Charity and Study Societies in Europe of the Sixteenth-Eighteenth Centuries." *Jewish Quarterly Review* 64:16–47; 164–75.

Field, Peter B. 1962. "A New Cross-Cultural Study of Drunkenness." In David

J. Pittman and Charles R. Snyder (eds.): *Society, Culture and Drinking Patterns*. New York: Wiley, pp. 48–74.

Freedman, Ronald, Pascal Whelpton, and Arthur Campbell. 1959. *Family Planning, Sterility, and Population Growth*. New York: McGraw-Hill.

———, ———, and ———. 1961. "Socio-Economic Factors in Religious Differentials in Fertility." *American Sociological Review* 26:608–14.

Frideres, James. 1973. "Offspring of Jewish Intermarriage: A Note." *Jewish Social Studies* 35:149–56.

Gans, Herbert. 1958. "The Origin and Growth of a Jewish Community." In Marshall Sklare (ed.): *The Jews: Social Patterns of an American Group*. New York: The Free Press.

Glazer, Nathan. 1957. *American Judaism*. Chicago: University of Chicago Press.

Glazer, Nathan and Daniel P. Moynihan. 1974. "Why Ethnicity." *Commentary* 58 (October):33–39.

Golden, Harry and Martin Rywell. 1950. *Jews in American History*. Charlotte, N.C.: Henry Lewis Martin Co.

Goldstein, Sidney. 1968. *A Population Survey of the Greater Springfield Jewish Community*. Springfield, Mass.: Jewish Community Council.

———. 1971. "American Jewry, 1970." *American Jewish Year Book* 72:3–88.

Goldstein, Sidney and Calvin Goldscheider, 1968. *Jewish Americans: Three Generations in a Jewish Community*. Englewood Cliffs, N.J.: Prentice-Hall.

Gordon, Albert I. 1959. *Jews in Suburbia*. Boston: Beacon Press.

———. 1967. *The Nature of Conversion*. Boston: Beacon Press.

Greeley, Andrew. 1964. *Mixed Marriages in the United States*. Chicago: National Opinion Research Center (mimeographed).

Heer, David. 1962. "The Trend to Interfaith Marriages in Canada." *American Sociological Review* 27:245–50.

Hollingshead, A. B., and F. C. Redlich. 1958. *Social Class and Mental Illness*. New York: Wiley.

Landes, Ruth, and Mark Zborowski. 1968. "The Context of Marriage: Family Life as a Field of Emotions." In H. Kent Geiger (ed.): *Comparative Perspectives on Marriage and the Family*. pp. 77–102. Boston: Little, Brown.

Landis, Judson T. 1960. "Religiousness, Family Relationships, and Family Values in Protestant, Catholic, and Jewish Families." *Marriage and Family Living* 22:341–47.

Lazerwitz, Bernard. 1970. "Contrasting the Effects of Generation, Class, Sex, and Age on Group Identification in the Jewish and Protestant Communities." *Social Forces* 49:50–59.

———. 1971a. "Fertility Trends in Israel and Its Administered Territories." *Jewish Social Studies* 33:172–86.

———. 1971b. "Intermarriage and Conversion: A Guide for Future Research." *Jewish Journal of Sociology* 13:41–63.

Leichter, Hope J., and William E. Mitchell. 1967. *Kinship and Casework*. New York: Russell Sage Foundation.

Lenski, Gerhard. 1961. *The Religious Factor*. New York: Doubleday.

Levinson, Maria, and Daniel J. Levinson. 1958–59. "Jews Who Intermarry:

Sociopsychological Bases of Ethnic Identity and Change." *YIVO Annual of Jewish Social Science* 12:103–30.

Liebman, Charles S. 1973. "American Jewry: Identity and Affiliation." In David Sidorsky (ed.): *The Future of the Jewish Community in America*. New York: Basic Books, pp 127–52.

Lippmann, Walter. 1969. "Australia Jewry in 1966." *The Jewish Journal of Sociology* 11:67–73.

Luria, Zella. 1974. "Recent Women College Graduates: A Study of Rising Expectations." *American Journal of Orthopsychiatry* 44:312–26.

Lurie, Olga R. 1974. "Parents' Attitudes toward use of Mental Health Services." *American Journal of Orthopsychiatry* 44:109–20.

Luschen, Gunther, *et al.* 1971. "Family Interaction with Kin and the Function of Ritual." *Journal of Marriage and the Family* 33:755–65.

Mandelbaum, David G. 1958. "Change and Continuity in Jewish Life." In Marshall Sklare (ed.): *The Jews, Social Patterns of an American Group*. New York: The Free Press, pp. 509–19.

Manners, Ande. 1972. *Poor Cousins*. New York: Coward, McCann and Geoghegan.

Massarik, Fred and Alvin Chenkin. 1973. "United States National Jewish Population Study." *American Jewish Year Book* 74:264–306.

Parsons, Talcott, and Robert F. Bales. 1955. *Family, Socialization and Interaction Process*. New York: The Free Press.

Pergola, Sergio Della. 1969. "Marriages and Mixed Marriages Among Jews of Milano, Italy." Paper given at the Fifth World Congress of Jewish Studies, Jerusalem. Available from the Institute of Contemporary Jewry, Hebrew University, Jerusalem.

Rehberg, Richard A., Judie Sinclair, and Walter E. Schafer. 1970. "Adolescent Achievement Behavior, Family Authority Structure, and Parental Socialization Practices." *American Journal of Sociology* 75:1012–34.

Roberts, B. H., and J. K. Meyers. 1954. "Religion, Natural Origin, Immigration, and Mental Illness." *American Journal of Psychiatry* 110:759–64.

Rose, Arnold M., and Halger R. Stub. 1955. "Summary of Studies on the Incidence of Mental Disorders." In Arnold M. Rose (ed.): *Mental Health and Mental Disorders*. New York: Norton, pp. 87–116.

Roseman, Kenneth D. 1974. "American Jewish Community Institutions in their Historical Context." *Jewish Journal of Sociology* 16:25–38.

Rosen, Bernard C. 1955. "Conflicting Group Membership: A Study of Parent-Peer-Group Cross Pressures." *American Sociological Review* 20:155–61.

Rosenthal, Erich. 1963. "Studies of Jewish Intermarriage in the United States." *American Jewish Year Book* 64:3–53.

Salisbury, Seward. 1964. *Religion in American Culture*. Homewood, Ill.:
———. 1969. "Religious Identification, Mixed Marriages, and Conversion." *Journal for the Scientific Study of Religion* 8:125–29.

Seeley, John R., R. Alexander Sim, and E. W. Loosley. 1956. *Crestwood Heights, a Study of the Culture of Suburban Life*. New York: Basic Books.

Seligman, Ben B. 1950. "The American Jew: Some Demographic Features." *American Jewish Year Book* 51:3–52.

Sidorsky, David. 1973. "Judaism and the Revolution of Modernity." In David Sidorsky (ed.): *The Future of the Jewish Community in America*. New York: Basic Books, pp. 3–21.

Sklare, Marshall (ed.). 1958. *The Jews, Social Patterns of an American Group*. Glencoe, Ill.: Free Press.

Sklare, Marshall. 1971. *America's Jews*. New York: Random House.

Sklare, Marshall, and Joseph Greenblum. 1967. *Jewish Identity on the Suburban Frontier: A Study of Group Survival in the Open Society*. New York: Basic Books.

Slater, Mariam K. 1969. "My Son the Doctor: Aspects of Mobility Among American Jews." *American Sociological Review* 34:359–73.

Snyder, Charles R. 1958. *Alcohol and the Jews*. New York: The Free Press.

Srole, Leo, Thomas S. Langer, Stanley T. Michael, Marvin K. Opler, and Thomas A. C. Rennie. 1962. *Mental Health in the Metropolis*. New York: McGraw-Hill.

Strodtbeck, Fred. 1958. "Family Interaction, Values and Achievement." In Marshall Sklare (ed.): *The Jews, Social Patterns of an American Group*. New York: The Free Press, pp. 147–65.

U.S. Bureau of the Census. 1958. "Religion Reported by the Civilian Population of the United States: March, 1957." *Current Population Reports*, Series P-20, No. 35. Washington, D.C.: U.S. Government Printing Office.

Wake, Sandra B., and Michael J. Sporakowski. 1972. "An Intergenerational Comparison of Attitudes toward Supporting Aged Parents." *Journal of Marriage and the Family* 34:42–48.

Weber, Max. 1961. *General Economic History*. New York: Collier Books.

Weinryb, Bernard D. 1958. "Jewish Immigration and Accommodation to America" in Marshall Sklare (ed.) *The Jews, Social Patterns of an American Group*. New York: The Free Press, pp. 5–25.

Whelpton, Pascal, Arthur Campbell, and John Patterson. 1966. *Fertility and Family Planning in the United States*. Princeton, N.J.: Princeton University Press.

Winch, Robert F., Scott Greer, and Rae L. Blumberg. 1967. "Ethnicity and Extended Familism in an Upper-Middle-Class Suburb." *American Sociological Review* 32:265–72.

Wirth, Louis. 1928. *The Ghetto*. Chicago: University of Chicago Press.

Young, Michael and Peter Willmott. 1962. *Family and Kinship in East London*. Baltimore: Penguin Books.

Zborowski, Mark. 1969. *People in Pain*. San Francisco: Jossey-Bass.

Zborowski, Mark, and Elizabeth Herzog. 1952. *Life is with People: the Culture of the Shtetl*. New York: Schocken Books.

The Mormon Family

The concept of family, the foundation of Mormon theology and social structure, is being modified as the church approaches its one hundred fiftieth anniversary in 1980. Several social scientists have identified certain strains that exist in the Mormon subculture between the routinized charismatic authority of the Mormon Church and the secular, urban, industrial American society. In this essay on the Mormon family Drs. Campbell attempt to present the normative system that was promoted by Joseph Smith, the founder of the religion and to examine the developing patterns of Mormon family life, paying special attention to the consequences of beliefs in the lives of those who hold them.

Like most of the authors in this book, Drs. Campbell are members of the group of which they are writing. They are aware of the possible sources of bias that may affect the validity of their study. They commented:

> The "insider" has the advantage of an intimate knowledge of his culture that could take the "outsider" years to develop. The structure of relationships, the idiom, or special nuances in a reply are clearer to the insider than the outsider. However, there are certain pressures on the insider which may introduce bias into his study making the role of disinterested scholar difficult to maintain in certain circumstances.

These problems are particularly so with a group such as the Mormons who they characterize as possessing "missionary zeal and concern with generation of self."

CHAPTER SIXTEEN

BY

BRUCE L. CAMPBELL and EUGENE E. CAMPBELL

EMERGENCE OF THE MORMONS AS A MINORITY GROUP

Mormonism had its beginning in an atmosphere of supernaturalism, millenialism, and religious revivalism that characterized the "burned-over" district of western New York during the first decades of the nineteenth century. Joseph Smith, Jr., the founder and prophet of the religion, in his early teens claimed to have experienced a series of heavenly visions beginning about 1820 in the vicinity of Palmyra, New York. According to Smith, in the first visitation God the Father and His Son, Jesus Christ, informed the youth that there was no true church of Christ on the earth, and that he should join none of them.

Other visions revealed the location of golden plates buried in a hill near his home on which were written the records and religious experiences of ancient inhabitants of America, including a visit of Jesus Christ to the American continent after His resurrection. After obtaining these plates and some spectaclelike instruments to aid in the translation of the record, Joseph Smith, with the help of several scribes, produced the Book of Mormon, which he claimed to be an inspired translation of the golden plates. The book was published in 1830 and became an effective missionary tool in the hands of the young prophet and his converts.

Smith also claimed to have received heavenly instructions and authority to re-establish what he said was the true restored Church of Christ. This church was organized in 1830 at Fayette, New York. In 1838 the phrase Latter-day Saints was added, reflecting the belief in the imminence of Christ's second coming and the end of the present age. Thus, Mormonism began as a restoration of primitive Christianity with a strong eschatological and millenial flavor.*

It may seem incredible that a movement based on such supernatural experiences should attract so many people, but its claim to charismatic authority—a living prophet and a new scripture—seemed to satisfy the religious needs of those who had been disoriented by the religious diversity that characterized nineteenth-century America. Smith also preached a brand of communitarianism that may have met some of the economic needs of his followers.

The young prophet emphasized the need to spread the word of this "restoration" to others, resulting in an active proselyting program. In 1830 four missionaries were sent to take the glad tidings to the Indians, a logical action since the Book of Mormon was proclaimed by Smith to be a record of the Hebrew origin of the aboriginal inhabitants of the Americas. It was expected that the Indians would find this record especially appealing, but such was not the case. Mormon missionaries continued to preach to the Indians whenever they met them but had little success.

---

*Eschatology is simply the doctrine or concept of the last days in a two-age view of history. This present evil age to be followed by a "Golden age" in which Christ will reign. Millenium refers to a thousand year period, usually associated with Christ's reign on earth.

Despite difficulties, the church continued to attract new converts, especially in an industrially depressed England, where a mission had been established in 1837. Preaching the need for conversion and the duty to "gather to Zion" the missionaries sent hundreds of converts to Mormon settlements in Ohio, Missouri, and Illinois. The early record of the Mormon movement can best be described as a cycle in which the Mormons created a new settlement, prospered, clashed with their non-Mormon neighbors, and were forced to move and create a new settlement. Hill's (1976) analysis of the strains between the Mormons and their neighbors is important in understanding this cycle. He suggests that:*

> in their peculiar theology as well as in their unusual social, economic and political institutions the Mormons sought to establish a monistic rather than a pluralistic community whose orientation would be entirely religious . . . But in so organizing their institutions, the Mormons encompassed and dominated the economic and political aspects of life around them, thus running counter to the more individualistic orientation of other 19th century Americans. The collective aspects of their culture go far to explain both the unique success they achieved in community building and the consistently recurring conflict with non-Mormons in New York, Ohio, Missouri and Illinois.

Nauvoo, located in western Illinois, was colonized in what proved to be the last attempt to create "Zion" in the Midwest. Within five years it became one of the largest cities in Illinois, but peace and prosperity there were short-lived. The beginning of the secret practice of plural marriage by Joseph Smith and other church leaders led to internal dissension, while political difficulties, militarism, economic solidarity, and religious fanaticism resulted in continued opposition by their non-Mormon neighbors. The destruction of an opposition press in Nauvoo led to the arrest and murder of Joseph Smith and his brother Hyrum in June 1844. When the community continued to thrive and grow, irate Illinois neighbors demanded that the Mormons leave the region.

The death of Joseph Smith was both functional and dysfunctional for the Mormon cause. In the eyes of his followers Smith became a martyr, and they viewed his death as an analogy to the life and death of Jesus. In death, Smith increased his charismatic authority, but disputes as to how to pass on this charisma also arose. Weber (1968:55) says, "Conflict between the charisma of office or of hereditary status with personal charisma is a typical process in many historical situations."

---

*Marvin S. Hill, "The Rise and Maturation of the Early Mormon Kingdom of God," in *Utah A Cooperative History,* Chapter Seven, now in preparation for publication by Brigham Young University Press. Projected date, Summer 1976.

In the Mormon situation Brigham Young claimed authority based on office, while others promoted hereditary claims for Smith's young son. Followers of Young moved to Utah and have become known as Mormons, the subject of this paper. Those opposed to polygamy and supporting hereditary claims remained in the Nauvoo area and became the other major inheritor of the charismatic legacy of Joseph Smith. Claims based on personal charisma were promoted by James Strange among others, but the groups organizing around such leaders were not successful.

Under the leadership of Brigham Young, the Mormons were determined to colonize an area in which they would be the first settlers, thus ensuring their right to practice their social and religious beliefs. The decision was made to settle somewhere in the Rocky Mountains, and they began to move westward across Iowa in February 1846. After delays occasioned by inadequate preparation, inclement weather, and the furnishing of a battalion of 500 men to aid in the Mexican War campaign to take California, the advance pioneer company completed their journey to the valley of the Great Salt Lake on July 24, 1847, and established the initial colony of their Great Basin Kingdom in what was then Mexican territory, but which was ceded to America, in the Treaty with Mexico in February, 1848.

Brigham Young and the other leaders were effective colonizers, and within 10 years approximately 100 towns had been established in Utah, with outlying colonies in California, Nevada, Idaho, and Wyoming. Missionary work continued in many parts of the world, and a steady stream of converts, mainly from the British Isles and northern Europe, poured into the Great Basin, resulting in expanding colonization. By the time of Brigham Young's death in 1877, approximately 300 colonies had been established, primarily in Utah, Idaho, and Arizona.

The gold rush to California in 1849 diminished their isolation, and the establishment of the Territory of Utah, as a result of the Compromise of 1850, terminated their political independence. Brigham Young was named to be governor of the Territory, but a series of conflicts with territorial officials plus the public announcement and defense of the practice of plural marriage in 1852 led to widespread opposition to the Mormons. Territorial difficulties increased resulting in the army being ordered to Utah to quell a reported rebellion and to install a non-Mormon governor in 1857–58. After almost a year of military resistance, the Mormons submitted to the political sovereignty of the federal government but continued to practice their theocratic domination of local government, their economic solidarity, and plural marriage. They proclaimed that they had established the Kingdom of God on earth, which kingdom commanded their first loyalty. Millenialism and eschatological predictions inspired loyalty to their church leaders despite governmental threats and opposition. The joining of the Union Pacific and Central Pacific Railroads in Northern Utah in 1869 signaled the completion of the nation's first transcontinental railroad and emphasized the end of Mormon isolation.

Territorial officials, intent on ending Mormon theocratic political power as well as the practice of plural marriage, used Congressional laws to disenfranchise Mormon voters and to disincorporate the church as a legal institution by 1889. Facing the loss of all church property and the legal existence of their institution, the church leaders finally capitulated and announced the end of polygamy in a manifesto issued in September 1890. They also renounced active political involvement as a church and encouraged the members to align themselves with the national political parties. These actions resulted in presidential amnesty, restoration of property and voting rights, and finally admission of Utah as a state on January 4, 1896.

Official action came more easily than individual compliance, and it was many years before the Mormons were regarded as loyal citizens. During the twentieth century, however, the church has become the epitome of patriotic Americanism. Mormons have served in the cabinet under Presidents Eisenhower and Nixon, and George Romney made an abortive run for the office of President in 1964. Being a Mormon no longer automatically disqualifies one from seeking and gaining high political office. Apparently they are no longer considered to be a "peculiar people" but are in the mainstream of American life.

The Mormon Family—Historical Developments

It has been asserted that all utopian movements have experimented with the family unit. Though Mormonism was utopian in spirit, as various experiments in communal living testify, it did not begin with a fully developed theoretical or theological blueprint for changing the family. In fact, the Mormon experiment with polygamy and the subsequent emphasis on the family as a divine unit did not appear until the movement was well under way.

There was nothing especially distinctive about early Mormon families. They tended to be large, close-knit, hard-working, and reli-

383

giously oriented. They reflected the social origins of the converts from Ohio, Pennsylvania, New York, Upper Canada, and the manufacturing, shipping, and mining centers of Great Britain.

Ellsworth's (1951) study of Mormon origins reveals that most of the early converts were proselytized by relatives and friends and came primarily from towns and cities rather than the frontier, as has often been assumed. A considerable number of the important leaders in the church came from New England stock, including the Smiths, Brigham Young, Heber C. Kimball, and Wilford Woodruff. Most were of the working class; farmers, unskilled and semiskilled laborers. Only a few were ministers or doctors.

The duty to gather to Zion and the unpopularity of the church often separated new converts from their family of orientation. Many sought to replace such ties within the developing structure of the church. By the middle of the Nauvoo period (1839–46) the family was welded to the core of Mormon theology, involving concepts of (1) the eternal family, (2) the extended family by adoption, (3) the patriarchal family, and (4) the polygamous family.

The Eternal Family

The family has long been recognized by religious and secular thought as a basic, if not the basic, institution of society. In Mormon doctrine, however, the family became the basic social organization in the eternal Kingdom of God.

Mormons assert that man is a dual being composed of a spirit body and a physical body, and that God was and is the literal father of the spirit in a pre-earth life called the pre-existence. Thus, God is not the creator of the spirit being but the *literal father* in the *same sense* that earthly fathers are the procreators of physical bodies. The Mormon poetess, Eliza R. Snow (born 1804, married polygamously first to Joseph Smith and later to Brigham Young), illustrated this Mormon belief when she wrote the words to what is now a favorite Mormon hymn:

> In the heavens are parents single?
> No, the thought makes reason stare.
> Truth is reason, truth eternal
> Tells me I've a mother there. [Mormon Hymnal:138]

This concept of a "Mother in Heaven" has little practical significance in the doctrine of the Mormon Church, but it is illustrative of the isomorphism that exists in the Mormon mind between the family in this earth life and the expected life after death.

In the Mormon view of man, not only is he a spirit child of God, but he is capable of achieving Godhood himself. In the process of becoming a God, a man must enter into the "new and everlasting covenant of marriage" by which he and his wife or wives will be married for all eternity and will have the privilege and duty of procreating spirit children throughout eternity even as God procreated us. Thus, man may become a god when he learns to organize a world and can people it with his own spirit children. Mormons call this celestial marriage, and *only* faithful members of the church who can gain authorization from priesthood leaders to enter the sacred temples, which have been built for solemnizing such ordinances, are so married.

To qualify for participation in temple marriage, one must be a member of the church in good standing and believe in the charismatic authority of the church. Some of the more important behavioral expectations are sexual purity, payment of tithing (10 per cent of gross income paid to the church), and obedience to the "Word of Wisdom," which requires abstaining from the use of tea, coffee, alcohol, and tobacco. It should come as no surprise that less than half of the membership of the church participate in this ordinance. Anything less than a temple marriage, however, is seen by many church members as failure, and entrance to the temple is one of the most effective sanctions the church has to exert control over its members. Mormons see life on this earth as a steppingstone to eventual Godhood and is essential for two basic reasons: (1) to gain a physical body, and (2) as a test of their willingness to obey God's commandments. According to Mormon teaching there are millions of spirit children of God who are waiting their chance to come to this earth in their continuing quest for Godhood. Brigham Young (1925:305) said:

> There are multitudes of pure and holy spirits waiting to take tabernacles (bodies), now what is our duty . . . to prepare tabernacles for them, to take a course that will not tend to drive those spirits into the families of the wicked, where they will be trained in wickedness, debauchery, and every species of crime. It is the duty of every righteous man and woman to prepare tabernacles for all the spirits they can.

Such doctrines at the heart of Mormon theology have a compelling impact on the modern Mormon family and account for some of its peculiar characteristics such as attitudes toward birth control and abortion.

The Extended Family

According to Mormon theology, the organizational structure of heaven is the extended family-kinship network. Closely tied to this concept is the Mormon practice of extending and unifying one's family through sealing ordinances in the temple for members of the family who did not have the opportunity to embrace Gospel during their lifetime. This "work for the dead," as it is called, is based on the belief that only by being "born of the water and the spirit," that is, baptized and confirmed a member of the Church of Jesus Christ, can one gain exaltation in the Celestial World and have the opportunity to be in God's presence and "become as He is." Since most of the human race has lived and died without a knowledge of the "true church," Mormons are taught that it is their obligation to seek out the names of their dead ancestors and to act as proxy for them by going to the temple and experiencing baptism and other sacred ordinances in the name of deceased relatives. This program has resulted in the building of over a dozen temples in various parts of the earth and the development of one of the greatest and most extensive genealogical library systems in the world. It has also resulted in extended family organizations for the promotion of genealogical research.

An interesting development of this extended family concept occurred early in Mormon history when leading men began adopting others to be a part of their extended family. Since many people had lost contact with their own families because of joining the unpopular movement, and since it was believed that church members would soon be the governing officials of Christ's millenial kingdom, it seemed to be a desirable thing to regain family ties within the church through adoption. Thus, Brigham Young, in addition to his own 56 children, had many more by adoption, usually adults. These adoptive family relationships served as a nucleus for groups migrating to Utah and in cooperative efforts colonizing the Great Basin.

The Patriarchal Family

The Mormon family, whether polygamous or monogamous, was patriarchal in nature. Following the Old Testament pattern was characteristic of the Mormons and is reflective of American religious thought of the time.

Every man is expected to hold some office in the Mormon priesthood and to preside over his family. The wife is to be subject to her husband "as he is subject to God." Thus, while the father is expected to preside and rule in the family, that rule should be based on religious principles.

The Polygamous Family

The concept of eternal marriage was closely tied to the practice of polygamy, or technically, polygyny. The practice was begun secretly by Joseph Smith and other church leaders as early as 1842, and probably earlier, and was based on the concept that the same God who had approved the Old Testament prophets who had many wives had revealed this principle to his modern prophet, Joseph Smith, with the command that the practice be instituted among the faithful and deserving Saints. Since polygamy remained secret until the public announcement in 1852, it is difficult to describe it in accurate detail. However, there is ample evidence that Joseph Smith married a number of wives before he was killed in 1844, and that Brigham Young and other leaders continued and enlarged the practice.

Since plural marriage in Nauvoo was clandestine, the church leaders denied the practice on several occasions when asked about such marriages. As late as 1850, representatives of the church in foreign lands continued to deny the doctrine and practice of polygamy. After the Mormons left Nauvoo, however, and began their epic trek to the valley of the Great Salt Lake, this practice could no longer be hidden from the membership of the church, but it was not until they were established in Utah that the practice was publicly announced and defended.

Some leaders in Nauvoo refused to accept the practice as inspired of God and asserted that Joseph Smith was a "fallen prophet." Opposition to the practice of polygamy was one of the reasons for the foundation of the Reorganized Church of Jesus Christ of Latter-day Saints in 1860.*

One of the most prominent reasons given for the institution of polygamy was the need for "righteous" men to bring as many children into this world as possible, and in order to do this, many wives were needed. It was also claimed that there were more women than men in the church at that time because women were more receptive to religious convictions than men. These women, from the Mormon point of view, needed protection and help on this earth, and their eternal salvation

---

*The practice of polygamy not only led to a major schism resulting in the RLDS, but it has led to numerous defections of small groups, since the Manifesto. These latter groups refuse to give up the practice and regard the Mormon Church as having apostatized from the true faith.

depended on their having a celestial marriage; thus it was a sacred duty for qualified men to take extra wives. This claim is subject to question since census reports of Utah Territory list more men to women in each decade.* However, in some communities there were more marriageable women than men. Some of the plural marriages were no doubt entered into in a spirit of charity.

Orson Pratt, an early Mormon theologian who was chosen by Brigham Young to make a defense of polygamy at the time of the public announcement, asserted that God would need plural wives to procreate all his spirit children. He also argued, and many Mormons have since concurred, that Jesus Christ himself must have been married. Just as Jesus needed to be baptized to set a perfect example for men to follow, the Mormons reasoned, he would need to be married in the celestial way, which presupposed polygamy. Pratt suggested that the miracle of turning water to wine at Cana was the celebration of Jesus' own marriage. Although the New Testament does not directly support this claim, Pratt argued:

> One thing is certain, there were several holy women that greatly loved Jesus—such as Mary, and Martha her sister, and Mary Magdalene; and Jesus greatly loved them, and associated with them much; and when he arose from the dead, instead of first showing himself to his chosen witnesses, the Apostles, he appeared first to Mary Magdalene. Now it would be very natural for a husband in the resurrection to appear first to his own dear wife, and afterwards show himself to his other friends (Young 1954:37–38).

While such arguments powerfully influenced and continue to influence Mormon thought, there is little wonder that the Christian world regarded the Mormons as being heretical. Eliza R. Snow (born 1804) wrote in her journal that among other things the practice of polygamy led to an elevation of character and "was also instrumental in producing a more perfect type of manhood mentally and physically, as well as in restoring human life to its former longevity." (Snow, 1971:129–30) She was, no doubt, alluding to the accounts of the Old Testament patriarchs who lived to be hundreds of years old. Heber C. Kimball (1858) made similar claims when he wrote:

---

*The U.S. Census Compendium records the following statistics for Utah Territory:

	Male	Female
1850	6,020	5,310
1860	20,178	19,947
1870	44,121	42,665
1880	74,509	69,454
1890	110,463	97,442

I would not be afraid to promise a man who is sixty years of age, if he will take the counsel of brother Brigham and his brethren, that he will renew his age. I have noticed that a man who has but one wife, and is inclined to that doctrine, soon begins to wither and dry up, while a man who goes into plurality looks fresh, young and sprightly. Why is this? Because God loves that man, and because he honors his work and word. Some of you may not believe this; but I not only believe it—I know it. For a man of God to be confined to one woman is small business; for it is as much as we can do now to keep up under the burdens we have to carry; and I do not know what we should do if we had only one wife apiece.

All such explanations and justifications are "after the fact," however, and the official position of the Mormon Church is that Joseph Smith began the practice because it was a revealed commandment of God. Religious conviction appears to be central to the acceptance of the practice.

As has been stated, polygamy had been practiced from at least 1842 but did not really get under way until after 1847 when the Mormons entered the Salt Lake Valley. Mormon polygamy differed from polygamy in other cultures in that it developed rapidly with little or no chance for the usual norms and other institutions of society to appear and regulate this custom. As a result, Mormon polygamy was not circumscribed by a set of generalized norms as is the case in other cultures allowing for polygamous marriages. There was no limit—formal or informal—on the number of wives a man might have or any strictly prescribed method of gaining extra wives.

The patterns of housing one's wives were varied. Some families lived under one roof, while others favored separate homes for each wife. At other times the families were spread throughout the city or even over the thousands of square miles of the Great Basin. The grandfather of a Mormon social scientist claimed he could "catch any streetcar in Salt Lake City and arrive *home*." Sometimes a man only visited his wives in the outlying regions often enough to bless his newest child and get another one started.

Theoretically, all of the wives in a family were to be social equals; however, in practice, the first wife was usually the most powerful because she was the only *legal* wife. She was also supposed to give her permission before her husband married other wives. Young's (1954) study indicates that in the case in which the man took several wives, he often continued to consult the first wife about subsequent additions but did not feel the need of consulting his other wives on the subject. If the first wife had a more powerful legal position vis-à-vis the law, the second or latest wife often had a position of power relating to her youth, beauty, or the romance of the courtship.

There was no structural demand such as sororal polygamy that specified the categories from which plural wives should be chosen. Though he says his records are limited, Young indicated that about one-fifth of the men had married sisters. Even more unusual, Ivins (1956:235) reports:

> John D. Lee gave the names of his nineteen wives, but modestly explained that "as I was married to old Mrs. Woolsey for her soul's sake, and she was nearly sixty years old when I married her, I never considered her really as a wife. . . . That is the reason I claim only eighteen true wives." (Mrs. Woolsey was the mother of two of his wives.)

Apparently immigrant girls or domestics or other such girls were likely to become a source of plural wives. An incident from the life of Apostle John W. Taylor illustrates this probability. His son Samuel Taylor, remembering a certain Christmas, related:

> Father was completely happy with these occasions with his family, except for one small thing. Mother had a hired girl who was surly, not very smart, and was ugly as a mud fence.
> "Nellie, why in heaven's name do you keep this scarecrow? Why don't you get a better girl?" "Because, John," my mother said with a bright smile, "you might marry her" (1972:10).

On the other hand, the belief in the "principle" was strong enough that some women took the initiative in forming polygamous unions.

Studies of Mormon polygamy by Young (1954), Ivins (1956), and Anderson (1937), indicate that during the 50-year period that polygamy was practiced, about 10 to 15 per cent of the eligible males were polygamous. Ivins' (1956:233) study reveals that

> of 1,784 polygamists, 66.3% married only one extra wife, another 21.2% were three-wife men, and 6.7% went so far as to take four wives. This left a small group of polygamists of less than 6% who married five or more women. The typical polygamist, far from being the insatiable male of popular fable, was a dispassionate fellow, content to call a halt after marrying one extra wife required to assure him of his salvation.

Of those who chose to have 5 or more wives, Brigham Young is the most prominent. He probably had at least 27 wives, 16 of whom bore him a total of 56 children. Heber C. Kimball, Young's first counselor, is said to have had at least 35 wives, but there were so many different arrangements that the term "wife" requires definition before totals can be determined.

Arrington (1958:152) argues that church pressure was the strongest motive for practicing polygamy. The coincidence of a rise in the rate of polygamous marriages and periodic religious "reformations" are cited. These reformations generally took place when the Mormons were threatened economically.

How did polygamy work? According to Young (1954:57), 53 per cent, or more than half of the cases examined, were either "highly success-ful" or reasonably successful. One-fourth of them were only moderately successful, and only 23 per cent rated as having considerable or severe conflict. He also found that there "was . . . a positive correlation of the practice of plural marriage and higher economic status." The relation-ship between polygamy and higher economic status is typical of other societies that practice plural marriage.

In theory, polygamous families were supposed to be ruled over by a patriarchal father. However, Young (1954) found that many of the women had considerable power in the home, especially in regard to the rearing of the children. In many cases, the husband was not physically present for much of the year, and the women were forced to take a rather independent, self-confident stance. Frontier living, the demands of the church on a man's time, and the need for equal interaction with his families tended to remove the man in some degree from the home. He did not exert the day-by-day influence on wife and children that his theology and his Western European cultural heritage would suggest. Polygamy, moreover, permitted an intelligent, ambitious woman to marry and bear children to fulfill her religious-social role as a woman and still allowed her some freedom to pursue a career (Arrington, 1972).

Do Mormons still practice polygamy? The answer is yes and no. In 1890, after great pressure from the federal government, Wilford Wood-ruff, the President of the Church, issued the Manifesto announcing the end of the practice of polyagmy in the Mormon Church. The real target of the government appears to have been the Mormon religious-political control of the Utah Territory. Polygamy provided a convenient "moral" issue around which anti-Mormon sentiment could be galvanized. Many of the Mormon leaders were either driven underground or jailed as a result of the Edmunds Act of 1882, which prohibited both polygamy and unlawful cohabitation. Because polygamy was so much more difficult to prosecute than unlawful cohabitation, most of the convictions of Mormon polygamists were for the lesser offense. U.S. Marshals conducted raids called "cohab hunts" in which over 1,000 polygamists were arrested and imprisoned, causing some Mormons to establish colonies in Mexico and Canada. Enforcement of the Edmunds-Tucker Act of 1887 threatened to destroy the power of the Mormon Church as a vital economic-political force. When the main goal of the government was accomplished, prosecution of polygamists declined and was winked at in some cases. Even after 1890 some polygamous marriages were solemnized by the Mormon Church, and President Joseph F. Smith and other polygamists lived openly with their wives. The Mormon Church leaders were forced to issue a second Manifesto in 1904 forbidding plural marriages to be solemnized anywhere in the church even if it were not a violation of the law of the land. However, those who were already married continued to live with their wives.

While the church has never renounced the doctrine of polygamy, those who are found practicing it are excommunicated from the church. There have been several groups that, while not officially members of the Mormon Church, are fringe members of the Mormon subculture who have continued or re-established the practice of polygamy. Polygamists in Short Creek, Arizona, raided by a large body of Arizona law-enforcement officers in 1953, are a good example. Other sporadic attempts have been made by state or local governments to wipe out the last traces of polygamy. There is, however, little support for "cohab hunts" now. In fact, if a grand jury is called to consider a few cases of polygamy or cohabitation, the public officials face hard questioning about the spending of the public's tax money on such trivial matters. Another method used by the polygamists to avoid arrest is the "flood of the welfare roles" approach. If a man practicing polygamy is prosecuted and placed in jail, his wives quit their jobs, and the whole clan goes on welfare. This can have a profound effect on the budgets of local governments and may be one reason why the practice of polygamy is not likely to die out in the Mormon subculture.

Although the Mormon Church no longer allows the practice of polygamy in terms of cohabitation, two situations remain that are polygamous in intent. First, if a Mormon couple is married in the temple, and the wife dies, the husband may marry another wife in the temple for time and eternity, which is a second celestial marriage. She is regarded as a "second" wife joining a polygamous eternal family unit. Second, if a man has only a legal and not a temple "divorce" from a woman, he may marry another woman in the temple. Since Mormons see the temple ceremony as an eternal marriage, the man is in effect a polygamist. The church, however, would feel that he would be committing adultery if he tried to cohabit with his first wife while legally divorced from her.

This view of eternal marriage does have one unfortunate consequence. If a woman is married to a man for eternity and her husband dies, she may have a difficult time finding an orthodox Mormon man who will marry her. The doctrine teaches that in the eternity she would belong to her first husband, as would all of her children, even though they might be fathered by her second husband. Few orthodox Mormon men will deny themselves the right to their own wives and children in eternity. This is especially difficult for a devout young Mormon widow, for she feels she must marry an active Mormon in order to find happiness in a second marriage. In recent years, there seems to be some sentiment among church leaders to modify this doctrine.

However, the practice left its mark on the church. Those who have polygamous ancestors are proud of this fact and see it as a mark of honor and loyalty. The practice of polygamy also seems to have increased the family orientation of the subculture and made the Mormon religion more family oriented than most. There remains some bitterness in families that can be traced to the practice. The family of the first wife may not recognize the family of subsequent wives as legitimate heirs to the family name or fortune. It also seems to have created a certain looseness in the marriage system. Some rather strange relationships were formed, and for many years there was a kind of marriage underground. In some ways this may help to account for a higher divorce rate in the Mormon subculture than one might expect.

THE MORMON FAMILY TODAY

In many, perhaps most, ways the Mormon family of today resembles the stereotyped white, middle-class American family. The outstanding differences are the attitudes Mormons have about their families and the extension of family life into the hereafter. Other outstanding features include larger family size, low divorce rates (for temple marriages), relative importance of parent-child relationship, the Church Family Home Evening, and perhaps a greater stress on sexual "purity" than is found in the general population.

Household and Its Members

The typical Mormon household is the *nuclear family*. So basic is this unit in the Mormon subculture that other living units are regarded with some suspicion. Single parent households are generally regarded as temporary units, and unmarried adults are the objects of concern because they are apparently not forming an eternal family unit. Failure to marry is not merely a matter of personal choice but hints at disobedience to the commandments of God. Marriage to a "good Mormon" and not marriage per se is the prime value. Those who do not find an "active" Latter-day Saint to fall in love with are cautioned to remain single, with the promise that in the millennium a suitable "righteous" partner can be obtained. Christensen (1965), in a study of 50 elderly Mormon couples, found that perhaps the greatest sadness they felt was the failure of some of their children to marry a "good Mormon" in the temple in spite of the fact that 70.1 per cent of their children had married in the temple.

Hagerty (1961) found that the divorced person in the Mormon Church is regarded with apprehension. This is especially true of those married in the temple who felt especially guilty about being divorced. Many of them expressed a belief that they should be more concerned than other people about being divorced because the breakup of a temple marriage was a greater failure than a "regular" marriage. Another problem is that the breakup of a temple marriage generally carries the stigma of sexual misconduct whether or not extramarital sex was involved in the rupture of the marriage.

Fertility, Contraception, and Illegitimacy

A high fertility rate is one of the outstanding features of the Mormon family. Mormons take very literally and seriously the biblical injunction to multiply and replenish the earth. The official church position seems to allow for little acceptance of birth control. An official letter issued in 1969 seemed to allow for child spacing and consideration for the physical and mental health of the women in making such a decision, but it also suggested that those practicing birth control would "reap disappointment by and by." Self-control was suggested as the only acceptable means of birth control. Studies spanning two decades (Moss, 1949; Peterson, 1971) suggest a rather consistent pattern of contraception in young Mormon families. The studies used rather different samples, but they suggest that between 70 and 80 per cent of the young couples sampled were practicing birth control. Of this group, around 50 per cent were using artifical means, especially the pill. It is interesting to note that the major justifications stated for practicing birth control is the protection of the wife's physical health (86.5 per cent) and the wife's mental health (76.6 per cent). The third most accepted reason was spacing of children (44.8 per cent). It would appear that when the Mormon couple decides to practice birth control, they are more concerned with its effectiveness than with doctrine. However, the reasons given for using birth-control methods conform to the church's officially stated position (Peterson, 1971).

As for other antifertility measures, the church has officially opposed any liberalization or modification of Utah's restrictive laws concerning abortion and sterilization. The First Presidency of the Church says that in some "rare cases" (rape, danger to health or life of the mother) abortion may be acceptable. However, they also say, "Abortion must be considered one of the most revolting and sinful practices of this day . . ." (*Priesthood Bulletin*, 1973 p. 1). Sixty-four per cent of the Mormon college students interviewed felt that abortion should *not* be legalized, with only 14 per cent approving such legalization (Peterson, 1971). These students appeared to be even more restrictive than the official position of their leaders because only 76 per cent agreed to abortion to save the life of the mother, and 38 per cent would agee with abortion when pregnancy results from rape (Peterson, 1971). These studies suggest that young couples are somewhat more liberal than their leaders in the area of contraception but more conservative in regard to abortion.

As a result, of course, Mormons have high fertility. DeHart (1941) found that the single best prediction of fertility rates in several intermountain states was the proportion of Mormons in the area examined.

Education, and the combined variables of urbanization and industrialization, have combined the world over to produce smaller families. Even the emphasis of Mormon theology has not eliminated the impact of these variables acting on the Mormon subculture. DeHart (1941) found that urbanization had an impact on the birth rate among Mormons in the urban counties of Utah, but they still had relatively large families. A more recent study by Pritcher and Peterson (1972) indicate some difference in urban-rural Mormon fertility rate, but their data show that the Mormon fertility rate remained high in some urban centers. For the Cohort 25–34 years of age in 1960, the urban Utah Mormon mean number of children was 3.55, while the overall mean family size for urban Utah that includes a substantial non-Mormon population was 2.84

children. Mormons living on the West Coast were compared to those living in Utah and other intermountain areas. While the mean family size decreased for all regions, the family size of Mormons living on the West Coast was 2.83 children per family. In 1940 the mean family size for Mormons in these areas was roughly equal at about 4.6 children per family, so that the last two decades found Utah Mormons decreasing the size of their family by about one child, while Mormons in the West Coast decreased their families by nearly two children (Mauss, 1972b). Though West Coast Mormons still have larger families on the average than their neighbors, life in West Coast urban centers seems to have more effect on fertility rate than life in intermountain urban centers. Merrill and Peterson (1972) report that the more mobile the family was geographically, the more children they had. While this surprised the authors, it does seem consistent with data presented earlier that relate high ambition and church membership as well as high ambition and the necessity to seek satisfactory employment outside the region. Also interesting was the finding that those who were converts to the church had larger families than those born in the church. Not surprising at all were data showing those married in the temple had larger families than those married outside the temple. Nelson (1952) showed that the higher the education, the smaller the family size, but that occupation or social class did not make nearly so much difference. It would appear that while many social influences are contributing to decreasing family size, Mormons are likely to continue having more children than other American groups. Not only the doctrine concerning the desirability of having children, but the negative attitudes toward most forms of birth control per se seem likely to support this conclusion.

Divorce

Even though the Mormon Church strongly opposes divorce, Utah is above the national average in its divorce rate (Christensen, 1972). Figures quoted by Christensen report:

Divorce (Including Annulments)
Per 1,000 Population

	UTAH	UNITED STATES
1940	2.7	2.0
1950	3.1	2.6
1960	2.4	2.2
1968	3.3	2.9

Christensen (1972:21) clarifies the influence of the church somewhat and reports the following divorce percentages: "Civil marriages, 13.4; Latterday Saint non-temple marriages, 10.2; non-Mormon religious marriages, 5.5; and Latter-day Saint temple marriages, 1.8 percent divorced."

Mitchell and Peterson (1972), studying divorce in 1,000 couples from four family histories covering the period from 1820 to 1960, report some interesting data on divorce among the Mormons. Of those married in the temple, 16.0 per cent had divorced, while 29.4 per cent not married in the temple had ended their marriage. This figure is somewhat higher than that found in other studies. A recent study by Cannon and Steed (1972) found the divorce rate considerably less than Mitchell and Peterson had found. In an extensive study of 548 couples married in 1955 and contacted in 1968, Cannon and Steed report only 2.8 per cent of those married in the temple were divorced. Where both partners were Latter-day Saints but not married in the temple, 12.3 per cent were divorced, but when only one of the partners was Latter-day Saints, 19.4 per cent were divorced.

These findings suggest that a temple marriage is significantly related to a low probability of divorce. This seems related to a statement of church-related values. Mitchell and Peterson (1972) report that high residential mobility, high education, and a large number of children are to be correlated with a low divorce rate for Mormon families. This seems to reflect the interesting relationship between religious orthodoxy, high educational aspirations, divorce, and large families found in the Mormon subculture. A low divorce rate is suggestive of stability in marriage that may result from couples having much in common before marriage. The strict requirements a person must meet before he or she can be married in the temple is likely to produce more harmony in such marriages than one might find in the general culture. Cannon and Steed (1972:29) also suggest that "it is very possible that individuals who marry in the temple have a very close identification with middle-class values; sobriety, ambition, hard work, family stability, strong religious beliefs, sexual morality, and so forth." Is it just the subscribing to similar values and a dislike of divorce per se that causes the low divorce rate, or are temple marriages actually happier and thus have fewer marriage failures? The data on this subject is limited and fraught with dangers in terms of measurement, but a matched sample of 50 couples married in the temple and 50 not married in the temple showed higher levels of marital satisfaction for those married in the temple (Nuttall, 1959). Women married in the temple were more secure in marriage than those not so married. Couples married in the temple had higher empathy scores than couples not united in the sacred edifice. This suggests that couples married in the temple may take their marriage vows more seriously than others and work to make it a pleasing relationship.

Hagerty (1961:72) found that the couples he interviewed who had been married in the temple and subsequently divorced experienced extreme trauma and stigma. Though he had a small sample,

> All but two indicated either actual attempts at suicide, serious consideration of suicide, or a wish for death as an escape. The central factor dissuading them from this action appears to be a belief that suicide is a greater sin than divorce and that they could not gain by this action.

However, one could not suggest such trauma for all Mormons who divorce, but it does suggest strong forces keeping marriages together that may not be satisfying.

The process of obtaining a "temple divorce" is not completely clear. There are no "canon laws" in the church that specify the conditions under which divorce will be granted. Such cancellations are granted reluctantly and are based on a careful investigation of each individual application by one of the leaders of the church.

Husband and Wife–Authority and Power

The normative authority pattern in Mormon family life is patriarchal. The man has the responsibility to act as leader of his family and officiates in a number of religious functions in the home. Every orthodox male member of the Mormon Church should be ordained to the priesthood at age 12 and from then on should have increasing responsibilities in the church. Mormons believe that the holding of this priesthood is extremely important. The Mormon father who holds this priesthood (as all active members do) performs such important functions in the religious aspects of family life as blessing and naming of children (christening), baptism of children, priesthood ordination of sons, some temple ordinances, and the blessing of sick family members, as well as leading in family prayers at each meal and on other occasions. In fact, almost all of the religious ordinances that a minister or priest might perform for members of other Christian churches is performed by the Mormon father for his family if he is "worthy." This activity, in addition to the Mormon conception of the eternal family unit, would seem to make the male dominant in the family and much more influential than his wife.

Christopherson (1956) found that the vast majority of Mormon couples believed that patriarchal authority is a divine endowment and is necessary, in this life as well as in eternity, as a system of family government. However, the majority of the husbands and wives felt that "the husband's authority operates chiefly in matters pertaining to religion" (p. 139). Christopherson (1963:151) makes the conclusion in another article that "the Mormon family has always exercised democracy in its family relations to a very high and pronounced degree." One interesting case that Christopherson (1956:326) reported indicated a curious discrepancy between the norm of male power and the principle in practice as follows:

> Typical of such instances was an interview with one family in which the woman had just finished expressing a point of view to the effect that in her family the husband and father was regarded as the ultimate seat of recourse with respect to most, if not to all, family disputes. Almost in the same breath, she interrupted her husband to correct him with an air of finality with regard to a point of Church doctrine.

Some Mormon women are fond of Eph. 5:22–24, which is interpreted to mean that wives need submit themselves only when the husband is acting "righteously" and that the wife can make such a judgment!

The findings on the actual balance of power in the Mormon home is somewhat contradictory. The power of the Mormon male remained high even when laboratory circumstance made him appear ineffective (Christenson, 1970). A study of Mormon women (Wise and Carter, 1965) indicated a preference for "traditional" rather than "companionship" marriages. Mote (1961) found Mormons accepting of "companionate" marriages as a general norm but had "traditional" expectations for their own marriage.

On the other hand, Black (1969) observed that most Mormon males in her study saw their relationship as equalitarian, with perhaps some slight male dominance. When compared to Catholics or Protestants, however, Mormons were not more "traditional" in their view of family ideology (patriarchal authority; Cannon, 1967). McBride (1963) found that the greater the activity in the Mormon Church, the more equalitarian the responses toward expected husband-wife roles for high school girls. We may conclude that while the Mormon male has authority in his home in certain functions, such authority does not always seem to increase his power in marriage. Thus, while there may be some patriarchal Mormon marriages based on Church teachings, these are by no means typical.

What about Women's Liberation? How has it affected Mormon women? Although Wise and Carter (1965) found that nearly 40 per cent of Mormon women in their sample were working, nearly one-fourth of them wished they were not employed. Church officials have long stressed that women should not work outside the home, especially when there are young children to care for. This may account for the ambivalence about working outside the home for these women. While many Mormon women might be attracted to elements of the Women's Liberation Movement, some Mormon women believe it to be antichild. The importance of children in Mormon life can hardly be overstressed. It is interesting in light of the fact that Mormons have always encouraged the higher education of their women, that there may be a fundamental ambivalence in the Mormon subculture about using the full potentials of their women.

The doctrines and practice of the church appear to place women in a second-class status. For example, the ultimate aim of the Mormons in their notion of eternal progression is that of becoming a God, but there is no expectation that women will become Gods. However, if they are "righteous" enough, they will become Goddesses, which in Mormon doctrine means being one of the wives of a God with whom they will procreate spirit children. Does this mean eternally barefoot and pregnant? This notion is not always accepted among educated Mormon women. As one prominent Mormon matron put it, "I cannot conceive of eternally conceiving." Many Mormon women have expressed the opinion that the inspiration for Women's Liberation is none other than Satan, the Devil himself. An even more revealing attitude, however, is found in an issue of *Dialogue: A Journal of Mormon Thought,* which was devoted to the subject of "Women's Rights and the Mormon Church." The group of women who produced this issue, half in jest, referred to themselves as the "L.D.S. Cell of Women's Liberation." These women are wives of professional Mormon men living in Boston and are college graduates, with several holding graduate degrees. They average 3.6 children each and remarked that "of the four children born to group members this year, one increased the family's children to five, one to six and one to eight." In this most liberal group of Mormon women, the articles written generally seem to conclude that a woman's place is in the home (Bushman, 1971:5–87). To say that the Women's Lib Movement has had no impact on the Mormon women would be unfair, but to say that it has had a great impact would be an exaggeration. It may be significant that the Equal Rights Amendment was easily defeated in the Utah State legislature early in 1975, and that Mormon Church opposition to the amendment was considered by supporters to have been the primary reason for its defeat.

Kinship Network and Extended Family Relationships

Mormons see the extended, eternal family unit as being very important. There are, however, no studies that have clarified the actual extent of extended family interaction. Life in the Mormon subculture convinced the observer that the kinship network must be at least as strong as those found by Sussman (1963), Litwak (1960), or Hill (1965) in other parts of America.

One of the strains on the kinship network in the Mormon subculture comes out of the emphasis on education, coupled with the lack of economic opportunities for highly educated people in Utah. Brown (1961) credited the Mormon emphasis on education with Utah's high ranking in all categories of educational achievement and effort. Studying three rural counties in which the demand for a college-educated person approaches zero, over half of the high school students planned to go to college. He found that parental encouragement is highly related to post high school educational aspirations as was the activity level in the Mormon Church. Of course, the variables of parental encouragement and the influence of the Mormon Church could not be completely untangled. It is a common saying in Utah that its chief export to other states is its highly educated young people.

Why is this so? Nelson (1952), in a study of rural Mormon villages, found that it takes about 40 to 50 years for these settlements to reach the maximum population they can maintain. Ephraim, home of Snow Junior College and a town that was included in both the Brown and Nelson studies "has been exporting practically all of its natural increases since 1900" (Nelson, 1952:148). For some time, the excess population of such small communities could be absorbed by Salt Lake, Ogden, Provo, Orem, Logan, and Tooele, the larger urban centers of Utah. Those leaving these small towns had the highest level of education and aspirations. They, along with their urban counterparts, formed a reservoir of highly educated, ambitious young people who could not enter into the economy of Utah and surrounding area of "Zion" and were therefore forced to leave. This factor has undoubtedly separated families that otherwise would have maintained high levels of interaction. One only needs to associate with Mormons away from "Zion" to recognize that if the economy of Utah and surrounding Mormon enclaves could support it, the population of these areas would double almost overnight. Living among the Mormons, one is much aware of men who have taken substantial cuts in salary and entered less attractive positions solely to return to "Zion" to be near their families. It is interesting to note that while Mormon doctrine indicates that extended family groups will be the social structure of heaven, very few choose or are encouraged to choose such a living arrangement now. The three generational household appears to be no more frequent among Mormons than other Americans.

Socialization

While most American marriages come to be child centered, Mormon marriages often start out child centered. Cook (1966) reported, for example, that 45 per cent of the young married college-student couples had a child within the first year of marriage. These are college-educated people who could be expected to be successful in a birth-control program if they had chosen such a course. This desire for children did not isolate the couples from experiencing crises at the birth of the first child. Marlow (1968) found that Mormon couples experience the same loss of marital satisfaction in at least the early stages of the family life cycle that has been reported among other American couples. This decline in other American marriages is related to some extent with child bearing and rearing, and it would appear that Mormons experience these same problems.

When asked to check their primary concern in married life, Mormon homemakers in Wasatch County (Bacon, 1964:84) indicated their first concern to be "helping your children to have faith in God and to be creatively active in Church." Issues centering around the marital relationship per se were near the bottom of the list of concerns. Kunz (1963) expected to find that Mormons would be more strict in their child rearing than non-Mormons but this was not the case. In fact, in certain social classes, non-Mormons were more strict than Mormons. Mormons were about the same as non-Mormons in timing of toilet training, but later in weaning their children. L.D.S. mothers encouraged their children to begin helping with household tasks earlier, but this could be a function of family size. Kunz concludes that the Mormons did take child rearing seriously. It appears that the prime value of Mormon parents is "proper" socialization in terms of end results rather than in terms of method. They do what they think will be effective in terms of making the child a good Mormon. They are, for the most part, quite willing to accept advice from non-Mormon or Mormon "experts" in the area of child rearing.

McKay, while President of the church (1969) said, "No success in the world can compensate for failure in the family." In this spirit, the church has long provided various organized programs to help *parents* become successful in raising *their* children. Failure, of course, is having a child who is not a "good Mormon." These programs have met with varying degrees of success, but in 1964 the church instituted a program called "family home evenings." Members of the church were urged to meet with their families one evening every week to learn about the gospel. In 1970, Smith told church members that "fathers and mothers who faithfully hold family home evenings and who built family unity in every way possible, fulfill with honor the greatest of all responsibilities—that of parenthood." Larsen (1967) analyzes this as an attempt at constructing family ritual. Mormons had tried to get families interested in such programs before, but never with as much power and authority on the part of the church leaders. A lesson manual was developed, a Sunday School class for training parents was instituted, and the church set aside one night of the week on which it was forbidden to hold any church meetings. This was an especially important concession due to the lay structure of church organization, which required numerous meetings of lay leaders. Laughing at themselves, Mormons have accepted the following definition: "A Mormon is one who is on his way to a meeting, at a meeting, or returning from a meeting." Most members appeared to have tried the program, but its regular practice is far from universal. Interestingly enough, it does not appear to be busy teen-agers who need to "break away" from home who have undermined the program, for Miller (1969) reports that teen-agers express the desire for more regular practice of family home evening than is the practice in their homes.

Adolescence

Since it is well recognized that a restrictive culture can be applied to children more readily than to teen-agers, it is important to examine Mormon success or lack of success with teen-agers. In some areas this question can be answered, but in other areas, drug abuse, for example, the information is only impressionistic. One piece of data to be examined is the church's missionary program. Presently, the church has about 19,000 missionaries in the various missions of the church, ranging from Japan to South Africa. The vast majority (90 per cent) are young men from 19 to 22 years old who have taken this time out of their lives to participate in what is considered a high calling and an honor. They are supported with funds they have saved or through money their parents contribute to them. These young men must meet strict standards of sexual morality, obey the Word of Wisdom, subject themselves to rigid conventions of dress while on the mission, and be willing to go any place the church should call them. That these young men are willing and able to go suggests they have accepted the standards and values of their parents.

A study by Lake (1963) suggests that many Mormon youths are quite willing to accept parental and church guidance in a wide range of behaviors and expectations.

The sexual revolution!—Has it hit the Mormon youth? Hatch (1968) found that somewhere between necking and light petting was the extent of acceptable sex relations before marriage for Brigham Young University students. A study of single men at the University of Utah shows Mormons with less sexual intercourse than non-Mormons. Christenson (1970), in a longitudinal study of sexual attitudes and behavior, found some increase in the percentage of students in the Utah area approving of sexual intercourse before marriage (males, 38 per cent; females, 23.5 per cent). As for actually having sex relations, 35 per cent of the males and 32.4 per cent of the females admitted to the experience. The most dramatic change was that of the females, with only 9.5 per cent admitting to premarital sex relations in the 1958 study. These findings suggest that there is likely a great deal of guilt surrounding sexual behavior in the Mormon subculture. These rates, however, are about half the rate reported by other college students. It appears that the church's stand on sex relations may be supported more in belief than in practice but still exerts a powerful influence on the young members of the church.

The Elderly

Surprisingly, there is practically nothing written on the elderly in the Mormon subculture. The top leaders in the Mormon Church keep their positions until they die. A kind of "date of rank" is important in determining who is president of the Quorum of Twelve Apostles, and the head of this quorum normally becomes president of the church when the current president dies. This seniority system is not followed elsewhere in the church, for young and middle-aged men dominate the leadership positions. It is only impressionistic, but it seems that the elderly, as in other churches, lose their positions and power.

Temple work, which involves participating in sacred dramas and rituals as proxy for the dead, is doctrinally important in the Mormon Church and is a regular source of activity among the elderly, who have looked forward to the day when they could retire and work in the temple. Since most do not receive money for this work, it is not motivated by a desire for income. The gratifications are religious in nature.

Many of the elderly are either not "worthy" or do not find temple work rewarding, so they do not have this outlet. It is difficult for the elderly person who has not been active in the church to be a part of it in his later years. The signs of his former "unworthy" life are all around him, and so he may not be willing to attend church. Recently there have been some centers for the elderly growing up in Utah towns that might fill a need for many non-Mormon or inactive Mormon elderly, although active Mormons also participate in these centers.

CHANGE AND ADAPTATION

As one examines the Mormon subculture, one fact is evident. The future of the Mormon Church and the Mormon family are inexorably welded. While the Mormon family depends on the church for direction and a theological explanation of its function and importance during the early decades of the Mormon movement, one cannot escape the conclusion that the church is dependent on the Mormon family for its very existence. An investigation of temple versus nontemple marriages is an interesting case in point. Throughout this chapter a number of Mormon family behavior patterns as encouraged by church officials have been examined. In *every* case, those married in the temple were much closer to the Mormon official norm than those married elsewhere. Many more cases were examined than can be presented here, but it is quite apparent that the church is dependent on couples married in the temple for most of its support.

What, then, is the major factor influencing couples to be married in the temple. Both Peterson (1969) and Rollins (1958), in examining reasons why Mormons choose the type of marriage ceremony they do, found the influence of the parents to be extremely important. Both of these studies examined only direct influence, however. Peterson found the person's individual religious commitment most strongly related to choosing a temple marriage, but it should be quite apparent that the individual's religious commitment is profoundly affected by the socialization he received from his parents. Apparently the church depends on temple marriages, and these occur in families that stress church activity and such marriages. Mauss (1972b) adds some interesting confirming evidence to this conclusion. Most Mormon young people attend seminary, which is a daily religious class for males and females in conjunction with their high school program. These classes are sponsored by the church education system and employ professional teachers to impart the gospel message to the young. Mauss (1972b:22) says, however:

> I found that respondents who had come from active L.D.S. homes were more likely to be active L.D.S. adults (and to have had missions, etc.) without regard to how much seminary experience they had. On the other hand, those who had come from religiously inactive homes were much more likely to be inactive as adults, again *without regard to seminary experience*.

The implication is clear. The church is dependent on the family for effective socialization of religious attitudes in the coming generation. Family orientation and religion classes on the college level appear to have an interactive effect, producing stronger beliefs in the adult, but here again the primacy of the home must be acknowledged.

The most significant influence on adult religious devoutness was the experience of serving on a mission that was interdependent on home experience. As Mauss (p. 22) concludes, "The major components in the socialization or indoctrination process for Mormon youth are the home and the mission. . . ." It is interesting to note that the mission is almost exclusively a male activity. Whitten (1928) concluded that the church was more effective in reaching its female than its male members. Few would doubt that this insight is also true today, but it appears that the mission experience results in developing more orthodox Mormon men than one might otherwise expect.

Perhaps the second most important factor in the future of the Mormon subculture is the sense of community, especially intimate friendship cycles. Anderson (1968) found Mormons to be rather strongly identified with their church and the Mormon community. The Mormons were more opposed to interfaith marriages than the other groups, and 80 per cent of them claimed that their three best friends were also Mormons. Beckstrand (1971) also found results similar to Anderson in that 80 per cent of the Mormons sampled felt that religiously endogamous marriages were very important, while only 39 per cent of Catholics made similar statements. These seem to indicate strong boundary-maintenance activity among the Mormons as a community.

A factor that seems to deserve more investigation is the matter of intimate community or friendship circles. Allred (1971:48) found a direct correlation between percentage of best friends who are Mormons and acceptance of the Latter-day Saint position on major national issues among teen-agers. He said, "It was found that the more non-Mormon friends the subject had, the more their attitudes were in agreement with national trends towards institutional reform, free and open expression of sex, women's rights for self-expression, military obligation and population." These matters cut to the very core of the life of Mormon families. Mortenson (1972) found that when friends held to the norm that sex with love is permissible, Mormon college students were more likely to have had premarital sex relations. Eighty per cent of the men and 84 per cent of the women had experienced sex relations when these circumstances held. This is considerably in excess of Mormon norms and behaviors reported earlier in this chapter and is inconsistent with temple marriage. If temple marriage is at the very heart of the peculiar Mormon subculture, then the peer group is near this heart. Many Mormons recognize this and wish to live where their children can have Mormon friends. The adults feel they are strong enough to resist the temptations of the world but wonder if their children can resist peer-group pressure to violate the norms of the church.

Smith (1959) found that Mormons living in urban areas were less likely to be active in church attendance than rural Mormons. Urban Mormons were much more likely than rural Mormons to have tea, coffee, or liquor in their homes. Smith (1959:360) predicts that "as Mormons become more urbanized (the current trend) they will become more and more like their non-Mormon neighbors unless Church policies are developed which can change the trend pattern." Mauss (1972a, and b) presents evidence that the attitudes held by Mormons in West Coast cities are substantially less orthodox than those held by their fellow members in Salt Lake City. It would thus appear that factors other than urbanization are at work.

It is contended here that percentage of Mormon friends will be a more important factor than urbanization. The Mormon congregation or ward often forms a community approaching the *gemeinschaft* ideal type presented by Toënnies. Mormons are likely to do business with Mormons when they can and stay within the ward (congregation) if necessary. Because a ward will include a variety of individuals, many primary relationships may be formed even in urban settings. Thus, the Mormon who is active in the church may have a ready-made community that will support him in his practice of the Mormon religion. It is likely, however, as the laws of propinquity apply to courtship, they also apply to the formation of friendships. Thus, as the percentage of Mormons in an area decreases, so does the Mormon percentage of "best friends." Mormons in large urban centers with low density of Mormons would be expected to begin to resemble their non-Mormon neighbors in attitudes and behavior.

The prognosis for Mormonism remaining a distinctive and vital religous group appears to depend on strong families socializing children to believe and on the ability of the church in an urban setting to maintain a network of primary relationships among its members.

Christensen (1972:23), as suggested earlier in this chapter, found a surprisingly high divorce rate in the Mormon subculture, especially those who had not married in the temple. He says:

> There seem to be about five major points of strain in Mormon family culture which are at least partly responsible for the marriage trouble we are experiencing: (1) a pattern of terminal petting; (2) a tendency to marry very young; (3) a guilt-laden premarital sexuality; (4) an unrealistic approach to family size; and (5) an overemphasis upon authoritarian control.

No doubt others could describe stress points in Mormon family culture that differ from those observed by Christensen. Such solutions as more sex education or less emphasis on procreation (Christensen, 1972) are not likely to be adopted by church leaders. Church leaders appear to be aware of problems families face and such programs as Family Home Evening and the creation of social services available to members are among the responses the church has developed. The viability of Mormonism rests on an accurate assessment of strains in the family and the effectiveness of programs that are developed to solve their problems.

REFERENCES

Allred, Garth L. 1971. "A Study of Expressed Attitudes of Selected L.D.S. Youth Regarding Social Trends." Unpublished Masters Thesis, Brigham Young University.

Anderson, C. LeRoy. 1967. "A Preliminary Study of Generational Economic Dependency Orientations." *Social Forces* 45 (June):516–20.

Anderson, Charles H. 1968. "Religious Communality among White Protestant, Catholics and Mormons." *Social Forces* 46 (June):501–08.

Anderson, Nels, 1937. "The Mormon Family." *American Sociological Review* 2 (October):601–08.

Arrington, Leonard J. 1958. *Great Basin Kingdom*. Cambridge, Mass.: Harvard University Press.

————. 1972. "Blessed Damsels: Women in Mormon History." *Dialogue: A Journal of Mormon Thought* 6 (Summer):22–32.

Bacon, Mary R. 1964. "A Comparative Study of Expressive and Instrumental Concerns of Homemakers in Wasatch County." Unpublished paper, Brigham Young University.

Beckstrand, Therald "C". 1971. "Religiously Endogamous and Religiously Exogamous Courtships as Perceived by Male College Students." Unpublished paper, Brigham Young University.

Black, Marybeth R. 1969. "The Relationships between Wives Simfam Relative Effective Power Scores and Husband's Marital Satisfaction." Unpublished paper, Brigham Young University.

Brown, Kenneth J. 1961. "Church Participation as a Factor Associated with the Educational Aspirations of Youth in Three Central Utah Counties." Unpublished paper, Brigham Young University.

Bushman, Claudia Lauper, 1971. "Women in Dialogue: An Introduction." *Dialogue: A Journal of Mormon Thought* 6 (Summer):5–8.

Cannon, John Q. Jr. 1967. "Traditional Family Ideology of University Students." Unpublished paper, Brigham Young University.

Cannon, Kenneth L., and Seymour Steed. 1972. "Relationship between Occupational Level, Religious Commitment, Age of Bride at Marriage, and Divorce Rate for L.D.S. Marriages." In *Developing a Marriage Relationship*. Utah: Brigham Young University Press, pp. 285–92.

Christensen, Harold T. 1972. "Stress Points in Mormon Family Culture." *Dialogue: A Journal of Mormon Thought* 7 (Winter):20–34.

Christensen, H. T. and C. F. Gregg. 1970. "Changing Sex Norms in America and Scandinavia." *Journal of Marriage and the Family* (November):626.

Christensen, Talmage. 1965. "Exploring the Golden Years of Marriage." Unpublished paper, Brigham Young University.

Christenson, Robert A. 1970. "The Effects of Reward and Expert Power on The Distribution of Influence in Mormon Couples." Unpublished paper, Brigham Young University.

Christopherson, Victor A. 1956. "An Investigation of Patriarchal Authority in the Mormon Family." *Marriage and Family Living* 18 (November):328–33.

————. 1963. "Is the Mormon Family Becoming More Democratic?" In Blaine Porter (ed.): *The Latter-day Saint Family*. Salt Lake City, Utah. Deseret Book Company, pp. 317–28.

Cook, Carole, I. C. 1966. "The Crisis of Parenthood as Experienced by L.D.S. Couples with One Child." Unpublished paper, Brigham Young University.

DeHart, William A. 1941. "Fertility of Mormons in Utah and Adjacent States." *American Sociological Review* 6 (December):818–29.

Ellsworth, S. George. 1951. "History of Mormon Missions in the United States and Canada, 1830–1860." Unpublished paper, University of California at Berkeley.

Hagerty, Everett Louis. 1961. "An Exploratory Study of the Effects of the Divorce Process and Post-Divorce Re-Adjustment on the L.D.S. Person." Unpublished paper, Brigham Young University.

Hatch, Gary Lee. 1968. "Patterns of Affection in Dating Approved by L.D.S. Students." Unpublished paper, Brigham Young University.

Hill, Marvin. 1976. Introductory chapter in text on Utah history presently being prepared for publication, David Miller (ed.), Brigham Young University Press.

Hill, Reuben, 1965. "Decision Making and the Family Life Cycle." In E. Shanas and G. Streibs (eds.): *Social Structure and the Family*. Englewood Cliffs, N.J.: Prentice-Hall, pp. 113–39.

Hilton, Jarold A. 1965. "Polygamy in Utah and Surrounding Area Since the Manifesto of 1890." Unpublished paper, Brigham Young University.

Ivins, Stanley S. 1956. "Notes on Mormon Polygamy." *Western Humanities Review* 10 (Summer):224–39.

Kimball, Heber C. 1858. "Temples and Endowments." *Journal of Discourses*, 5:22.

Kunz, Philip. 1963. "Religious Influences on Parental Discipline and Achievement Demands," *Marriage and Family Living* 24 (May):224–25.

———. 1964. "Mormon and Non-Mormon Divorce Patterns." *Journal of Marriage and the Family* 26 (May):211–13.

Lake, Bruce M. 1963. "A Measure of Attitude Change Toward Courtship and Marriage." Unpublished paper, University of Utah.

Larsen, Robert E. 1967. "Factors in the Acceptance and Adoption of Family Home Evening in the L.D.S. Church: A Study in Planned Change. Unpublished Masters Thesis, Brigham Young University.

Litwak, Eugene. 1960. "Occupational Mobility and Extended Family Cohension" *American Sociological Review* 25:9–21.

Marlow, Roy H. 1968. "Development of Marital Dissatisfaction of Mormon College Couples Over the Early Stages of the Family Life Cycle." Unpublished paper, Brigham Young University.

Mauss, Armand L. 1972a. "Moderation in All Things: Political and Social Outlooks of Modern Urban Mormons." *Dialogue: A Journal of Mormon Thought* 7 (Spring):57–64.

———. 1972b. "Saints, Cities, and Secularism: Religious Attitudes and Behavior of Modern Urban Mormons." *Dialogue: A Journal of Mormon Thought* 7 (Summer):8–27.

McBride, Gary P. 1963. "Marriage Role Expectations of Latter-day Saint Adolescents in Utah County." Unpublished paper, Brigham Young University.

McKay, David O. 1969. "Saving the Family." *Improvement Era* (June):2–5.

Merrill, Stan W., and Evan T. Peterson. 1972. "Some Aspects of Family Size: Stress and Utility." Institute of Genealogical Studies: Working Papers, Brigham Young University, Number 4 (August).

Miller, Don LeRoy. 1969. "A Study of Factors which May Influence Attitudes of L.D.S. Teen-agers Towards Family Home Evening." Unpublished paper, Brigham Young University.

Mitchell, Sidney, and Evan T. Peterson. 1972. "A Longitudinal Study of Factors Associated with Divorce Among Mormons." Institute of Genealogical Studies: Working Papers, Brigham Young University.

Mortenson, Ramah P. 1972. "Affectional Attitudes and Behavior Patterns of Selected L.D.S. Students from Universities and Colleges in Utah." Unpublished paper, Brigham Young University.

Moss, Joel J. 1949. "A Comparison of the Attitudes and Practices of Two University Housing Groups of Married Veterans Concerning Family Size and Family Limitations." Unpublished paper, Brigham Young University.

Mote, Herbert I. 1961. "The Wife's Role in the Family: A Comparative Study of Three Educational Levels with a Male and Female Group at Each Level." Unpublished paper, Brigham Young University.

Nelson, Lowry. 1952. *The Mormon Village*. Salt Lake City, Utah: University of Utah Press.

Nuttall, Paul E. 1959. "Comparison of L.D.S. Couples Married in the Temple in Respect to Marital Adjustment, Feelings of Security and Empathy." Unpublished masters thesis, Brigham Young University.

O'Dea, Thomas F. 1957. *The Mormons*. Chicago: University of Chicago Press.

Packer, James D. 1951. "A Study of Fertility Changes in Mormon Society Based on the Use of Genealogical Records." Unpublished paper, University of Utah.

Pennock, John A. 1949. "A Study of the Sexual Attitudes and Behavior of Two Hundred Single College Men." Salt Lake City, Utah: University of Utah Press.

Peterson, Erlend D. 1971. "Attitudes Concerning Birth Control and Abortion as Related to L.D.S. Religiosity of Brigham Young University Students." Unpublished paper. Brigham Young University.

Peterson, Jack W. 1969. "A Study of Selected Family Background Factors Influencing Women to Marry Outside of the L.D.S. Church." Unpublished paper. Brigham Young University.

Pratt, Orson. Defense of Polgamy. (As found in K. Young, *Isn't One Wife Enough?*) New York: Henry Hold & Co. 1954.

Priesthood Bulletin, 1973. Vol. 9. No. 1.

Pritcher, Brian L. and Evan T. Peterson. 1972. "Residential Differentials in Mormon Fertility." Institute of Genealogical Studies: Working Paper, Brigham Young University, Number 1 (October).

Rollins, Boyd C. 1958. "Factors Influencing the Decision of Latter-day Saint Youths Concerning the Selection of a Temple or Non-Temple Type of Marriage Ceremony." Unpublished paper. Brigham Young University.

Smith, Joseph F., Sr. 1917. *The Relief Society Magazine* 4:318.

Smith, Joseph Fielding. 1966. Doctrines of Salvation, 13th ed. Salt Lake City, Utah: Bookcraft.

Smith, Wilford E. 1959. "The Urban Threat to Mormon Norms." *Rural Sociology* 24:355–61.

Snow, Eliza R. 1971 "Sketch of My Life: Reminisances of One of Joseph Smith's Plural Wives." (Ed. Spencer J. Palmer) Brigham Young University Studies 12:129–30.

Sussman, Marvin B. 1963. "The Help Pattern in the Middle Class Family." *American Sociological Review* 18:22–28.

Taylor, Samuel W. 1972. "The Second Coming of Santa Claus: Christmas in a Polygamous Family." *Dialogue: A Journal of Mormon Thought* 7:7–10.

Thomas, W. I., and D. S. Thomas. 1928. *The Child In America*. New York: Knop.

411

Weber, Max. 1968. "The Sociology of Charismatic Authority" In S. N. Eisenstadt (ed.): *On Charisma and Institution Building*. Chicago: University of Chicago Press, pp. 18–28.

————. 1968. "The Nature of Charismatic Authority and its Routinization." In S. N. Eisenstadt (ed.): *On Charisma and Institution Building*. Chicago: University of Chicago Press, pp. 46–65.

Whitton, Nathan L. 1928. "Response of a Mormon Village Population to the Religious Institutions as Measured by Attendance at Meetings." Unpublished masters thesis, Brigham Young University.

Wise, Genevieve M., and Don C. Carter. 1965. "A Definition of the Role of Homemaker by Two Generations of Women." *Journal of Marriage and the Family* 27:4 (November):531–32.

Young, Brigham. 1925. Discourses of Brigham Young arranged by John A. Widtsoe. Salt Lake City, Utah: Deseret Book Co.

Young, Kimball. 1954. *Isn't One Wife Enough*. New York: Henry Holt and Co.

The American Ethnic Family: Protean and Adaptive

Most edited works in sociology are without a final, concluding chapter. Whatever the reasons—editor's fatigue, the press of publication schedules, the difficulties of summarizing and integrating materials not one's own, or perhaps the paralyzing suspicion that nothing can be concluded and that no summing of the parts into a greater whole is possible—many scholars have closed up shop with the last contributed chapter to their book. All along we, the present editors, have hoped to write the kind of conclusion that would leave the reader with a somewhat better comprehension of the common, parallel, and more or less shared experiences and contingencies of ethnic life in America, particularly as it gets institutional expression in the ethnic family.

However, rather than engaging in the space-consuming task of summarizing the life history of each of the 15 ethnic families already compactly presented in the book, we have chosen to deal with them first in historical perspective and then more or less analytically, searching for propositions or general statements that might help the reader get a handle on ethnic family diversity without doing too much violence to the historical uniqueness that each author has taken such pains to depict. Finally, we will attempt a brief discussion of some of the problems that have emerged or loom on the horizon as recent social changes bear on current ethnic family organization and life style.

CHAPTER SEVENTEEN

BY

ROBERT W. HABENSTEIN and CHARLES H. MINDEL

THE HISTORICAL SCENARIO

In the century after 1830 some 35 to 40 million immigrants came to America. They came crowded beyond belief in sailing vessels whose unsanitary conditions and disease-ridden voyages gave rise to the term "fever ships" (Feldstein and Costello, 1974:1–141). The West Coast received Chinese by the tens of thousands, "coolie" labor for the building of the transcontinental railroads and for working in the mines. Hispanic peoples were added as America "gained" Texas, and later French Canadians sifted across the northeast border into the New England states.

That abysmal chapter of our nation's history, the two centuries of enslavement and shipping African Black peoples to America for plantation and other labor-intensive enterprises, precedes the great ethnic migration. But exploitation of Blacks continues throughout this time, emancipation marking a political but not significant shift in economic circumstances as Black migrants move toward cities to compete with a growing white urban proletariat.

Scholars have subdivided this century of inpouring peoples into the period 1830–82, as that of the "new," or early, and 1882–1930, as the "old" immigration. The 10 million who made up the first period were predominantly Irish Catholics, Germans, and Scandinavians. The ethnic composition changed after 1882, as did the character of the country's economy, and the great influx of southern, eastern, and central European migrants mostly of peasant stock coincided with the rapid surge of industrial and urban growth in America. No longer needed to build the railroads or settle the virgin land of the Western states, the new arrivals, Bohemians, Slovaks, Polish, Russians and Russian/Polish Jews, Czechs, and Italians were directed to the factories and sweatshops of America's slum-ridden cities (Feldstein and Costello, 1974:3). Also, after 1882 federal control replaced that of the states, and immigration became a matter of increasing public concern, eventuating in a social movement after World War I to "Americanize" all immigrants (Hartmann, 1948) and at the same time to change immigration laws (1921, 1924) to the virtual exclusion of all ethnic peoples other than those of Nordic and Anglo-Saxon stock.

The denigration of Asiatics, Jews, Slavs, and others of southern and central European ancestry resulted to some extent in their sharing the stigma heaped on Blacks, enslaved or emancipated, American Indians, decimated, subjugated, and virtually driven into reservations, and Mexicans, whose exploitation for an expanding labor force in the Southwest gave rise to a long-lasting form of peonage. It is against this historical backdrop that the authors have chronicled the experiences of the specific ethnic groups, from which groups in most cases they are descended, and on whose family and kinship organization they have focused their scholarly energies and attention.

414

The Initial Ethnic Family in America

Initially, the ethnic family of mid- and late nineteenth-century America represents a transplanted, adaptive, primary social unit engaged in the business of conserving and rebuilding ethnic culture, and through a distinctive socialization process, of creating new generations in the image of the old. In its typical form, which might vary somewhat from group to group, we find the patterning of structural characteristics, the operation of distinctive principles of organization, and a set of discernible functions.

Somewhat static, stationary, and resistant to geographical mobility, the initial ethnic family remains kin involved and community situated. Families and kin generate neighborhoods, which combine into communities, perhaps better identified as colonies, or in Gans' terminology, particularly appropriate for city-dwelling migrants, "urban villages." Once established, ethnic colonies become known as collective refuges and along with kinship ties attract fellow immigrant countrymen.

STRUCTURE. Prototypically, the family is large, or becomes large, with nuclear units of husband, wife, and children embedded in households comprised of some extended kin and possibly a boarder, some nonrelated compatriot. The norm is three generations under one roof. Family organization consists in the more or less habituated role enactments of the members, with executive command in the male head, management skills developed by the wife and mother, and a division of labor that includes all members of the household.

The initial ethnic family in America, then, is most likely "father headed and mother centered." But the long hours of arduous work away from home, often compounded by long journeys to work, meant that many if not most heads of households were limited in their contacts with the family and might remain important yet shadowy figures in the socialization experiences of the children. The reverse, of course, might obtain if the family set up a shop or other type of small family enterprise. In such cases the family members would be thrown into almost continuous interaction, the authority becoming more diffuse as personality factors of wife, children, and husband as well would interact with cultural values. In any event, family loyalty, respect for the family name, the adjudicating of squabbles and conflicts within households, or perhaps in the context of extended kin circles, and a rather pronounced au-

415

thoritarianism were typical organizational features that kept the head of the household in a dominant position.

It is axiomatic that ethnic groups maintain their distinctive character through rules prescribing and proscribing marriage, residence, kinship obligations, and to some extent, division of labor. Endogamy, marrying within the group, is a normative prescription, and as a mode of achieving kinship integration, cousin marriages may also be allowed, or even preferred. For ethnic groups suffering discrimination, exploitation, and sometimes threats to life and property, kinship organization, with its mutual and reciprocal aid system, has operated as a social mechanism for survival. Patrilocality, endogamy, service of daughter-in-law to the mother, some form of dowry system that offered a modicum of protection to the marrying-in wife, and a wide network of kin obligations, all help in structuring and giving viability to a family-centered existence in a new world of strange persons, external institutions, and unforeseeable contingencies.

Uncles, aunts, and cousins interpenetrate the social life of family members, serving as sources for affection, support, advice, and to a considerable extent, control. Mother's sister becomes at times mother's surrogate, father's brother the "dutch uncle" for nieces and nephews. The family remains adult centered and maintains a place in the sun for the elderly, whose contributions to the household continue so long as they are able to help, and who serve as storehouses of wisdom, legend, and lore, cautionary and exemplary tales all part of the cultural heritage.

CHAIN MIGRATION AND TRANSPORTATION. The initial ethnic family in America cannot, however, be seen as a simple transplant, a family system lifted out of its Old World context and deposited intact in the New. Few if any complete family systems, with all personnel included, would have made the journey. The first moves might be made by single young men seeking opportunities and prospects for better work, jobs that would permit the saving of money for an eventual return to the home community. Or as was very often the case, the young husband would leave first, hoping to be able to bring his family across the ocean as soon as possible—which might turn out to be years rather than months. When intact nuclear families made the crossing, some members of the extended family group might, if able, come to swell the group. But in the context of chain migration, single men, women, families, or parts of families would immigrate in some sort of sequence that seemed to make sense to the family members involved at the time. Thus, families would seek to reassemble in the image of family systems left behind. Often

416

single men would not return but would marry and settle down and into an ethnic community. The most important generalization to be made, perhaps, is that immigrants initially, and at least through the first generation, clung to the same family orientation in the New World as they had in the old, and that this orientation would play a central role in the structuring of the initial New World ethnic family. The family as a primary unit of social organization, as a source of identity and a repository for men's strongest affections and loyalties, could not easily leave the minds of men as they exchanged living in one land for another.

FUNCTIONAL DEPENDENCE AND INDEPENDENCE. Yet the exigencies and contingencies of the new life were as many as they were threatening. The ethnic family was in the first instance a refuge *par excellence,* a place of first and sometimes last resort within which coping responses to threat might be traditional, virtually automatic, and unthinking; or they might be tempered with the realization that things are done differently in America, and that adaptation and accommodation must also be part of the struggle for survival.

The economic factor could hardly have been more important, yet the responses of the ethnic groups and families were never completely captured by nor prefigured in the economic stimulus. The labor-intensive needs of a rapidly developing rational and amoral capitalist economy produced new imperatives, functionaries, and roles. Immigrants were subject to the influence of the recruiting agent, the labor boss, the ethnic labor contractor, the hired strikebreaker, and even the national-guard trooper, all working in the service of a system that had little regard for, if it did not stand in opposition to, the urban villager of peasant stock with his traditional family-centered mores. Yet the economy's demands, no matter how generally they came to be met, never determined in what specific form and in what actual ways ethnic family members would respond. Opportunities might be taken advantage of immediately to dig ditches, carry hod, build, transport, or engage in protective or personal services. An industrial tropism would draw many into mills and factories. Nevertheless, the decisions to respond, the strategies of coping and surviving, were ethnic-specific, most often made in a family context or with implications for the family as a first consideration.*

Italians in Buffalo at the turn of the century, as Virginia Yans McLaughlin demonstrates, showed "a definite preference for occupa-

---

*A friend of one editor recounts how after receiving a Ph.D. at Columbia in the late 1960s he worked one year more at his Italian father's family-operated, small grocery store even though there were five other less highly educated brothers available to help out!

tions that permitted minimal strain on their traditional family arrangements" (Gordon, 1973:137). Females worked, but only at jobs that could be done in the home, sewing, basting, and artificial flower making; while first-generation Italian males preferred occupations in the fringes of Buffalo's industrial structure "where customary family relationships could be and were effectively maintained" (McLaughlin, in Gordon, 1973:137).

Another more sweeping example of the family's strength in channeling and mediating occupational behavior is found in Richard Sennett's innovative historical research on later nineteenth-century middle-class families in Chicago's Union Park. Rather than pushing the members outward into society to achieve social mobility and societal recognition, the families closed in on themselves, withdrawing to some extent from the fluctuating, potentially dangerous (anarchists were thought to be everywhere) world about them into the sanctuary of their homes. In the process, the father, who does not aggressively set a role model as the socially mobile head of the family "on the make," finds his authority eroding, and at the same time the wife and mother's role expands. The result is a form of more or less mother-centered middle-class family, going nowhere in particular, sheltered, nuclear, privatistic, and emanating a "dull respectability" (Sennett, in Gordon, 1973:111–34).

IDEOLOGICAL CONTENT. Beliefs tend toward the concrete rather than the abstract. The physical and social world is personalized, suffused with the sacred and a body of folk beliefs expressed in folk sayings, discrete aphorisms, and maxims providing explanation, meaning, and guidance to everyday life. The focal concerns of the initial ethnic family are survival, acquisition of necessities, and, if possible, developing resources against hard times. Kinship, family name, family honor, good marriage, sociability among one's relatives and familiars, wariness in dealing with outsiders who may or may not prove worthy of trust, complete the constellation of focal concerns that constitute early ethnic family ideology.

COHESION AND INTEGRATION. The initial ethnic family develops unity through division of labor and attendant habituated role playing; and, significantly through family rituals, ceremonies and group participation in sacred and pragmatic activities. Holidays, festivals, religious observances, storytelling, with much reference to magic, spirits, and the mysteries of the unknown, draw family members closer and serve to keep alive meanings that undergird the everyday more prosaic practices.

Gatherings of related families for marriages, baptisms, funerals, and other *rites de passages* are as important as they are ubiquitous. Out-group threats, perceived or real, contribute to in-group solidarity. Such ethnic families have it as an article of faith that they must first and always protect their own. Philanthropy, social and public service conceived of in the abstract, and effort expended for which few if any immediate concrete rewards can be foreseen are all rejected out of hand. The family, kin, quasi-kin bonded through godparenthood, blood vows, and the like remain insular, resistant to the society of institutional and voluntary associations that mark the structural rearrangements and *gesellschaft* bonds of a developed industrial society with its impersonal market economy.

Institutional Relationships of Early Ethnic Families

Ethnicity presupposes antecedent culture: traditions, symbols, meanings, and practices. But the patterns of behavior that are rooted in and express the emotions, beliefs, and ideals of any ethnic group do not exist inside a social vacuum. Particularly is this the case where ethnic groups formerly separated by long-secured boundaries are thrown into contiguity, if they are not actually mixed together, in urban milieus. In these cases, local institutions arise; or those that are already present in antecedent Old World societal organization of the ethnic peoples are adopted to ensure some form of cultural and social survival.

The initial ethnic family, then, may further be viewed as a *primary* social unity embedded in a constellation of indigenously developed or adapted limited-purpose local institutions. For example, the ethnic boarding house sheltered, fed, and offered its residents some psychological security, functioning at best as a surrogate family household, at worst as minimum shelter for unattached migrants and sojourners in a land they did not intend to make their own. Since immigrant families often included a lodger, there might be some overlap of function, but for the most part the ethnic family and the ethnic boarding house served complementary purposes.

The neighborhood-tavern relation to the initial ethnic family is more complex. Male members of the family might look to the tavern as a refuge, a source of conviviality with age mates, an interesting social milieu in which the long hours of arduous work, the vexations and troubles, and the coarseness of daily life might be forgotten or put aside. Drunkenness was not invented in ethnic taverns, but by the same token it was not an unexpected nor surprising happenstance. Family visits to neighborhood taverns, on the other hand, as a form of family ritual would likely contribute to cohesiveness and tone up family morale. The services of the saloonkeeper beyond serving drinks to patrons might well include tendering advice and information, and often the keeping of savings for fellow ethnics who found commercial banks strange, if not forbidding.

The settlement house mixed social uplift, training in self-help, and instruction by example with sociability and groupish activities. The family, however, remains the arbiter or medium through which the new learning must pass muster. Along with the boarding house and the tavern the settlement house operates socially at a secondary level of community organization. Labor bosses, on the other hand, span a continuum of relationship to labor gang members. Father figures, operating in highly personalized and particularistic contexts marked one pole; at the other were men whose power over the job could lead to anything from petty tyranny to total and unmerciful exploitation.

Finally, labor unions extended ethnic power but in the course of work-force convolutions interethnic solidarities or accommodations would bring about secondary levels of association. Ethnicity then became only one of many factors in what was eventually to become large craft guilds or industry-wide union organizations. In any event family involvement and interchange of influence with, upon, or from unions might be close and supportive, that is, with workers meeting in each others homes at the earlier stage and later separated by formal organizational structures and more universalistic ideologies as big unions rise to meet the challenge of even bigger corporate power.

The Ethnic Family in Modern Perspective

Each of the ethnic families portrayed in this work has its distinctive social biography. By their having taken up existence in America at a particular point in history, and consequently having been exposed to the forces and elements of societal organization extant at that time, the life course of each will not only vary, but will vary in relation to the historical experiences of the others. The composite picture, similar to an automobile race in which some drivers would lap others and in turn be lapped, so that only by each driver's time being kept separately can the winner be determined, is extremely complex. In all candor it must be admitted that the patterning of experiences of the earlier ethnic groups, particularly for those who came during the previous century, seems easier to discern, label, and typify. Generalizations about *the* ethnic family of the present time are not impossible, but at every turn we would be first to note exceptions and to point out that intra-ethnic differences further compound the problem set by differences that separate one kind of ethnic family from another.

RESIDUAL CHARACTERISTICS OF THE INITIAL ETHNIC FAMILY. Currently, ethnic families in America, excluding Cubans and Vietnamese, are no longer transplanted social entities but have become integral to a distinctive type of pluralist society whose internal differences are more likely to be home grown than imported. The anticipated assimilation of the immigrant groups and the merging of Old World traits into one cultural whole is by no means complete; to the contrary, there are strong recent arguments contending that ethnics, particularly of southern and eastern European provenance, have all the while remained "unmeltable" and are in fact capable of a renascence whereby identities partially lost or obscured by the passage of time may be recovered (Nowak, 1973; Greeley, 1969 and 1974; Glazer and Moynihan, 1970). While we will have more comment on this matter at the end of the chapter, our present judgment is that although the spirit of ethnicity and ethnic consciousness may vary rather significantly from time to time, many indubitably important changes in ethnic family structure and function *have* taken place, and that when these changes are juxtaposed against the model of the initial ethnic family developed above, it can be argued that what remains is an institutional *residuum*. This residuum of what was a discernible historical type of family in our opinion remains of undeniable social import, but it is neither as unitary and viable as the "unmeltable ethnics" position holds, nor is it a mere vestigial remnant of some bygone set of rapidly fading institutional arrangements, as the assimilationists have wanted us to believe over the past half century.

STATICITY AND MOBILITY. The modern ethnic family remains to a considerable extent place-centered. Geographic mobility in America is high, and it is true that we are indeed a nation of movers. Moreover, today's ethnic family, particularly in urban centers, finds itself subject to ecological and social forces that make clinging to a homestead around which a body of symbols, images, and memories have long developed increasingly problematical. As always, one or more members of the younger generation may be encouraged to strike out for a new location in which prospects for a better livelihood seem possible, or likely. But no ethnic family (except the Gypsy) uproots itself as a matter of course. Home ownership has always been a central value to American ethnics, particularly because saving for, buying, and owning a home, often a dream in their countries of origin, has always been feasible, and thus transformable into a social reality. But, as intimated, there are many contingencies associated with maintaining local community residence in urban milieus: impinging and threatening invasions of other ethnic groups, physical deterioration of neighborhood, declining economic life chances, reduced political power—the Polish in Detroit as a prime example—the demise, flight, or structural change of local institutions, the erosion of civility, that indispensable product of interethnic accommodation, and the suburban movement which in recent times suggests a species of mass collective behavior. All these, and the reader can certainly add more, combine in inner cities in which ethnic colonies traditionally took roots to lay a heavy burden upon the home-centered, place-minded, ethnic family.

The familiar response, migration, through succession, that is, in a slow centripetal movement with families of one ethnic group taking up residence areas of other ethnic groups; or by jumping over these areas to the suburbs; or yet by migrating to more distant places, remains the most viable solution for ethnic youth seeking in the acceptable American style to found their own homes away, but usually not too far away, from the family homestead. For the adults, the old and the very old, however, mobility with attendant destruction of established neighborhood folkways, and the attenuation of kinship and sociability networks, moving out can only mean leaving a lot of one's life behind. Enmeshed in a welter of social and ecological contingencies, the established adult ethnic family, having committed itself to stay in or near the family homestead, can be expected to close in on itself, to resist the blandishments of mobility, to maintain as best it can personal and social ties, and to aid in the structuring of the group solidarity necessary to forestall rapid and destructive neighborhood change. In times of crises, of course, when a "state-of-siege" mentality suffuses an embattled ethnic enclave, efforts to move out inevitably produce charges of disloyalty to one's ethnic heritage; thus, family, neighborhood, and community values converge into a united front against potential leavers.

STRUCTURE. With the passing years the established ethnic families become smaller in members, the nuclear units of husband, wife, and children become more visible and free standing, family households are less likely to have three generations under one roof, and other nonrelated members such as boarders become almost nonexistent. Yet in all respects except the last these changes have been at a slower pace than for families in the society at large. Extended family organization, for example, continues to remain important both as a back-up system of social support and as a resource for services, sponsorship, and often financial assistance. Aged parents still find shelter in children's homes when independent living no longer becomes feasible—at least until impairments dictate the necessity for hospitalization or nursing-home care. For many ethnic families the latter is anathema, and resistance to institutionalization of their elderly remains strong.

Meanwhile, the "father-headed and mother-centered" ethnic family has not disappeared even though the roles of both parents, particularly the father's, are becoming less institutionalized. The area of negotiation of internal family matters has expanded at the same time and values of companionship and spontaneity are emerging where once controls and restrictive norms held families together somewhat in a state of compression. But in spite of all this, the truly "equalitarian," "companionship," "democratic," or "open" family is at least one full step beyond the ethnic family as we discern it in the chapters of this work. Granted that street culture, peer groups, nonlocal institutions, and the evocations of mass popular culture create values and structure sentiments that work at cross purposes to ethnic-family cohesion, the total effect of these influences does not seem to jell toward the creation of a new mode or system of family organization. For rather than disorganized or resolutely organized, the ethnic family appears to be somewhat unorganized, susceptible to strain in matters involving the acceptance and enactment of roles, distribution of authority, and recognition of individual rights— drifting rather than headed in any easily chartable direction.

By and large rules of marriage have tended to be prescriptive rather than proscriptive, with emphasis placed on categories of persons acceptable, even preferred as potential marriage partners. But parents do little if any matchmaking; they may have strong marriage preferences for mates for their children, but to be effective these must be applied through indirection. Head-on clashes with children over marriage partners are to be avoided, although feelings on the matter need not be hidden. Ethnic endogamy remains a norm, as does marriage within the same religion, but again controls either through sanctions or rewards are at best only partially effective. The chances remain about even that youth will marry within their own ethnic group.

Uncles, aunts, and cousins still continue as important relatives, but the locus of family control seems to be shifting away from them and to a lesser extent from the parents. Socialization of children includes traditional practices, often involving and reinforced by close relatives, mixed with the prescriptions found in the popular culture, in books, manuals, and an infinite number of articles in newspapers, pulp and slick journals. Ethnic families have, then, multiple foci: Parents, grandparents, children, relatives, all find themselves ambivalently involved in each other's personalities; but variation, chance, external factors, the easing of social controls, and a somewhat heightened ego consciousness of all principals make for a blurred rather than a clearly discernible product.

FUNCTIONAL DEPENDENCE AND INDEPENDENCE. Many of the contingencies, even threats to the physical existence of the early arriving ethnics, have over the past century been disposed of or otherwise dealt with successfully. In part through their own efforts, but also in great measure reinforced by a national ideology stipulating an equal chance for all immigrant groups to survive, even prosper, ethnic groups in America have never found themselves permanently locked into a rigidly stratified caste system. Many local institutions—ethnic boarding homes, taverns, groceries, unions, protective associations, cultural organizations, and the like—have either grown and become society-wide (the Bank of America, an excellent example), incorporated into broader ranging organizations or continue to exist on a marginal basis. The back-up or bulwarking function of these entities has meanwhile shifted appreciably.

The modern ethnic family becomes much less a refuge and creator of protective, educational, and religious functions. The socialization process has been shared with external, increasingly abstract, and bureaucratic agencies. Within the past several decades millions of federal dollars insinuated into community affairs have had as their goal the development of more viable systems of community organization and the strengthening of the family. Data on the success or failure of literally dozens of plans, demonstration projects, and programs aimed at activizing local citizenry have yet to be decisively analyzed and evaluated. Our perspective, which emphasizes both differentiation and patterning, is not primarily evaluative. We can generalize, on the basis of the data of the contributing authors, that modern as opposed to earlier ethnic families will be likely to have fewer uninterrupted hours together, will be less likely to operate as a social unity, and less likely to keep its members on a short tether, particularly as peer groups, school affairs, and age-specific mass entertainment provide strong inducements for family members to go their own way. Certainly the family is less likely to operate as an economic unity. Paying board is now a rarity as working youth squirrel away their earnings for purchases in markets that cater to and help define their age groups or save toward acquiring the standard package of household furnishings and other commodities that become part and parcel of their marriages—the business of such sales and acquisitions is estimated at 15 billion dollars a year!

After World War II the educational and training assistance provided service veterans began an enormous expansion of education that was further exacerbated by Sputnik and the subsequent national concern for this country's retaining world leadership in research and technology. And while the initial response was commensurate with the promise that education was infinitely expansible, with the greater payoffs correlated with increasing exposure to education for management, technicians and the professions, the counterculture youth in the 1960s, continuing to the end of the war in Vietnam, questioned both the methods and goals of education and rejected the traditional expectation that one's major portion of his waking life be allocated to participation in the work force.

The role of the ethnic family in all this remains somewhat obscure, but it appears that ethnic family norms have continued to stress the need for ethnic youth to prepare themselves for life with a vocation, a "good steady job," that only as much education as is consistent with this goal is deemed necessary (Jewish families apparently an exception), and that youth should settle down fairly early in life to job, marriage, and homemaking. Moreover, despite the long-held and deep-seated patriotism found in ethnic families, military service has become an object of considerable ambivalence, particularly since the new wars have lost their simple black and white character, and also because the lower the socioeconomic status of the ethnics involved, the apparent higher their casualty rates. In addition, that ethnics, particularly those of darker pigmented skins, are overrepresented on the rolls of the unemployed, with additional prospects for a "permanent army of the underemployed" (O'Toole, 1975:1), does little to support the notion that America's ethnics should simply seek to immerse themselves wholeheartedly in the work force and let the problems of the economy be worked out without their attention. If jobs are to remain a central issue to our ethnic populations, one has some right to expect that ethnic youth will reverse the emphasis of the 1960s on doing one's own thing to finding something vocationally to do and, not finding it, to find themselves caught up in a new activism.

Again, the internal response of ethnic families to the vagaries of the business cycle and the propensity for many businessmen to subject the disadvantaged to exploitation has not been for these families to become seedbeds of revolt with children socialized toward the acceptance of revolutionary roles. Rather, the family, adapting in a protean manner, tends to reorganize around new modes, some truly innovational, and new values for ensuring continued existence. The ethnic mother with the steady, reasonably well paying job, by virtue of her new responsibilities in and to an external social world becomes less a source of nurturance and care, less the heart and more the operating head of the family. Her mother may now become indispensable to the home, and other blood-related females serve as resources for the reorganization of the family. The resultant product, a matricentric, partially extended family is compounded out of lower socioeconomic class position and an ethnic heritage that contains great latent strengths in females despite the patriarchal overcast of immigrant families. For the modern middle-class ethnics, with husband and wife both often holding well-paying job, the ethnic family may move toward the equalitarian or companionship mode. Yet as intimated above, all reports seem to suggest that cultural residues still have their effect. Equality in work disposes ethnic families toward sharing in authority, responsibilities, and in relating to external society; but there is no evidence across our broad spectrum of families that all who share roughly the same economic contingencies are headed in a single direction and at the same rate of development.

IDEOLOGICAL CONTENT. Members of the modern ethnic family more or less tenuously hold beliefs that in the larger society have long ago passed into receivership. The expressive dimension of ethnic family life still contains images, symbols, mystical, magical, and folk beliefs, superstitions, religious credulity involving strong beliefs in miracles, the efficacy of prayer, spiritual intercession, patron saints, personalized deities, demonic spirits, evil eyes—an immense and amorphous uncritical ideational mass, the function of which remains as unclear as it is pervasive.

If these are remnants of a sacred society, their presence suggests some well-anchored resistance by the ethnic family and its members to emancipation from nonrational thought. Contrariwise, if the modern freewheeling, secularized, nuclear family that constantly engages in rational decision making turns out to be critically lacking in social and personal bonds, and only with great difficulty reaching consensus on anything, then these same ethnic-related, nonrational ideological elements may exist instructively as resources for other families and persons who as groups and as individuals have reached the end of the line.

Other ideological elements of ethnic families may be viewed similarly: the sense of honor backed up with appropriate codes of prescribed behavior, fierce loyalty toward kin, interfamilial sociability and primary relationships structured along kinship lines, godparenthood, the sanctity of the adult mother, protectiveness toward the female sex generally, respect and fondness for the aged, all still present in some degree or another and well worthy of comparison with those "melted down" ethnic groups whose attachment to such ideological elements are presumably more attenuated.

COHESION AND INTEGRATION. It should be fairly clear to the readers of this work that while the early or initial ethnic family develops considerable unity through division of labor and authority, habituated role playing, and through family rituals and ceremonial participation in sacred and pragmatic activities, today's counterpart has been unable to display or assemble a clearly agreed upon, integrated set of definitions of what all members might best be doing at all times. Looking at the complexity of American society and its changing position in world affairs, the product of its evolutionary growth and convolutionary spasms remain for students of ethnic families somewhat blurred—as a moving object caught by a camera whose shutter speed is too slow. The outlines are discernible, particularly in our case in which the initial ethnic family model is available for comparison. Hard thought on the matter suggests difficulty in achieving a sharp analytical focus on the manifold of variables, happenstances, differential rates of change, different things changing (divorce rates, intermarriage, achievement norms, social and geographical mobility) and the effects of large-scale economic and political developments across the land and around the world.

To be an ethnic in America means something different each time a major shakeup occurs in domestic or international affairs. The continuing function of the ethnic family has been to orient its members pragmatically to the here and the now, but always against a cultural backdrop. The culture of the "old country" may lose meaning in one instance, only to gain meaning in another. Old World cultures may become articles for mass consumption by leisured ethnics with money for travel and a curiosity to see the land of their fathers. The revivalistic impulses of some modern ethnics have brought new attention to themselves, and sociological literature expands accordingly. But how to relate what nearly four generations ago E. A. Ross called the "planes and currents" of society to such a stuck-in-place social unity as the family?

We have suggested that the ethnic family is adaptive, that it does not lose cultural content and social meanings so rapidly that new meanings, new foci of attention (bussing school children, urban demolition,, employment jeopardy, bureaucratic machinations) may not arise, first as problems, then changing to adaptations, then becoming the folkways of

427

groups whose identities may shift and blur only to become reorganized around new foci, and, finally for these folkways as community, neighborhood, and group preoccupations to become central to family belief and behavior.

There is little chance that this process will give way overnight to a new family form expressing the rational-purposeful, means-ends-dominated, instrumentally oriented features of a family that serves only the functional requisites of a corporate-business-dominated society. Neither will the modern ethnic family simply reflect the overarching and homogenizing forces of a mass, consumption-oriented society. Somewhere between these great grindstones that would pulverize traditional family organization a type of family, once consigned to oblivion—being ground or melted down—persists: protean, adaptive, conservatizing, generating meanings, and forming a sense of identity partly from the realities of an earlier time, partly from the exigencies of the present. The bonds of ethnicity are reminiscent of the life forces of those desert creatures that, buried in the earth for years, come "alive" again when it rains. It is not the task of the authors to proclaim nor to look askance at ethnic groups and their constituent families, in their variegated forms, in their dropping from sight, their re-emergence, growth, and change. Their existence is *sui generis,* to be studied as our authors have studied them, and to be a continuing object of the thinking sociologist's scrutiny.

REFERENCES

Feldstein, Stanley and Lawrence Costello (eds.). 1974. *The Ordeal of Assimilation*. New York: Anchor Press/Doubleday.
Gans, Herbert H. 1962. *The Urban Villagers*. Glencoe: The Free Press.
Gersuny, Carl and William R. Rosengren. 1973. *The Service Society*. Cambridge: Schenkman.
Glazer, Nathan and Daniel Patrick Moynihan. 1970. *Beyond the Melting Pot*. Cambridge, Mass.: M.I.T. Press.
Gordon, Michael (ed.). 1973. *The American Family in Social-Historical Perspective*. New York: St. Martin's Press.
Greeley, Andrew M. 1969. *Why Can't They Be Like Us?* New York: Institute of Human Relations Press.
————, 1974. *Ethnicity in the United States: A Preliminary Reconnaissance*. New York: Wiley.
Greenstone, J. David. 1975. "Ethnicity, Class, and Discontent: The Case of Polish Peasant Immigrants." *Ethnicity* 2 (March):1–9.
Handlin, Oscar. 1963. *The American People in the Twentieth Century*. Boston: Beacon Press.

Hartmann, Edward G. 1948. *The Movement to Americanize the Immigrant*. New York: Columbia University Press.

Higham, John. 1968. *Strangers in the Land*. New York: Atheneum.

Horowitz, Irving Louis. 1975. "Race, Class and the New Ethnicity." *Worldview* 18 (January):46–53.

McLaughlin, Virginia Yans. 1971. "Patterns of Work and Family Organization: Buffalo's Italians." *Journal of Interdisciplinary History* 2 (Augumn). Reprinted in Gordon, Michael (ed.) 1973. *The American Family in Social-Historical Perspective*. New York: St. Martin's Press.

Nowak, Michael. 1973. *The Rise of the Unmeltable Ethnics*. New York: Macmillan.

O'Toole, James. 1975. "The Reserve Army of the Underemployed: I—The World of Work." *Change* 7 (May):26–33 *passim*.

————, 1975a. "The Reserve Army of the Underemployed: II—The Role of Education." *Change* 7 (June):26–33 *passim*.

Park, Robert E. and Herbert Miller. 1969. *Old World Traits Transplanted*. New York: Arno Press and The New York Times.

Patterson, Orlando. 1975. "Ethnicity and the Pluralist Fallacy." *Change* 7 (March):10–11.

Schermerhorn, R. A. 1970. *Comparative Ethnic Relations*. New York: Random House.

Sennett, Richard. 1969. "Middle Class Families and Urban Violence." In Thernstrom, Stephen, and Richard Sennett (eds.): *Nineteenth Century Cities: Essays in the New Urban History*. New Haven: Yale University Press. Reprinted in Gordon, Michael (ed.). 1973. *The American Family in Socio-Historical Perspective*. New York: St. Martin's Press.

Sennett, Richard. 1970. *Families Against the City*. Cambridge: Harvard University Press.

Van den Berghe, Pierre. 1970. *Race and Ethnicity*. New York: Basic Books.